WAGING INSURGENT WARFARE

WAGING INSURGENT WARFARE

LESSONS FROM THE VIETCONG
TO THE ISLAMIC STATE

SETH G. JONES

OXFORD
UNIVERSITY PRESS

OXFORD
UNIVERSITY PRESS

Oxford University Press is a department of the University of Oxford. It furthers
the University's objective of excellence in research, scholarship, and education
by publishing worldwide. Oxford is a registered trade mark of Oxford University
Press in the UK and certain other countries.

Published in the United States of America by Oxford University Press
198 Madison Avenue, New York, NY 10016, United States of America.

© Oxford University Press 2017

Library of Congress Cataloging-in-Publication Data
Names: Jones, Seth G., 1972– author.
Title: Waging insurgent warfare : lessons from the Vietcong to the Islamic
State / Seth G. Jones.
Other titles: Lessons from the Vietcong to the Islamic State
Description: New York, NY : Oxford University Press, [2016]
Identifiers: LCCN 2016009582 (print) | LCCN 2016011273 (ebook) |
ISBN 9780190600860 (hardcover : alk. paper) | ISBN 9780190600877 (E-book) |
ISBN 9780190600884 (E–book)
Subjects: LCSH: Insurgency. | Insurgency—Statistics. | Guerrilla warfare. |
Counterinsurgency.
Classification: LCC U240 .J64 2016 (print) | LCC U240 (ebook) | DDC
355.02/18—dc23
LC record available at http://lccn.loc.gov/2016009582

1 3 5 7 9 8 6 4 2
Printed by Sheridan Books, Inc., United States of America

CONTENTS

LIST OF FIGURES

——❖——

LIST OF TABLES

I

Introduction

Without question, the fountainhead of guerrilla warfare is in the masses of the people.[1]

—MAO TSE-TUNG

It is necessary to be on the side of the oppressed masses in their struggle against foreign invasion, the imposition of a vile dictatorship, etc. If this prerequisite is not met, the guerrilla will always be defeated. Whosoever starts an uprising against the will of the masses or against a popular regime will fail.[2]

—GENERAL ALBERTO BAYO

ON SEPTEMBER 17, 2009, I had just sat down for a meeting at NATO's headquarters in Kabul, Afghanistan, when there was a thunderous explosion. I was working for the commanding general of US Special Operations Forces in Afghanistan at the time, and the meeting was, somewhat ironically, focused on the Taliban's goals, strategy, tactics, and organizational structure. As we soon learned, insurgents in a white Toyota sports utility vehicle had pulled out of a side street, maneuvered between two Italian armored vehicles traveling from Kabul International Airport, and detonated explosives. The weight of the main charge was between 600 and 800 pounds, and it left a massive, smoking crater in the middle of the road. The force of the blast threw the front Italian vehicle thirty-five meters to a dirt patch on the shoulder and peeled the roof off the passenger compartment like a tin can. It also left a twisted pile of bicycles, cars, and bodies along the road. As with many suicide attacks in the country, innocent Afghans absorbed most of the casualties. Sixteen civilians were killed and another sixty were wounded, in addition to the six Italian soldiers and four Afghan police officers that died.

"It was a mess," said one of my colleagues who was near the attack site. "Shrapnel was coming down like rain. And car fragments, dirt, rocks, and chunks of nearby trees came hurtling at us."[3]

The suicide bombing was a common insurgent tactic in Kabul and other areas, alongside ambushes, raids, targeted assassinations, kidnappings, and other types of attacks. Earlier that year, in April 2009, the Taliban had announced the beginning of Operation Nasrat (Victory) and vowed to use "ambushes, offensives, explosions, martyrdom-seeking attacks and surprise attacks."[4] They ostensibly had several goals in conducting these attacks. One was to coerce the withdrawal of international forces from Afghanistan by making it too costly—politically, financially, and militarily—for foreign forces to continue fighting. After the September 2009 attack in Kabul, Italian Prime Minister Silvio Berlusconi promptly announced that his country had begun planning to "bring our young men home as soon as possible" and declared that "it would be best for everyone, whoever they are, to remove our conspicuous presence from Afghanistan quickly."[5] Taliban leaders had other goals, such as creating a climate of fear and a perception that the Afghan government's security services were too weak and inept to stop the attacks. The Taliban also warned Afghans to stop cooperating with international and Afghan forces. If they refused to listen, the Taliban warned, "the Mujahideen will take action against such inadmissible deeds, and if something happens to them as a result of these actions, then responsibility will lie with them."[6]

More broadly, the September attack was part of a wider strategy of guerrilla warfare, which involved the use of military and political resources to conduct hit-and-run attacks (rather than face the enemy directly on the battlefield), mobilize the local population, and undermine the government's will to fight. Taliban leaders were remarkably consistent over time about the importance of a guerrilla strategy. In 2016, for instance, Taliban leaders announced their 2016 spring offensive, named Operation Omari, in honor of former Taliban leader Mullah

Mohammad Omar. They stressed the importance of guerrilla "attacks on enemy positions across the country, martyrdom-seeking and tactical attacks against enemy strongholds, and assassinations of enemy commanders in urban centers."[7] As discussed in more detail in Chapter 3, the primary goal of a guerrilla strategy is to defeat the *will* of the government by undermining its support base and raising the costs of continued fighting.

In addition, outside support from Pakistan was critical to the attack against the Italian convoy. NATO's assessments and those by Afghanistan's intelligence agency, the National Directorate for Security, concluded that the Haqqani Network had perpetrated the bombing. The suicide bombers had been brought in from Pakistan, kept at a safe house, and then maneuvered the white Toyota to the target area. The link to Pakistan was not a surprise, though the reality of outside support was much darker. Throughout the insurgency, Pakistan's spy agency, the Directorate for Inter-Services Intelligence (ISI), provided several types of assistance to the Taliban and other insurgent groups. One was sanctuary to Afghan groups and their senior leadership. Some ISI officials sent money and logistical supplies to insurgents, and ISI agents kept in regular contact with insurgent leaders. Indeed, the ISI was helpful in providing strategic and operational advice to the Afghan Taliban and the Haqqani Network.[8]

To conduct political and military operations, the Taliban established a somewhat centralized organization. At the top was the Taliban's senior leadership shura (or council), which was divided into committees that oversaw finances, military operations, propaganda, religious affairs, and other tasks. As in many other insurgencies, the Taliban's chief decision-making body was a *political*, rather than a military, one. Below the senior shura were three regional shuras—in Peshawar, North Waziristan, and Quetta (all in Pakistan)—whose job was to coordinate operations in nearby Afghan provinces. Below the regional shuras, the Taliban appointed a shadow governor and a military commander for Afghan provinces. In Afghan districts, the Taliban appointed shadow district governors to collect taxes, ensure commanders were conducting operations in accordance with strategic-level guidance, and pass information up to the shadow provincial governors. Finally, the Taliban had a range of low-level fighters, justice officials, mullahs, and other supporters that collaborated with a heterogeneous mix of drug-trafficking organizations, tribal and subtribal allies, and other groups.

Those of us involved in fighting the Taliban and other insurgent groups routinely examined their strategy, tactics, organizational structure, outside support, and other key factors important to the insurgency. But this was only one case and one point in time.

This book seeks to better understand how groups start, wage, and end insurgencies. It asks several sets of questions. First, what factors contribute to the rise of an insurgency? Second, what are the key components involved in conducting an insurgency? Insurgent groups need to decide on a strategy, select an organizational structure, secure outside aid from state and nonstate actors, conduct an information campaign, and utilize a range of tactics. They routinely reassess these aspects over the course of an insurgency. Third, what factors contribute to the end of insurgencies? Fourth, what do answers to these questions mean for the conduct of counterinsurgency warfare?

In analyzing these questions, this book is designed to be a practical handbook to help understand insurgent warfare. It also provides relevant implications for counterinsurgency warfare. It is not an academic treatment of insurgency and, for example, does not offer a new theory of insurgency. But it does examine a range of qualitative and quantitative data on insurgencies and provides novel insights into such issues as what strategies, tactics, organizational structures, information campaigns, and types of outside support insurgents have used; how these factors interrelate; and how insurgencies end. Unfortunately, there remains a significant barrier between the work of academics and practitioners. Some of the academic work on insurgencies is virtually impenetrable for policymakers and often focuses on breaking new theoretical ground or utilizing new research methods, not on better informing policy. At the same time, many practitioners are woefully ignorant of historical trends in past insurgencies, and make decisions based on selective cases or intuition rather than sound, objective analysis.

This barrier is regrettable, since insurgencies are a reality of international politics—and have been for centuries.[9] They can also have significant geopolitical implications. Take Iraq. Despite the 2011 departure of US military forces, which had been conducting operations since

2003, US forces returned in 2014 to help Iraqi and local forces conduct counterinsurgency operations against a resurgent Islamic State, also referred to as Da'ish (*al-Dawla al-Islamiya fi al-Iraq wa al-Sham*), the Islamic State of Iraq and the Levant (ISIL), and Islamic State of Iraq and al-Sham (ISIS). In nearby Syria, the United States and other outside state and nonstate actors supported insurgent groups against the Assad regime, which received assistance from Iran and Russia. In Ukraine, Russia provided direct aid to rebels in eastern Ukraine. And in Yemen, Saudi Arabia conducted air strikes and deployed overt and covert operatives in Yemen to overthrow the Houthi government.

Between World War II and 2015, there were 181 insurgencies. They averaged over twelve years in duration, with a median of seven years.[10] As Figure 1.1 shows, the number of insurgencies per year peaked at sixty in 1992 at the end of the Cold War. By 2015, the number had decreased to thirty-eight per year, levels comparable to the mid-1970s but still higher than the early Cold War years. Of these thirty-eight insurgencies, six countries faced multiple insurgencies at the same time: India, Ethiopia, Burma/Myanmar, Pakistan, the Philippines, and Yemen.

In addition, the conduct of insurgent warfare rapidly evolved because of technological and other changes. For example, it took insurgents less time to achieve relatively high levels of technical sophistication in

FIGURE 1.1 Number of active insurgencies annually

manufacturing improvised explosive devices (IEDs).[11] Insurgent groups also used the Internet and social media to communicate, distribute propaganda, recruit individuals, and accomplish other tasks. The evolution of information technology will likely continue to be driven by demand from governments and businesses, but there will be a resulting cascade of uses by insurgents. Internet-based propaganda and tailored social media provided a way for the Islamic State to communicate with adherents and inspire them to perpetrate attacks like the June 2016 shooting in the Orlando, Florida night club "Pulse;" conduct information operations; send money; and otherwise support the organization. The Islamic State drew on a variety of social networking applications, such as Facebook, Instagram, Tumbler, Telegram, Ask.fm, and Twitter. Based on these developments, it is vital to revisit the theory and practice of insurgency.

Despite the frequency of insurgencies, there has been comparatively little policy-relevant research devoted to waging insurgent warfare. After the US and other Western militaries became involved in the wars in Iraq and Afghanistan, for instance, counterinsurgency attained a lofty pedestal among policymakers and academics. In 2006, for instance, the US Army and Marine Corps jointly published the *Counterinsurgency Field Manual*, over sixty years after the US Marine Corps published its seminal *Small Wars Manual*.[12] The same year, the US military, CIA, US State Department, and Iraqis had some success supporting the Anbar Awakening—or *Sahawa al-Anbar*—in which a range of Iraqi tribes and other groups revolted against al Qaʾida in Iraq. By 2007, General David Petraeus oversaw the US military surge that severely weakened Iraqi insurgents and began to turn the tide of the war, at least temporarily. In 2009, General Stanley McChrystal established a campaign plan in Afghanistan that was heavily influenced by the *Counterinsurgency Field Manual*, predicated on the assumption that NATO and the Afghan government needed to adopt a population-centric counterinsurgency strategy.[13] Many of these decisions were buttressed by works from David Kilcullen, John Nagl, and others.[14] Much of this literature, in turn, relied heavily on a selective body of historical work on counterinsurgency by David Galula, Robert Thompson, Roger Trinquier, and others.[15] After the withdrawal of US combat forces from Iraq and Afghanistan, there was another flurry of books on counterinsurgency as researchers critiqued US, British, and other approaches.[16]

But most of these works neglected a systematic treatment of insurgency itself, focusing almost exclusively on *counter*insurgency.[17] The decision to eschew insurgency is somewhat puzzling since the United States and other Western countries have frequently supported insurgencies. In 2001, US Special Operations Forces and CIA operatives helped overthrow the Taliban government in Afghanistan, along with local Afghan groups and US air power. In 2011, NATO forces helped local militia forces unseat the Libyan government of Muammar el-Qaddafi. In 2012, several NATO countries began to support Syrian insurgents against the regime of Bashar al-Assad. And beginning in 2014, Russia provided direct assistance—and then deployed ground forces—to insurgents in eastern Ukraine. Overall, the United States, France, and United Kingdom supported rebel groups in a combined nineteen insurgencies since World War II, while Russia provided assistance to insurgent groups in 18 cases.[18]

This study aims to rebalance the scales by focusing on insurgents.

WHAT IS AN INSURGENCY?

In its *Guide to the Analysis of Insurgency*, the CIA defines an insurgency as "a protracted political-military struggle directed toward subverting or displacing the legitimacy of a constituted government or occupying power and completely or partially controlling the resources of a territory through the use of irregular military forces and illegal political organizations."[19] Along these lines, this study defines an insurgency as *a political and military campaign by a nonstate group (or groups) to overthrow a regime or secede from a country.* Insurgent groups are clandestine organizations, which impacts virtually all aspects of their activity. Leadership actions such as monitoring the compliance of lower-level operatives, planning and conducting operations, and fundraising may involve risky electronic communications and book-keeping. These actions must be balanced by the need to preserve secrecy in the face of aggressive government operations.[20]

The definition of insurgency used in this book includes several components. First, insurgent groups are nonstate organizations. The primary role of nonstate actors differentiates an insurgency from an interstate conflict, which involves war between two or more states.

Outside states may provide aid and even soldiers to either side in an in- surgency, but the main opposition group or groups are nonstate actors. Second, insurgent groups use violence—and the threat of violence— to achieve their objectives. Insurgent violence often includes assassi- nation, terrorism, subversion, sabotage, ambushes, and raids.[21] This differentiates an insurgency from purely nonviolent political mobiliza- tion, public demonstrations, legal political action, strikes, agitation, and other steps.[22] Third, insurgent groups have political objectives and seek to govern a specific territory by overthrowing a regime or seceding from a country.

Consequently, insurgency can be understood, in part, as a process of alternative state-building. Groups often tax populations in areas they control, establish justice systems, and attempt to provide other services.[23] The political objective of insurgent groups makes it impor- tant for them to mobilize a population against a national government or foreign occupier. As the Chinese leader and insurgent philosopher Mao Tse-Tung explained, "Without a political goal, guerrilla warfare must fail, as it must if its political objectives do not coincide with the aspirations of the people."[24] Insurgents attempt to gain control of a population or a territory, which distinguishes them from some terror- ist groups that have narrower goals, such as changing specific policies within a country.[25] Terrorism, after all, is a tactic. While there is no broadly accepted definition, terrorism generally involves the use of po- litically motivated violence against noncombatants to cause intimida- tion or fear among a target audience.[26] In addition, terrorist attacks are often episodic, while insurgency is protracted warfare.

Indeed, insurgents should integrate politics into virtually every aspect of their campaign. They need to establish a political vanguard at the beginning of an insurgency; closely integrate security and political re- sources to defeat the government on the battlefield through their choice of strategies; establish a political arm in their organizational structure; minimize tactics, such as suicide attacks, that undermine political goals and popular support; utilize information operations that maximize po- litical support for insurgents and undermine political support for the government; and carefully choose the types of outside support and sup- porters that minimize political costs. Politics is ubiquitous in all aspects of insurgent warfare.

A counterinsurgency, which is discussed in the final chapter, is *a political-military campaign to prevent insurgent groups from overthrowing a regime or seceding from a country.* A counterinsurgency campaign does not necessarily result in the military defeat of groups, since some insurgencies end through a political settlement rather than through battlefield victory.[27] Most counterinsurgencies include an assortment of political, security, economic, psychological, and civilian actions aimed at weakening insurgents and bolstering the government's legitimacy.[28]

As Figure 1.2 highlights, insurgencies generally involve three sets of actors. The first are insurgents and their local allies, which can include tribes, militias, and other actors. In Iraq, for example, Sunni tribes shifted allegiances based on such factors as their perception of who was winning and local grievances. The second is the indigenous government and its local allies, which can include a range of actors, such as tribes and militia forces, who oppose insurgents. The third set includes external states and nonstate entities, which can support the indigenous government or the insurgents. Special operations forces have used terms like "unconventional warfare" to discuss operations conducted by, with, or through irregular forces to coerce or overthrow a government or occupying power.[29] Outside actors can play a pivotal role in tipping the war in favor of insurgents or the government.

Support from—and sometimes coercion of—the population is a common goal for all actors in an insurgency, particularly insurgent groups and the government. With support comes assistance—money, logistics, recruits, sanctuary, intelligence, and other aid—from the local population. But the population is a means to an end (victory for one side or the other), not an end in itself.

KEY FINDINGS

This book makes several broad arguments. First, insurgents are more successful than some policymakers realize. Since World War II, insurgent groups achieved victory by overthrowing a government or gaining independence in 35 percent of insurgencies that ended. Governments defeated insurgents on the battlefield another 36 percent of the time. Insurgencies ended in a draw another 29 percent of the time, though the percentage of settlements increased over the last few decades. This means that roughly three quarters of insurgencies ended with a battlefield victory by either the government or insurgents. Like it or not, insurgencies have usually been settled on the battlefield—not the peace table.[30]

Second, while insurgents need to think judiciously about all aspects of an insurgency, several factors can substantially impact a group's chances of achieving victory. Securing combat support from great powers *increases* an insurgent group's chances of achieving victory. International relations realists have long noted the importance of great powers in international politics. The most effective combat support has often come from external special operations forces, intelligence units, and air power, not from large numbers of outside conventional forces. In addition, several factors *decrease* a group's odds of victory. Insurgent groups that use punishment strategies and seek secession, rather than regime change, are less likely to achieve victory. Great-power support to governments—particularly combat support—also decreases the probability of insurgent victory, especially when insurgent groups don't enjoy great-power support themselves. These factors provide a useful contribution to the understanding of insurgent activity, since there has been comparatively little quantitative work that examines what factors contribute to insurgent success.[31]

Third, insurgents need to carefully weigh the pros and cons of their options in key areas of an insurgency: strategy, tactics, organizational structure, information operations, and outside support. These areas are

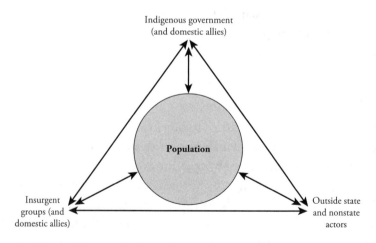

FIGURE 1.2 Key actors in an insurgency

interrelated, and groups need to assess how these areas connect to each other to achieve their goals.

- *Strategy*: Insurgents can choose from three main strategies: guerrilla warfare, conventional warfare, and punishment. These strategies are not mutually exclusive, and insurgents often use more than one strategy during an insurgency. The choice of strategy depends on such factors as control of territory, performance on the battlefield, and balance-of-power with the government. Guerrilla strategies, for example, are generally more effective when insurgents are weaker than government forces, and conventional strategies are more effective when the balance-of-power is favorable to insurgents.

- *Tactics*: Groups can choose from a range of tactics, such as ambushes, raids, sabotage, subversion, assassinations, mutilations, and bombings. But insurgents should avoid using tactics that undermine local and international backing, including ones that lead to indiscriminate civilian casualties. Tactics that inordinately punish the local population risk decreasing support and undermining a group's chances of victory.

- *Organizational structures*: In designing their organizations, centralized structures are generally more effective because they help insurgent leaders identify and punish those engaged in shirking behavior or defections. Centralization can also help groups better govern territory they control. In insurgencies with more than one group, leaders have several options. They can establish an umbrella structure to coordinate activities, stovepipe efforts, or compete against each other.

- *Information operations*: Insurgents have a wide range of forums to conduct information campaigns and propaganda, including word of mouth, print, radio, video, the Internet, and social media. While insurgents have long used traditional media such as print and radio, there was a dramatic quantitative increase in insurgent use of the Internet and social media. These mediums can reach a broad audience, help mobilize key populations, and overcome collective action problems by facilitating coordination of insurgent operations. But insurgent use of mobile technology and social media also poses risks that need to be countered, since governments can monitor their use and conduct operations using this information.

- *Outside support:* External states and nonstate actors can provide a range of services (such as combat support, sanctuary, training, and intelligence) and goods (such as money, lethal material, and non-lethal material). But combat support from great powers is most strongly correlated with insurgent victory, and great-power support to governments can undermine insurgent odds of success.

Fourth, there was a historical shift in the type of insurgencies, with an increase in the number of insurgencies involving extremist Islamic groups. During the Cold War, a high percentage of insurgent groups were motivated by Communist ideology, though the percentage of Communist insurgencies dramatically declined in the post–Cold War era. Over time, there was a rise in Islamic-motivated insurgencies, as Figure 1.3 highlights, and a notable increase in the slope of the line after 2001. Extremist Islamic groups and donors proactively supported insurgencies in multiple regions—such as Africa, the Middle East, and Asia—by moving fighters, money, and material to existing or new

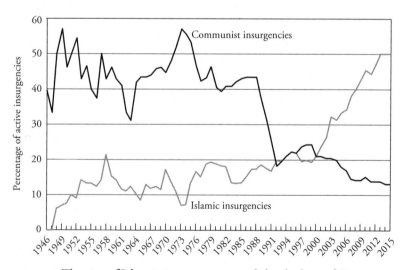

FIGURE 1.3 The rise of Islamic insurgencies and the decline of Communist insurgencies

battlefields.[32] The Islamic State and al Qa'ida were particularly active in trying to spread insurgencies.

RESEARCH DESIGN

To analyze insurgencies, this book combines both qualitative and quantitative data. On the qualitative side, it examines thousands of firsthand accounts from insurgents themselves. It should be obvious that insurgent warfare cannot be understood without carefully scrutinizing the writings and statements of field-level insurgent commanders and low-level operatives who were directly involved in starting and waging insurgent warfare. Consequently, this study leverages primary source documents from such insurgents as Mao Tse-Tung, Ernesto "Che" Guevara, Mullah Mohammad Omar, Chin Peng, Pushpa Kamal Dahal (also known as Prachanda), General Alberto Bayo, General Vo Nguyen Giap, and many others that fought in insurgencies in Asia, Latin America, Africa, the Middle East, and Europe. It also examines a range of primary source documents from such sources as the Harmony Database at the Combating Terrorism Center at West Point.

On the quantitative side, the book compiles data on all 181 insurgencies between 1946 and 2015, which are listed in Appendix A.[33] For each insurgency, it includes data on over one hundred factors, such as the outcome of the war, insurgent strategies, size of rebel groups, insurgent goals, types of organizational structure, and types of outside support. Included in the universe of insurgencies were any armed conflict that began after World War II and which satisfied each of the primary criteria: they involved a nonstate group or groups fighting against agents of a sovereign state; the group or groups used violence—and the threat of violence—to achieve their objectives; and the group or groups had political objectives and aimed to govern a specific territory by overthrowing the incumbent regime (including by ousting colonial authorities) or creating a new state by seceding from an existing one. In order to be coded as an insurgency, the level of violence had to meet two thresholds: at least 1,000 combatant battle-deaths were sustained over the course of the conflict, with a yearly minimum of at least 25 deaths; and at least 100 combatant battle-deaths were sustained by each side (government and insurgent) over the course of the conflict.[34]

The book uses bivariate correlations and multivariate analysis. Most of the chapters include simple bivariate correlations between key factors—such as insurgent strategies—and the percentage of insurgent victories, defeats, and draws. This provides an opportunity to assess, for example, how frequently insurgent groups that used a guerrilla strategy were successful in achieving victory. It does not, however, show causation or control for other factors that might be contributing to victory. The results of the cross-tabulations are discussed in each chapter. In addition, Chapter 8 includes a multivariate analysis that statistically examines the relationship between these factors and insurgent victory. For the multivariate correlations, regression analysis is used. Full results of the regression analysis are provided in Appendix B.

The quantitative and qualitative pieces complement each other to provide different parts of the same story. The quantitative findings highlight the explanatory factors most strongly correlated with insurgent success, such as the importance of great-power support to insurgents. But the qualitative cases illustrate the hows and whys, as well as provide empirical context about key aspects of an insurgency. Examples include cases in which groups started (and failed to start) an insurgency, adopted one or more of the primary strategies, developed efficient (and inefficient) organizational structures, utilized effective (and ineffective) tactics, conducted successful (and unsuccessful) information campaigns, and secured (or failed to secure) outside support. For instance, the quantitative data suggests that combat support from great powers is correlated with victory. Examples include Indian support to East Pakistan (now Bangladesh) in its war of secession in 1971, NATO support to the Kosovo Liberation Army in 1998 and 1999, US support to Afghan insurgents in 2001, and NATO support to Libyan insurgents in 2011.

There are, of course, limitations with any quantitative analysis. Coding an insurgency in this way—including identifying violence thresholds—means that there is some selection bias. To be included in this data base, groups have to "succeed" to a large degree. The vast majority of would-be insurgents are eliminated well before they get to this point.[35] Consequently, this is a book about established insurgencies, including what works—and doesn't work—for insurgent groups. Where feasible, such as in Chapters 2 and 9, this study examines hopeful insurgents that never succeeded in starting an insurgency, as in Singapore from the 1940s to the 1960s, Peru in the 1960s, Macedonia in the 1990s, and Saudi Arabia in the 2000s.

ROAD MAP OF THE BOOK

Insurgencies will continue to be an important component of international politics. Aggrieved, power-hungry, or greedy insurgent leaders and groups will attempt to overthrow regimes or secede from them, and governments will need to counter them. Like it or not, governments must continue to grapple with what works—and what doesn't—in insurgent warfare. The rest of the study is organized around key components of an insurgency, and each of these chapters begins with a brief anecdote.

Chapter 2 examines the barriers inherent in starting an insurgency and analyzes what factors increase the likelihood of war. Chapter 3 outlines and evaluates insurgent strategies, from traditional Maoist-style guerrilla warfare to conventional and punishment strategies. It also gauges historical patterns and explores why groups choose some strategies rather than others. Chapter 4 analyzes the range of battlefield tactics available to groups, such as ambushes and raids, subversion, assassinations, mutilations, kidnappings, and terrorism. Chapter 5 assesses organizational structures. It identifies organizational challenges faced by insurgent groups, options to organize an insurgent group, and options where there are multiple groups in the same insurgency. Chapter 6 focuses on propaganda and information tactics, including the growing use of the Internet, social media, and mobile technology by insurgent groups. Chapter 7 examines the impact of outside support from state and nonstate actors, including which types of actors can be most useful to insurgents. It also analyzes the types of outside assistance that states and nonstate organizations can offer, including goods and services, as well as the potential pitfalls of outside support. Chapter 8 highlights those factors that increase and decrease the odds of insurgent victory. Chapter 9 outlines implications for counterinsurgency warfare.

2

Starting Insurgencies

At the outset, the essential task of the guerrilla fighter is to keep himself from being destroyed.[1]

—Ernesto "Che" Guevara

We want you young men to join us in the struggle for freedom and the return of our stolen land. That is why we have brought you here to swear an oath joining you with us in this struggle.[2]

—Mau Mau insurgent, Kenya

ON MAY 15, 1952, local villagers spotted two bodies tangled in the dense weeds of the Kirichwa River near Nyeri, a gritty town nestled in the Central Highlands of Kenya. The two men had been executed and their bodies mutilated. One was a headman from the Kikuyu, the largest ethnic group in Kenya. The other was an alleged police informer. A few weeks later, Mau Mau insurgents assassinated the villager that identified the bodies and had reported them to the police.[3] Over the next several months, violence levels increased as Mau Mau operatives targeted government sympathizers in their campaign to secure independence from Britain and, more importantly, to take back Kikuyu land seized by European settlers. Disaffected Kikuyu had flocked to impoverished, teeming urban centers like Nairobi's African quarters, which became ripe for Mau Mau recruitment.[4] By mid-1952, Kikuyu guerrillas openly targeted wealthy European farms and property.[5]

As part of the political indoctrination process, Mau Mau recruits were expected to recite oaths before entering into the group. In some cases, recruits were bound together with a *rukwaro* (a cow-hide thong), which was placed around each neck, symbolizing unity and confidence. Each recruit passed several times through an arch, then squatted. An oath administrator brought forward a *calabash* (a fruit that can be hollowed out, dried, and used as a food container) containing blood, soil, and other parts of a slaughtered goat, which the recruits were ordered to eat. They then repeated an oath:

> I swear that I will fight for the African soil that the White man has stolen from us. I swear that I will always try to trick a White man and any imperialist into accompanying me, strangle him, take his gun and any valuables he may be carrying. I swear that I will offer all available help and further the cause of the Mau Mau. I swear that I will kill, if necessary, anybody opposed to this organization. I swear that I will never in any way betray a member of this organisation. I further swear that I will never reveal any Mau Mau secret or any thing regarding this oath, either directly or indirectly, to any of the enemy. And if I don't keep my word, MAY THIS OATH KILL ME.[6]

Mau Mau recruits usually took at least four additional oaths before becoming full-fledged members.[7]

By August 1952, the acting governor of Kenya, Henry Potter, expressed concern about the "deteriorating situation" to senior British officials and warned that "drastic legislation" might be needed to regain control.[8] Between August 1 and October 20, Mau Mau insurgents assassinated thirty-four people and caused an uproar among Kenya's apoplectic settler community, who demanded an expeditious and decisive government response. Mau Mau operatives also conducted arson attacks against settler properties, with over sixty attacks around the town of Nyeri alone from January to March 1952.[9] On October 9, 1952, Sir Evelyn Baring, the newly appointed British governor in Kenya, cabled London requesting permission to declare a State of Emergency, which would give him powers to detain suspects under special emergency legislation and use the military against Mau Mau insurgents. On October 14, Oliver Lyttleton, Secretary of State for the Colonies in Winston

Churchill's Conservative government, gave his consent and, on October 20, Governor Baring declared a State of Emergency.[10] Baring immediately launched Operation Jock Scott to capture some 150 Mau Mau operatives. The insurgency—and counterinsurgency—was underway.

For upstart insurgents like the Mau Mau in the early 1950s, the barriers to beginning an insurgency are staggering. Most have limited popular support, little money, few weapons and supplies, and only a handful of recruits.[11] Indeed, most would-be insurgents may only make it to the "pre-insurgency" stage, where they attempt to build a political and military infrastructure but never transition to violence.[12] These barriers are not isolated to start-up insurgent groups. About three quarters of new venture-backed companies fail.[13] Most firms flop because of too little legitimacy, resources, and human capital—not unlike insurgent groups.[14]

So what can insurgents do to increase their odds? This chapter examines a range of quantitative and qualitative data on causes of insurgency, including the statements and writings of insurgent leaders, to help answer this question. Unlike most chapters in this book, which generate and analyze new data, this chapter relies on an already-existing and rich body of literature on how insurgencies and civil wars begin. The goal is to identify factors that increase the probability of an insurgency. None of the factors identified below, either by themselves or in combination with others, guarantees that an insurgency will occur. They are not deterministic. Rather, they should be viewed as impacting the *probability* of an insurgency occurring. If groups are fortunate enough to get an insurgency started, it is difficult for governments to stop the war quickly. Insurgencies persist more than ten times longer than international wars, draining the blood and treasure of governments and their outside backers.[15] So getting it right from the beginning is important for insurgents. And getting it started *at all* is most important.

One challenge for would-be insurgents is that the list of social, political, religious, economic, and ethnic problems that could potentially motivate an insurgency are regrettably common in much of the world. It is therefore important to identify those factors that affect the viability of—or opportunity for—rebellion. The evidence suggests that three sets of factors increase the probability of an insurgency: grievances tied to a handful of specific conditions, weak governance, and greed.

The first are local grievances, particularly ones associated with low per capita income, ethnic dominance, and religious dominance. Groups need a cause that charismatic leaders can use to help mobilize a local population. Insurgents have long recognized the importance of co-opting and sometimes coercing the population. As Mao Tse-Tung argued in one of the most common axioms of insurgent warfare, a "primary feature of guerrilla operations is their dependence upon the people themselves."[16] Mao likened the local population to water and insurgents to fish that need water to survive.[17] Second, a weak government with incompetent police and military forces is generally an important cause. Since insurgents start with few resources, a weak state provides a welcome opportunity for rebellion. A weak state also increases the likelihood of a "security dilemma," in which each side's efforts to increase its own security inadvertently threaten the other side. Third, the availability of lootable resources like oil or drugs increases the probability of an insurgency by creating an opportunity for nonstate actors to challenge the state. Competition for resources makes insurgents more like bandits or pirates, using insurgency as an opportunity to generate economic profits.

These causes—local grievances, weak governance, and greed—are sometimes viewed as competing explanations. But the interaction between them best explains the outbreak of specific insurgencies. As political scientist Stathis Kalyvas highlighted, "rather than positing a dichotomy" between them, it is the interaction of these and other factors that increases the possibility of war.[18]

GRIEVANCES

Insurgencies are caused, in part, by grievances that motivate rebels. If rebels didn't have these motivations, insurgencies wouldn't happen. Charismatic leaders that use hyper-nationalist, religious, or other types of rhetoric are generally important to mobilize individuals and organize rebellion.[19] Insurgent leaders can use grievances instrumentally like an advertising campaign: to persuade individuals to join and to retain those loyalists that already support the cause. After all, insurgents generally view themselves as agents of change. As Che Guevara wrote, "We must come to the inevitable conclusion that the guerrilla fighter is a social reformer . . . and that he fights in order to change the social system that keeps all his unarmed brothers in ignominy and misery."[20] In order to do this, insurgents need an effective political campaign to highlight grievances and a narrative to convince locals to participate in the struggle. This campaign requires denouncing the current government, providing a counter-narrative, and explaining how insurgents will govern when they come to power. The narrative should include both rewards and threats. Marxist insurgents, for example, championed the proletariat, which threatened the bourgeoisie and landed classes.[21]

The challenge, however, is to understand what types of grievances actually increase the probability of an insurgency. There are dozens of possibilities, such as inequality, authoritarian governments, ethnic and religious diversity, state discrimination of a particular ethnic group or religion, rapid economic growth that could destabilize rural social systems, societies with a surplus of young males, or foreign assistance.[22] David Galula argued in his classic study *Counterinsurgency Warfare* that "problems of all natures are exploitable for an insurgency," including social, economic, religious, political, and racial grievances.[23] For example, it is conceivable that democratic states decrease the possibility of insurgency since citizens have political opportunities—such as voting—to voice their grievances, which they don't enjoy in dictatorships. Or perhaps government policies that discriminate in favor of a particular group's language or religion increase grievances, raising the possibility of war.

However, the empirical evidence suggests that most of these factors are not correlated with the onset of insurgencies. Among the nearly limitless possibilities, grievances associated with three types of conditions are particularly important: low per capita income, ethnic dominance, and religious dominance.

Low per capita income: Insurgents have successfully rebelled—and encouraged others to rebel—in countries with low per capita income.[24] Those suffering may blame the government for their travails, increasing their willingness to support an insurgency. Low income may decrease the opportunity cost of fighting, since people have less to lose.[25] In addition, low-income and -growth rates in poor countries may indicate a lack of economic opportunity, making it easier for insurgents to recruit fighters.[26] There may be other factors at work. Governments in low-income countries, for example, often raise less revenue from taxes and have weaker security forces, which are unable to root out rebels.[27] Regardless of the reason, there is considerable evidence that countries with a lower per capita income are at a higher risk of insurgency.[28]

During the Cold War, Communist insurgent groups were motivated by a desire to improve economic conditions, particularly among the proletariat. In an essay titled "Guerrilla Warfare," Vladimir Lenin wrote that starting an insurgency was necessary to support "the mass struggle in practice." As class consciousness of the masses increased, Lenin argued, it would create a more acute crisis and give rise to "new and more varied methods of defense and attack" among insurgents.[29] Lenin's writings and actions inspired insurgencies across the globe, from Latin America to Africa and Asia. One of the quintessential cases was Cuba, where Fidel Castro, Che Guevara, and a small band of revolutionaries began an insurgency in 1953. Their goal, in Che Guevara's words, was to improve economic conditions among "small farmers, peasants, and slaves of the eastern estates of Cuba" and to "defend together the right to possess land."[30] But there are many other cases. During the Malayan Emergency, which lasted from 1948 to 1958, the Malayan Communist Party (MCP) advocated overthrowing the government and supporting poor, rural peasants to establish a classless society and create common ownership of the means of production.[31] In 1948, the first year of the insurgency, the Central Committee of the MCP explained, "Under the increased exploitation and oppression and even use of violent attacks of the British imperialists, the working classes launched a violent strike, followed by an outbreak of peasant struggle in certain places."[32]

In Colombia, poor economic conditions helped cause "La Violencia" in 1948, an insurgency that persisted until 1958. A slow process of industrial and financial modernization triggered a series of agrarian movements in the 1920s and 1930s in Colombia, which had low per capita income levels. Land tenants demanded better working conditions and the right to cultivate coffee, and native Indians demanded the restitution of their communal land. Thousands of peasants in the frontier regions also invaded the newly formed land properties, or *haciendas*, reclaiming public land they had lost. The Liberal party, which promoted agrarian reform during the 1930s, lost power in 1946 and the assassination of liberal leader Jorge Eliécer Gaitán in April 1948 helped trigger La Violencia.[33] In nearby Peru, the propaganda campaign of Sendero Luminoso (Shining Path) focused on the economic challenges of rural peasants and was heavily influenced by the writings of José Carlos Mariátegui.[34]

In Peru, which also had low per capita income levels, Sendero Luminoso took advantage of income grievances among peasants in the southern highlands. And in Kenya, poor economic conditions caused, in part, by limited access to land was a motivating factor for Mau Mau insurgents during the insurgency beginning in 1952. The Kikuyu wanted the land taken from them by European settlers to be returned. Over time, disaffected Kikuyu flocked to impoverished, teeming urban centers like Nairobi's African quarters, which became ripe for Mau Mau recruitment. Mau Mau operatives appealed to the mass of unskilled and illiterate Kikuyu, who had been disadvantaged and dispossessed.[35] By early 1952, Kikuyu guerrillas openly targeted wealthy European farms and property.[36]

In short, the evidence suggests that the conditions for an insurgency are more propitious in countries with low per capita income. Would-be insurgent leaders may be more likely to develop narratives tied to economic grievances and mobilize populations in these countries.

Ethnic polarization: Some groups have successfully used ethnicity to jump-start an insurgency. But the details are important since research on ethnicity shows nuanced findings. Countries that are highly homogenous (they have one ethnic group) and highly heterogeneous (they include numerous groups) are less prone to insurgency.[37] Instead, would-be insurgents have a better chance of starting a war in countries where a large, well-organized ethnic minority faces an ethnic majority.[38] As one study found, "Coordination costs would be at their lowest when the population is polarized between an ethnic group identified with the government and a second, similarly sized ethnic group, identified with the rebels."[39] The probability of an insurgency can increase in cases where there is hyper-nationalist rhetoric from ethnic leaders, in reaction to atrocities committed by one or both sides, or if there is a history of ethnic conflict.[40] In these cases, small groups of radicals can pull moderates into the fray.[41] In practical terms, this means that insurgents may be more successful in starting an insurgency in polarized countries where there is a dominant ethnic group associated with one side (like the government) and a large minority that is unified and associated with another side (like the rebels).[42]

There are numerous examples of insurgencies starting in response to concerns about ethnic polarization, including in Angola, Burma, Burundi, Chad, Indonesia, and Sudan.[43] When an insurgency began in Sri Lanka in 1983, the Tamils were a minority of around 18 percent of the population.[44] In Burundi and Rwanda, the Tutsi were 14 and 9 percent of the population when conflict erupted in 1993 and 1994, respectively.[45] In both cases, minority ethnic populations were alarmed at the prospect of ethnic domination. In southern Thailand, insurgent groups were motivated by a belief that their unique Patani identity was under threat from a Bangkok government that unilaterally interfered in their affairs.[46] In the Caucasus, ethnic dominance was a cause of several insurgencies. In Abkhazia, there was a large Georgian population and a small portion of Abkhazians, which comprised about 18 percent of the population. By 1992, grievances about Georgian dominance among the Abkhazian population led to violence. In nearby South Ossetia, Ossetians comprised two thirds of the population. The Georgian parliament's decision to strengthen the status of the Georgian language, among other steps, increased Ossetian concerns about ethnic discrimination and helped trigger conflict in 1991. In Chechnya, ethnic Chechen dominance and a collapsing Russian state helped spark a secessionist movement and violent reaction after the Russian invasion in 1994.[47] Over a decade later, Russia used Abkhazian and Ossetian grievances as a pretext for its 2008 invasion of Georgia.

Religious polarization: Some groups have effectively used religious grievances to start an insurgency. Yet research on the links between religion and insurgency highlights some important subtleties. Like ethnic diversity, broad religious diversity makes a country *less* vulnerable to an insurgency.[48] Instead, a country faces a higher risk of insurgency when it has a majority religious group and a well-organized minority group. This suggests that religious minorities in polarized countries dominated by one main religion may feel excluded from the political process and economic opportunities, leaving them strongly motivated to rebel. In addition, insurgencies with deep religious (and ethnic) cleavages may also be more barbaric than insurgencies motivated by more shallow cleavages.[49] Consequently, insurgent groups have a better chance of starting an insurgency in polarized countries where there is a dominant religious group that is associated with one side (like the government) and a well-organized minority associated with another side (like the rebels).[50]

There are numerous examples. In Lebanon, Muslim leaders increasingly called for more equal power-sharing arrangements with Christians in the early 1970s. These demands had the potential to shift economic benefits in favor of Muslims, arising from greater access to public sector employment and opportunities to participate in—or control—private economic enterprises that were largely in the hands of the Christian community.[51] By April 1975, armed clashes broke out in a Beirut suburb between members of the Maronite Christian Kataeb party and Muslim Palestinian organizations, which triggered a war that lasted until 1990.

After its establishment in 1988, al Qa'ida was involved in multiple insurgencies to overthrow regimes in Africa, the Middle East, and Asia to establish a pan-Islamic caliphate. In Iraq, for example, al Qa'ida operatives led by Abu Mus'ab al-Zarqawi helped start an insurgency by supporting a minority Sunni opposition movement against what they viewed as a United States—and Christian—occupation. Sayyid Qutb, the Egyptian theorist and an inspiration for Ayman al-Zawahiri and Osama bin Laden, was particularly adamant that the long-term goal was to overthrow apostate Muslim rulers (the near enemy, or *al-Adou al-Qareeb*) and their Christian backers (the far enemy, or *al-Adou al-Baeed*). In their place, they aimed to establish a pan-Islamic caliphate that implemented an extreme version of Islamic law.[52] In his book *Knights under the Prophet's Banner*, Zawahiri wrote, "it is the hope of the Muslim nation to restore its fallen caliphate and regain its lost glory."[53] For bin Laden and Zawahiri, the envisioned caliphate included a swath of territory in North Africa, the Middle East, and Asia, as highlighted in Figure 2.1. As one al Qa'ida insurgent manual outlined, a key goal in starting an insurgency was to "fight for the sake of God to make the shari'a the law of the land and for the word of God to come supreme."[54] The Islamic State followed a similar pattern after its formal break with al Qa'ida in 2014, reigniting an insurgency in Iraq by supporting a well-organized minority Sunni opposition against what they viewed as an Iran-supported, majority Shia government led by Nouri al-Maliki.

FIGURE 2.1 Map of Ayman al-Zawahiri's envisioned pan-Islamic caliphate

Motivations tied to low income, ethnic dominance, and religious dominance increase a group's chances of starting an insurgency. But most other measures that one might think increase the level of grievances in a country—such as degree of inequality, democracy, government observance of civil liberties, ethnic and religious diversity, state discrimination of a particular language or religion—are not associated with higher risks of insurgency. There is little evidence, for example, that establishing a democratic state decreases a group's odds of starting an insurgency, since authoritarian regimes are no more vulnerable than democracies to insurgencies. Nor is there evidence that state discrimination against regional languages, anti-colonialism, or other factors increase the likelihood of insurgency.[55]

WEAK GOVERNANCE

A fragile state with a weak or collapsed government is generally an important condition for starting an insurgency.[56] This cause is not about the motivations of insurgents, like grievances, but about what factors distinguish countries with insurgencies from those that don't have insurgencies. Most countries have intensely aggrieved people or groups. Weak governance, it turns out, is an important structural factor that helps explain where these aggrieved populations may have a good opportunity to start an insurgency.

Governance, as used here, is defined as the set of institutions by which authority in a country is exercised.[57] It includes the ability to establish law and order, effectively manage resources, and implement sound policies. German sociologist Max Weber defined the state as "a human community that (successfully) claims the monopoly of the legitimate use of physical force within a given territory."[58] A key essence of governance, then, is enforcement. Can the government force people to comply with the state's laws? Can the government establish law and order? Governance can also include the quality of public services, the quality of policy formulation and implementation, and the credibility of the government's commitment to such policies.[59] Does the population have confidence in the rules of society, including the quality of contract enforcement, the police, and the courts? Is the government involved in corruption, which can undermine legitimacy? Corruption includes the extent to which public power is exercised for private gain, including both petty and grand forms of corruption, as well as "capture" of the state by elites and private interests.[60]

When state institutions are weak, opportunistic elements in society are able to take advantage.[61] State weakness is particularly likely in remote areas of the country, where insurgent groups can establish rural strongholds.[62] The more extreme the decline or absence of authority in a region, the more the population becomes "virgin territory" for those who would become an alternative government.[63] Mountainous terrain or external sanctuaries, for example, can be helpful to upstart insurgents. It is easier for rebels to hide in mountainous areas, with jagged peaks and cave complexes, and more difficult for government security forces to operate there.[64] A country that is half mountainous has an estimated 13.2 percent chance of insurgency over the course of a decade, according to one assessment. A similar country that is not mountainous has a 6.5 percent risk.[65] Mountainous terrain and other factors allowed some groups—such as those in Zomia in Southeast Asia—to live virtually stateless.[66] It is possible that other types of terrain, such as swamps and jungles, may be favorable to insurgents.[67]

In these areas, insurgents then set up institutions and use violence against alleged spies.[68] Weak governance fuels alternative power centers and warlords often flourish.[69] Poor governance increases the likelihood of insurgency because the state's security forces are weak and lack popular legitimacy. These forces may be badly financed and equipped, organizationally inept, corrupt, politically divided, and poorly informed about events at the local level.[70] While military and paramilitary forces play a key role, the police are perhaps the most critical component of local forces. They are the primary arm of the government focused on internal security matters. Unlike the military, the police usually have a permanent presence in cities, towns, and villages; a better understanding of the threat environment in these areas; and better intelligence. This makes them a direct target of budding insurgent forces, who often try to kill or infiltrate them.[71]

State collapse may also increase the likelihood of an insurgency by creating a "security dilemma," a situation in which each side's efforts to increase its own security inadvertently threaten others.[72] The partial or entire collapse of a regime can lead to a condition of emerging anarchy, where groups left in the wake of the disintegrating state compete with each other for security. Since it may be difficult for groups to distinguish between offensive and defensive weapons, even efforts by one side to protect itself may motivate others to arm, creating a spiral of countermeasures that lead to the outbreak of war.[73] One of the quintessential examples is the former Yugoslavia, where the collapse of the Tito regime contributed to a violent insurgency.[74]

A large body of quantitative evidence suggests that weak and ineffective governance is critical to the onset of insurgencies. One study, for example, analyzed 161 cases over a fifty-four-year period and found that financially, organizationally, and politically weak central governments render insurgencies more feasible and attractive due to weak local policing or inept counterinsurgency practices.[75] The reverse is also true: strong governance decreases the probability of insurgency. Another study found that governance is critical to prevent insurgencies, arguing that success requires the "provision of temporary security, the building of new institutions capable of resolving future conflicts peacefully, and an economy capable of offering civilian employment to former soldiers and material progress to future citizens."[76] In addition, governmental capacity is a negative and significant predictor of civil war, and between 1816 and 1997 "effective bureaucratic and political systems reduced the rate of civil war activity."[77] Weak governance also contributes to lengthier insurgencies and civil wars.[78]

A number of cases suggest a link between weak states and the onset of insurgency. A weak state in Mozambique led to infighting in various regions of the country in 1976.[79] After the collapse of the Soviet Union, weak state institutions in Georgia played a major role in a series of insurgencies. One study deduced that the "causes of the three Georgian wars shared some similarities. Institutional weakness was a shared element in all three."[80] In Bosnia, state failure caused by the crumbling Communist Party apparatus gave way to insurgency across the Balkans in the early 1990s. As one study concluded, war in the Balkans was caused by "the collapse of central authority in Yugoslavia. The secession of Slovenia and Croatia led quickly to the disintegration of this weakly held together ethnofederal Republic."[81] Another study concluded that the "dissolution of Yugoslavia was an important shock that increased the risk of civil war onset."[82] In Lebanon, a delicate political balance led to the emergence of a weak state in the 1970s and, as a consequence, the inability to implement substantive administrative reforms. The prevailing political system tended to foster corruption and laxity in upholding the public interest. The weak state fueled competition between local groups and contributed to the war that lasted from 1975 to 1991.[83]

A number of cases also highlight the importance of mountainous areas, where governments are weaker. In the North Caucasus, for example, mountainous terrain was a boon for would-be insurgents. Georgia is squeezed between the Black Sea to the west, the Greater Caucasus mountain range to the north, and the Lesser Caucasus range to the south. Approximately 65 percent of its territory is above 2,265 feet, with several peaks above 5,000 feet.[84] Rebel groups used this terrain—particularly the Greater Caucasus mountains in the north—to launch guerrilla campaigns in Abkhazia and South Ossetia. In nearby Chechnya, Russian troops had difficulty establishing control over the southernmost portion of the republic. The mountainous terrain allowed guerrillas to ambush Russian forces, conceal ammunition and weapons, and move almost unhindered between Chechnya and safe havens across the border in Georgia, Dagestan, and Ingushetia.[85] In the Philippines, the Moro Islamic Liberation Front utilized mountainous areas in Mindanao to establish a safe haven and wage a guerrilla campaign against the government. There are numerous other examples of rebel groups using mountainous terrain to help start an insurgency, such as the Taliban and other Afghan groups in the Hindu Kush, Cuban rebels in the Sierra Maestra mountains, Farabundo Martí National Liberation Front (FMLN) guerrillas in El Salvador's rugged mountain ranges along the Honduran border, MR-13 insurgents in Guatemala's mountainous east, and Bosnian rebels in the former Yugoslavia.[86] As Che Guevara acknowledged, "fighting on favorable ground and particularly in the mountains presents many advantages" for insurgent groups.[87]

While Mau Mau insurgents enjoyed some support in urban areas, such as Nairobi, their primary sanctuary was the area around Mount Kenya. The deeply ridged slopes of Mount Kenya and the Aberdares hills provided a key hideout for Mau Mau insurgents like Waruhiu Itote, better known as General China.[88] In Algeria, insurgents from the Armed Islamic Group (GIA) utilized the mountains of Kabilya to plan operations and hide from Algerian security forces.[89] PKK militants utilized the mountains along the Turkish–Syrian border to launch their insurgency against the Turkish government. "We stayed in the mountains, moving from mountain to mountain," outlined one PKK fighter. "The goal was to learn the geography, figure out where the guerrillas could hide, find out the views of the people to the struggle and learn where the Turkish soldiers were based."[90] In Nicaragua, the Sandinistas relied on the mountains near Matagalpa for sanctuary and training.[91]

While weak governments may increase the possibility of an insurgency, groups generally have a more difficult time starting an insurgency in strong states. Security forces are competent and the government can provide basic services to the population. There are numerous examples of groups that tried—and failed—to start an insurgency in a strong state, such as al Qa'ida's unsuccessful effort to start an insurgency in Saudi Arabia beginning in 2002.[92]

GREED

A final cause is greed. Prospective insurgents are more likely to start an insurgency if they have access to resources that can help finance rebellion—such as oil, diamonds, or drugs.[93] Outside powers can also provide resources to start an insurgency, as Russia did with Donbass rebels in eastern Ukraine beginning in 2014. Regardless of an insurgent group's motivations, they still need money to buy weapons and supplies, pay fighters, and fund a range of activities such as propaganda operations and housing.[94] Some have referred to this as the "feasibility" of rebellion.[95] Where an insurgency is feasible, it will occur. Consequently, insurgents may be more successful in starting an insurgency in countries with greater opportunities for profit. An insurgent group, for example, is more expensive than a political party and usually faces more serious organizational difficulties. The Tamil Tigers spent between $200 million and $350 million per year in the early 2000s to finance their insurgent operations. This was equivalent to between 20 percent and 34 percent of the gross domestic product of northeast Sri Lanka, where the Tamil Tigers fought to establish an independent state.[96] In the United Kingdom, the Conservative Party spent around $50 million per year in 2005—or about 0.002 percent of gross domestic product. While the Tamil Tigers were not the best-funded rebel group in the world, they still commanded a share of gross domestic product 10,000 times greater than one of the world's major political parties.[97]

There are multiple examples of the importance of lootable resources. The Katangan insurgency occurred in the copper-mining region of Zaire, the Biafran insurgency in Nigeria took place in the oil-producing region, and the Aceh insurgency in Indonesia was fought in an oil-producing region with per capita gross domestic product three times the national average.[98] In Aceh, for example, rebels from the Aceh Freedom Movement (Gerakan Aceh Merdeka, or GAM) leveraged the area's liquefied natural gas.[99] In 1971, Mobil Oil discovered immense deposits of gas in Aceh, with enough to generate $2 billion to $3 billion annually in export revenues over a 20- to 30-year period. GAM guerrillas mounted a campaign to kidnap ExxonMobil employees to extort money. As Muzakir Mualim, a GAM regional commander in the Lhokseumawe area, remarked in March 2001, "We expect [ExxonMobil] to pay income tax to Aceh. We're only talking about a few percent of the enormous profit they have made from drilling under the earth of Aceh."[100]

In Sierra Leone, the Revolutionary United Front (RUF) benefited from access to diamond mines, most notably the Kono and Kenema districts, in their effort to overthrow the government of Joseph Momoh. The RUF used funds harvested from the alluvial diamond mines to purchase weapons and ammunition from neighboring Guinea, Liberia, and even Sierra Leone Army soldiers. In Colombia, the FARC funded its insurgency against the Colombian government partly through the drug trade. They charged taxes, or *gramaje*, for providing armed protection and services to drug producers, smugglers, plantations, laboratories, and airstrips. The FARC also worked with other drug cartels, including Mexican ones, to move cocaine from Colombia to foreign markets. In addition to drugs, FARC operatives were involved in legal businesses, such as agricultural cooperatives, transport cooperatives, security companies, and cattle.[101]

In addition, insurgent groups invariably tax locals in areas they control. In Peru, Sendero Luminoso imposed "taxes" on local landowners and foreign companies, the targets of their propaganda campaign.[102] In Algeria, the GIA forced locals to pay a "revolution" tax in areas they controlled. Those who didn't have money gave what they could, such as blankets, mattresses, and food. As one firsthand account summarized, "some people cooperated with the group because they believed in what it was doing, but a lot did so out of fear."[103]

FAILURE TO START AN INSURGENCY

Among the dozens of possible factors that might increase the probability of an insurgency, the empirical evidence indicates that three sets are most important: local grievances (particularly those related to low per capita income, ethnic polarization, and religious polarization); weak governance; and available resources to start a rebellion. In general, the more that these conditions exist, the more likely it is that would-be insurgent leaders can successfully mobilize a local population. How these factors interact is different in every insurgency, making it impossible to generalize about various combinations. Since each insurgency is distinct, it is important to understand the political, social, cultural, and economic nuances within each country. Still, groups that are successful in starting an insurgency generally enjoy some combination of grievances that motivate the local populations (and leaders that help organize them), weak governments that fail to stop them, and sufficient resources to fund their efforts.

Insurgents can use this information in at least two ways. The first is to gauge the probability of successfully starting an insurgency. If, for example, aspiring rebels attempt to start an insurgency in a country with a strong government, few available resources, and limited grievances (such as high per capita income and little ethnic or religious polarization), they may want to rethink the wisdom of their endeavor. Second, insurgents can focus on exploiting those factors that maximize their chances. They can exploit certain grievances, such as mobilizing the local population by highlighting low income. They can leverage geographic areas where the government is weak by building bases in mountainous terrain or neighboring states. They can also focus at the beginning on acquiring funding from high-payoff sources, such as lootable resources or outside powers.

Despite these steps, however, the barriers to initial entry are substantial. One problem for hopeful rebels is that an insurgency is a "public good." If the war succeeds in overthrowing the government or seceding from it, many will benefit whether or not they participated. Consequently, insurgencies face a collective action problem in trying to start an insurgency, though these costs may decrease during war.[104] In the early stages, it makes more sense for an individual to let others fight—to "free ride" on their activities—than to take part. After all, starting an insurgency is dangerous, time-consuming, and inconvenient. The government's police, military, and intelligence units will invariably attempt to capture or kill the rebels, who are often forced to live a spartan, clandestine lifestyle. Yet if every one free rides, nothing happens. So the trick for insurgents is to rally enough supporters to join the fight, provide resources, and help start a cascade—or tip—that draws in more locals to join the insurgency.[105] Over the course of insurgencies collective action costs can substantially decrease and the risks of non-participation may actually rise, creating a situation where not supporting insurgents may be *more dangerous* for individuals.[106]

Groups generally start to contemplate armed resistance when all other options fail. As one member of the Malayan Communist Party remarked on the eve of the Emergency in February 1948,

> I feel we have tried our best. We have used every peaceful means to further the cause of the masses . . . Yet we have had no impact whatever on even a single clause in the Constitution which is coming into force at this very minute. If we continue like this, what future lies ahead for the movement?[107]

Yet there is no clear-cut road map to starting an insurgency, and would-be insurgents will likely encounter a wide range of factors that point in different directions. Some may enjoy mountainous terrain and access to resources like oil, but find a strong state that crushes their fledgling efforts. Others may discover inhospitable local conditions, but are able to take advantage of a weak state and a popular cause.

The reality is that most groups fail to start an insurgency. In Peru, the National Liberation Army (ELN) failed to start an insurgency in the 1960s despite establishing a cause focused on overthrowing the government and replacing it with a Communist one, creating a political organization, and building a limited military infrastructure. As ELN leader Héctor Béjar summarized, the group was unable to start an insurgency for several reasons. Peruvian security forces were stronger than anticipated, capturing or killing most ELN members. In addition, the ELN failed to mobilize Peru's rural population, many of whom were not sympathetic to the goals of the organization. "In 1965," Béjar concluded, "the guerrillas were not able to make their methods one with those of the peasantry."[108] The ELN also failed to cooperate with other anti-government groups, including the Revolutionary Left Movement (MIR). As Béjar remarked, "This competition led not only to wasteful duplication of efforts and tasks, but also worked against the development of a unified political line."[109] This competition meant that MIR and ELN guerrillas fought the same enemy in close proximity—but had no little or no contact with each other.

In Singapore, the Malaysian Communist Party (MCP) also failed to start an insurgency despite repeated efforts in the 1940s, 1950s, and early 1960s. Their goal was to oust the British colonial government and replace it with a Communist one. As one assessment concluded, part of the reason was that "the army and the police were very strong."[110] They were manned by British, Gurkha, and Malay personnel, none of whom had any reason to support a Chinese Communist revolution. Using a football analogy, the MCP's achievements were like "a football team which trains for a number of championship matches but loses every one."[111] It also helped that Singapore lacked the mountainous terrain and large population size that facilitated other insurgencies. Despite predictions of an insurgency in Macedonia after the collapse of Yugoslavia, it did not materialize, though Macedonia did experience limited violence in 2001.[112] One study that examined ethnic violence in Africa found that despite the conventional wisdom that conflict is ubiquitous, the mean figure of actual violent events as a percentage of potential events hovered around zero.[113]

In general, there are often too many hurdles for insurgents, who lack sufficient resources, fighters, leadership, and popularity. This handicap explains why Che Guevara warned that the "essential task" of an insurgent at the beginning is "to keep himself from being destroyed."[114] But with a better understanding of the causes of insurgency, groups may be able to increase their odds.

3

Strategies

As the momentum for armed struggle gathered, I became worried that British intelligence had probably infiltrated our ranks to a degree that a number of our decisions had become known to the authorities. This consideration, in itself, tended to accelerate our activities. I reconvened the Central Committee on May 5, [1948] this time in northern Johore . . . The aim now was to discuss the implementation of armed struggle.[1]

—CHIN PENG, leader of the Communist Party of Malaya

ON OCTOBER 6, 1947, Archibald Nicolson, manager of the Gunong Pulai Rubber Estate, was driving home with his wife along the Skudai–Pontian road in a southern district of British-run Malaya. The couple had been dining with the chairman of the South Johore District Planters Association, A. J. Boyd, and his wife. At approximately 10:00 p.m., they came across a crude roadblock at a double bend in the road. It was constructed of rubber tree logs and debris, which cluttered the road. Nicolson clutched the steering wheel and drove toward a gap at the left-hand end in an effort to break through. But his front tire caught a soft embankment in the roadblock and his car rolled violently across the road, settling in a shallow ditch next to a clump of rubber trees. Nicolson was instantly killed. Four masked men approached the car and one of them wrestled a gold watch from the wrist of Nicolson's wife, who had survived. When a second bandit demanded her diamond solitaire wedding ring, she refused to hand it over. He cracked her over the head with the butt of his Sten gun, a cheap British-made 9-mm submachine gun commonly used by British and Commonwealth forces.[2]

Nicolson's death quickly became a rallying point for the European planter community and further polarized Malayan society, contributing to an upsurge in militancy across the country. For the Communist Party of Malaya, the event provided an opportune moment to overthrow Malaya's capitalist class and ultimately its government. On May 5, 1948, the party convened a meeting in Johore to discuss strategic options. According to Chin Peng, head of the Communist Party of Malaya, the group settled on a guerrilla strategy: "We decided on setting up, state-by-state, guerrilla force nuclei. We went on to analyze the best means of inserting them into jungle camps."[3] This was a critical decision for the Malayan Communist Party. They had previously agreed on long-term objectives in Malaya, which included overthrowing the government. But now they had agreed on a strategy for action.

This chapter examines insurgent strategies. As used here, a strategy includes a group's resources and methods to degrade or defeat adversaries, including a government.[4] Insurgent leaders need to consider how to use their security forces and political resources to defeat the government on the battlefield or coerce it to achieve other insurgent aims. A strategy forces insurgents to foresee the nature of the war. Does the plan of attack—the proposed strategy—promise success at a reasonable cost?[5] The British soldier and military theorist B. H. Liddell Hart referred to strategy as "the art of distributing and applying military means to fulfill the ends of policy."[6] In insurgent warfare, strategy includes more than just military means, but political and other instruments as well. The political dimension is particularly critical to strategy. For instance, insurgents need to mobilize the local population when they use a guerrilla strategy, which is often more about political mobilization than military resources.

Strategy in this sense is different from a "grand strategy," which is the broader process (usually by a state) of determining vital security interests, identifying the threats to those interests, and deciding how best to employ political, military, and economic resources to protect those interests.[7] Strategy should also be distinguished from tactics, which is examined in Chapter 4 and includes the techniques for using weapons or military units in combination to engage and defeat an adversary.

Contrary to many accounts that conflate insurgent strategies with guerrilla warfare, this chapter finds that insurgents can choose from three main strategies: guerrilla warfare, conventional warfare, and punishment.[8] However, these strategies are not mutually exclusive. Groups may adopt one or more over the course of a war, depending on several factors. Insurgents may switch strategies if one fails to achieve results. Groups may use different strategies depending on the balance-of-power with the government, which can change over the course of a conflict and even vary in different areas. Mao advocated three stages of insurgency, which began by building up political and military capabilities, moving to a guerrilla campaign, and finally concluding with sustained conventional operations. In addition, groups may use different strategies depending on their control of territory, which can vary within and across urban and rural areas. Guerrilla strategies, for example, are generally more effective when insurgents are weaker than government forces, and conventional strategies are more effective when the balance-of-power is favorable to insurgents.

The rest of this chapter is organized into four sections. The first outlines a guerrilla strategy. The second section discusses a conventional strategy and provides historical examples. The third analyzes a punishment strategy. The fourth section examines historical patterns in insurgent strategies, and explores why groups choose some strategies rather than others.

GUERRILLA WARFARE

A guerrilla strategy involves the use of military and political resources to mobilize a local population, conduct hit-and-run attacks (rather than face the enemy directly on the battlefield), and undermine the government's will to fight.[9] The primary goal of a guerrilla strategy is to defeat the *will* of the government by mobilizing the civilian population, undermining government support, and raising the costs of continued fighting. It is not necessarily to defeat the capacity of its adversary to fight, nor is it to bring the government to its knees by punishing the population and raising the costs of continued resistance. A guerrilla strategy is often palatable to insurgent groups that are significantly weaker than government security forces, which is why a guerrilla campaign is sometimes likened to a "war of the flea."[10]

Guerrilla warfare was popularized in the writings of Mao and Che Guevara, but it is much older.[11] Sun Tzu, the Chinese military philosopher, emphasized the importance of attacking an adversary's weak points, avoiding its strengths, and maximizing patience—all key tenets of a guerrilla strategy.[12] Groups adopted guerrilla strategies against European colonial powers in the nineteenth and twentieth centuries, such as in Burma (1824–1825, 1852, and 1885), Algeria (1830–1847), Madagascar (1844–1895), West Africa (1882–1898), the Boer Wars (1880–1881 and 1899–1902), and the Caucasus (1836–1859).[13] Napoleon's Grande Armée was defeated, in part, by the guerrilla operations of Spanish peasants.[14]

Guerrilla war is distinguished from other insurgent strategies by three main characteristics. First, insurgents attempt to mobilize the local population to obtain adequate resources to sustain an insurgency, including fighters, food, shelter, supplies, and intelligence.[15] The logic for leveraging the local population is straightforward: insurgents are weaker than the government, believe they would be defeated if they fought the government directly, but assess there is sufficient latent support among the population to begin the fight. As Mao concluded, "A primary feature of guerrilla operations is their dependence upon the *people* themselves to organize battalions and other units."[16] Indeed, Mao's most important contribution was not his focus on guerrilla warfare per se, which was not novel, but rather his emphasis on the participation of peasants in the struggle, either as a combat force or as an underground political structure. Prachanda, leader of the Unified Communist Party of Nepal, remarked that "guerrilla war can be developed only if it is conducted for the masses and by the masses."[17] Many Latin American revolutionaries argued that the social, political, and economic oppression of local populations in the region made insurgency virtually inevitable.[18]

The challenge for a guerrilla strategy, then, is to mobilize the population. An important component is persuading as many people as possible—by co-opting or coercing them—to commit to the group. In South Africa, for example, African National Congress (ANC) leaders began preparations in 1963 for Operation Mayibuye, which involved organizing and implementing a guerrilla strategy against the government. It was orchestrated by the ANC's military wing, Umkhonto we Sizwe. The ANC's six-point plan for Operation Mayibuye emphasized the need to begin "well prepared guerrilla operations during the course of which *the masses of the people will be drawn in and armed.*"[19] The

ANC sent hundreds of activists to neighboring countries for training in the techniques and art of guerrilla war.[20]

While a guerrilla strategy has often been implemented in rural areas, and was conceived by Mao and Che Guevara for that purpose, it has also been utilized to mobilize populations in urban areas.[21] In fact, 25 percent of total cases where insurgents used a guerrilla strategy involved fighting in an urban area. Guerrilla campaigns in urban areas peaked in the 1960s and 1970s, when they were 40 percent of total guerrilla campaigns. They decreased to 20 percent in the 1980s, 15 percent in the 1990s, and then rose again to 30 percent of total guerrilla campaigns after 2000.

An important component of mobilizing the local population is building a viable political structure.[22] Guerrillas need to establish political cells to develop a coherent narrative and engage in propaganda activities. Insurgents also try to infiltrate enemy institutions, foment strikes and demonstrations, and carry out sabotage missions. As part of their political effort, insurgents may appeal to religious, ethnic, economic, or other grievances and provide social services to demonstrate their sincerity and gain support. A key objective is the recruitment of local leaders, who, once in the organization, play a key role in separating the people from the government. To institutionalize support, insurgents often attempt to build government structures that will provide de facto control of the population.[23] This aspect of mobilization is a political rather than a military task, and the primacy of political over military concerns became a hallmark of Mao's theorizing about warfare.

Second, groups employing a guerrilla strategy rely on irregular forces that are organized in small and highly mobile units against government forces and their allies. A guerrilla strategy typically emphasizes campaigns of assassination, sabotage, and hit-and-run attacks designed to impose significant costs on the enemy, rather than engaging in conventional battles that seek to defeat the opposition directly. In short, a guerrilla strategy places a high priority on mobile warfare.[24] There are numerous examples of insurgents relying hit-and-run attacks, from El Salvador (1979–1992) and Peru (1980–1996) to Nepal (1996–2006). In those and other wars, rebels relied on harassment, surprise, stealth, and raids.[25] After the end of the Cold War, insurgents adopted a guerrilla strategy when fighting great powers like the United States in Afghanistan and Iraq, primarily because of the insurgents' disparity in power.

Rebels believe they have the capacity to harass the state, but lack the capacity to confront their security forces directly. Put otherwise, since states can mount a devastating response to a direct armed challenge, insurgents conclude that the only viable option is to fight asymmetrically.[26] Based on his experience in the Spanish Civil War and several Latin America insurgencies, Cuban General Alberto Bayo remarked that "every good guerrilla must rely on surprise, the skirmish, the ambush and always attack when the enemy is confident and does not expect attack. When the enemy begins to counterattack, we must disappear from sight and withdraw to a safer place."[27] For T. E. Lawrence, the British officer and advisor to Arab insurgents against the Ottoman Empire, mobility was essential. He wrote in *Evolution of a Revolt* that "granted mobility, security (in the form of denying targets to the enemy), time, and doctrine (the idea to convert every subject to friendliness), victory will rest with the insurgents, for the algebraical factors are in the end decisive."[28] According to Nepalese insurgents, the key to success was to "apply the tactics of hit and run" and to "make surprise attack[s]" when targeting government forces.[29] And Mao similarly advised:

> In guerrilla warfare ... avoid the solid, attack the hollow; attack; withdraw; deliver a lightning blow, seek a lightning decision. When guerrillas engage a stronger enemy, they withdraw when he advances; harass him when he stops; strike him when he is weary; pursue him when he withdraws.[30]

Guerrillas may also try to force government army and police units to scatter, or at least wait for them to do so, to make them more vulnerable. As one MPLA leader in Angola outlined, "You know, according to the laws of guerrilla war, we can't afford a concentration of enemy forces. We must make them disperse so that we can attack them in small groups."[31] Counterinsurgency forces sometimes mistakenly conclude that hit-and-run attacks are a sign of cowardice and weakness. In Afghanistan, for example, US military and civilian officials frequently derided Taliban ambushes, raids, or suicide attacks as signs of "weakness" and "desperation."[32] But these conclusions are generally mistaken, since they reflect a strategic calculation by insurgents.

Third, guerrilla warfare is a long-term strategy designed to exhaust the political will of the government and its outside backers.[33] Over the long run, the objective of a guerrilla strategy is to cause demoralization, lethargy, and defections from the government. Insurgents may also want to intimidate the police and other security forces to further weaken government capacity and control. In Uganda, for instance, the National Resistance Army organized themselves into four sections and began a series of hit-and-run operations in the Luwero Triangle during the Ugandan Bush War between 1980 and 1986.[34] The long-term aim of insurgents is to isolate the people from the government. But guerrilla strategies should be conceived of as lasting a decade or more, not months or years. This is why Mao titled one of his key essays on the subject "On Protracted War," emphasizing the lengthy, protracted nature of guerrilla warfare.[35]

In Guinea-Bissau, for example, Amilcar Cabral and his African Party for the Independence of Guinea-Bissau and the Cape Verde Islands (PAIGC) developed a guerrilla strategy to win independence from Portugal. The PAIGC spent over a decade conducting hit-and-run attacks against Portuguese forces until Guinea-Bissau became independent from Portugal in 1974, thanks in part to the coup in Portugal.[36] The same was largely true in Northern Ireland. According to one Provisional IRA document, the group's guerrilla strategy was designed to "create such psychological damage to the Brits that they'll withdraw. Sick of the expense, the hassle, the coffins, coming back to England. But we know we can't defeat them in a military sense, no more than they can beat us."[37] The Provisional IRA's guerrilla strategy had five main goals, which are worth quoting at length:

1. A war of attrition against enemy personnel which is aimed at causing as many casualties and deaths as possible so as to create a demand from their people at home for their withdrawal.
2. A bombing campaign aimed at making the enemy's financial interest in our country unprofitable while at the same time curbing long-term financial investment in our country.

3. To make the Six Counties as at present and for the past several years ungovernable except by colonial military rule.
4. To sustain the war and gain support for its ends by National and International propaganda and publicity campaigns.
5. By defending the war of liberation by punishing criminals, collaborators and informers.[38]

Several influential leaders led by Che Guevara and Régis Debray, a French academic who fought with Che Guevara in Bolivia, argued that insurgents could skip the political mobilization process of guerrilla warfare and immediately resort to violence. It became known as "focoism."[39] As Che Guevara contended, "It is not necessary to wait until all conditions for making revolution exist; the insurrection can create them."[40] Che Guevara and Debray contended that a revolutionary force, using violence, can mobilize popular support more quickly by taking on the government directly.[41] A guerrilla strategy assumes that effective political mobilization, beginning with careful recruitment in rural villages, will eventually create sufficient local support to build a military force that can fight the government. Foco arguments reverse the causal logic: military conflict itself can help mobilize the local population. Violence is the catalyst. Proponents of focoism hoped that locals would be motivated by insurgent attacks, angered and encouraged by the brutality and ineptitude of governmental response, and alienated if the government seeks help from a foreign power.[42] Insurgents and would-be insurgents adopted foco approaches in such countries as Paraguay, Colombia, Ecuador, Peru, the Dominican Republic, Venezuela, Guatemala, Bolivia, and even the Congo.[43] But most of these efforts were unsuccessful and were crushed by their respective governments.[44] Following his failed effort in the Congo, Che Guevara later wrote:

> The soldiers are of peasant stock and completely raw, for whom the main attraction is to have a rifle and a uniform, sometimes even shoes and a certain authority in the area. Corrupted by inactivity and the habit of ordering peasants around, saturated with fetishistic notions about death and the enemy, devoid of any coherent political education, they consequently lack revolutionary awareness or any

TABLE 3.1 Duration of insurgencies by strategy

Insurgent strategy	Average duration of insurgency[106]
Conventional strategy	7 years
Guerrilla strategy	16 years
Punishment strategy	15 years

forward-looking perspective beyond the traditional horizon of their tribal territory. Lazy and undisciplined, they are without any spirit of combat or self-sacrifice.[45]

As Table 3.1 highlights, insurgencies lasted an average of 16 years when groups adopted a guerrilla strategy, compared to only seven years for conventional campaigns. As discussed in more detail later in the chapter, punishment campaigns can also last for a significant period averaging 15 years. Guerrilla wars frequently turn into wars of attrition, where ultimate success depends on wearing down the adversary until resistance is no longer feasible.[46] There may be several reasons for this variation in duration. It is possible, for example, that insurgents strong enough to mount a conventional campaign against the government are able to end wars more quickly.

A large number of studies equate insurgent strategy with guerrilla warfare.[47] But insurgents have two other options when designing a strategy, the first of which is conventional warfare.

CONVENTIONAL WARFARE

A conventional strategy involves the use of insurgent forces to capture or destroy the government's armed forces, thereby gaining control of the government's values—its population, territory, cities, or vital industrial and communications centers. The goal is to win the war in a decisive engagement or a series of battles by destroying the adversary's physical capacity to resist. An attacker's force, for instance, may advance to capture a defender's strategic assets—such as a city or base—and the defender moves to counter that effort. A battle or series of battles ensue, sometimes marked by lulls in the fighting, until one side is defeated.[48]

Unlike a guerrilla strategy, a conventional strategy focuses on defeating the government's security forces, rather than winning over the local population. The principal military objective is to destroy the government's main forces; the principal political aim is the displacement of the governing authorities.[49] In conventional wars, military confrontation is direct, either across well-defined front lines or between armed columns. Clashes often take the form of set battles, trench warfare, and town sieges.[50]

Many insurgents would happily adopt a conventional strategy—but can't, at least in the early stages of an insurgency. They are simply too weak. This is, in part, why Mao advocated waiting until a third stage. Outside assistance, especially from states, can help insurgent groups acquire heavy weapons—tanks, artillery, and surface-to-air missiles—and other resources necessary to adopt a conventional strategy.[51] Of the eighty-nine cases since World War II in which insurgent groups used a conventional strategy at some point during the war, groups received state support 70 percent of the time. States are usually the largest external donors during insurgencies since they have the most significant resources. External assistance provides a way to help tip the balance in favor of whichever side increases a state's security. In addition, insurgents can acquire weapons and ammunition by capturing them from government forces.[52] Given the basic constraints posed by numerical weakness, insurgents need arms and matèriel, money to buy them, or goods to trade for them. They also need a supply of recruits. During the Cold War, the United States and Soviet Union provided significant assistance to insurgent groups across Africa, Latin America, and Asia, enabling some of them to amass substantial resources, achieve rough parity with the government, and adopt a conventional strategy.

A number of insurgent leaders and theorists eschewed guerrilla warfare, arguing that victory ultimately necessitated a conventional strategy. Abdul Haris Nasution, an influential thinker and Indonesian general, contended that "final victory must be achieved by a regular army in a conventional war, because only such an army can stage an offensive of the nature that will subdue the enemy."[53]

Insurgents adopted conventional strategies in such cases as Greece (1946–1949), Vietnam (1955–1975), the Biafra conflict in Nigeria (1967–1970), Angola (1961–1974), Sierra Leone (1991–1997), the Croatian and

Bosnian wars in the former Yugoslavia (1992–1995), Afghanistan (1996–2001), Syria (2011–), Iraq (2014–), and Ukraine (2014–). These conflicts included the deployment of artillery and tanks in a landscape often dominated by trenches.

In Greece, for example, the Democratic Army of Greece established brigades and divisions in late 1948 to fight against the Greek government and engaged in positional warfare to defend areas they controlled. They built an army that peaked at 25,000 soldiers equipped with anti-aircraft and anti-tank guns, machine guns, heavy mortars, and rocket launchers.[54] To support a growing conventional army, Greek insurgent divisions required logistics bases, lines of communication, and other support necessary for a conventional military.[55] Unfortunately for Greek insurgents, the decision to shift to a conventional strategy was ill-timed and they were soundly defeated. As King Paul, who assumed the Greek throne in 1947, remarked, "The bandits made a mistake. They went in for the regular military form of warfare in large units. That's when they got it in the neck. Before that, we would give them a punch and they would disappear into thin air, then reappear and attack a village to get food."[56]

By the late 1960s, the Viet Cong adopted a conventional strategy. As Generals Vo Nguyen Giap and Van Tien Dung explained, "we used military attacks by our mobile strategic army columns as the main striking force to wipe out and smash the enemy's army. That is the application of the common law of war: *using our armed forces to destroy the armed forces of the enemy.*"[57] In April 1975, the North Vietnamese Army launched the Ho Chi Minh campaign to deliver a decisive conventional blow to the crumbling South Vietnamese army. As Giap and Dung acknowledged, "We had made great efforts to build many large strategic army columns composed of many modern technical units, especially tank, armor, artillery and anti-aircraft units capable of conducting combined offensives on a large scale."[58]

In the Biafran conflict in Nigeria, the principal goal of the Igbo, the dominant ethnic group in eastern Nigeria, was to secede. The Igbo focused on conventional operations thanks, in part, to their ability to secure arms and ammunition from Nigerian army stockpiles and donations from France, Spain, and Portugal. The Biafran military acquired airplanes and helicopters for a small air force, and boats fitted with machine guns for a small navy. Many Igbo officers had attended the Royal Military Academy Sandhurst, the British Army's national training center, where they took courses in conventional operations. Aside from a bold, though ultimately failed, attempt to seize the midwestern region of Nigeria in the summer and fall of 1967, conventional military operations took place in the east, and included artillery and mortar duels.[59]

UNITA rebels also adopted a conventional strategy in Angola, engaging in heavy fighting and controlling several provinces.[60] The battle of Cuito Cunavale, which took place in September 1987 between the pro-Soviet People's Movement for the Liberation of Angola (MPLA) and South African–backed UNITA fighters, entailed clashes between heavily armored columns.[61] In Sierra Leone, the Revolutionary United Front (RUF) adopted a conventional strategy against the government of Sierra Leone, especially in the early stages of the conflict. As one RUF document outlined, "we fought a semi-conventional war relying heavily on vehicles of mobility" intended to defeat the government's armed forces.[62] In Angola, MPLA insurgents adopted a conventional strategy in cases where their units were equipped with conventional weapons and had enough fighters to take on government forces. As one MPLA commander explained, "Now, with mobile columns that can move in large numbers with heavy weapons, we can carry out much larger attacks. We are better able to annihilate whole enemy units and attack and occupy Portuguese positions."[63]

During the war in Yugoslavia, the main Croat and Bosnian insurgent groups adopted conventional strategies and utilized their forces in a series of decisive military engagements. As a CIA assessment concluded, "virtually all of the fighting was done by professionally led, relatively well-organized citizen armies."[64] Much like government armies, Bosnian and Croat groups developed military structures with a centralized staff that controlled a hierarchy of units, such as air defense, transport, training, military police, and communications. They also planned and executed complex military operations involving tens of thousands of combatants over fronts that spanned tens or hundreds of miles, some of which included trench warfare.[65]

After the September 11, 2001, terrorist attacks in the United States, Northern Alliance rebels developed a conventional strategy to overthrow the Taliban regime with help from CIA and US Special Operations teams. Gary Schroen, who headed the first CIA team in Afghanistan in 2001, explained the Northern Alliance–US strategy in a cable to CIA headquarters: "If we smash the Taliban front lines, the [Northern Alliance] will take the Shomali Plains and Kabul. The Taliban will not try to hold Kabul but will flee to the south and east, down into Paktia, Paktika, and Gardez."[66] Beginning in October 2001, the Northern Alliance and US teams attacked Taliban positions with T-55 tanks, M-30 artillery, 14.5-mm machine guns, and other heavy weapons, with support from US aircraft that targeted Taliban fighting positions. Insurgents such as the Islamic State of Iraq also utilized a conventional strategy in the conflicts in Syria and Iraq.

Some al Qa'ida leaders, such as Saudi operative 'Abd Al-'Aziz Al-Muqrin, have encouraged jihadist insurgents to consider using a conventional strategy when appropriate. Muqrin noted, for example, that "these are wars in which all weapons are used, with the exception of weapons of destruction, and this is a war waged between two conventional armies."[67] The Islamic State used a conventional strategy in 2014 as part of its blitzkrieg campaign to seize territory in western and northern Iraq. It began with an attack on Samarra on June 5, 2014, followed by the seizure of Mosul on June 10, Tikrit on June 11, and then a range of other cities and towns. The Islamic State secured weapons from Iraqi and Syrian bases and checkpoints—such as surface-to-air missiles, tanks, Humvees, anti-aircraft guns, rockets, and rocket launchers—that allowed it to conduct conventional operations against Iraqi forces.[68]

PUNISHMENT

Punishment strategies involve deliberately targeting noncombatants, such as killing civilians or destroying infrastructure, in order to raise the societal costs of continued resistance and coerce the government to concede to insurgent demands.[69] The common feature of punishment campaigns is that they inflict suffering on civilians, either directly or indirectly.[70] Their goals may include decreasing civilian morale by exposing large portions of the population to terror or by causing severe shortages of consumer goods and services (such as food, textiles, and industrial goods), as well as deterring the population from cooperating with the government. A decline in civilian morale, it is hoped, then produces internal turmoil, which causes grass-roots opposition against the local government. Unlike a guerrilla strategy, insurgents that employ a punishment strategy don't focus on winning popular support from a local population. Instead, they seek to coerce and manipulate support through brute force, since their objective is targeting the population—not necessarily the government. Insurgents may still engage government forces. Their goal, however, is not to win by defeating the government's capacity to fight, but rather to undermine its morale by targeting its population.

Insurgents rarely, if ever, use a punishment strategy by itself, but they generally mix punishment with other strategies. Insurgents can gradually manipulate the risk of punishment instead of immediately resorting to large-scale brutality.[71] The focus in some punishment campaigns is to raise the threat of civilian damage slowly and deliberately, compelling governments to concede defeat and avoid suffering future costs. Punishment can be inflicted directly by killing a selective group of civilians, or indirectly by destroying economic infrastructure and depriving the population of essential goods and services. The key is not to destroy the entire target set in one fell swoop. Since coercive leverage comes from the anticipation of future damage, insurgents should be careful to spare a substantial part of the opponent's civilian assets in order to threaten further destruction.[72]

It may seem puzzling why groups use a punishment strategy *at all*. Indiscriminate violence can engender discontent among civilian populations, create high levels of resistance to rebel advances, and damage the reputation of a rebel group within the country and internationally.[73] But insurgent groups may use a punishment strategy for several reasons.

First, insurgents may attempt to coerce locals in areas they do not control.[74] As one study concluded, such coercion may involve "partial annihilation, intended to convince the target population that one is resolved to go the whole way."[75] There may also be an identification problem in areas that insurgents don't control. In the midst of war, insurgents may have difficulty identifying friends and enemies, since spies and agents of both sides hide among the civilian population. Government forces face the same challenge. One US soldier patrolling in an Afghan village remarked, "Two out of 10 people here hate you and want to kill you. You just have to figure out which two."[76] Insurgents generally don't need to use violence against civilians where they already enjoy high levels of control. Instead, they may resort to indiscriminate violence where they have no control of territory, and more selective violence in cases where they have dominant—but incomplete—control. As political scientist Stathis Kalyvas found, "The key resources around which the process is arrayed are information and violence. Political actors need information in order to be able to target selectively, to distinguish from among the sea of civilians those who are abetting the enemy."[77]

The objective of coercion was neatly illustrated with the FLN in Algeria, as one observer noted: "The FLN with one killing, would set an example strong enough to scare a large crowd into acquiescence and, once successful, would stop."[78] In Colombia, FARC rebels resorted to massacres in the 1990s in areas where they had no control.[79] The same was true in Colombia in the late 1940s and early 1950s during La Violencia, when both sides committed large-scale brutality against villagers in an effort to control rural areas.[80] Insurgents in Malaya targeted resettlement centers and towns controlled by the British.[81] The FRELIMO in Mozambique mortared and rocketed the *aldeamentos* (government-protected villages) on a routine basis during the decolonization struggle.[82] The Nicaraguan contras used violence against Sandinista strongholds, the Sendero Luminoso against villages that formed militias, the RUF in Sierra Leone against villages that formed kamajor militias, and the National Liberation Army in Colombia against villages that rose up against them.[83] In Uganda, the Lord's Resistance Army adopted a punishment strategy. As LRA leader Joseph Kony remarked in reference to the Acholi ethnic group from Northern Uganda, "If the Acholi don't support us, they must be finished."[84] Insurgents that used a punishment strategy did not just target competing ethnic or sectarian groups. Many punished their co-ethnics who collaborated with the enemy, such as in the wars of decolonization in Africa and the Kurdish insurgency in eastern Turkey.[85]

Mau Mau insurgents adopted a punishment strategy in some areas of Kenya against ethnic Kikuyu that supported the British-backed government, leaving civilian victims hacked and mutilated. The vast majority of insurgent violence was directed at fellow Kikuyu, not white settlers. As one assessment concluded, "It was a war in the Kikuyu reserves, in the labour lines where African families resided on the farms, and in the squalid African estates of Nairobi; it was a war fought between and among Kikuyu communities."[86] One of the most egregious examples of the Mau Mau punishment strategy was in the town of Lari, Kenya in March 1953. Mau Mau operatives slaughtered men, women, and children because they had friends or family members that were outspoken opponents of Mau Mau. To be clear, these types of attacks were not random, but were part of a deliberate effort to punish government supporters and deter future support. Indeed, attacks like the one at Lari were facilitated by neighbors of the victims, many of whom supported the Mau Mau campaign.

Second, insurgents may adopt a punishment campaign to bait the government into overreacting. The hope is that government security forces may be so appalled at the killing of civilians that they will overreact and massacre insurgents and their alleged supporters, undermining local hearts and minds in the long run.[87] In Algeria, the FLN targeted *pieds-noirs*—settlers from France, Italy, and Spain that had migrated to Algeria—along with French security targets to provoke a French overreaction and encourage more locals to support the insurgency.[88]

Third, insurgents sometimes adopt a punishment strategy in cases where they have abundant resources to finance warfare, which minimize the costs of brutality. When insurgents have access to natural resources or external support from an outside patron, they may become opportunistic and primarily interested in short-term, material gains. The short-term behavior of combatants sometimes leads to incidents of looting, destruction, and indiscriminate killing. Groups are thus permissive, if not encouraging, of attacks on civilian populations in order to maintain their membership and prevent organizational collapse, since the group is held together by members with short-term interests.[89] As Table 3.1 highlights, wars in which groups use a punishment strategy are often long, averaging fifteen years. The long duration of punishment campaigns may occur, in part, because groups have access to abundant resources, allowing them to fund insurgent operations over a prolonged period.

In Mozambique, for example, RENAMO was involved in wide-spread killing and brutality. As one civilian recalled, "In the beginning, they only abducted boys and took them. But they came back and said that the objective was to kill everyone who belonged to the Grupo Dinamizador. They began by killing those people, but then began to kill people who had nothing to do with the Grupo Dinamizador or anything else."[90] RENAMO's use of violence was partly a result of the short-term, material motivations of its membership, which rendered RENAMO's commanders unable or unwilling to prevent defection within their units. RENAMO augmented its financial base by systematically looting household property, trading illegal goods, and extorting payments from private enterprise in exchange for protection. In areas it controlled, RENAMO used traditional authorities to maintain a consistent supply of food, abduct new members from schools and homes, and seize women as wives for the soldiers.[91]

Fourth, groups may adopt a punishment strategy to sow discord and disorder among government officials, including raising concerns among the population that the government can no longer protect them.[92] The primary responsibility of a government is to guarantee order to its population, and insurgent groups may attempt to disorient the population by demonstrating that the government cannot provide adequate support and security. The insurgent rationale in this case is to affect the psychological well-being of locals, isolating them from the government and destroying their social and personal stability.[93]

Fifth, insurgents may use punishment for ideological reasons, particularly when they view the enemy as subhuman or illegitimate. For example, some groups inspired by religious extremism, including Salafi-jihadist groups like the Islamic State and al Qa'ida, argued that it is legitimate to kill civilians they consider apostates.

Al Qa'ida leader Ayman al-Zawahiri maintained that it was legitimate to kill civilians, including Muslims, under some conditions. One was during night raids, in which al Qa'ida targeted specific individuals, and only accidentally killed women or children. "If they are not separated from the others," he wrote, "it is permitted to kill them including old people, women, young boys, sick persons, incapacitated persons, and unworldly monks."[94] A second condition involved killing those who supported infidels by providing money, information, or other aid. While not engaged in actual fighting, abetting the enemy was just as condemnable. "It is permitted to kill women, young boys, and the old and infirm if they help their people," Zawahiri wrote.[95] A third condition was when civilians were interacting directly with infidels. "If they mix with others and one cannot avoid killing them along with the others," Zawahiri insisted, "then it is permitted to kill them."[96] By 2007, four years after the start of the insurgency in Iraq, al Qa'ida in Iraq had conducted 6,210 attacks that caused 13,612 deaths. Approximately 70 percent of the victims were civilians and over 50 percent of victims were Muslims.[97]

TRENDS IN INSURGENT STRATEGIES

Given these strategic options, what are key historical trends? This section examines aggregate data on insurgent strategies, with a particular focus on how frequently these strategies are used, how use of these strategies has evolved over time, and how insurgents choose among strategies. Since World War II, guerrilla warfare was the most common strategy adopted by insurgent groups, though it was used more frequently during the Cold War. As Table 3.2 illustrates, insurgents adopted a guerrilla strategy in 69 percent of cases, a conventional strategy 49 percent of the time, and a punishment strategy in only 36 percent of cases. In 44 percent of insurgencies, groups used more than one strategy.

What explains the frequency of different insurgent strategies? One possibility is that most groups adopt a guerrilla strategy because of their relative weakness—or perceived weakness—compared to the government. With limited popular support, fighters, and resources—at least

TABLE 3.2 Frequency of insurgent strategies

Strategy	Percentage of total insurgencies where the strategy was used
Guerrilla	69%
Conventional	49%
Punishment	36%

initially—it may be suicidal to fight the government directly using a conventional strategy. Another possible explanation for the prevalence of guerrilla strategies is that they are more successful. The data, however, do not support this conclusion. In conflicts that have terminated, insurgents that adopted a conventional strategy were victorious in 41 percent of cases and battled the government to a draw in another 23 percent (for a total of 64 percent), according to the data compiled for this book. Put another way, insurgents that adopted a conventional strategy achieved either a victory or draw nearly two thirds of the time. Insurgents that adopted guerrilla and punishment strategies achieved outright victory 34 percent and 31 percent of the time, respectively.

As Chapter 8 highlights, however, none of these strategies is strongly correlated with insurgent victory, suggesting that other factors are more decisive in winning—at least in the 181 cases since World War II.[98] There are also likely selection effects at work with conventional strategies. Groups may adopt conventional strategies when the government is weak—or they perceive the government is weak. Consequently, the results may indicate a weak government rather than a more effective strategy. Another possibility is that groups choose a conventional strategy when they have combat support from outside governments, augmenting their capabilities. In nearly half the cases since World War II in which insurgents adopted a conventional strategy, they enjoyed combat support from outside states.

Patterns in insurgent strategies have not remained static over time. As Figure 3.1 shows, groups utilized a guerrilla strategy in over 90 percent of insurgencies at various points since World War II, though the percentage temporarily dipped at the end of the Cold War. Conventional strategies dropped in the post–Cold War era, with groups using a conventional strategy decreasing from 38 percent of insurgencies in 1992 down to 24 percent in 2015. The decline of conventional strategies may be caused, in part, by the decrease in great-power support to insurgent groups, which is discussed in more detail in Chapter 7. Great powers have historically provided insurgent groups with financial aid, arms, and equipment, which can increase their power relative to the government. With the end of the Cold War, both the Soviet Union and United States substantially cut their support to insurgents. The decline may also be a result of the breakup of some states, such as Yugoslavia

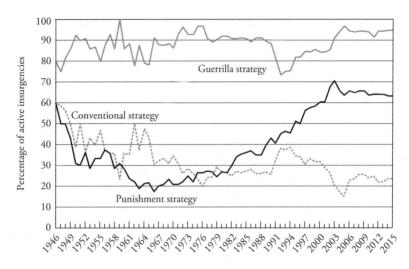

FIGURE 3.1 Trends in insurgent strategies

and the Soviet Union, where there was a condition of emerging anarchy in which groups left in the wake had sufficient weapons to fight conventionally.[99] Finally, punishment strategies have been on the rise since the end of the Cold War. This rise may be caused, in part, by the rise of Islamic extremist groups, highlighted in Chapter 1, which have adopted punishment strategies and tactics.

Some individuals have used such terms as "hybrid warfare" to describe a mixture of conventional and other strategies, as Ukrainian rebels and their Russian supporters utilized in eastern Ukraine beginning in 2014.[100] But insurgent groups have long used a mixture of strategies. In fact, groups used more than one strategy in 44 percent of insurgencies. The data suggest several reasons why groups use more than one strategy.

First, insurgents may switch strategies if one fails to achieve results. In Sierra Leone, for example, the RUF moved from a conventional to a guerrilla strategy because of poor results on the battlefield. As one RUF assessment concluded,

> Initially we fought a semi-conventional war relying heavily on vehicles of mobility. This method proved fatal against the combined fire power of Nigeria, Guinea and Ghana ... We dispersed into smaller units, whatever remained of our fighting force. The civilians

were advised to abandon the towns and cities, which they did. We destroyed all our vehicles and heavy weapons that would retard our progress as well as expose our locations. We now relied on light weapons and on our feet, brains and knowledge of the countryside. We moved deeper into the comforting bosom of our mother earth—the forest.[101]

Second, groups may use different strategies depending on the balance-of-power with the government, which can change over the course of a conflict. It can even vary by area, where government forces in some regions may be weaker than in other areas. Mao advocated a three-phased approach to insurgency. In the first stage, when opposition forces had a significant advantage in numbers and military power, insurgents should focus on building their political apparatus and securing support from outside powers. In the second stage, which Mao termed "strategic stalemate," insurgents should shift to a guerrilla strategy, focusing on hit-and-run attacks. As Mao wrote, "In this stage, our form of fighting will be primarily guerrilla warfare, supplemented by mobile warfare."[102] The duration of this stage "will depend on the degree of change in the balance of forces between us and the enemy and on the changes in the international situation."[103] In the third stage, insurgents should focus on offensive, conventional operations as their military power increases.[104]

Third, groups may use different strategies depending on their control of territory, which can vary across urban and rural areas. Insurgents may adopt a punishment strategy, for example, in areas where they have little local support and limited control of territory, but a guerrilla strategy in areas where they have some support and greater territorial control.[105] In Algeria, the Armed Islamic Group (GIA) used little violence against civilians in areas it controlled, preferring a guerrilla strategy and targeting the Algerian government. But the GIA adopted a punishment strategy in some contested areas.

In sum, strategies are a critical component of insurgent warfare. Insurgent groups need to decide how to use their military and political resources to defeat the government on the battlefield or coerce it to achieve their objectives. Contrary to accounts that conflate insurgent strategies with guerrilla warfare, insurgents can choose from three main strategies: conventional warfare, punishment, and guerrilla warfare. As this chapter suggests, blindly focusing on a guerrilla warfare strategy could be catastrophic for hopeful insurgents. In the end, insurgents should choose a strategy that matches means to ends. They may need to vary their strategies by area (depending on territorial control), phases of the insurgency (depending on the balance-of-power with the government), the government's strategy, or other factors. But without an adequate strategy, insurgents have little chance of achieving their objectives.

4

Tactics

In guerrilla warfare, select the tactic of seeming to come from the east and attacking from the west; avoid the solid, attack the hollow; attack; withdraw; deliver a lightning blow, seek a lightning decision.[1]

—Mao Tse-Tung

Tactics are dictated by the existing conditions. Here again the logic is quite simple. Without support Volunteers, Dumps, Weapons, Finance, etc., we cannot mount an operation, much less a campaign.[2]

—Irish Republican Army, *Green Book*

BEGINNING IN 2011, SYRIAN insurgent groups adopted a broad suite of tactics against the Assad regime. These tactics ranged from attacks using vehicle-borne improvised explosive devices (VBIEDs) to targeted assassinations and ambushes, with insurgent groups frequently relying on the Internet and social media to broadcast the results. In one of the most brazen attacks in the early phase of the war, rebel groups led by the Islamic State staged a sophisticated attack in 2012 on Minakh Air Base, a Syrian Air Force installation near Aleppo that was home to the Syrian military's 4th Flying Squadron and housed MBB 223 Flamingo trainer aircraft, Mi-8 helicopters, ammunition, and other supplies. It was a strategic target for insurgent groups since the Syrian government had used aircraft from the base against rebel forces in northern Syria, including in Aleppo city. The siege of Minakh began in August 2012, when rebel forces attacked the base using small arms, rocket-propelled grenades, and captured army tanks.[3] The battle intensified in late

December 2012 as insurgents advanced to the edge of the base and government aircraft bombarded insurgent positions.[4]

Over the first half of 2013, groups conducted multiple attacks against the air base and, on August 5, 2013, finally breached Minakh's walls. Two suicide bombers from Jaish al-Muhajideen wal Ansar, a group led by Syria-based Chechen leader Abu Umar al-Shishani, carried out the initial assault by driving an armored BMP, a Russian-made infantry-fighting vehicle, packed with six tons of explosives, into the perimeter wall.[5] Fighters from several groups—such as the Islamic State, Jaish al-Muhajideen wal Ansar, Liwa al-Fateh, and the Northern Storm Brigade—then successfully stormed Minakh. The operation against Minakh Air Base was coupled with an aggressive Internet and social media campaign. A video uploaded to YouTube on August 6, 2013, for example, showed rebel commanders reporting on the operation from inside the base.[6]

As the Minakh Air Base attack highlighted, Syrian insurgents adopted a broad mix of tactics—from bombings to ambushes—in their struggle to overthrow the Assad regime.

This chapter focuses on insurgent tactics. As used here, tactics refer to the employment and arrangement of forces—including arms, equipment, and personnel—in battle or in the immediate presence of the enemy in an insurgency.[7] While strategy involves a group's plan for using military and other instruments, tactics are about what insurgents and counterinsurgents do—and how they do it. As the military theorist Carl von Clausewitz noted, tactics are "the use of armed forces in the engagement; strategy, the use of engagements for the object of the war."[8] British Field Marshall Archibald Wavell similarly argued that "tactics is the art of handling troops on the battlefield; strategy is the art of bringing forces to the battlefield in a favorable position."[9]

This chapter makes several arguments. First, effective tactics tend to be those that exploit government weaknesses (such as ambushes against exposed government forces), undermine government legitimacy (such as subversion), strengthen insurgent forces (such as raids that seize government arms and supplies), or provoke the government into overreacting. These objectives are just as much political and psychological as they are military. To be effective, tactics need to be closely linked with strategy and other elements of an insurgency, including information campaigns and propaganda. Second, ineffective tactics tend to be those that weaken local support for insurgent groups or expose insurgent weaknesses. Tactics that inordinately punish the local population risk decreasing local support and undermining a group's chances of victory, much like with punishment strategies. Some tactics, such as suicide attacks, have often been counterproductive in achieving long-term objectives. No insurgent group that has utilized suicide terrorism has yet won an insurgency that has ended. The data indicate that there is no correlation between most tactics and whether insurgents win, since virtually every insurgent group uses a wide range of tactics from ambushes and raids to assassinations. But *how* insurgents use tactics is critical.

The rest of this chapter is organized into two major sections. The first examines the range of tactics available to groups. The second analyzes trends in the use of insurgent tactics, including the lethality of insurgent tactics, the loss of popular support, and urban versus rural tactics.

BATTLEFIELD TACTICS

Insurgent groups have used multiple tactics—usually in combination with each other—to fight governments. This section focuses on several tactics: ambushes and raids, subversion and sabotage, assassinations and mutilations, kidnappings, and bombings (including suicide attacks). This list is not meant to be exhaustive, but rather to highlight some of the tactics most frequently utilized by insurgents on the battlefield. These tactics can be used in all the strategies discussed in Chapter 3: guerrilla warfare, conventional warfare, and punishment. And they are not mutually exclusive since insurgents can use them in combination.

Ambushes and raids: Both ambushes and raids are designed to achieve a range of military and political objectives, such as killing or capturing enemy personnel, destroying or seizing enemy vehicles and supplies, and coercing and deterring enemy forces or the local population.

An ambush is an attack from a concealed position on a moving or temporarily halted enemy. Ambushes usually stop, deny, or destroy enemy forces by maximizing the element of surprise, though they generally do not involve seizing and holding territory. Insurgents conducting an ambush can employ direct fire and indirect fire.[10]

Insurgent groups sometimes organize ambushes into three teams: assault, support, and security. The assault team fires into the "kill zone" where counterinsurgent forces are located. Insurgents also attack and attempt to clear the kill zone, and some may be assigned additional tasks like searching for items of intelligence value and capturing prisoners. Next, the support team aids the assault force by firing into and around the kill zone. The support team attempts to destroy the majority of counterinsurgent combat power before the assault team moves into the kill zone. Finally, the security team warns of the arrival of counterinsurgent forces and provides security for the assault and support teams.[11]

A raid is an offensive operation to temporarily seize an area to secure information, confuse or threaten an adversary, capture or kill personnel, or seize or destroy equipment. It is then followed by a planned withdrawal.[12] Unlike an ambush, in which insurgents are generally in place when enemy forces move into the kill zone, the government force is usually in place in a raid. 'Abd Al-'Aziz Al-Muqrin, head of al Qa'ida in the Arabian Peninsula until his death by Saudi security forces in June 2004, explained in his book *A Practical Course for Guerrilla War* that "the technical difference between an ambush and a raid is that an ambush consists of lying in wait in a good position, whereas a raid is a planned and organized attack on a target selected with precision and care."[13]

Ambushes and raids have been particularly valuable in striking much better equipped local government or foreign forces. In Vietnam, the Viet Cong conducted ambushes and raids against South Vietnamese and US forces to undermine morale, among other aims. They also spent considerable time planning operations, sometimes using a sand table or a stake-and-string replica of the target during rehearsals. The Viet Cong also carefully chose terrain that provided concealment for insurgents to encircle and divide government forces; utilized heavy weapons emplacements to provide sustained fire; set up observation posts for early detection of government or allied forces; and permitted the clandestine movement of troops to positions and the dispersal of troops during withdrawal.[14] In Angola, MPLA insurgents utilized ambushes, in part, "to demoralize the Portuguese troops, to prevent them from living peacefully in their barracks."[15]

During the Chechen insurgency in Russia, rebels repeatedly carried out ambushes and raids against Russian forces.[16] The head of the main operational staff for Russia's Unified Grouping of Federal Forces (OGV), Col. Gennadii Zhilin, noted that Chechen ambushes often initiated contact by detonating a roadside bomb: "After the explosives are detonated, especially if the convoys are relatively small, the bandits move in and are on the troops' vehicles relentlessly for 5–15 minutes, using all types of weapons. They then seize as many weapons, documents, and prisoners as they can and swiftly disappear into the thickets of the surrounding mountains and forests."[17] In addition, Chechen insurgents conducted raids against Russian bases and camps. These raids were designed to "create a constant, high level of psychological stress on [Russian] servicemen and to undermine their morale."[18] Ambushes were particularly lethal in areas of the North Caucasus where the road system was virtually nonexistent and Russian military vehicles used well-known routes.[19]

One Russian commander warned in 2004 that the "constant ambushes along the roads" in Chechnya killed a "worrying number" of Russian soldiers, and that the insurgents' "systematic attempts to expand the scope of their combat operations" created a dire situation in the North Caucasus.[20] The Ministry of Internal Affairs and the army were subsequently criticized for their "appallingly slow and disorganized response" to the raids and ambushes.[21]

In Afghanistan after the 2001 overthrow of the Taliban regime, ambushes were a staple insurgent tactic. Afghanistan is a sparsely populated country with poor roads. The long lines of US communication presented easy targets. The Taliban employed a wide variety of ambush tactics against mounted and dismounted patrols in mountainous terrain and along key roads. Most ambushes were hit-and-run attacks, lasting less than thirty minutes. Insurgents used scouts to observe the movement of Afghan, US, and other NATO forces. Forward observers often reported the details of a convoy, such as the number and type of vehicles, the presence of tactical air controllers, and whether the convoy was carrying artillery. Insurgents lying in wait in the Gulistan valley in Farah Province in October 2007, for example, appeared to know that air support was unlikely, giving them ample time to maneuver on their target. The insurgents also knew the route the convoy would take and when it would arrive. Figure 4.1 highlights the Gulistan ambush on October 31, 2007, in which insurgents killed twenty Afghan security personnel and wounded two US soldiers.[22]

In some cases, insurgent groups can mass forces against government troops in raids and ambushes that start to resemble conventional fights. In Colombia, for example, FARC insurgents conducted ambushes against battalion-sized units of the Colombian army, decimating the 52nd Counterguerrilla Battalion (52 BCG) of the 3rd Mobile Brigade (3 BRIM) in February 1998.[23] In addition, insurgent groups

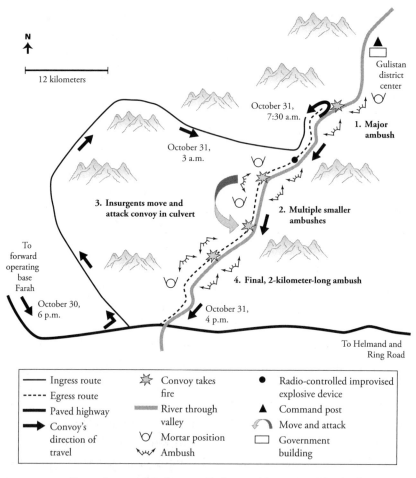

FIGURE 4.1 Complex ambush in Gulistan District, Farah Province, October 2007[116]

have conducted ambushes and raids against militias and other non-state actors allied to the government. In Kenya, for example, Mau Mau insurgents regularly ambushed Home Guard patrols in an effort to intimidate them.[24]

While insurgents have frequently utilized ambushes to kill, capture, or destroy enemy personnel, they are also used to confiscate arms, ammunition, vehicles, food, medical equipment, and other supplies from opposition forces.[25] The FARC in Colombia raided farms to obtain food, and later attacked small military outposts or patrols to seize weapons, clothing, communications equipment, and ammunition. According to one account, FMLN guerrillas in El Salvador gathered a range of their "weapons, including even mortars and other artillery pieces . . . by way of captured government troops."[26] Sendero Luminoso in Peru and Boko Haram in Nigeria sustained themselves, at least partly, by raiding locations like police stations and mining camps to collect weapons, explosives, and supplies.[27] So did Huthi insurgents in Yemen, who acquired weapons, ammunition, and vehicles from raids and ambushes against government forces.[28] Mau Mau fighters in Kenya were constantly short of weapons and other equipment, and resorted to raids and thefts to seize them.[29]

Subversion and sabotage: Subversion involves efforts by insurgent groups to undermine the military, economic, psychological, or political strength of a government by individuals working clandestinely.[30] The legitimacy of a government hinges on providing security and delivering basic services. Subversion tactics attempt to undermine public perception of the government. They can also help mobilize social unrest without resorting to more large-scale and overt action. Insurgencies may not be able to seize power by fomenting disorder, but efforts to undermine regime legitimacy are important for insurgent groups to establish control.[31] As one al Qa'ida insurgent manual summarized, "The objective of [subversion] targets is to shake the security and sense of stability necessary for work to go forward and for the economic wheels to turn, as happened with the attack against the oil wells and pipelines in Iraq, which caused foreign companies to pull out."[32] Unlike ambushes and raids, which involve a direct, overt confrontation with counterinsurgent forces, subversion generally does not include direct engagement.

In Angola, MPLA insurgents focused their subversive operations in 1961 in Luanda at freeing political prisoners held in the town's police stations and prisons. They also seized arms from police posts.[33] In Vietnam, the Viet Cong developed a doctrine termed *binh van*, which focused on desertion and defection from the Vietnam government.[34] Through agitation, persuasion, coercion, and threats, the Viet Cong's subversion campaign attempted to weaken the government's popularity and swell the ranks of the insurgency. It helped decrease the will of Vietnamese soldiers to fight for their government who, in some cases, provided intelligence on government activity or defected to the Viet Cong.[35] In Nicaragua, locals in the barrios lit bonfires as a symbol of subversion against the Somoza regime and support for the Sandinistas. As one Sandinista rebel explained, "Fire took on this subversive character because everybody in the opposition, all the anti-Somoza people and all the pro-Sandinistas, clung together around the flames. So the bonfire was a sign of subversion, a symbol of political agitation, of revolutionary ideas brought by the students into the barrios."[36]

Propaganda is an important component of subversion, but is examined in more detail in Chapter 6. Insurgents can also utilize subversive techniques to manipulate crowds and civil disturbances to advance their overall strategy.[37] Groups like university students, unions, and political organizations are prime targets for insurgent mobilization because they can facilitate strikes, protests, and other types of social and political unrest.[38]

In addition, sabotage is an important subversive tactic and involves "an act or acts with intent to injure, interfere with, or obstruct the national defense of a country by willfully injuring or destroying, or attempting to injure or destroy, any national defense or war matèriel, premises, or utilities, to include human and natural resources."[39] Sabotage can include both violent and nonviolent activities. In selective sabotage, insurgents may try to destroy or incapacitate installations that cannot be easily replaced or repaired. In some cases, insurgent groups may receive training from other insurgent groups, such as Provisional IRA members who traveled to Colombia to train the FARC in improvised explosives.[40] Sabotage can help undermine the military, economic, psychological, political strength, and morale of a governing authority by damaging military production, economic resources, industrial facilities, food production, public morale, and public security.[41]

In South Africa, African National Congress (ANC) operatives utilized sabotage operations to undermine support for the white government. As outlined in ANC documents like Operation Mayibuye, key targets included strategic roads and railways, power stations, major industrial installations, and dams.[42] Sabotage served a number of purposes in the early 1960s. The ANC hoped it might inspire some young militants to join underground combat units. In addition, the ANC used sabotage to threaten further escalation if the government did not change its policies toward blacks. In the words of ANC operative Jack Hodgson, the goal was straightforward: "When they have to guard everything that opens and shuts in the country, they'll have no one available to control the people."[43] The ANC leadership gave its operatives specific instructions to avoid attacks which would lead to injury or loss of life in hopes that the regime might change its policies. According to one ANC operative,

> The point was strongly featured in the proclamation accompanying the first sabotage acts which expressed the hope that "even at this late hour" the actions would awaken everyone to a sense of realization of the disastrous situation to which the regime's policy was leading, and could bring the government and its supporters to their senses before it was too late and before matters reached the desperate stage of civil war.[44]

The economist Thomas Schelling referred to this logic as the "diplomacy of violence." It was the threat of further violence—of more damage to come—that could make the state yield or comply.[45] In a letter to Fidel Castro, the Cuban military leader General Alberto Bayo emphasized that sabotage was one of the most important aspects of an insurgent campaign and encouraged Castro to "begin a wave of sabotage aimed in particular against the sugar centers of the interior."[46] Similarly, Che Guevara remarked that "acts of sabotage are very important" for insurgents and "well-managed sabotage is always a very effective arm."[47] Roads, railroads, bridges, and rivers are vulnerable because they are key transportation hubs, labor-intensive for government forces to defend, and costly and time-consuming to rebuild.

In El Salvador, the FMLN effectively cut the country in two for part of the insurgency by destroying all the main bridges that crossed the Lempa River, an economic lifeline. The FMLN also destroyed dozens of coffee, sugarcane, and cotton installations, including many of the largest and most important ones. And the FMLN continuously interrupted the electrical system in more than 80 percent of the country.[48] In Nigeria, the Movement for the Emancipation of the Niger Delta was successful in shutting down sections of the Niger Delta's oil infrastructure because of sabotage operations.[49] In Yemen, Huthi insurgents conducted multiple sabotage operations against the Yemen government and its supporters in the war that began in 2004, including against water pumps in Baqim.[50]

In the Iraq war that began in 2003, insurgents targeted key infrastructure, which disrupted oil exports, electricity production, and fuel distribution.[51] A US government assessment of critical infrastructure noted that Iraqi insurgents "demonstrate some agility in switching their attacks between Oil, Power and Rail—but greater ruthlessness should be anticipated. Damage to pylons, oil pipes and rail track is unacceptable but relatively easily repaired; sabotage of a power plant or refinery (Critical Infrastructure) is catastrophic."[52] The problem was daunting in Iraq with 23,500 km of infrastructure, well above what the US and Iraqi security forces could protect. The solution, the US assessment argued, was to focus on critical infrastructure, develop intelligence-directed patrolling and air surveillance capabilities, and invest in rapid repair techniques.[53]

Iraqi insurgents targeted railroads as well. As one US government report concluded, "the extent to which normal operations are disrupted remains unacceptable if the railway is to function as a vital transport element in the movement of cargoes."[54] Several of these sabotage efforts were effective in undermining support for the US-led Coalition Provisional Authority. According to a military assessment for US Secretary of Defense Donald Rumsfeld, "the emerging threats and attacks against the Iraqi infrastructure are reaching a level that requires immediate and unprecedented action. We are losing the consent of the Iraqi people by failing to meet their expectations in some of the most basic areas of life support. As such we risk losing the peace."[55]

In Peru, Sendero Luminoso jump-started their insurgency in May 1980 during the presidential elections by conducting attacks against polling stations in Ayachucho designed to undermine the government's legitimacy. In subsequent years, Sendero orchestrated a series of high-profile sabotage campaigns, including against the country's electric power grid. In August 1982, Sendero bombed five high-tension towers supplying electricity to the Lima-Callao area, plunging nine million people—half the nation's population—into darkness for 48 hours. Several months later, Sendero launched another attack on Lima's electrical grid that caused a complete power failure in the capital and six other cities. Minutes after the blackout, Sendero lit a large flaming hammer and sickle that burned on a mountaintop overlooking the darkened city of Lima.[56]

Assassinations: This tactic is designed to coerce, deter, or simply eliminate civilians or government officials through the *precise* use of violence. Assassinations involve the targeted killing of counterinsurgents, collaborators, and others that sympathize with the government. As one al Qa'ida guerrilla manual summarized, an assassination is an "operation involving a surprise killing of a designated target, done in order to eliminate the harm someone is doing and to deter others like him."[57] There are several objectives of assassinations: to eliminate counterinsurgent civilian or security personnel; cause discord within the government; encourage defections from within the government or civilian population; and deter locals from collaborating with the government. Insurgent groups can use multiple methods to assassinate enemies, from small-arms fire to improvised explosive devices (IEDs).

In Kenya, Mau Mau insurgents began their campaign in 1952 with grisly assassinations against ethnic Kikuyu that supported the government. Victims died as a result of multiple blade wounds, with the bodies hacked and mutilated. Mau Mau assassination squads targeted collaborators with the British government and its allies, including the Home Guard militias. As one Mau Mau insurgent leader summarized, one of the first activities of the "secret committee" established in 1952 was the "elimination of informers."[58] In Algeria, the GIA assassinated friends and family members for supporting the government, including those who voted during elections.[59] In Yemen, Huthi insurgents targeted sheikhs and their family members that supported the government, as well as destroyed their houses, agricultural plots, and other property.[60] In Uganda, Lord's Resistance Army (LRA) commanders sometimes forced children to kill their own family members to ensure that the child's loyalty was to the group—not the family.[61]

In Northern Ireland, the Provisional IRA regularly targeted the Royal Ulster Constabulary (RUC) and other forces. This included a range of assassinations, such as the IRA women who lured three British sergeants to a party on the Antrim Road in Belfast. The sergeants were captured, lined up, and machine-gunned to death. An IRA squad also caught two off-duty RUC sergeants buying wine to take home and executed them. As one IRA official glibly noted, "We've nothing against them personally. It's the uniform we are after. It's just business."[62]

Mutilations: While they are banned under Article 3 of the Geneva Conventions, mutilations involve cutting off, wounding, or permanently destroying a limb or other part of the human body.[63] Numerous insurgent groups and governments have resorted to mutilations to coerce or deter locals through fear. Unlike assassinations, which are designed to kill the target, this tactic ensures that the victim survives—but with a visible wound. Much as in Nathaniel Hawthorne's fictional book *The Scarlet Letter*, the goal is to leave the victim with a publicly identifiable symbol that sends a message to others.

In Uganda, the LRA severed off the lips, ears, noses, fingers, and hands of victims. They also sewed shut the eyes of some victims and padlocked lips together. LRA fighters cut off the ears, lips, and fingers of one 17-year-old boy. They then wrapped his ears in a letter that warned locals not to join local defense forces, explicitly threatening, "We shall do to you what we have done to him."[64] The LRA used mutilation to influence or control the local population. Cutting off the ears and lips, for example, was a deliberate tactic to deter civilians from informing on the LRA.[65] Mau Mau insurgents in Kenya were notorious for conducting mutilations. Members in some areas were given the following instructions: "Any enemy captured in a fight or in a raid shall be cut into small pieces with a sharp *simi* [knife]. First the right-hand wrist shall be severed and thrown away for the vultures, and this will be continued until the body is separated. The flesh shall then be thrown away for the hyenas."[66] In Northern Ireland, the Provisional IRA conducted a range of mutilations—including "kneecapping," which is inflicted by a gunshot to the knee—designed to cripple British collaborators.[67] In some cases, insurgents may stop short of mutilating individuals, but instead destroy their property. In Algeria, for example, the GIA destroyed the property of collaborators, including burning down the houses of collaborators and torching their property.[68]

As discussed later in this chapter, assassinations and mutilations (along with other insurgent tactics) can backfire if they cause substantial casualties among the civilian population, undermining local—and even international—support for insurgents. As many insurgents and counterinsurgents alike have argued, support of the local population is a *sine qua non* of insurgent warfare. And significant brutality can be counterproductive.

Kidnappings: Kidnappings involve the seizure of individuals by force. Insurgents have used kidnappings and related tactics, such as hostage-taking, to accomplish several objectives: force the government to accede to specific demands, such as releasing insurgent prisoners; cause the government political embarrassment; secure intelligence from the kidnapped individual; acquire money through ransom payments; and highlight a group's cause through media coverage of the incident.[69] Insurgents have also seized civilians, including children, and forced them to join their organization.[70]

Ransom is one of the most frequent goals of insurgent kidnapping. Numerous groups—such as the FARC in Colombia, Taliban in Afghanistan, al Qa'ida in the Islamic Maghreb in North Africa, and Movement for Emancipation of the Niger Delta in Nigeria— kidnapped individuals to collect ransom money. These organizations often utilized an elaborate network of middlemen and negotiators to exchange their captives for funding.[71] According to one assessment, al Qa'ida and its affiliates earned at least $125 million in revenue from kidnappings between 2008 and 2014.[72] Most of the payments, the assessment concluded, were made almost entirely by European governments, who funneled the money through proxies. This may be why the former head of al Qa'ida in the Arabian Peninsula, Nasir al-Wuhayshi, remarked, "Kidnapping hostages is an easy spoil, which I may describe as a profitable trade and a precious treasure."[73]

Similarly, some insurgent groups have coerced individuals or companies into making donations under the tacit or direct threat of reprisals, including kidnapping. In Colombia, the FARC obtained funds through extortion and other forced contributions, and they punished individuals and companies—including through kidnapping—that did not provide funds. In one case, FARC operatives burned forty-eight delivery trucks owned by a Coca-Cola distributor that refused to provide funds, kidnapped eleven of its workers, and robbed the company approximately 400 times.[74] In 2014, Boko Haram captured nearly 300 schoolgirls in northeastern Nigeria and asked for the release of Boko Haram operatives that had been jailed. As Abubakar Shekau, the leader of Boko Haram, explained in a video, "We do not release them, unless you release our brothers."[75] In Uganda, the Lord's Resistance Army frequently kidnapped individuals for use as a bargaining chip to gain money, free prisoners, or acquire other goods such as food.[76]

Groups have also utilized kidnapping and related tactics, such as hostage-taking, to secure the release of jailed insurgents and highlight the strength of insurgents. In Nicaragua, for example, two dozen Sandinista operatives headed by Edén Pastora attacked the Nicaraguan National Palace in August 1978 when Congress was in session. Pastora demanded $500,000 and the release of fifty-eight political prisoners. "The raid's success," one assessment concluded, "sparked an uprising against the regime in the slums around Managua" and, perhaps more important, "showed the Nicaraguan people, Somoza, and officials in Washington that the Sandinistas were a formidable guerrilla outfit— one capable of dramatic and successful operations."[77]

But insurgent groups need to be careful. Kidnapping and similar tactics, such as hostage-taking, can backfire if they alienate the local population. In Russia, for example, Chechen insurgents did severe damage to their reputation—both domestically and internationally— by orchestrating such hostage situations as the September 2004 Beslan school hostage crisis, which led to the death of 334 civilians—including 186 children.[78]

Bombings: Insurgents frequently use bombings to demoralize troops and force counterinsurgents to seek safety in fortified bases, cutting them off from the local population.[79] They are low-risk, high-payoff weapons, particularly the use of improvised explosive devices (IEDs).

Insurgents have utilized an assortment of types: radio-controlled IEDs; suicide attacks; pressure-activated circuits with diamagnetic, low-metal switch components; and explosively formed projectiles.[80] More generally, insurgents have developed sophisticated radio-controlled IED switches (using cell phones, personal mobile radios, handheld transceivers, vehicle security systems, garage door openers, and high-power cordless phones), timed switches (that are electric, mechanical, or chemical), and victim-operated switches that come in numerous types.

The growing use of IEDs may be a reaction to the counterinsurgent adoption of more advanced vehicles, platforms, and systems and their subsequent asymmetry with insurgent groups.[81] To counter these developments and to make up for the asymmetry in power, insurgents have developed a range of asymmetric tactics, including IEDs, to target counterinsurgent innovations and separate armies from the local population.

In Chechnya, the use of explosives by insurgent groups posed significant challenges for Russian troops, causing roughly 40 percent of the casualties during some parts of the war.[82] Col. Gen. Nikolai Serdtsev, the head of the Russian army's engineering forces, remarked that mine-clearing units were overwhelmed because of IEDs and sometimes had to contend with as many as twenty devices per day:

> [Chechen fighters] are using booby-trap mines and explosives made from aerial bombs, artillery shells, mortars, or some combination more widely than before. . . . If we compare the scale of the "mine war" in the current campaign with the earlier one, we find that its intensity has sharply escalated and the number of casualties among combat and technical personnel has sharply increased. All of this confirms that the terrorists are now more organized in their preparations, in their accumulation of stockpiles of high-explosive munitions, in their development of a network of clandestine laboratories to construct improvised explosive devices and radio-controlled detonators, and in their plans for laying mines and explosive barriers.[83]

More broadly, insurgents became more proficient at achieving high levels of technical and tactical sophistication for IEDs. It took the Irish Republican Army about thirty years to progress from command-wire

improvised explosive devices (CWIEDs) to remote-controlled improvised explosive devices (RCIEDSs) and then to shaped charges. By
contrast, it took about six years for Chechen insurgents to make the
same improvements, three years for fighters in Gaza, and about twelve
months for insurgents in Iraq.[84] In Afghanistan and Pakistan, fighters began with RCIED technology in hand, and quickly progressed to
innovations such as diamagnetic, low-metal switch components. This
can be explained at least partially by the widening availability of bomb-
related information exchanged through person-to-person communications, printed manuals, and the Internet. It may also be attributable in
part to the proliferation of consumer electronic and other commercially
available technologies that were suitable for making bombs.[85] In addition, insurgent exploitation of global positioning systems allowed them
to more accurately target fixed or slow-moving vehicles.

Many of these bombings were terrorist attacks. Terrorism involves
the use—or threat—of violence against noncombatants in pursuit of
political aims.[86] In insurgencies, terrorism is designed to achieve multiple objectives like coercing locals to support insurgents, deterring them
from aiding the government, and creating propaganda. As the French
practitioner Roger Trinquier concluded, with effective terrorism the
"silence and collusion of the unprotected inhabitants have been won."[87]
Virtually every insurgent group has used terrorist tactics.

Most notably, there has been a rise in the use of *suicide* attacks, which
provide insurgents with a relatively cheap and maneuverable weapon
that can often kill with chilling precision.[88] According to the data in
this book, the use of suicide tactics in insurgencies is a relatively rare
phenomenon, with groups using suicide tactics in only 23 insurgencies
(12.7 percent). But the use of suicide tactics has grown. Of the thirty-
eight active insurgencies in the dataset, for instance, groups in twenty
cases (52.6 percent) used suicide tactics. With few exceptions, such as
the LTTE in Sri Lanka, most insurgent groups that used suicide tactics
were extremist Islamic groups. Table 4.1 highlights the use of suicide
attacks by insurgent groups.

As one study argues, terrorists and insurgents learned that this strategy works.[89] But does suicide terrorism pay in insurgencies? The data
suggest several broad conclusions about the use of suicide terrorism in
insurgencies.

TABLE 4.1 Use of suicide attacks in insurgencies, 1946–2015[118]

Conflict case	Year of first attributable suicide attack	Lag time between conflict onset and use of suicide attacks	Conflict[119] outcome
Afghanistan, 2001–present	2001	0 years	ongoing
Algeria, 1992–present	1995	3 years	ongoing
China/Xinjang, 1991–present	2002	11 years	ongoing
Egypt/Sinai, 2013–present	2013	0 years	ongoing
India/Kashmir, 1989–present	1998	9 years	ongoing
India/Assam, 1990–present	2007	17 years	ongoing
Indonesia, 1990–2005	2003	14 years	draw
Iraq, 2003–present	2003	0 years	ongoing
Israel/Occupied Territories, 1987–present	1989	2 years	ongoing
Lebanon, 1975–1990	1982	7 years	govt. victory
Libya, 2014–present	2014	0 years	ongoing
Mali, 2012–present	2012	0 years	ongoing
Nigeria, 2009–present	2011	2 years	ongoing
Pakistan, 2007–present	2007	0 years	ongoing
Pakistan/Baluchistan, 2004–present	2011	7 years	ongoing
Philippines/Mindanao, 1970–present	2000	30 years	ongoing
Russia/Chechnya, 1994–present	1999	5 years	ongoing
Somalia, 2006–present	2006	0 years	ongoing
Syria, 2011–present	2011	0 years	ongoing
Sri Lanka, 1984–2009	1987	3 years	govt. victory
Turkey/Kurdistan, 1984–present	1996	12 years	ongoing
Ukraine, 2014–present	2014	0 years	ongoing
Yemen, 2008–present	2008	0 years	ongoing

First, suicide tactics are extremely lethal. The average lethality of suicide attacks occurring in insurgency campaigns included in our dataset is nine people killed and twenty-four wounded per attack.[90] In particular, when the delivery device used by insurgents is a truck bomb, these statistics climb to seventeen people killed and sixty-two people wounded per attack, as illustrated in Table 4.2. These averages are much higher than for other types of attacks, as explained in more detail in the next section. Still, suicide attacks did not become notably more lethal over time. In fact, the average number of individuals killed and wounded per attack dropped somewhat after 2009. Second, suicide attacks do not appear to be correlated with insurgent victory. No insurgent group that used suicide attacks succeeded—at least yet—in overthrowing the government or establishing independence, the long-term objectives of most insurgent groups. While there does not appear to be a correlation between suicide attacks and success in insurgent campaigns, it is not clear whether the use of suicide terrorism actually causes a decline in insurgent success. After all, there are multiple factors that may impact insurgent outcomes. Still, suicide and other terrorist attacks can backfire and reduce popular support. Al Qaʾida in Iraq, for example, lost considerable support beginning around 2005 because

TABLE 4.2 Impact of suicide attacks by type, 1982–2015[120]

	Number of suicide attacks by insurgents	Number killed (excluding insurgents)	Number wounded (excluding insurgents)	Average killed	Average wounded
Belt bomb	1,620	16,373	39,125	10.1	24.2
Boat bomb	43	569	242	13.2	5.6
Car bomb	2,217	17,628	44,350	8.0	20.0
Motorcycle bomb	219	1,237	3,370	5.6	15.4
Truck bomb	332	5,540	20,537	16.7	61.9
Other/mixed[121]	189	1515	4,073	8.0	21.6
Total	**4,616**	**42,861**	**111,697**	**9.3**	**24.2**

of its widespread brutality, which included the use of suicide attacks against local Iraqis.[91] Third, suicide tactics have almost exclusively been used by insurgents where the government side was either supported by a great power or was itself a great power.[92] This was the case in 95 percent of the insurgencies in which suicide attacks were employed since World War II.[93]

TRENDS IN INSURGENT TACTICS

After reviewing battlefield tactics, we now turn to broader trends by asking three questions. First, is there variation in the lethality of these tactics, both between tactics and over time? Second, is there a danger in losing hearts and minds? After all, killing, maiming, or intimidating individuals can be counterproductive if it undermines local support and benefits counterinsurgents. Third, are there differences between the use of these tactics in urban and rural environments?

Lethality: As Table 4.3 highlights, there are notable differences in the lethality of tactics. As might be expected, since sabotage and assassinations involve the precise use of violence, they have the lowest numbers of victims killed per attack—with less than one killed per attack for sabotage operations and about one and a half people killed per assassination. The average lethality of ambushes and raids is significantly

TABLE 4.3 Average lethality by insurgent attack type, 1970–2015[122]

Tactic	Frequency	Total confirmed killed (including insurgents)	Average lethality per attack
Ambushes and raids[123]	30,049 attacks	133,788 killed	4.5 killed per attack
Sabotage attacks[124]	4,508 attacks	3,427 killed	0.8 killed per attack
Assassinations[125]	13,327 attacks	18,959 killed	1.4 killed per attack
Kidnappings[126]	7,140 attacks	64,049 taken	9.0 seized per attack
Bombings	50,499 attacks	103,230 killed	2.0 killed per attack
Suicide attacks[127]	3,668 attacks	34,533 killed	9.4 killed per attack

higher than for bombings, with an average of five killed per attack for ambushes and raids but only two killed per attack from bombings.

There may be several reasons for the difference. One is that insurgent bombings can range from Iraq-style vehicle-borne improvised explosive devices designed to kill dozens of people to some Provisional IRA bombings, such as the June 1996 attack in Manchester, designed to cause economic damage and undermine support of the British government—but to kill few or no people. This difference in lethality may also result from the larger number of insurgent forces used for ambushes and raids, the direct engagement of government forces, and the ability of insurgent groups to take the initiative—all of which may increase the likelihood of higher casualties. As already noted, suicide attacks are the most lethal tactics, killing twice the number as ambushes and raids at over nine people killed per attack. Finally, kidnappings tend to be large in insurgencies, with groups seizing an average of nine people per attack.

The average lethality of several tactics has declined over time (see Figure 4.2). It is unclear why this is the case, but it may be a result of counterinsurgent responses. There is some evidence that counterinsurgent

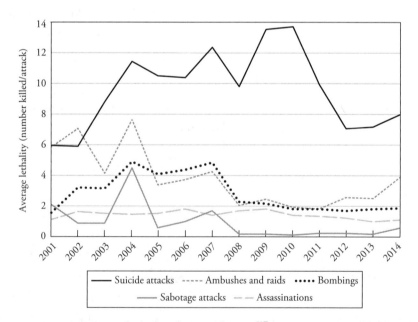

FIGURE 4.2 Average lethality by attack type[117]

forces have developed better equipment and technology to protect vehicles, structures, and individuals from insurgent attacks. Several Western armies, for instance, have spent considerable resources on Mine Resistant Ambush Protected (MRAP) vehicles and improved the armor plating on Humvees (High Mobility Multipurpose Wheeled Vehicles), trucks, and other vehicles. By 2011, the US Department of Defense alone had invested $35 billion in developing and producing MRAPs.[94] In addition, some counterinsurgent militaries developed electronic jamming devices and other technological innovations to improve intelligence, surveillance, and reconnaissance against insurgent attacks. Numerous counterinsurgent personnel also utilized more advanced body armor, which may have contributed to the decline in lethality of rebel attacks.

Losing hearts and minds: Despite these developments, however, one of the most striking trends in data on tactics is the lack of correlation between tactics and insurgency outcomes. Virtually every insurgent group since World War II has used these tactics in combination against governments. A range of other factors—such as outside support—likely has more of an impact than the tactics employed. Still, *how* insurgents use tactics against the government and its allies can be important. Effective tactics tend to be those that exploit counterinsurgent vulnerabilities, decrease government legitimacy, strengthen insurgents, or bait the government into overreacting. Ineffective tactics tend to be those that weaken local support for insurgent groups or expose insurgent weaknesses.

Mao Tse-Tung warned that it is "only undisciplined troops who make the people their enemies and who, like the fish out of its native element, cannot live."[95] He established three tactical rules for insurgent conduct: all actions are subject to command, do not steal from the people, and behave neither selfishly nor unjustly. They were meant to be practical rules for operating among the local population. Mao also urged guerrillas to abide by eight "remarks" that would endear rebels to local populations or, at the very least, minimize the likelihood of local hostility:

- Replace the door when you leave the house
- Roll up the bedding on which you have slept

- Be courteous
- Be honest in your transactions
- Return what you borrow
- Replace what you break
- Do not bathe in the presence of women
- Do not without authority search those you arrest[96]

Brutal tactics tend to undermine insurgent support.[97] As one first-hand account of GIA activity summarized, "when the GIA started massacring civilians, including people who had nothing to do with the government at either the national or local levels, and especially after they began indiscriminately slaughtering entire families, the empathy the people felt for the movement turned to horror."[98] GIA leaders like Djamel Zitouni launched an increasingly bloody campaign against civilians, Algerian government officials, French citizens, and even opposition factions within the GIA. A growing number of extremist Salafi-jihadist groups, including Egyptian Islamic Jihad, condemned Zitouni as shedding "forbidden blood" and rescinded their support for the GIA. As one assessment concluded, the "GIA was especially split in Algiers, where the devoted middle class, fed up with the endless violence and racketeering by gangs of young men in the name of jihad, participated en masse in the presidential elections of 1995."[99]

In Afghanistan, Taliban leaders attempted to increase local support by establishing a tactical-level code of conduct, or *Layha*. Article 78, for example, argued that "Mujahedin are obliged to adopt Islamic behavior and good conduct with the people and try to win over the hearts of the common Muslims and, as mujahedin, be such representatives of the Islamic Emirate that all compatriots shall welcome and give the hand of cooperation and help."[100] At the tactical level, this included such steps as not destroying private property or killing civilians. In practice, however, Taliban commanders did not always faithfully follow the *Lahya*, killing significantly more civilians than Afghan government and NATO forces. In 2015, for instance, the United Nations attributed nearly three quarters of civilian deaths and injuries to Taliban and other insurgent attacks, with only 16 percent attributed to Afghan government and allied forces.[101]

Urban and rural tactics: Some have argued that changing demographic trends and the growth of sprawling cities and peri-urban environments will increase the likelihood of urban combat—including urban insurgency.[102] But insurgents have long used the tactics described in this chapter in both urban and rural environments. In Latin America, for example, a range of organizations—from the Rebel Armed Forces in Guatemala to the Montoneros in Argentina and the Sendero Luminoso in Peru—conducted operations in cities and the countryside. As Gordon McCormick concluded in his study of Sendero Luminoso, "Organized urban rebellion has a long tradition in Latin America."[103] In some insurgencies, urban tactics were more useful in later stages of the insurgency. For Sendero Luminoso, which began its campaign against the Peruvian government in 1982, urban operations increased when the group consolidated greater control in the rural highlands. The inclusion of urban operations was virtually inevitable based on demographic changes in Peru. There were approximately three million people living in cities in 1961. But this number doubled in 1972 and then nearly doubled again to 11 million in 1985. Indeed, where urban dwellers accounted for less than 30 percent of the national population in the mid-1960s, they were estimated to account for well over 50 percent of the national total in the mid-1980s.[104]

Urban tactics—from ambushes to assassinations and bombings—have been common in other insurgencies. In Algeria, the urban struggle was immortalized in the 1966 film *The Battle of Algiers* (*La Bataille d'Alger*), directed by Gillo Pontecorvo, which took place in Algiers' Casbah. In Kenya, a key battleground for Mau Mau insurgents in Kenya was in the alleyways and dirt streets of Nairobi, particularly in the shanties in Eastlands that included hordes of jobless, disenfranchised Kikuyu. Mau Mau operatives focused on assassinating ethnic Kikuyu that supported that government, which they referred to as *tai-tai*. The Mau Mau presence in cities like Nairobi forced the British to conduct a range of urban campaigns, including Operation Jock Scott in 1952, Operation Rat Catcher in 1953, and Operation Anvil in 1954.[105] More recently, insurgent groups in Iraq, Syria, Yemen, Pakistan, Chechnya, Palestinian territory, and Somalia conducted a range of tactics in urban terrain—from the densely populated neighborhoods in

Baghdad, Damascus, Sana'a, Karachi, Grozny, and Mogadishu to the teeming refugee camps in Jenin and Gaza.

Still, there are differences in urban and rural warfare.[106] There are some advantages for insurgents in urban environments. Urban centers represent the government's seat of power, and insurgent attacks can demonstrate the weakness of the government. Most journalists and media outlets are also located in urban areas, increasing the likelihood that attacks will be broadcast nationally and internationally. This explains why one al Qa'ida in the Arabian Peninsula manual said, "Since the operations are in cities, people will see them and will see the targets that are attacked, so that the media will not then be able to lie about them."[107] In addition, insurgents may be better able to mobilize larger numbers of people against the government, including using social media forums. Finally, the indiscriminate use of force by the government in urban environments may cause more civilian casualties than in rural areas, undermining local support.

But urban environments also pose serious challenges for insurgents, which can blunt the effectiveness of insurgent tactics. First, states often have a greater ability to concentrate firepower and security forces against insurgents in urban areas. As one assessment concluded, "There is a simple, grim way to decisively shatter an urban rebellion that has escalated into an insurgent challenge—using conventional firepower to annihilate the city or cities in which it is based. Cities present easier targets to conventional military forces than the pacification of vast swaths of rural terrain, regardless of their social characteristics."[108] In Chechnya, for example, Russian forces were able to mass forces and firepower using long-range artillery (including tactical ballistic missiles, thermobaric rockets, and laser-guided 240-mm mortar rounds) and air strikes against Chechen insurgent positions in Grozny. The result was the destruction of Grozny and the successful reclamation of territory from insurgents.[109]

Second, government military, police, and intelligence units can more readily control movement and access to urban areas than they can in rural areas. The inevitable road network that defines urban areas creates numerous chokepoints that can be used to control movement. State forces can take advantage of these chokepoints by creating an array of active measures (such as checkpoints) and passive measures (such as berms, minefields, and cameras) to control and monitor access to urban areas and movement within them.[110] This may be, in part, why Shaykh Yusuf Al-'Ayyiri, founder and leader of al Qa'ida in Saudi Arabia, re-marked, "The dangers surrounding a *mujahid* within cities are many times greater than the dangers in the mountains and in the bush."[111]

Third, urban areas are also typically more fruitful environments for intelligence collection for counterinsurgents. This is true of both human intelligence and technical intelligence collection. For human intelligence collection, the urban environment presents a more atom-ized and anonymous environment than rural areas, allowing collectors greater opportunities to recruit sources. Rural communities are fre-quently characterized by intimate, overlapping social networks, making it easier to identify government collaborators. For technical collection, urban areas typically have denser electronic communications networks than rural areas, which can be monitored by counterinsurgents.[112] The ease of counterinsurgent intelligence collection is why one insurgent handbook notes that insurgent operations and tactics are more difficult because "a city is full of eyes and spies" and it "is the cities that usu-ally represent a state's prestige."[113] Che Guevara also warned insurgents that the urban guerrilla "must be considered as situated in exceptionally unfavorable ground, where the vigilance of the enemy will be much greater and the possibilities of reprisals as well as of betrayal are in-creased enormously."[114]

In short, tactics are critical in insurgent warfare because they help groups execute their strategies and operations. While there does not appear to be a correlation between the tactics used by a group and whether insurgents win, lose, or draw, insurgent groups still need to be mindful of how their tactics affect the local population. Tactics may not guarantee success, particularly in the absence of a good strategy. But the poor use of tactics can undermine local support and potentially seal the fate of insurgent groups. The Provisional IRA *Green Book* offers a useful warning to insurgents:

> The enemy through our own fault or default is the one we create
> ourselves through our personal conduct and through our collective
> conduct of the struggle: the wee woman whose gate or back door gets
> pulled off its hinges by a volunteer evading arrest and who doesn't get

an apology as soon as possible afterwards or more preferably has the damage repaired by one of our supporters; the family and neighbours of a criminal or informer who has been punished without their being informed why. In brief our personal conduct as well as our conduct of our Republican activities must be aimed at if not enhancing support, at least not creating enemies unnecessarily.[115]

5

Organizational Structures

By early 1984 [ISI head] General Akhtar was determined that some sort of formal alliance be formed by the [Afghan insurgent] parties. Some recognized high-level body was vital to act as a filter for the supply of arms and money to the users, and through whom we could attempt to coordinate action inside Afghanistan.[1]

—Mohammad Yousaf

Many of those who decide to participate in guerrilla activities do not know the methods of organization.[2]

—Mao Tse-Tung

IN OCTOBER 1983, MOHAMMAD Yousaf, who had just been appointed to head the Afghan Bureau of Pakistan's Inter-Services Intelligence (ISI) Directorate, traveled to Peshawar, Pakistan. Peshawar was a bustling frontier town 30 miles from the Afghanistan border and the much-coveted capital of successive Buddhist and Hindu kingdoms. Its bazaars had attracted visitors for centuries with their rich assortment of carpets, pottery, arms, and artwork. Yousaf's task was unenviable: to establish a functioning organizational structure for the insurgency in neighboring Afghanistan, which the ISI was supporting. There were seven main Afghan insurgent groups, but virtually no coordination among them in late 1983. "I could only meet the Leaders separately. This was because they would not sit in the same room with each other," Yousaf recounted. "I was speaking to men who, although devout Muslims, although committed to Jehad, were fueled by personal rivalries, prejudices and hatreds, which often clouded their views and dictated their actions."[3]

Over the next several months, the seven groups agreed to establish a more defined organizational structure, but only after significant cajoling by the Pakistan government. The arrangement consisted of two parts. The first was a Military Committee, located in Peshawar, that included the heads of the seven major parties: Gulbuddin Hekmatyar, Yunus Khalis, Burhanuddin Rabbani, Abdul Rasul Sayyaf, Mawlawi Muhammad Nabi Muhammadi, Pir Sayyid Ahmad Gailani, and Sibghatullah Mujaddadi. Every Afghan commander had to belong to one of these seven groups. Otherwise, he received no arms, ammunition, training, or other aid from the ISI. The second was a political headquarters in Quetta, Pakistan, that included party representatives. Pakistan's ISI acted as the main liaison with the groups. Each of the seven groups also had its own political and military command-and-control structure in Afghanistan. While there were still coordination problems for the rest of the war, this structure was adequate to effectively fight the Afghan government and the Soviet military. By 1989, Soviet leaders withdrew the Red Army from Afghanistan and, three years later, the Afghan government led by Mohammad Najibullah collapsed. At that point, however, the insurgent organizational structure broke down and the groups began fighting each other for control of the state.

As highlighted in the Afghan experience, establishing a viable organizational structure is a key challenge for insurgent groups. As used here, an insurgent organization refers to the internal characteristics of an insurgent group, such as its membership, policies, and structures.[4] In insurgencies with multiple groups, insurgent leaders often establish umbrella structures to facilitate coordination and cooperation between groups. Conducting an insurgency involves building an organization capable of militarily and politically challenging a government.[5]

Consequently, this chapter asks three major questions: What are the organizational challenges for insurgent groups? What options do insurgent leaders have in structuring their own groups? What options do leaders have when there is more than one insurgent group? The data suggest several findings.

First, insurgent groups face collective action and principal–agent problems that can severely impact their ability to accomplish key organizational tasks, such as recruiting members, fighting a war, securing finances, collecting intelligence, and governing territory. Consequently, insurgent leaders need to find ways to overcome these problems, such as providing sufficient monetary or other incentives to overcome the costs of participation. Second, in designing their organizations, centralized structures are generally more effective because they help leaders identify and punish those engaged in shirking behavior or defections. Centralization can also help insurgent groups better govern territory they control and enable leaders to coordinate logistics. While a centralized organizational structure is preferable, there are several factors that can make it difficult to implement. Government repression, for example, can force groups to disperse and delegate in order to survive. Insurgent leaders whose members include a mix of ethnic, religious, and other groups may also find it difficult to centralize control because of heterogeneous preferences. Third, in insurgencies with more than one group, leaders have several options. They can establish an umbrella structure to coordinate activities, stovepipe efforts, or compete—including fight—against each other. Groups have generally been more successful if they can create an umbrella structure and coordinate activities.

The rest of this chapter is organized into four sections. The first examines organizational challenges and tasks faced by insurgent groups. The second section analyzes options to organize an insurgent group. The third assesses options where there are multiple opposition groups. And the fourth section outlines the challenges of decentralized structures.

ORGANIZATIONAL CHALLENGES AND TASKS

Insurgent groups need to accomplish multiple tasks while trying to remain secure and elude government surveillance. This creates a dilemma for insurgent leaders. The tools leaders use to control insurgent organization, management, fundraising, and other activities create operational vulnerabilities and increase the possibility that operatives will be caught and the group compromised.[6] Insurgent groups must recruit members, prevent defections, conduct military operations, secure funding, collect and analyze intelligence, and govern areas they control—all while attempting to remain covert. But they face organizational challenges in doing so.

Challenges: Two of the most difficult organizational challenges are collective action and principal–agent problems. Both impact an insurgent group's ability to achieve its primary tasks. First, insurgent groups need to overcome what economist Mancur Olson termed the "collective action problem."[7] Individuals—including would-be rebels—value numerous goods that can be produced only through collective action. Collective goods are non-excludable; everyone can take advantage of them regardless of whether they play a role in securing the good. If an insurgent group overthrows an oppressive government, many people may benefit. Yet individuals also value purely personal goods, such as the time, opportunity cost, and risk involved in acting collectively. In other words, the benefits of collective action are often public, while the costs are private. Under these circumstances, every person's best move is to stay home and let someone else work for the public benefit.

In insurgencies, the injury or death of participants (and sometimes their friends, family members, and neighbors), financial difficulties, unpleasantness of living a clandestine lifestyle, and forced relocation dissuade many people from participating in the initial stages of an insurgency. The recruitment pitch to one soon-to-be Sandinista in Nicaragua, Omar Cabezas, was simple: "Skinny, look . . . uh . . . do you think you might be interested in a greater commitment to the people and to the organization?" Cabezas, who eventually joined the organization, quickly understood the danger. "I was scared . . . of getting myself killed," he later recalled.[8] After war has started, however, this paradox may change, and it may be more dangerous for individuals to refrain from supporting insurgents in some areas. Individuals may participate in rebellion not in spite of the risks involved, but in order to better manage them.[9]

The central implication of the collective action paradigm is that rebel activists face tremendous obstacles in launching insurgencies. The Provisional IRA ensured that its recruits understood the difficulties inherent in joining an insurgent organization. As the Provisional IRA explained in its *Green Book*, "All potential volunteers must realize that the threat of capture and of long jail sentences are a very real danger and a shadow which hangs over every volunteer . . . He should examine fully his motives, knowing the dangers involved and knowing that he will find no romance within the Movement."[10] Mau Mau insurgents in Kenya provided similar advice to their recruits. As one Mau Mau leader summarized, "Some of you, too, will be imprisoned, and some of you will be killed. But when these things happen, my sons, do not be afraid—and we must buy our freedom with our blood."[11] As one scholar summarized, rebellion is a substantial commitment and is extremely dangerous for participants.[12]

Insurgent groups can overcome collective action problems in several ways. They can provide selective incentives that are powerful enough to overcome the costs of participation. Rebels enjoy several types of benefits, including profits from the production and trade in diamonds, oil, drugs, and other licit and illicit activity. Rebels often receive private material incentives for participation beyond any anticipated public goods.[13] As the American envoy in Greece, William McNeill, described, referring to the Greek People's Liberation Army (Ellinikós Laïkós Apeleftherotikós Stratós, or ELAS): "[A] soldier in ELAS lived a good deal better than did the ordinary peasants, and did not have to work with the same drudging toil . . . Under the circumstances, many a peasant's son found himself irresistibly attracted to the guerrilla life; and an over abundant peasant population made recruitment easy."[14] Another way is to appeal to nonmaterial interests, such as ideology, ethnic and religious identification, and social acceptance.[15] Insurgents can also provide security to those individuals that cooperate and target those that don't cooperate, altering their cost–benefit calculations and creating a situation where *not* supporting insurgents is more costly and risky than supporting them.[16]

Second, insurgents face a "principal–agent problem."[17] A principal (an insurgent leader) needs to set in place a system of incentives and penalties so that an agent (a member of the group) will perform as the principal expects. Minimizing principal–agent problems is particularly important to prevent "shirking" and defections, especially when lower-level operatives have different preferences and motivations from senior leaders. Shirking occurs when members take actions that do not contribute to the maximum efficiency of the organization.[18] Shirking may arise, for example, when a fighter takes a nap instead of setting up a roadside bomb to attack a government convoy. With no one around to monitor behavior, the fighter may calculate that he or she won't be caught. An organization's success depends on its ability to motivate members and encourage them to behave in ways consistent with its broader goals and objectives. A lack of discipline among lower-ranking members can waste resources, alienate potential supporters, and undermine military and political efforts. Leaders need to make decisions about how to shape, manage, and control the behavior of their members.[19] Insurgent groups also need to worry about defections because of material or other incentives.

In Vietnam, the Vietcong considered defection one of their greatest problems.[20] Vietcong guerrillas were ruthless in dealing with defectors. According to one account, when they regained control over a village that had defected to the government in Quang Ngai Province, they seized "the headman and his family, disemboweled his wife in front of him, hacked off his children's arms and legs and then emasculated him."[21] In Oman, the Popular Front for the Liberation of Oman faced repeated setbacks following steadily increasing desertions during the 1970s. In Thailand, there were a series of defections among Thai insurgents in the 1980s following a return to civilian rule and an amnesty program.[22]

Insurgent fighters take actions that cannot easily be observed and evaluated by their superiors. Moreover, rebel combatants sometimes operate under the command of multiple principals. The difficulty of monitoring dispersed rebel forces and the complications introduced by multiple principals contribute to a related challenge of management in rebel organizations: incentives to shirk are magnified by the level and immediacy of the risks combatants face.

But insurgent leaders can design tools to help minimize shirking. When hiring members, for example, insurgents can design screening mechanisms to select among potential recruits and evaluate their competence. Leaders can also monitor the actions of their members through direct oversight mechanisms (such as patrols), or they can clandestinely monitor them by having third parties report on bad behavior through counterintelligence activity. Monitoring alone, however, is usually not enough. It must be coupled with credible threats that insurgent leaders will punish members for bad behavior. The credibility of the threat is particularly important since issuing punishments can be costly for the leader as well.[23]

Tasks: Groups that effectively overcome collective action and principal–agent problems are in a better position to perform important tasks. First, insurgents need to develop a political strategy, recruit members, and mobilize local populations. Like employers in a private firm, rebel leaders wish to attract qualified, committed, and able recruits interested in the long-term goals of the organization.[24] Recruitment is a classic organizational challenge for rebel organizations and requires them, in particular, to overcome the collective action problem. Leaders sometimes establish a political arm to help with recruitment and other political steps, including negotiating with governments and other insurgent groups. Sinn Féin served as the political wing of the Provisional Irish Republican Army, leading negotiations with the British government that culminated in the 1998 Good Friday Agreement. Lashkar-e-Taiba created a political arm in Pakistan, Jamat ud Dawah, which served in part as a welfare organization. In total, about half of insurgent groups had an overt political arm.

For Sendero Luminoso leader Abimael Guzman, the political organization of an insurgency should take precedence over the military. His first priority was to establish a party of core activists who could be tasked with the objective of guiding the revolutionary struggle. The party's political vanguard was "a select organization" that was the strategic center of the organization.[25] In Angola, MPLA leaders emphasized political above other aspects in starting their insurgency. "We know our basic problem is a political one, but it cannot be solved without violence. So, while the military aspect is secondary to the political, there is an interdependence between the two."[26] And in Vietnam, Viet Cong leaders stressed the need to mobilize "the political forces of the masses," which could then be used to assist with military operations.[27]

Second, insurgent groups need to fight a war.[28] Leaders need to design organizational structures that educate and train soldiers, procure and maintain equipment, collect and analyze intelligence, oversee the logistics of getting material to soldiers, build infrastructure, feed and clothe soldiers, fight on the battlefield, and conduct numerous other tasks that militaries need to accomplish. It is a massive and complicated undertaking. Mao and Che Guevara devoted considerable time and space to outlining how to organize rebel units to fight, including dividing and subdividing units in the field.[29] Several of the figures later in this chapter—including ones that lay out the organizational structure of such groups as the National Liberation Front/Army of National Liberation, Taliban, and Islamic State—show detailed military wings that deal with training, logistics, security, operations, and other tasks of fighting a war.

Third, insurgents need to build a financial infrastructure to secure and transfer funds necessary to sustain the insurgency. Groups need to pay salaries, build infrastructure, and purchase lethal and non-lethal material. Financing can come from many sources. Some insurgent groups are able to extract natural resources, including timber, gemstones, poppy, diamonds, and other minerals. Many rely on the taxation of local production or the conduct of criminal business, including the drug trade. Many also receive donations from supporters in the diaspora or contributions from external patrons.[30] Local commanders are often expected to fund some or most of their day-to-day activities. In Turkey, for example, PKK fighters were expected to finance their own operations. PKK operatives in the cities frequently had jobs that helped cover some of their operational costs.[31]

Fourth, insurgents need to collect and analyze intelligence. The development of an intelligence network impacts virtually all aspects of insurgent warfare, from strategy to tactics. Insurgents need to understand such questions as what counterinsurgent forces are planning, how they are organized, where they are located, what and where are their vulnerabilities, and who and where are their spies.[32] As General Alberto Bayo remarked, "It is necessary that all guerrillas must practice intelligence and counter-intelligence work, since wars are won more through cunning and shrewdness than by pulling the trigger finger."[33] In Nicaragua, the Sandinistas recruited spies from the universities. Nicaraguan university students spearheaded nationalistic, anti-Somoza groups, and the schools became recruiting grounds and intellectual seedbeds for the Sandinistas and other anti-Somoza groups.[34] In fact, the Sandinista Front for National Liberation (FSLN) was founded in 1961 by men such as Carlos Fonseca Amador, Tomás Borge, and Silvio Mayorga, who were young leaders from the anti-Somoza student movement. In Kenya, Mau Mau insurgents heavily recruited informants from urban and rural areas, which they relied on for information about British forces, Home Guard militias, and collaborators.[35]

Fifth, insurgents need to govern areas they control.[36] After all, insurgency is often a process of alternative state-building, where insurgents provide governance to the population in areas they control.[37] Leaders want to extract what they can from noncombatants to sustain their groups, such as information, food, housing, and supplies. But they generally try to avoid extracting so much that civilians become alienated and defect to the opposition. Rebel leaders also need to make choices about the structure of the governments they build in liberated zones and govern them accordingly. Groups need to establish organizational structures that can secure funds through taxation and other means, organize policing, administer justice, and provide health benefits (including care to wounded soldiers).

According to one account of Sendero Luminoso in the Canipaco Valley of central Peru, the group "assumed control and organized every aspect of the inhabitants' daily life. Sendero undertook the administration of justice and played the role of a moralizing force."[38] They were also involved in a range of other activities, such as adjudicating marriage conflicts. As the Viet Cong explained in their ten-point policy for areas under their control, they intended to abolish "the regime and administrative machinery, armed forces and all organizations, all regulations, and all forms of repression and coercion of the puppet administration." In their place, they advocated "the speedy establishment of the people's revolutionary administration at all levels in the newly liberated areas."[39] In Algeria, the GIA banned French from being taught in areas it controlled. When girls reached the age of nine, they couldn't go to school anymore and had to cover their heads when they went outside.[40]

In Iraq, the Islamic State and its predecessor organizations, al Qa'ida in Iraq and the Islamic State of Iraq, designed an organizational structure to help control territory. The group's province-level structure for al-Anbar around 2006, for example, was outlined in a series of documents seized by a local militia cooperating with US forces in al-Anbar Province in March 2007. As highlighted in Figure 5.1, the documents depicted an organizational structure similar to that of core al Qa'ida with a legal (sharia) committee, military committee, administrative committee, security committee, and media committee. Over time the Islamic State of Iraq made some modifications to the structure.[41] In an internal memorandum, an Islamic State of Iraq manager named As'ad

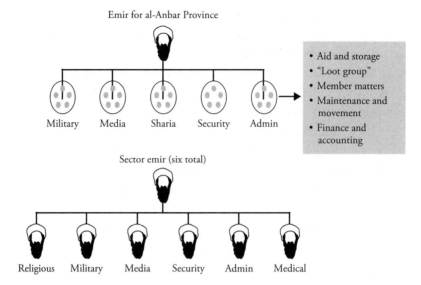

FIGURE 5.1 Islamic State of Iraq structure for al-Anbar Province, circa 2006[115]

suggested that the financial organization be expanded in two steps.[42] As As'ad noted, this new structure

> makes the issue of monitoring the Treasury easier and makes the Administration of Finance distinct from the Taxation of Treasury [sic], and the Administration of Taxation distinct from the Administration of Finance, and this issue is important to minimize the problem of embezzlement and fraud, first, and second, [to allow] the Finance Administrator to secure the mission and operations from destruction of the Sunni at the hands of the enemy.[43]

In sum, faced with collective action and principal–agent problems, insurgent groups need to design their organizations in ways to attract new members and prevent them from shirking, conduct effective military operations, secure and sustain funding, and govern territory they control.

ORGANIZING AN INSURGENT GROUP

So how do insurgent groups structure their organizations? This section focuses on one important aspect of organizational design: the degree of centralization. Centralization, sometimes called hierarchy, refers to the measure of power distribution over decision-making within an organization.[44] Decision-making involves such steps as formulating strategy, distributing resources, controlling communication, and enforcing discipline.[45] As defined here, an organization is centralized when the leadership directly controls operations and resources. The key issue is control. In centralized groups, leaders exert some measure of control over operations and resources. Small teams of US Special Operations Forces, for instance, can operate in a dispersed fashion overseas, but they remain part of a centralized organization because they are under the control of a higher decision-making body.[46]

There are other important organizational components of insurgent groups, such as interconnectedness (the nature of connections among cell leaders and units) and specialization (the distribution of skills within cells).[47] But centralization is a particularly important aspect of organizational management. In order to succeed, insurgent leaders need to establish some measure of control over the use of violence and other aspects of conducting an insurgency.[48] Centralization can help groups become more effective by facilitating resource-sharing, improving economies of scale, and reducing contracting costs.[49]

Centralized groups: The vast majority of insurgent groups since 1946 (91 percent) have set up centralized structures.[50] But there is wide variation in the *degree* of centralization. Groups can have a high level of central control (the leadership directly controls virtually all operations and resources), a moderate level of central control (the leadership directly controls some, but not all, operations and resources), and a low level of centralized control (the leadership directly controls few operations and resources).[51] Simple cross-tabulations of the data suggest that groups with high levels of centralization are more likely to achieve victory (46 percent) than ones with moderate (34 percent) or low (15 percent) levels of centralization. In fact, among insurgencies that have terminated since World War II and in which groups have had a high degree of centralization, four out of five conflicts have ended in insurgent victory or draw.

Insurgent groups generally employ centralized structures rather than decentralized ones for at least two reasons. First, groups are shaped by the initial core of leaders who start the rebellion and who overcome collective action problems. These individuals have a great deal at stake and often demand control over the trajectory of the organization, including over the selection of members. Leadership is critical to insurgent groups, including in centralized organizations. As an al Qa'ida insurgent manual concluded, "Leadership is what unifies, shapes, and executes. Leaders unify in the sense that they integrate under one umbrella all the cadres, efforts, capabilities, and experience that the movement possesses."[52]

Second, centralization is often more effective in dealing with principal–agent problems because it is easier to identify and punish those engaged in shirking or defections. This is why many insurgent leaders, such as the Cuban insurgent Alberto Bayo, stressed that "there should be no arguments over who exercises the direction of the unit and whoever is in command should be respected by all."[53] In centralized organizations, leaders have tighter command and control of their members. The scale and scope of insurgent activity makes decentralization less efficient, especially if lower-level cells are not working in unison toward common objectives.[54] Centralization can also be useful when insurgent groups turn to the difficult task of governing territory, since it minimizes the likelihood that local cells can usurp power and resources for their own interests. Overall, a centralized structure generally makes it easier for leaders to accomplish the key tasks identified at the beginning of this chapter: recruit new members, prevent defections, conduct military operations, secure funding, collect and analyze intelligence, and govern areas they control.

There are numerous examples of centralized groups. During the Algerian insurgency from 1954 to 1962, for instance, the National Liberation Front (Front de Liberation Nationale, or FLN) established a centralized structure that succeeded in gaining independence from France. On August 20, 1956, FLN leaders met in Soummam Valley in Algeria and produced a forty-five-page document that codified guiding principles for gaining independence.[55] The attendees also established two political institutions to govern the FLN: a legislative body known as the National Council of the Algerian Revolution, and an executive body known as the Committee of Coordination and Execution.

The National Council of the Algerian Revolution was the FLN's supreme governing body. On September 19, 1958, it announced the creation of the Provisional Government of the Algerian Republic to act as an Algerian government-in-exile. As illustrated in Figure 5.2, the government included a president, vice president, and heads of key ministries such as defense, foreign affairs, information, social affairs, economic affairs and finance, and interior. This hierarchical structure allowed the FLN to streamline decision-making in several areas, over-coming potential principal–agent problems. It also facilitated the execution of key tasks, such as securing funds to sustain the insurgency (including from foreign backers such as Egypt, Libya, Tunisia, and

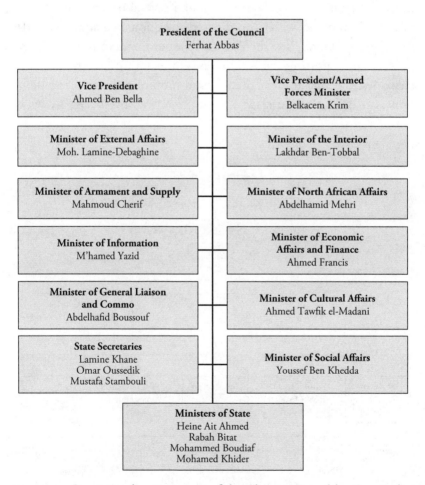

FIGURE 5.2 Provisional government of the Algerian Republic, September 1958[116]

Morocco) and governing areas under FLN control. The structure of the provisional government indicates that the leadership was committed to establishing an alternative state apparatus that could govern the country if the FLN succeeded in winning Algeria's independence. In areas under FLN control in Algeria, the political-military structure operated somewhat openly; in areas controlled by the French it was clandestine.[56]

On the military side, the FLN divided Algeria into six administrative provinces, or *wilayas*. The FLN's military arm, the Algerian Army of National Liberation (Armée de la Libération Nationale, or ALN), was divided into two commands: the Eastern Command, which coordinated operations in *wilayas* 1, 2, 3, and several other areas; and the Western Command, which coordinated operations in *wilayas* 4, 5, and 6. As Figure 5.3 highlights, the ALN was subordinate to the provisional government, ensuring the preeminence of political leaders over military ones. In order to fight the war and minimize shirking and defections, an inter-ministerial war committee oversaw the ALN, which

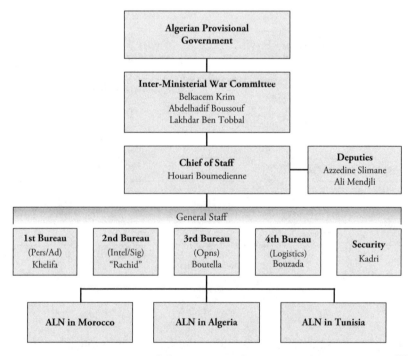

FIGURE 5.3 Organization of the ALN High Command, January 1960[117]

also included a General Staff composed of personnel, intelligence, operations, logistics, and security units.[57] The Second Bureau, for instance, was instrumental in running the collection, analysis, and distribution of intelligence. It oversaw activities in each of the *wilayas*, which included the development of an intelligence network with agents, clandestine communications, safe houses, and letter drops.[58] The Fourth Bureau oversaw a massive logistics system dedicated to the procurement, distribution, storage, and maintenance of food, clothing, weapons, ammunition, vehicles, fuel, and other supplies. Logistics was a complex process, in part since it involved the secret coordination of supplies in Algeria, North Africa, Europe (including France), and as far away as China.

The political and military structure of the FLN allowed it to become a fairly unified and effective insurgent group. It was able to suppress internal dissent, overcome external competitors, and gain assistance from outside powers. The FLN was also able to raise, organize, equip, train, and direct ALN military units capable of challenging French forces and paramilitary groups like the Organisation de l'armée secrète (OAS). The OAS was a far-right paramilitary organization that used violence to prevent Algeria's independence from French colonial rule.

There are other examples of centralized insurgent groups. In Peru, Sendero Luminoso established a centralized organizational structure under the control of Abimael Guzmán, though Sendero's regional commanders operated with a degree of tactical independence.[59] So did M-19 in Colombia.[60] In Algeria, insurgents from the Armed Islamic Group kept detailed records of virtually everything they did. As one firsthand account summarized, "There was a list of everyone who was collaborating with the GIA and what his or her connection was. The group put everything in writing. Even when they decided to kill someone, they wrote it down."[61]

In Vietnam, the Viet Cong established a highly sophisticated five-level "shadow" administrative infrastructure by the end of 1968. According to one assessment, which was based on approximately 2,400 interviews of Vietnamese familiar with the activities of the Viet Cong and the North Vietnamese army, the Viet Cong believed that "an efficient, centrally managed organization [was] a major tool of revolutionary war."[62] The most significant decision-making body was the People's

Revolutionary Party, highlighting a common theme in insurgent organizations: the tendency to place political (rather than military) bodies in charge. Indeed, the Viet Cong's military organizations, the Liberation Army and National Liberation Front, executed party decisions. This hierarchical structure allowed the Viet Cong to recruit members in North and South Vietnam, minimize defections, fight, sustain funding, and govern areas under their control. It also allowed the Viet Cong to keep comprehensive centralized records, including after-action reports, lesson plans, field manuals, and operations research reports.[63]

In the Afghan insurgency that began after September 11, 2001, the Taliban devised a fairly centralized organization that included multiple levels. As Figure 5.4 highlights, it included a centralized structure, the senior leadership shura, which was divided into committees that oversaw finances, military operations, propaganda, religious affairs,

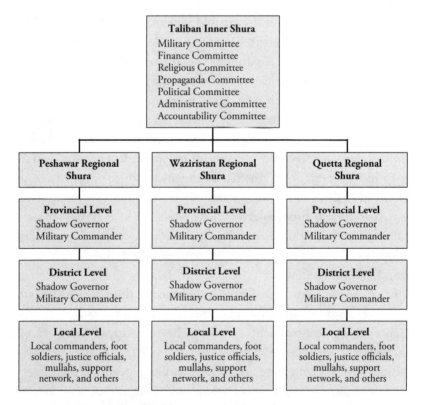

FIGURE 5.4 Example of Taliban organizational structure

and other tasks to run an insurgency. In 2013, key members included such individuals as Mullah Mohammad Omar (*Amir al-Mu'minin*, or Commander of the Faithful), Mullah Gul Agha (head of the finance committee), Mullah Abdul Qayum Zakir (head of the military committee), Mullah Mohammad Hassan Akhund (chief of commissions and head of the recruitment commission), and Mullah Akhtar Mohammad Mansour (head of the senior leadership shura). The Taliban also established an Accountability Commission to help solve principal–agent problems. It reviewed the effectiveness of Taliban commanders and leaders, helped resolve disputes between members, and appointed new leaders. As in many other insurgencies, the Taliban ensured that the primary decision-making body was a political, rather than a military, one. Among its most important tasks was overseeing propaganda, which included establishing relations with international and local media outlets; publishing newspapers and magazines, such as *Al Somood*; overseeing websites and the distribution of information on a variety of social media forums; issuing and publishing books; and preparing and distributing videos.[64]

Below the senior leadership shura were three regional shuras in Pakistan (in Peshawar, North Waziristan, and Quetta); provincial shadow governors and military commanders; district shadow governors and military commanders; and then low-level fighters, justice officials, mullahs, and others that provided local support.

While most groups prefer centralized organizations to decentralized ones, a hierarchical structure is not sufficient for success. Insurgents still need, for example, outside support as discussed in Chapter 8. Centralized structures can also be highly resistant to change, slow to innovate, overly bureaucratic, vulnerable to decapitation, and inflexible over the course of a war.[65] There are numerous groups—such as the Democratic Army of Greece (1946–1949) and the Republic of Biafra in Nigeria (1967–1970)—that possessed centralized structures but lost on the battlefield. So did the LTTE in Sri Lanka, which had a centralized structure under Vellupillai Prabhakaran that included the Sea Tigers (naval attack unit), Baby Tigers (child soldiers), Black Tigers (suicide bombers), Air Tigers (air force), and the Women's Military Units of the LTTE.[66] By 2009, the LTTE was decimated after a brutal counterinsurgency campaign by the Sri Lankan government.[67]

Decentralized groups: Despite the frequency of centralized structures, 9 percent of insurgent groups were decentralized after World
War II.[68] An organization is decentralized when there is little or no
centralized control and the leadership directly controls few or no
operations and resources. Local cells may fund themselves, recruit
locally, and plan and execute the majority of their operations. The
more control that lower-level operatives wield over the formulation of
operations and resourcing, the more decentralized the organization.[69]
As previously noted, however, decentralized groups are more likely to
face principal–agent problems because it is more difficult to detect and
discipline operatives engaged in shirking or defection. Decentralized
groups may also find it challenging to control territory, since lower-
level cells are more likely to usurp power and resources for their own
interests with limited oversight. Insurgent groups don't necessarily
choose to be decentralized, but may adopt decentralized structures for
several reasons.

First, government repression can force groups to disperse and delegate in order to survive. Some hierarchical groups are vulnerable to
decapitation strategies, in which governments attempt to weaken or
destroy the group by capturing or killing its leadership.[70] Government
pressure can force insurgent cells and members into hiding, increasing
the likelihood of dispersal. Insurgent groups generally choose greater
levels of hierarchy when the operational environment allows, and are
forced to decentralize when they face government pressure. Centralized
activities, which may involve regular electronic communications or
record-keeping to solve agency problems, make insurgents vulnerable.
Indeed, groups under significant government pressure will generally
give up control and efficiency relative to otherwise similar groups under
less pressure.[71]

During the Malayan Emergency that lasted from 1948 to 1957,
the Malayan Communist Party established an increasingly decentralized structure. Initially, the political apparatus included a Central
Committee and a series of State, District, and Branch Committees—
partly in the jungle and partly outside the country. The Malayan People's
Anti-British Army, the military arm, initially mobilized eight regiments
and subsequently increased them to ten regiments.[72] Beginning around
1951, however, the Malayan Communist Party decentralized in response

to British infiltration and battlefield successes. This reorganization created serious problems for the Malayan Communist Party, whose lower-level echelons did not receive specific orders or instructions either from outside the country or from their own superior headquarters.[73]

Second, insurgent groups that receive substantial benefits from natural resources or outside sponsors often encounter difficulties exerting control and discipline over their membership. Combatants are more likely to loot, destroy property, and attack civilians indiscriminately. Indeed, groups organized largely on the basis of economic endowments, such as RENAMO in Mozambique or Sendero Luminoso in the Upper Huallaga Valley of Peru, had difficulty controlling their members and restraining them from committing widespread abuses against civilians.[74]

Third, insurgent leaders whose members include a mix of ethnic, tribal, religious, cultural, and other constituencies may find it difficult to centralize control because of heterogeneous preferences. Decentralized structures, in turn, make it difficult for leaders to control messaging, public statements, and negotiations. In some cases, the inclusion of diaspora populations outside the country can increase the likelihood of decentralization. In Sudan, the Anya Nya was fragmented for much of the war, which lasted from 1963 to 1972. As one analysis concluded, the Anya Nya "did not develop into a politically organised movement under a disciplined military leadership," but rather "consisted of scattered local resistance bands."[75] There were rivalries among exiled members of Anya Nya, as well as those within Sudan, inhibiting its military effectiveness and political legitimacy. In Angola, the Front for the Liberation of the State of Cabinda (FLEC) had an increasingly decentralized structure. In the mid-1970s, the FLEC fractured because of competition from other groups (such as the Popular Movement for the Liberation of Angola) and personal rivalries, breaking into three factions. There were additional splits in 1977 and 1979 that further decentralized the organization and undermined its effectiveness.[76] In Senegal, the Movement of the Democratic Forces of the Casamance (MFDC) had a decentralized structure. As one report concluded, the MFDC's leadership had little "control over its own armed units."[77] This made it difficult for the MFDC to recruit members, prevent defections, and ultimately prosecute a war against Senegal.

In Ethiopia, the Eritrean Liberation Front (ELF) had a decentralized organizational structure. Founded in 1961 in Barka, a western lowland region of Eritrea, the ELF initially recruited from among Eritrea's semi-nomadic Muslim lowlanders. In the mid-1960s, the ELF started to attract Christian highlanders and, by 1965, ELF leaders established four zones along ethnic, religious, and regional lines. With the growing influx of urban and educated Christian highlanders, ELF leaders created a fifth zone in 1966. The leadership lived abroad in Sudan and Saudi Arabia, and thus lacked engagement in daily activities of the group. The rank and file, however, included a diverse contingent of religious and ethnic representatives that made it difficult to establish a centralized command-and-control apparatus. By the late 1960s, the ELF fractured and several groups broke away to form the Eritrean People's Liberation Front in 1970.[78]

Even in Kenya, Mau Mau insurgents suffered from a decentralized organizational structure. As one assessment concluded, "Mau Mau was a significant fighting force by the middle of 1953, but it would never be a unified guerrilla army."[79] By the mid-1950s, the decentralized structure of Mau Mau resistance made it easier for the British to sow discord among guerrilla units with "pseudo-gangs" (pro-government units sent into the forest disguised as rebels) and encourage defections among Mau Mau units. Mau Mau commanders, such as Dedan Kimathi and Stanley Mathenge, competed with each other for power in a decentralized apparatus.[80] As one assessment summarized, "This failure, with the internal dissent it bred, was to prove fatal to the Mau Mau cause."[81] In Yemen, Huthi insurgents adopted a decentralized organizational structure that was influenced by *qabyala*, the ethical code of tribalism in northern Yemen, which stressed individual autonomy. Area commanders had substantial autonomy to organize, fund, and conduct operations.[82]

In some countries with a weak state or a heterogeneous mix of ethnic, tribal, religious, cultural, and other groups, insurgents have leveraged local militias, which contributed to a decentralized apparatus. In Angola, for example, local militias were crucial for the MPLA. "Without the militias," remarked one MPLA leader, "the semiregular forces of the MPLA couldn't control this area. Moxico [Province] itself, you know, is four times larger than Portugal. So, to control this area, we need the help of the militia."[83] Even in Vietnam, the Viet Cong established local militias at the hamlet and village levels. These militias served multiple purposes: to assist in the defense of villages against the Army of the Republic of Vietnam, collect intelligence for Viet Cong units, counter the infiltration of government spies in villages, conduct offense operations against government military and police posts, and conduct sabotage operations.[84]

More broadly, insurgents have been forced to deal with numerous local forces that are not necessarily pro-government or pro-insurgent. In Iraq, for example, Sunni tribes shifted sides during the insurgency that began in 2003. In South Vietnam, the Binh Xuyen, a gang of opium-smuggling river pirates based in Saigon's Cholon district, were initially aligned with the insurgent Viet Minh in 1945 against the French. However, the two soon fell out and the Viet Minh actively sought to assassinate the leader of the Binh Xuyen, Bay Vien.[85] The Binh Xuyen were reportedly effective in combating the Viet Minh in Cholon, and later expanded to protect much of Saigon. But as one report concluded, at the end of the Indochina war the Binh Xuyen "maintained semi-autonomous fiefs to the south and southeast of Cholon, controlled the Saigon-Cholon police, ran lucrative gambling and prostitution establishments, and controlled the opium trade, much of the fish and charcoal commerce, and several hotels and plantations."[86] In Algeria, the nominally pro-state *pieds noirs* eventually birthed the radical anti-government Organization of the Secret Army.[87] Insurgent efforts to co-opt local militias and other forces have sometimes contributed to the decentralization of insurgent groups.

Fourth, there may be other reasons why insurgent leaders opt for decentralized structures. As political scientist Jacob Shapiro argued, leaders may choose decentralized organizational structures under several conditions: when groups don't want or need to be discriminate in their use of violence; when there is little uncertainty between leaders and operatives about which targets serve the group's political goals; and where there is substantial agreement (or low "preference divergence") between insurgent leaders and lower-level operatives about how best to use violence to accomplish their stated goals.[88]

Consequently, while decentralized organizational structures may not necessarily be preferable for insurgent leaders, several factors increase their frequency. Government repression, the widespread availability of economic endowments, and heterogeneity among groups can increase the likelihood of more decentralized structures.

OPTIONS WHEN THERE ARE MULTIPLE GROUPS

Another organizational challenge for insurgent groups is weighing options when there is more than one group. After all, there was more than one insurgent group in half (50 percent) of insurgencies since 1946. Multi-group insurgencies lasted longer than single-group insurgencies. Among insurgencies that ended, multi-group insurgencies averaged 13 years, compared to only seven years for single-group insurgencies.[89] Simple cross-tabulations suggest that single-group insurgencies may also be more likely to end in a decisive government victory than multi-group insurgencies. Excluding ongoing cases, 44 percent of single-group insurgencies resulted in government victory, compared to only 25 percent of multi-group insurgencies. Of multi-group insurgencies that ended since World War II, three quarters (75 percent) ended in rebel victory or draw, compared to a little more than half (56 percent) of single-group insurgencies.

In addition, the percentage of multi-group insurgencies increased over time, as highlighted in Figure 5.5. Of the 100 insurgencies that began in the 1940s through the 1970s, two thirds were single-group insurgencies, while only one third were multi-group insurgencies. In the last three and a half decades, though, these ratios nearly flipped. Among insurgencies that started after 1980, only 36 percent consisted of a single group, while 64 percent consisted of multiple groups. Of the thirty-eight insurgencies active throughout the world in 2015, 82 percent consisted of multiple groups. There may be several reasons for the increase in multi-group insurgencies. It may be caused, for example, by a decline in outside government support to insurgent groups, since outside powers have frequently tried to streamline insurgencies. It may also have been caused by the rise in Islamic insurgencies, which tend to include multiple groups.

Insurgent leaders have several strategic options in wars with more than one group. They can coordinate activities, compete with each other, or conduct stovepiped operations. These are not mutually exclusive

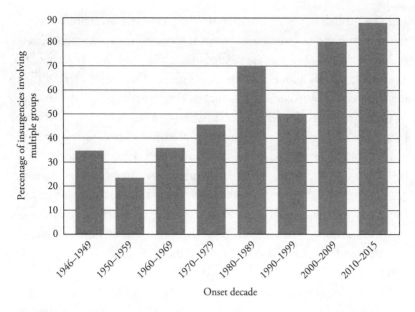

FIGURE 5.5 Percentage of multi-group insurgencies by onset decade

options, since groups may choose more than one—even all three—over the course of an insurgency. A group may also choose alternative strategies toward different groups simultaneously—for instance, cooperating with one rival group while fighting another. This is particularly true in insurgencies with multiple groups, such as in Syria beginning in 2011, Iraq beginning in 2003, and Lebanon from 1975 to 1990.

First, groups can *coordinate* their activities, either informally or by developing an umbrella structure.[90] Groups often choose to coordinate when they have similar ideologies or other common traits, such as recruitment from the same ethnic group. Coordination can also bolster capacity. Just as defense manufacturers sometimes gain from joint production by achieving economies of scale, groups can join forces to aggregate their capabilities and present a more serious threat to the government. Coordination can help groups increase their access to tactical and technological information and weaponry. Finally, coordination provides groups with the opportunity to jointly train, develop new skills, and transmit knowledge and expertise—much as some firms do when they collaborate.[91]

In two thirds of cases involving multiple groups, insurgents attempted to cooperate and coordinate activities at some point during the life of the insurgency. However, they succeeded in establishing a formal umbrella organization in only about half of these conflicts. This indicates the difficulties inherent in overcoming personal rivalries and ideological differences in order to institutionalize a power-sharing arrangement—as opposed to simply forming tactical "marriages of convenience." In some cases, as in Afghanistan in the 1980s, an outside power can be helpful—even necessary—by acting as a neutral mediator, overcoming collective action problems. Pakistan's ISI was pivotal in the Afghan insurgency in the 1980s, helping design a structure to bring together the seven major insurgent groups.[92] In Libya in 2011, the United States, France, and the United Kingdom helped coordinate a fractured network of insurgents and militia that overthrew the Qaddafi government.[93]

But outside actors are not always necessary. In Pakistan, several militant commanders coalesced under the banner of the Tehreek-e-Taliban-e-Pakistan (TTP), led by Baitullah Mehsud. They sought to establish a radical interpretation of *sharia* across the Pashtun belt. In late February 2008, two commanders, Mullah Nazir and Hafiz Gul Bahadur, appeared to temporarily set aside their differences with Baitullah Mehsud and forged an umbrella organization.[94] One of their most successful methods was to exploit local grievances: socioeconomic concerns among local Pakistanis; Pakistan governance failures, including adequate and timely security and justice; and frustration with government corruption. They established functional—if draconian—police functions and dispute resolution mechanism. The *qazi* courts established in Swat, run by Islamist jurists, required the addition of new *qazis* (Islamic jurists) when their caseload exceeded 150 cases. No such provision existed in the mainstream courts.

TTP-linked groups also established "love marriage bureaus" to solemnize love marriages. This had the advantage of appealing to youth who resented forced marriages and ameliorated the economic requirement of young men to pay large bride prices.[95] Over time, however, TTP unity broke down because of internal disagreements over leadership, tactics (including civilian casualties), ideology, and other factors.[96] Beginning in 2014, the Islamic State took advantage of fissures within the TTP to recruit members to its Islamic State Khorasan branch, initially under the leadership of Hafiz Saeed Khan, the former chief of the TTP's Orakzai branch in Pakistan's tribal areas.

During the Cold War, there were numerous examples of Latin American guerrilla groups coordinating their activities. In El Salvador, the Farabundo Martí National Liberation Front (FMLN) was formed with the help of Cuba as an umbrella group in October 1980 from several left-wing guerrilla organizations: Fuerzas Populares de Liberación Farabundo Martí, Ejército Revolucionario del Pueblo, Resistencia Nacional, Partido Comunista Salvadoreño, and Partido Revolucionario de los Trabajadores Centroamericanos. They established a manifesto that coordinated political and military efforts, declaring that "there will be only one leadership, only one military plan and only one command, only one political line."[97] In Colombia, several leftist groups created the National Guerrilla Coordinating Board in 1985 to coordinate activities, including negotiations with the Colombian government. In 1987, it was renamed the Simon Bolivar Coordinating Board and included members of the Revolutionary Armed Forces of Colombia (FARC), April 19 Movement (M-19), National Liberation Army (ELN), Popular Liberation Army (EPL), Workers' Revolutionary Party (PRT), and the Quintin Lame Command. And in the Guatemalan insurgency that began in 1965, rebel groups formed the umbrella Guatemalan National Revolutionary Unity in 1982 to coordinate political and military activities. It eventually reached a peace agreement with the Guatemalan government in 1996, which ended the war.

Still, insurgent groups sometimes try—and fail—to coordinate their efforts. They may be unable to overcome collective action problems; disagree on a common cause; face competing interests from groups with diverse ethnic, religious, or other constituencies; or clash over whether—and how—to enter into political negotiations. In the Syrian insurgency that began in 2011, for instance, rebel organizations and their outside backers repeatedly attempted to coordinate efforts through organizations like the Supreme Military Council, Syrian National Army, and Joint Military Command for the Syrian Revolution. In December 2012, an assortment of rebel leaders established the Syrian Military Council and elected a thirty-member unified command structure. The Syrian Military Council worked to strengthen its command and control of insurgent groups and was a mechanism by which international actors and foreign donors could deliver lethal and non-lethal aid to Syria. However, it had little influence over the day-to-day operations of groups or their campaign plans.[98]

In addition, numerous Syrian opposition groups refused to participate, including the al Qa'ida–affiliated group Jabhat al-Nusrah and the Islamic State. In fact, Jabhat al-Nusrah attempted to co-opt other Sunni groups beginning in 2012, creating the Mujahideen Shura Council in Dayr az-Zawr. The council was formed to "unite the ranks of the jihadi brigades in the Cause of Allah, organize the efforts and the attacks against the soldiers of disbelief and apostasy, and distinguish the ranks of truth from falsehood," according to a statement released by the group in December 2012. It continued: "We call upon our sincere mujahideen brothers all over the strong Levant to unite their ranks in groups, pure of the filth of suspicious groups and the infiltration of people who have no qualities or faith, in order to clarify their banner and purify their path."[99] But these objectives put them at odds with other Syrian opposition groups, undermining the likelihood that groups could coordinate their activities.

A second option is *competition*. Groups can attempt to co-opt or coerce members of other groups, including by fighting them. Competition may be more common when groups don't share similar ideologies or other common traits. The logic for competition is straightforward: a group may decide that the best way to preserve the purity of its cause and ensure that its leaders retain power is to defeat other groups on the battlefield or co-opt them short of violence. Competition among groups is fairly common in insurgencies, occurring in nearly one third of those insurgencies with more than one group.

During the Sri Lankan insurgency from 1984 to 2009, there was intense competition among Tamil groups. By the 1970s, there were five main groups: the Tamil Eelam Liberation Organization, the Eelam Revolutionary Organization of Students, the People's Liberation Organization for Tamil Eelam, the Eelam People's Revolutionary Liberation Front, and the Tamil National Tigers (later renamed the Liberation Tigers of Tamil Eelam, or LTTE).[100] Outside of these five, there were at least twenty others in the Jaffna Peninsula of Sri Lanka, all locally based. Around 1985, Vellupillai Prabhakaran and other LTTE leaders decided to eliminate the other four major resistance groups. Prabhakaran had envisioned himself as president of an inde-pendent Tamil Eelam in Sri Lanka. He began with People's Liberation Organization for Tamil Eelam. LTTE operatives targeted fighters from the People's Liberation Organization for Tamil Eelam in Madras and attempted to kill their leader, Uma Maheswaram.[101] Prabhakaran then sent coded messages detailing how Tamil Eelam Liberation Organization members based in Jaffna should be eliminated. Over a fif-teen-year period culminating around 1986, the LTTE effectively elimi-nated its main rivals. As one assessment concluded, "One by one their rivals and opponents among the Tamil separatist groups succumbed to the relentless violence of the LTTE. An essential feature of the pro-cess was the physical elimination of the leadership of several important Tamil separatist groups, rivals and onetime associates of the LTTE."[102]

In France, the FLN carried out one battle against the French and an-other to suppress rival nationalist elements, ethnic separatists, and even dissent within the FLN. The most important rival was the Algerian Nationalist Movement, formed by dissident elements of Messali Hadj's Movement for the Triumph of Democratic Liberties just before the out-break of the rebellion. The conflict between the FLN and the Algerian Nationalist Movement extended to metropolitan France, where the two groups vied for the support of the Algerian population and car-ried out a war of terrorism against each other. Between October 1956 and October 1957 alone, some 550 Algerian Muslims were killed, and over 2,200 were wounded in terrorist incidents in France. The FLN eventually triumphed over the Algerian Nationalist Movement, but only after independence was achieved.[103] In Peru, Sendero Luminoso conducted a ruthless campaign against another insurgent group, the Tupac Amaru Revolutionary Movement, at the same time it fought the government. Until 1984, Sendero had retained a virtual monopoly of the insurgency.[104]

In Iraq, al Qa'ida created the Islamic State of Iraq to bring together groups that opposed the United States, some Anbar tribes, and the Iraqi government. Al Qa'ida's goal remained expelling US forces and estab-lishing an Islamic caliphate in Iraq. Al Qa'ida's decision to establish the Islamic State of Iraq was, in part, an attempt to increase its power by preventing the further fracturing of insurgent groups. By claiming to be a state, al Qa'ida also sought to gain legitimacy. Less publicized, but probably more important, was al Qa'ida's attempt to unify Sunni Arabs by cracking down on corruption and assassinating recalcitrant sheiks. One al Qa'ida communiqué implored its foot soldiers to "avoid any awful act and replace it by nothing but a good deed."[105] Recognizing the importance of winning local support, al Qa'ida then began an intense propaganda campaign centered on Islamic motifs, which threatened defectors and attempted to shame them into rejoining its thinning ranks.

For those who refused al Qa'ida's olive branch, it was all-out war. Al Qa'ida began a string of deadly attacks: 202 killed and 257 wounded in suicide bombings on November 23, 2006; 117 killed and 270 wounded on March 6, 2007; 152 killed and 347 wounded on March 27; 140 killed and 160 wounded on April 18; and 156 killed and 267 wounded on July 2. The casualty figures were unprecedented. Al Qa'ida targeted the public faces of the new alliance: key sheikhs and the police.[106] Harith Zaher al-Dhari, son of the leader of the Zobai tribe and head of the Association of Muslim Scholars, was assassinated, an act attributed to his organization's refusal to join the Islamic State of Iraq. Some thirty commanders of 1920 Revolution Brigade and Jaysh al-Islami were assassinated by al Qa'ida or killed in battles over arms caches in al-Anbar. In October, Sheikh abu Osama al-'Iraqi called on Osama bin Laden to denounce al Qa'ida in Iraq for killing Sunnis and targeting jihad fighters from other Sunni factions.

A third option is *stovepiping*. Groups that stovepipe choose to operate as separate organizations and neither coordinate nor directly compete with each other. Stovepiping often occurs when insurgent leaders fail to resolve collective action problems among groups, develop personality clashes with other leaders, or operate in different geographic regions. The result is often a duplication of efforts and a waste of resources. In Argentina, the activities of the Revolutionary Worker's Party (which was a Trotskyite group heavily influenced by the Tupamaros) and the Monteneros Peronist Movement (which was committed to the return of Juan Peron and his policies) were fairly stovepiped between 1974 and 1977. In Indonesia, there was significant stovepiping between groups during the insurgency from 1953 to 1961 in Sumatra. In Kashmir, a number of insurgent groups that sought to incorporate Kashmir into Pakistan or secure an independent Kashmiri state operated autonomously, with little or no coordination. And in Chad during the war that began in 1991, there was substantial stovepiping among numerous opposition groups such as the Forces Armées pour la République Fédérale and the Mouvement pour la Démocratie et le Développement.

Which of these options—coordinating, competing, or stovepiping—is preferable? Simple cross-tabulations suggest that groups have sometimes been more successful when they established a formal umbrella structure, an organizational body that synchronized strategy and operations across groups. Umbrella structures are particularly helpful to insurgents for a draw, including efforts to negotiate a peace settlement. But umbrella structures are relatively rare. Of the thirty-one insurgencies in which groups established an umbrella structure, only 3 percent ended in a government victory. The other cases either ended in an insurgent victory (26 percent), a draw (32 percent), or were ongoing (39 percent). When groups stovepiped operations or fought each other, they were less likely to succeed. Somewhat counterintuitively, violent competition between groups did not eliminate their chances of overthrowing the government. In fact, the probability of insurgent victory when groups competed with each other in the same insurgency was just as likely (21.4 percent) as government victory (21.4 percent).

THE CHALLENGE OF DECENTRALIZATION

As this chapter highlights, if groups can overcome collective action and principal–agent problems, it helps them perform a range of important tasks. They are generally better able to recruit members, prevent defections, conduct military operations, secure funding, collect and analyze intelligence, and govern areas they control—all while attempting to remain covert. In addition, centralized organizational structures are generally helpful to overcome these problems.

Decentralized groups, on the other hand, are often less successful in dealing with principal–agent problems because it is more difficult to identify and punish those engaged in shirking or defections. The scale and scope of insurgent activity makes decentralization less efficient, especially if lower-level cells are not working in unison toward common objectives. Decentralization can also be problematic when insurgent groups turn to the difficult task of governing territory, since local cells can usurp power and resources for their own interests. This reality may be why Régis Debray, a contemporary of Che Guevara, remarked that the "lack of a single command puts the revolutionary forces in a situation of an artillery gunner who has not been told which direction to fire. . . . The absence of a centralized executive (political and military) leadership leads to such waste, such useless slaughter."[107]

Still, a range of transnational terrorist, criminal, and insurgent groups have adopted decentralized structures.[108] In the United States, for example, some urban gangs, rural militias, and militant single-issue groups have developed networked attributes. Anti-government activist and white supremacist Louis Beam advocated an organizational structure that he termed "leaderless resistance" to target the United States government. As Beam noted, "Utilizing the Leaderless Resistance concept, all individuals and groups operate independently of each other, and never report to a central headquarters or single leader for direction or instruction, as would those who belong to a typical pyramid organization."[109] In addition, a range of left-wing revolutionaries, radicals, and anarchists have adopted networked organizational structures. As John Arquilla and David Ronfeldt argue,

> The organizational structure is quite flat. There is no single central leader or commander; the network as a whole (but not necessarily each node) has little to no hierarchy. There may be multiple leaders. Decision-making and operations are decentralized and depend on consultative consensus-building that allows for local initiative and autonomy. The design is both acephalous (headless) and polycephalous (Hydra-headed)—it has no precise heart or head, although not all nodes may be "created equal."[110]

Even al Qa'ida established an increasingly decentralized structure composed of several tiers, which were involved in insurgencies across northern Africa, the Middle East, and Asia.[111] One was core al Qa'ida, which included the organization's leaders, most of whom were based in Pakistan. Al Qa'ida leaders referred to this broader area as Khorasan, a historical reference to the territory that included Persia, Central Asia, Afghanistan, and parts of northwestern Pakistan during the Umayyad and Abbasid caliphates.[112] The next tier included affiliated groups that became formal branches of al Qa'ida. What distinguished "affiliates" from other types of Salafi-jihadist groups was the decision by their emirs to swear *bay'at,* or loyalty, to al Qa'ida leaders, which was then accepted by al Qa'ida leaders. These organizations included groups like al Qa'ida in the Arabian Peninsula (based in Yemen), al Shabaab (based in Somalia), al Qa'ida in the Islamic Maghreb (based in Algeria and neighboring countries), and Jabhat al-Nusrah (based in Syria).

Next were a series of allied Salafi-jihadist groups that established a direct relationship with al Qa'ida.[113] But they were not created by core al Qa'ida, did not become formal members, and their leaders did not swear *bay'at* to core al Qa'ida. This arrangement allowed these Salafi-jihadist groups to remain independent and pursue their own insurgent goals in general, but to work with al Qa'ida for specific operations or training purposes when their interests converged. Examples included a number of groups across Africa (such as Ansar al-Sharia Libya and Harakat Ansar al-Din), Asia (such as Jemaah Islamiyah and the East Turkestan Islamic Movement), the Middle East (such as Ansar Bayt al-Maqdis and Ziyad al-Jarrah Battalions), and the Caucasus (such as Imarat Kavkaz). Finally, there were inspired individuals and networks with no direct contact to core al Qa'ida, but who were inspired by the al Qa'ida cause and outraged by the perceived oppression of Muslims in Afghanistan, Chechnya, Palestine, and other countries.

Decentralized groups like al Qa'ida that are unable to control their members—particularly when they resort to brutal tactics—can severely undermine the support of insurgent groups. As discussed in Chapter 4, undisciplined and barbarous tactics can weaken local support for insurgent groups over the long run. As one study that examined al Qa'ida in Iraq (AQI) and other groups concluded, "AQI repeatedly had problems with local units taking actions that led to conflicts with other insurgent organizations and alienated non-combatants."[114]

6

Information Campaigns and Propaganda

The printing press is the greatest weapon in the armory of the modern commander.[1]

—T. E. LAWRENCE

The Internet offers the insurgent the ability to use e-mail, chat rooms, blogs, and other forums both for propaganda and for direct messaging. Operatives capture digital video imagery, upload it within minutes, and broadcast it round the world almost instantaneously.[2]

—United States Army Special Operations Command

IN SEPTEMBER 2013, AL Shabaab operatives from the Somalia-based group grabbed international headlines by conducting a deadly attack at the upscale Westgate shopping mall in Nairobi, Kenya, killing at least 59 people and wounding nearly 200 others. The attackers carefully selected the Westgate mall among possible alternatives; conducted intelligence, surveillance, and reconnaissance on the target; moved operatives and equipment into place; performed rehearsals; executed the attack; and implemented an information campaign before, during, and after the attack.[3] During the attack, they utilized the social media site Twitter to update followers and orchestrate a propaganda campaign. Following are a sampling of tweets during the attack, with al Shabaab referring to itself as Harakat al-Shabaab al-Mujahideen (HSM) and using the Twitter account @HSM_Press:

HSM has on numerous occasions warned the #Kenyan government that failure to remove its forces from Somalia would have severe consequences

By Land, air and sea, #Kenyan forces invaded our Muslim country, killing hundreds of Muslims in the process and displacing thousands more

The attack at #WestgateMall is just a very tiny fraction of what Muslims in Somalia experience at the hands of Kenyan invaders. #Westgate

The Mujahideen entered #Westgate Mall today at around noon and are still inside the mall, fighting the #Kenyan Kuffar inside their own turf

Since our last contact, the Mujahideen inside the mall confirmed to @HSM_Press that they killed over 100 Kenyan kuffar & battle is ongoing

The message we are sending to the Kenyan govt & Public is and has always been just one: remove all your forces from our country #Westgate

BREAKING: HSM Press has just made contact with the Mujahideen inside #Westgate Mall. They are still fighting and still strong. Stay tuned!

Only Kuffar were singled out for this attack. All Muslims inside #Westgate were escorted out by the Mujahideen before beginning the attack

They Kenyan govt is pleading with our Mujahideen inside the mall for negotiations. There will be no negotiations whatsoever at #Westgate[4]

Al Shabaab also released a special edition of its magazine, *Gaidi Mtaani*, in late 2013 devoted to the mall attack. An article in the magazine justified the attack as retaliation for Kenya's alleged "blatant aggression against Islam and Muslims," as well as Kenya's purported "blind and aimless bombardment of civilians by Kenyan jets and ships."[5] Al Shabaab's use of social media was one of countless examples. In October 2015, the Islamic State's branch in Sinai, Egypt claimed responsibility for taking down a Russian airplane, killing all 224 passengers on board. The Twitter statement read: "#Egypt #ISIS Claim Responsibility for shot down the Russian Aircraft over Sinai #IS #ISIL pic.twitter.com/tBCRt7Xen1."

This chapter examines the use of information campaigns—including propaganda—by insurgent groups. As used here, an "information campaign" refers to insurgent efforts to spread information (or disinformation) to aid the insurgent cause, damage or otherwise undermine counterinsurgents and their supporters, influence local and international audiences, and achieve other goals.[6] The chapter does not, however, systematically assess the effectiveness of insurgent information campaigns. Virtually all groups use word of mouth, print, radio, television, social media, and other forums, which suggests that there is not a correlation between the type of forum and the effectiveness of an information campaign—or the success of an insurgency. In addition, it is often difficult to understand the causal linkage between information campaigns and outcomes. Did they cause a specific outcome, or was it a product of other factors? Instead, this chapter compiles a range of quantitative data and qualitative material on insurgent use of information campaigns and propaganda.

Based on a review of insurgent information campaigns, this chapter comes to several conclusions. First, while insurgents have long used traditional media such as print and radio, there was a dramatic quantitative increase in insurgent use of the Internet and social media in two waves: the late 1990s, which involved the establishment of independent websites and private, password-protected chat rooms; and the rise of public social media forums beginning in the late 2000s. Insurgent groups increasingly used a sophisticated mix of Internet and social media sites and services to recruit members, raise funds, perpetrate limited cyber attacks, and conduct psychological operations. Second, communications technology like mobile devices appear to help insurgent groups overcome collective action problems, discussed in Chapter 5, by increasing their ability to distribute information to supporters and allowing for real-time coordination of insurgent operations. Third, insurgent use of mobile technology and social media forums also poses risks, since counterinsurgents with signals intelligence capabilities can better monitor their use for intelligence collection and strike operations. Counterinsurgents increasingly used formal and informal "electronic armies" to launch cyber attacks against insurgents and their supporters, spread false information, block websites, spam targets, and collect intelligence on insurgent activity and locations.

The chapter is divided into four sections. The first examines traditional media, including word of mouth, print, radio, and television. The second analyzes the rise of the Internet and social media in insurgent campaigns. The third outlines implications of the growing use of mobile technology and social media, including helping overcome collective action problems. And the fourth section explores counterintelligence challenges.

TRADITIONAL MEDIA

Insurgent groups are faced with the complicated task of trying to communicate with numerous audiences during an insurgency—such as potential recruits, the local population, donors, diaspora populations, counterinsurgents and their allies, and a range of other national and international audiences—while minimizing government targeting. Information campaigns need to be designed to deal with one or more of these audiences. T. E. Lawrence, for example, emphasized the criticality of designing propaganda to influence multiple groups, including fellow insurgents. "We had to arrange their minds in order of battle, just as carefully and as formally as other officers arranged their bodies," he wrote. But it was "not only our own men's minds, though them first: the minds of the enemy, so far as we could reach them; and thirdly, the mind of the nation supporting us behind the firing-line, and the mind of the hostile nation waiting the verdict, and the neutrals looking on."[7]

Insurgents use information campaigns for several purposes. First, they can be helpful to recruit new members and supporters, a task outlined in Chapter 5. Rebels require foot soldiers willing to risk their lives in battle against a stronger government force, intelligence agents to collect information on counterinsurgents and collaborators, and other dedicated members to conduct a range of tasks from logistics to training.

Attracting recruits is not an easy task. The work of an insurgency is arduous and often dangerous.[8] Insurgent groups attempt to attract new recruits with messages designed to gain support for a cause, such as overthrowing a corrupt and ineffective government. Second, insurgents use information campaigns to conduct psychological operations: spread propaganda and disinformation, encourage defections from counterinsurgents, sow fear and discord, portray insurgents as likely to win, and disseminate images of recent operations. Third, information campaigns can be helpful in raising funds and securing material resources from local and international donors. As with recruits, the goal is to use specifically designed messages to persuade and resource individuals to fund the insurgency. Fourth, insurgents use information campaigns to accomplish other goals, such as sharing operational and tactical information, planning and coordinating specific attacks, and providing eulogies for deceased members. In addition, some have used mass media to organize demonstrations, riots, and other forms of violent and nonviolent protests during an insurgency.

Insurgents have long used word of mouth, print, radio, and television to distribute information. Mao Tse-Tung argued that propaganda was critical to insurgent success, noting that "every large guerrilla unit should have a printing press and a mimeograph stone."[9] So did Che Guevara, who suggested that guerrillas should focus on distributing newspapers, bulletins, and other written proclamations to influence both supporters and counterinsurgents.[10] Table 6.1 highlights some of the key types and examples of traditional propaganda used by insurgents since World War II.

Word of mouth: Most insurgent groups use word of mouth because it is cheap and can be persuasive, especially if it comes from legitimate locals. Just as all good politicians understand, there are few substitutes in insurgencies for classic "retail politics." Shaking hands in the living room of one's constituents is sometimes profoundly more powerful than messaging on the airwaves. Effective messages often involve leveraging feelings of doubt, uncertainty, and anger about the government. In Cuba, insurgents emphasized the importance of spreading disinformation through word of mouth and other forums. As General Alberto Bayo remarked, "All rumors which discredit the tyranny should be repeated. Gossip should spread such rumors rapidly

TABLE 6.1 Traditional types of insurgent media

Type	Explanation	Examples
Word of mouth	Leverage influential individuals (such as religious figures and tribal leaders), hold public meetings, and meet directly with locals	Sandinista campaign to influence campesinos in rural Nicaragua through face-to-face engagements; disinformation campaign by Cuban insurgents
Print	Use multiple print forums, such as leaflets, books, newspapers, and magazines	Taliban use of *Shabnamah* (night letters) in Afghanistan; Viet Cong use of leaflets in South Vietnam
Radio	Spread information using radio, cassettes, CDs, and songs	FMLN use of Radio Venceremos in El Salvador; Islamic State use of radio
Video	Spread information using cable television, satellite, DVDs, and other video recordings	Hezbollah establishment of Al-Manar based in Lebanon

and should amplify and slant the facts against the government."[11] In Nicaragua, the Sandinistas used word of mouth to spread information and disinformation. Sandinista guerrillas regularly visited houses in rural areas, often at night. "The first thing we would ask," recalled one guerrilla, "was if they owned the land they lived on, and the answer was always no, it belonged to 'rich folk.' Or they would laugh, as if making a joke, or they would hang their heads. Because, for the campesinos, the land was a dream."[12] Sandinista rebels would then attempt to exploit local grievances. "The callouses," on their hands, the Sandinistas asked, "how did you get them?" Their goal was to influence the campesinos by directing their anger at the wealthy landowners and the government. "We wanted to make him see that though the dream was dangerous—since it implied struggle—the land was their right. And we began to cultivate that dream."[13] The Sandinistas invited the campesinos to fight for the land—for *their* land.

Print: In addition to word of mouth, mass media can be a powerful tool for insurgent groups. Newspapers and other printed material help spread insurgent information and ideas, which can be instrumental in tying their readers into a close-knit community. In Yemen, Huthi insurgents created campaigns using print messages designed to resonate with the Sa'da population. These motifs included a revival of Zaydi identity and practice, Arab humiliation, and Arab regime complicity in collaborating with the United States and Israel. In disseminating its messages, Huthi rebels utilized culturally acceptable mechanisms such as poems (*qasa'id*), lectures (*muhadarat*), and anthems (*anashid*). More broadly, the development of Huthi information campaigns illustrated a conscious effort to combine culturally resonant modes of influence with cutting-edge mechanisms commonplace among various militant Islamist organizations. To reach a broader international audience, Huthi leaders also conducted interviews with a wide range of media outlets in the West and the Arab world, such as the British Broadcasting Corporation and Al Jazeera.[14]

In Algeria, GIA leaders faxed communiqués to foreign news organizations. In El Salvador, FMLN guerrillas used graffiti to intimidate locals. During the 1982 elections, the Salvadoran government allowed the FMLN to participate in the vote if they first laid down their arms. But the FMLN dismissed the offer and warned Salvadorans not to vote, arguing that a power-sharing agreement needed to precede any election.[15] In a graffiti campaign across the country, FMLN propaganda warned, "Vote in the morning, die in the afternoon."[16]

In Afghanistan, the Taliban attempted to influence local villagers by distributing *Shabnamah*, or night letters, which were leaflets that warned villagers not to cooperate with foreign forces or the Karzai regime.[17] More broadly, the Taliban used religion as a propaganda tool. They argued that "Western countries are trying to destroy Islam" in their propaganda campaigns.[18] As one Taliban leader argued, "God be praised, we now are aware of much of the US plans. We know their target, which is within the general aim of wiping out Islam in this region."[19] The Taliban and other insurgent groups also used anti-government religious leaders to influence the local population. One Afghan intelligence report noted, "There are 107 mosques in the city of Kandahar out of which 11 are preaching anti-government themes."[20]

Radio: Radio broadcasts can reach a large number of people over an expansive territory, depending on such factors as the strength of the transmitting antennas and help from diaspora communities in outside countries. The same coverage by newspaper takes longer and is more dangerous for publishers, distributors, and recipients. In Cuba, Fidel Castro and his fellow insurgents from the July 26 Movement established Radio Rebelde, which broadcast pro-revolutionary propaganda to increase support among locals. In El Salvador, the FMLN established Radio Venceremos as an underground radio station to broadcast ideological propaganda, provide acerbic commentary, and ridicule the Salvadoran government.[21] The Islamic State launched a local radio station in 2014 in Syria's ar-Raqqah governorate to improve its public image and broadcast recitations of the Qur'an, reading of the Hadith (the teachings, deeds, and sayings of the Prophet Muhammad), *anashid*, and other material.[22] In the Mozambique insurgency, RENAMO broadcast *Voz da Africa Livre* (Voice of a Free Africa), which condemned the FRELIMO government.[23]

Television: The introduction of television—and then satellite television—allowed insurgents to expand their reach. The creation and transmission of television messages do not necessarily require origination or dissemination from within the country where insurgents are fighting, since they can broadcast television from foreign-based areas while claiming transmission from inside the country.[24] In 1991, Hezbollah established its own television station, Al-Manar (the Lighthouse), to supplement its newspapers and radio stations. In 2000, Hezbollah began broadcasting Al-Manar via satellite from its base of operations in the Shi'a-controlled neighborhood of Harat Hurayk in the southern suburbs of Beirut. In the 1990s, PKK sympathizers fighting against the Turkish government established MED TV, broadcasting out of London until the British government revoked its license in 1999. After British authorities refused to renew its licensing, the station moved to France and then to Belgium.

Some insurgents have attempted to co-opt already-existing national and international television stations—or at least use them to broadcast propaganda—rather than establish their own stations. After the overthrow of Saddam Hussein's regime in Iraq, for example, some members of the Iraqi Governing Council accused Al Jazeera television of sympathizing with insurgents.[25] On September 22, 2003, the Council agreed to issue Decision 48, which ordered the closure of Al Jazeera and another station, Al Arabiya, for one month for "repeated violations committed by the two networks in broadcasting voices that call for political violence in Iraq, at times to the point of blatant incitement to kill."[26] In addition, US officials secured affidavits "stating that the Al Jazeera reporters confirmed that they had advance knowledge of a bomb being placed in the area, and had come there seeking exclusive footage. They indicated they would be paid a bonus if they produced such an exclusive."[27]

Information campaigns should use these forums—word of mouth, print, radio, and video—in a complementary fashion. South African insurgents led by the African National Congress (ANC) and its armed wing, Umkhonto we Sizwe, established a national and global information campaign designed to overthrow the South African government and end apartheid. The goal was to use multiple information media to highlight the insurgent cause in South Africa. As outlined in such documents as Operation Mayibuye, the ANC strategy involved using "massive propaganda to win world support" for their struggle and to encourage a political and economic boycott of South Africa, "raising a storm at the United Nations which should be urged to intervene militarily," securing funding (including large-scale credits) to finance the struggle, and establishing radio facilities "for daily transmission to the world and to the people of South Africa."[28] This campaign also needed to be closely linked to the military campaign. As the ANC outlined in Operation Mayibuye, "Although we must prepare for a protracted war we must not lose sight of the fact that the political isolation of South Africa from the world community of nations [through propaganda] . . . may result in such massive assistance in various forms, that the state structure will collapse far sooner than we can at the moment envisage."[29]

INTERNET AND SOCIAL MEDIA

By the late 1990s, insurgents also began to utilize the Internet and, eventually, social media. As with print, radio, television, and other forums, groups used social media for numerous purposes, such as recruiting members, raising funds, and conducting psychological operations. Figure 6.1 shows trends in Internet use between 2005 and 2015 by region. Of particular note was the growing use of the Internet across

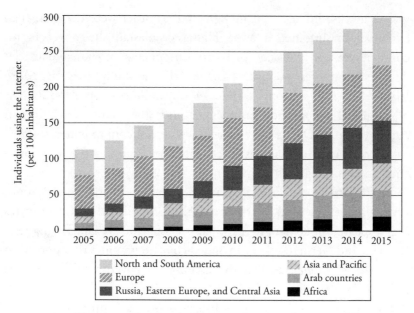

FIGURE 6.1 Number of individuals using Internet by region[70]

insurgent-affected areas, with Internet use increasing over 760 percent in Africa, nearly 350 percent in Arab countries, and 84 percent per 100 inhabitants in North and South America between 2005 and 2015. The increase was also significant with mobile cellular subscriptions, including a nearly 500 percent increase in mobile cellular subscriptions in Africa, 300 percent in Arab states, and 100 percent per 100 inhabitants in North and South America between 2005 and 2015.[30]

Insurgent use of the Internet and social media occurred in two waves. The first was in the late 1990s, when insurgent groups began to develop their own Internet pages and communicate on jihadist forums.[31] The Internet enabled insurgents to research and coordinate attacks, expand the reach of their propaganda to a global audience, recruit overseas, and search for new sources of funding to audiences they couldn't access through word of mouth, print, and radio. For most groups, building and financing television stations was too expensive.

Among the first to start a website was the LTTE in Sri Lanka, which established www.eelam.com in 1996. Over the next several years, the LTTE initiated other sites, such as www.tamiltigers.net around 2001 and www.eprlf.net in 2004. In Palestinian territory, Hamas created www.palestine-info.com in 1998, as well as other websites later, such as www.hamasinfo.net. In 2002, Hamas even established a website for children, www.al-fateh.net, with cartoons, poems, puzzles, and articles designed to interest younger audiences. In the Philippines, the Moro Islamic Liberation Front started www.luwaran.com in 2000 as part of its global propaganda campaign against the Manila government. Around 2001, al Qa'ida established www.alneda.com to increase global support for its efforts against the United States, other Western countries, and local regimes it aimed to overthrow.

In Colombia, the FARC initiated www.farc-ep.org around 2000. Over the next several years, the FARC established other websites that appeared in six languages (Spanish, English, Italian, Portuguese, Russian, and German). They included colorful graphics that portrayed the FARC's struggle against the Colombian government, as well as links to news releases, historical documents, and other information for supporters and curious Internet surfers. Insurgent groups in more remote locations also created websites. In Angola, the Front of Liberation for the State of Cabinda launched websites in 1999 (www. cabinda.org) and 2000 (www.cabinda.net). In Ethiopia, the Oromo Liberation Front started www.oromoliberationfront.org in 1998, and the Ogaden National Liberation Front started www.onlf.org in 2000.[32] Many insurgents and supporters were also active in posting information on other nonofficial websites and forums.

Most of these groups included information on their websites about the history of the group, biographies of their leaders, aims of the organizations, and news bulletins.[33] They occasionally discussed tactics. On one Hamas website, for example, a man who identified himself as Abu Jendal wrote in 2003, "My dear brothers in Jihad, I have a kilo of Acetone Peroxide. I want to know how to make a bomb from it in order to blow up an army jeep; I wait your quick response." An hour later, a Hamas supporter who called himself Abu Hadafa responded, "My dear brother Abu Jendal, I understand that you have 1,000 grams of Om El Abad. Well done! There are several ways to change it into a bomb."[34] Om El Abad was the Hamas nickname for the explosive triacetone triperoxide (TATP). Abu Hadafa explained how to put together the bomb and attached a file with instructions on how to make detonators.[35] The conversation occurred between two anonymous Palestinians who, it appeared, never met each other face-to-face. As Figure 6.2 highlights, approximately 60 percent of active insurgencies made use of official websites in 2004. Over the next decade, the percentage increased to nearly 80 percent in 2008 and 90 percent by 2014.

In addition to websites, a growing number of insurgents began to use chatrooms, e-groups, forums, and virtual message boards by the late 1990s and early 2000s for communication and information operations. These online platforms were designed to ensure as much anonymity as possible to safeguard the identity of participants and allow them to communicate in a password-protected environment.[36]

The second wave occurred in the late 2000s, when insurgent groups increasingly utilized social media sites. Figure 6.2 highlights the percentage of insurgencies active between 2004 and 2015 in which at least one group had established a website, Facebook account, and Twitter account. The data only show official, sanctioned accounts established by insurgent groups, so may understate the number of sites affiliated with insurgent groups. Some groups and their supporters used informal, surrogate sites that could be quickly shut down and re-created to elude government surveillance or in response to government campaigns to shut down their sites. Insurgents became increasingly attracted to

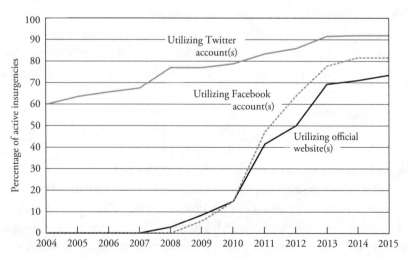

FIGURE 6.2 Percentage of active insurgencies using websites, Twitter, and Facebook

microblogging and other social media platforms because it was easy to use, had large numbers of users, and was accessible across numerous electronic devices. This was true even with the availability of traditional dissemination mechanisms such as web forums.

Twitter was created in 2006 as an online social network and microblogging service that enabled users to send and read short 140-character text messages, or "tweets." In 2008, only 3 percent of active insurgencies operated an official Twitter account, as highlighted in Figure 6.2. But this increased to 9 percent in 2009, 15 percent in 2010, 42 percent in 2011, 50 percent in 2012, 69 percent in 2013, 71 percent in 2014, and 74 percent in 2015. There were similar trends with Facebook, which was founded in 2004 to facilitate online social networking. In 2009, only 6 percent of active insurgencies made use of an official Facebook page. But this increased to 15 percent in 2010, 47 percent in 2011, 64 percent in 2012, 78 percent in 2013, and 82 percent in both 2014 and 2015.

Insurgents also utilized other social media forums. One was YouTube, which began in 2005 as an online repository to share video content.[37] For insurgent groups, YouTube was an easily accessible platform for the dissemination of propaganda and radicalization videos. Such organizations as Hezbollah, Hamas, the LTTE, and Sendero Luminoso uploaded propaganda videos on YouTube by the late 2000s. A decade after its creation, virtually every active insurgent group had videos on YouTube that were uploaded by the group or its supporters.

In many cases, there was a rough time lag of three to five years between the commercial introduction of social media sites and substantial use by insurgents. It is unlikely that this delay was caused by a lack of technical capabilities by insurgent groups, which have not struggled to understand how to use the technology. Instead, the time lag appeared to reflect, in part, caution by insurgents that government intelligence agencies might collect data about their identity and social networks. In response to a participant's request to become friends on Facebook, for instance, some members of the Pakistan group Ansar al-Mujahideen worried that such a network of friends could be a danger to members and sympathizers. Several wondered whether the risks of tying their real identity to their online identity outweighed the potential gains from networking with other supporters. A member of a jihadi forum warned readers that a Facebook network would allow intelligence agencies to trace entire groups of insurgents:

> Don't make a network in Facebook . . . Then Kuffar will know every friend you have or had in the past. They will know location, how you look, what you like, they will know everything! Join Facebook if you want and use it to keep in touch with friends and brothers far away but not as a network.[38]

But many insurgents began to rethink these initial conclusions since social media had numerous benefits. It provided an opportunity to recruit new members, raise funds, and influence local and foreign audiences.[39] It also increased the opportunities for external actors, such as states and diaspora populations, to become involved in the insurgency and help shape international perceptions of the conflict.[40] In Syria, insurgent groups and sympathizers uploaded a steady stream of information about the insurgency on Facebook, Twitter, YouTube, and other forums.[41] As one study concluded, "every serious political or militant actor with a stake in what is happening in Syria has a presence on social media."[42] For some rebel factions, social media was integrated into military and political strategy. Other technological developments, such as cell phones, allowed Syrian groups to distribute information to fighters and supporters and allowed for real-time coordination of insurgent activity.[43] In short, Syrian insurgents adopted a broad mix of tactics— both on the battlefield and the information realm—in their struggle against the Assad regime.

In addition, Islamic insurgent groups increasingly adopted social media tools. In mid-2012, Asad al-Jihad and Wamid Qalam were among the first Sunni extremist pundits to join Twitter and encouraged other prominent extremists to join. Their Twitter posts provided commentary on topical issues, guidance on the logistics and details of undertaking violent jihad, and previewed forthcoming or past attacks. The next year, al Qa'ida in the Arabian Peninsula and the al Qa'ida–linked Ziyad al-Jarrah Battalions created new official Twitter accounts shortly before conducting high-profile attacks. Syrian insurgent groups, such as Jabhat al-Nusrah and the Islamic State, utilized Twitter to coordinate activities and distribute propaganda.[44] As noted at the beginning of this chapter, al Shabaab used Twitter to claim responsibility for the Westgate shopping mall attack in Nairobi in September 2013 as it unfolded. Al Shabaab had created some of the Twitter "handles" (the username and the accompanying URL) it used to publicize the attack at least a year earlier.[45]

In Iraq, the Islamic State had a large and sophisticated presence on social media during its insurgency against the Iraq government. Its presence ranged from official media centers and spokesmen, such as Minister of Information Dr. Wa'il 'Adil al-Fayyad, to individual supporters like @Abu_Dujana_ and @muhajirbritanni on Twitter, who were independently creating or proliferating propaganda without direction from the Islamic State. The Islamic State was one of the first insurgent groups to successfully conduct Twitter hashtag campaigns. The group and its supporters used the campaigns to attract attention to the Islamic State's battlefield successes and threatened retaliation for Western intervention in Iraq or Syria, reaching far larger audiences than was typical for extremist Twitter users.

MOBILE TECHNOLOGY AND COLLECTIVE ACTION

In addition to the Internet and social media, insurgent groups increasingly utilized mobile technology to communicate, conduct information campaigns, and overcome collective action problems.[46] As one study of political violence in Africa concluded, "When cell phone coverage is present, the likelihood of conflict occurrence is substantially higher than otherwise. We consistently find a relationship between cell phone coverage and violent conflict."[47]

As noted in Chapter 5, organizing violence is fraught with challenges. Successful insurgent activity requires solving various collective action problems.[48] This is particularly true when it comes to organizing an insurgency, where participation is risky and benefits are often unclear.[49] Even if rebel groups can convince members to fight and the local population offers tacit support, insurgent political and military action needs to be carefully coordinated to be successful. Warfare against governments with superior military technology, firepower, and training relies on carefully plotting attacks, timing operations, coordinating groups in target areas, and managing the retreat to safe havens. Insurgent leaders need to coordinate the interplay of independent groups across distant geographic locations and time.[50]

In contrast to mass media, access to individual communication technology like cell phones can undermine the effects of government propaganda and help overcome other collective action and coordination problems inherent in insurgent violence.[51] Cell phones allow the distribution of information to tacit supporters among the population and permit real-time coordination of insurgent operations.[52] At the same time, free-riding behavior can be curbed through repeated interaction, increased communication, and improvement in the monitoring of group members' actions. Interaction between group members becomes easier since cell phones make long-distance communication possible, especially in insurgencies where factions operate far apart from each other for long periods of time.[53]

Tipping-point models of protest and popular support suggest that if citizens are able to communicate their privately held beliefs about the regime, without fear of reprisal, public support for the regime can transform into widespread opposition.[54] The spread of cell phones makes the transmission of news to citizens through the country more likely. The support for insurgent activity can increase in the general population when news about governance failures, including predatory action and corruption, is communicated through citizen communication. Apart from affecting a group's ability to address collective action problems, the distribution of cell phones aids the coordination of insurgent actions.[55] Syrian rebels used cell phones to spread information on government activity, greatly aiding insurgent efforts.[56] Charles Taylor successfully utilized mobile phone technology to coordinate and control his rebel commanders in Liberia's insurgency.[57]

More broadly, a range of other technological developments have impacted insurgent tactics, supporting what MIT professor Eric von Hippel called "democratizing innovation."[58] Users of products and services, including insurgents, have been able to innovate because of the improving quality of computer software and hardware, better access to easy-to-use tools, and information from the Internet and other sources. These advances have made it easier for insurgents to recruit, distribute propaganda, communicate, and identify and track people.

Any insurgent with a cell phone camera, for example, can case a target and collect information. Virtually all insurgent groups have websites, enabling geographically dispersed insurgents to establish relationships with one another and raising the possibility of collaboration and cross-pollination. The social networking features of these websites re-create the cohesive virtual communities of traditional extremist forums on more stable and technically reliable sites. When used in combination with more conventional password-protected private forums, main-stream websites can provide insurgents with alternate channels for communication.

Some insurgent groups, such as the Taliban, took advantage of these developments by disseminating propaganda through mobile phones. Taliban commanders uploaded content to mobile phone flash media cards or directly onto a phone's hardware and included Taliban pro-paganda videos, martyrdom photos, and fight songs. In addition, the Taliban developed a short-message service (SMS) network, where posts on the group's websites and Twitter feeds were sent to individual mobile phones. These users then forwarded the messages to a network of phones through SMS.[59] In Indonesia, Jemaah Islamiyah and other groups adopted many of these technologies as a new generation became more comfortable working with Internet sites, mobile phones, and computers.[60]

The proliferation of readily available, inexpensive online communi-cations and location-masking tools also complicated counterinsurgent efforts to collect and exploit insurgent communications. The Tehreek-e-Taliban Pakistan, for example, used social networking and file-sharing services, remote desktop access software, voice-over Internet protocol, and anonymizers to conceal their operational activities, identities, and locations. Some insurgents also used encryption, location-masking tools, and other related technologies to protect their online activities.[61]

GOVERNMENT INFILTRATION

Yet there is a danger with some insurgent information campaigns, includ-ing with the use of the Internet, social media, and mobile technology. They are vulnerable to government spying. The increase in mobile tech-nology, for example, is a two-way street since governments with signals intelligence capabilities can intercept cell phones, satellite phones, and computers. In Iraq, for example, US and Iraqi forces could track insurgent movement, understand insurgent activity by reviewing the transcripts of intercepted calls, and ensure that locals could share information with them by placing calls from more secure locations than with fixed land-line phones.[62] In addition, the use of social media can be risky for insurgents by allowing governments to collect information about their social networks, including who some of their supporters are and where they're located. Insurgents can also lose control of their narrative in the chaotic miasma of social media, since individuals can stray off message.

Government penetration is not confined to the Internet, social media, and cell phones. For the Provisional IRA, "loose talk" allowed British spies to identify IRA members and confidential information. Figure 6.3 shows an IRA poster that warned its members from talking about their activities in taxis, on the phone, in restaurants, or even at sporting events. As one IRA memo warned its members, "Don't be seen in public marches, demonstrations or protests. Don't be seen in

FIGURE 6.3 IRA "loose talk" poster

the company of known Republicans, don't frequent known Republican houses. Your prime duty is to remain unknown to the enemy forces and the public at large."[63] The IRA also warned its members to be careful in their use of alcohol: "Volunteers are warned that drink-induced loose talk is the MOST POTENTIAL DANGER facing any organisation, and in a military organisation it is SUICIDE."[64]

Most insurgent groups established a suite of tactics, techniques, and procedures to blunt government human and signals penetration. Some also developed anti-interrogation techniques in case operatives were captured. One Provisional IRA training manual bluntly concluded, "The best anti-interrogation [technique] is to SAY NOTHING."[65] Other groups established organizational structures where insurgents had little knowledge of what was happening outside their own cell. Sendero Luminoso, for example, created local cells that had limited day-to-day contact with Sendero's leadership *at any level.* This ensured that many of Sendero's operatives that were captured had limited knowledge outside of their immediate area of responsibility, protecting the group's operational security.[66] In Nicaragua, the Sandinistas adopted a practice of "compartmentalization," which meant that few of the operatives— or compañeros—knew the details of the organization as a whole.[67]

Despite these challenges, however, information campaigns are a significant component of insurgent operations along with effective strategies, organizational structures, tactics, and outside support. Information campaigns can't take the place of a poorly executed or disorganized insurgency. But they can help groups spread information and disinformation, damage or otherwise undermine counterinsurgents and their supporters, and influence local and international audiences. Traditional types of media—such as word of mouth, print, radio, and video (including television)—remain important. Even word-of-mouth campaigns can be powerful in sowing local ire about the government and providing a deeply personal forum to explain insurgent motivations, much like the rationale behind door-to-door grassroots politics during an election campaign. In addition, the growth of the Internet and social media provided insurgent groups with a new avenue to recruit members, raise funds, issue propaganda, communicate, and conduct other activities—helping solve some collective action and coordination problems inherent in insurgent warfare.

Shortly after the death of Osama bin Laden, al Qa'ida leader Ayman al-Zawahiri commented, "The strength of al-Qa'ida, however, is derived from the message it spreads to the ummah and the downtrodden all around the globe. It spreads a message calling on them to rise up against the world order of tyranny, the international arrogance, and the global robbery."[68] Former al Qa'ida in the Arabian Peninsula leader Nasir al-Wuhayshi remarked, "Our most important weapon is the media. You are kindly requested to put in place the right people, who can express themselves well and convey our message."[69]

7

Outside Support

Conditions are ripe for triumph. We will win. And we will wield great power here.[1]

—Daniel Ortega Saavedra

ON JULY 19, 1979, the Sandinista National Liberation Front (Frente Sandinista de Liberación Nacional, or FSLN) marched into the Nicaraguan capital of Managua and seized control of the government. FSLN leaders had created a political organization among university students, intellectuals, the Catholic Church, and peasants in the 1960s dedicated to establishing a Marxist government in Nicaragua and overthrowing the regime of President Anastasio Somoza Debayle. In the 1970s, the FSLN attacked Nicaraguan forces from bases in neighboring Honduras and Costa Rica, which triggered a series of bloody reprisals. In 1978 the FSLN, then headed by Daniel and Humberto Ortega Saavedra, stepped up its campaign of violence after the death of the Nicaraguan politician Pedro Joaquín Chamorro, eventually defeated the National Guard, and overthrew Somoza.

Outside support was helpful to FSLN success. The FSLN received aid from several countries, including the Soviet Union and Cuba. According to declassified KGB documents, Carlos Fonseca Amador, one of the founding members of the FSLN, was recruited by the KGB in 1959 on a trip to Moscow and given the code name GIDROLOG ("hydrologist"). In 1960, the KGB organized funding and training for twelve individuals that Fonseca handpicked, who were core members of the FSLN. Over the next several decades, the KGB retained agents within the FSLN and provided money, training, and other types of assistance.[2] One of the main objectives of KGB support to the FSLN was to expand the Soviet beachhead in Latin America and to increase Soviet power and influence at the expense of the United States. In November 1961 Aleksandr Sakharovsky, head of the First Chief Directorate, which was responsible for the KGB's foreign operations and intelligence collection, reported to KGB Chairman Vladimir Yefimovich Semichastny:

> In accordance with the long-term plan for the KGB's intelligence operations in Latin America and Decision No. 191/75-GS of the highest authorities dated 1 August 1961, our residency in Mexico has taken measures to provide assistance in building up the national liberation movement in Nicaragua and creating a hotbed of unrest for the Americans in this area. The Residency, through the trusted agent GIDROLOG [Fonseca] in Mexico, selected a group of Nicaraguan students (12 people), headed by the Nicaraguan patriot doctor PRIM [Manuel Ramón de Jesus Andara y Ubeda], and arranged for their operational training. All operations with PRIM's group are conducted by GIDROLOG in the name of the Nicaraguan revolutionary organization "The Sandinista Front," of which he, GIDROLOG, is the leader. The supervision of the group's future activities and financial aid given to it will also be provided through GIDROLOG. At the present time PRIM's group is ready to be dispatched to Honduras, where it will undergo additional training and fill out its ranks ... In order to equip PRIM's group and provide for its final training in combat operations, assistance amounting to $10,000 is required. The highest authorities have given their consent to using the sum indicated for these purposes. I request your approval.[3]

Semichastny gave his approval the next day. Cuba also provided support to the FSLN. By the late 1960s, the Cuban government's intelligence service, the Dirección General de Inteligencia (DGI), had heavily infiltrated the FSLN and provided substantial money, arms, and operatives. As DGI head Manuel Piñeiro Losado remarked, "Of all the countries in Latin America, the most active work being carried out by us is in Nicaragua. Aid is being given to partisan groups headed by C[arlos] Fonseca. This movement has influence and could go far."[4]

Moving forward, the DGI provided training, money, weapons, and equipment to the FSLN before—and after—its successful overthrow of the Somoza government in 1979.

Outside support is common in insurgencies. Of the 181 insurgencies since 1946, 148 cases (82 percent) involved some form of outside support. But simply acquiring any type of outside support does not necessarily increase an insurgent group's chances of success. The problem is that "outside support" is too generic to be of much value. To provide a more nuanced understanding of outside support, this chapter asks two main questions. What kinds of outside supporters, such as states and diaspora populations, are most useful to insurgents? And what types of outside support, such as goods and services, are most useful?

The data suggest several trends. First, great-power support to insurgent groups—especially combat support—is more likely to tip the outcome in favor of insurgents than support from other actors. Simple cross-tabulations show that insurgents won almost half the time when they received support from a great power and nearly two thirds of the time when they received aid from a superpower such as the United States or Soviet Union.[5] This is intuitive since great powers have access to more resources than other actors, which made Soviet aid to the FSLN particularly helpful. Perhaps more surprising, however, the data indicate that support from other types of actors is less likely to be decisive—from states writ large, neighboring states, diaspora populations, and outside terrorist and insurgent groups. Second, the type of support matters. Outside actors can provide a range of services (such as combat support, sanctuary, and training) and goods (such as money, lethal material, and non-lethal material). Direct combat support from great powers to insurgent groups is most closely correlated with insurgent victory, especially when it comes from a major power.

The rest of this chapter is organized into three sections. The first examines the impact of outside actors that provide assistance, including which types can be most useful to insurgents. The second section analyzes the types of outside assistance that states and nonstate organizations can offer, including goods and services. The third discusses the potential pitfalls of outside support.

OUTSIDE SUPPORTERS

Several types of actors can provide support to insurgent groups: states, diaspora populations, refugees, and a range of other nonstate actors like terrorist and insurgent organizations.

States: Since World War II, states have supported insurgent groups in nearly three quarters (70 percent) of insurgencies—compared to 54 percent for diasporas, 35 percent for refugees, 35 percent for outside terrorist and insurgent groups, and 5 percent for international organizations.[6] Some research suggests that state support can help increase the probability of insurgent victory.[7] One study, which examined 286 insurgencies fought between 1800 and 2005, found that 70 percent of all insurgent groups that received external support either won or negotiated a settlement to the conflict; groups without any external support won or negotiated a settlement only 28 percent of the time.[8] But is this true for all states? Does it make a difference, for instance, whether support comes from a great power, a neighbor, or other types of states? To help answer these questions, I divided state support into several categories: support from all states, great powers, and neighboring states.

Preliminary evidence suggests that support from great powers is more strongly correlated with insurgent victory than from other actors.[9] The impact of great-power support is intuitive. Unlike other types of states, great powers have access to more resources and generally can sustain support for longer periods of time.[10] Some studies suggest that state support is most valuable early in a campaign, when it can help establish the insurgent group's viability and enhance its longevity.[11] In general, great powers and superpowers are primarily motivated by geopolitics rather than ideological, ethnic, religious, or other sentiments in supporting insurgents.[12]

A simple cross-tabulation of supporters and the outcome of insurgencies indicates that insurgent groups which received support from great powers were victorious more than half the time (52 percent) and battled the government to a draw in 17 percent of cases. Put another way, insurgents that received great-power support achieved either victory or a draw nearly seven out of ten times. Somewhat surprisingly, support from neighboring states does not reach the same level. The probability of insurgent victory in cases where there is support from border states (42 percent) is almost identical to all states (40 percent).

Great powers: There are multiple examples of the utility of great-power support. In Afghanistan during the 1980s, US aid to the mujahideen began at a relatively low level, but then increased as the prospect of a Soviet defeat appeared more likely, totaling as much as $5 billion between 1980 and 1992.[13] The CIA provided about $60 million per year to the Afghan mujahideen between 1981 and 1983, which was matched by assistance from the Saudi government. Beginning in 1985, the United States increased its support to the Afghans to $250 million per year. This shift culminated in National Security Directive 166, which was signed by President Ronald Reagan and set a clear US objective in Afghanistan: to push the Soviets out.[14] The United States provided money, arms (including heavy machine guns, Stinger missiles, and Oerlikon anti-aircraft cannons), technical advice on weapons and explosives, strategic advice, intelligence, and sophisticated technology such as wireless interception equipment. Most of this assistance went through Pakistan's Directorate of Inter-Services Intelligence (ISI), rather than directly from the CIA to the mujahideen.[15]

There are numerous other examples. During the insurgency in Angola from 1961 to 1974, for instance, the Soviet Union provided substantial assistance to rebel groups. As one US Air Force assessment summarized, "In Angola, Soviet aid was *decisive* in creating a viable movement, the Popular Movement for the Liberation of Angola (MPLA)."[16] In Ethiopia, the United States and other countries—including Sudan and Saudi Arabia—provided support to the Ethiopian People's Revolutionary Democratic Front (EPRDF) in its successful war from 1976 to 1991. In Namibia, the Soviet Union provided assistance to the South West African People's Organization (SWAPO) in its victorious insurgency from 1966 to 1988. As one declassified CIA analysis concluded, "The Soviets . . . provided SWAPO with almost all of its military equipment. SWAPO troops based in Angola have used this equipment in their guerrilla raids into northern Namibia, where operations are aimed at undermining the government's authority and its ability to maintain security."[17] In Malaya, the Soviet Union provided instructions to the Malayan Communist Party about the organization of an insurgency against the British government.[18]

Insurgent failure to secure great-power support can be significant. Without great-power support, insurgents in Burundi (1965–1972),

Central African Republic (1996–1997), Democratic Republic of Congo (1960–1962), Dominican Republic (1965), Greece (1946–1949), Indonesia (1965–1978), Kenya (1952–1956), Peru (1982–1989), and the Philippines (1946–1954) lacked sufficient resources to achieve their objectives. Greek groups failed to secure Soviet support, which contributed to their ultimate defeat since the United States provided substantial aid to the Greek government. The Philippines case is also telling, since the Magsaysay government, with US help, successfully defeated Hukbalahap insurgents who never enjoyed outside support from such states as China. As one study concluded, "while they had more than enough men under arms, the Huks lacked a potent external sponsor who could provide scarce weapons and ammunition."[19]

Diaspora populations: Diaspora support is fairly common in insurgencies, especially from ethnic kin, religious affiliates, and exiled elites. Groups received support from diaspora communities in half of insurgencies. Diaspora motivations differ from those of state sponsors. Governments back insurgencies for strategic reasons. Diaspora communities, in contrast, are largely motivated by a desire to support a kinship group or homeland. But how significant is this aid? The data suggest that diaspora populations are less likely to decisively impact insurgencies than great powers, with diaspora support correlating with victory 38 percent of the time in insurgencies that have ended. The difference between great powers and diaspora support may be due to the inability of diaspora populations to contribute large amounts of aid over a sustained period of time. In addition, there is usually little coordination among diaspora populations, increasing inefficiency and duplication.

While diaspora support is not strongly correlated with insurgent victory, diaspora populations can still have an impact. Cross-border diaspora populations, for example, increase the likelihood of insurgency onset.[20] They can also increase the likelihood of interstate conflict.[21] Based on the ninety-seven cases since 1946 in which diasporas provided aid to insurgent groups, diaspora populations can be most helpful in providing several types of assistance: recruits, training, money, political support, sanctuary, and propaganda.

In Sierra Leone, the RUF received some assistance—including fighters—from diaspora populations in neighboring countries. As one

RUF document concluded, "We entered Sierra Leone through Liberia and enjoyed the sympathy of Sierra Leonean migrant workers, some of whom joined us to cross the border to start our liberation campaign."[22] In the Balkans wars in the early 1990s, there was extensive financial and propaganda support for insurgents. Ethnic diaspora abroad raised substantial funds. One example was Gojan Susak, the Croatian defense minister, who ran a pizzeria in Toronto. As a member of the North American diaspora, Susak was instrumental in financing the Croatian rebels through donations from Canada.[23] Support from the wider Islamic community was also available to the Bosnian Muslims. The Islamic lobby in the United States was critical in efforts to lift the Bosnian arms embargo, and the Croat lobby in Germany influenced Germany's decision to recognize Croatian independence in 1992.

In the insurgencies in Chechnya, Ossetia, and Abkhazia, diaspora populations provided substantial money to insurgent groups. Support took the form of donations from households, voluntary war taxes, and profits from the legal or illegal businesses of entrepreneurs operating in Russia and abroad.[24] The LTTE in Sri Lanka also received substantial financial assistance and propaganda support from the Tamil diaspora in the United Kingdom, India, Canada, Australia, France, and Switzerland.[25]

In Turkey, the PKK relied on a diaspora network of Kurds in locations like Europe to fund their operations. The PKK also operated an extensive network of cultural clubs, political offices, and publishing ventures that were spread out over a half dozen countries. They organized festivals that attracted tens of thousands of supporters and sold magazines and other propaganda to attendees. "Our goal was to organize people [in Europe] and tie them to the PKK's struggle," said one former spokesman. "This meant everything from getting new people for the war to getting them out to marches."[26] The Somali diaspora community became an increasingly important source of funds and recruits for al Shabaab beginning around 2007. According to some estimates, the Somali diaspora population sent over $1 billion in remittances back to the country annually.[27] Although it is unclear how much of these financial flows reached al Shabaab's coffers, it was likely significant in al Shabaab's early years. Additionally, the organization's increasing alignment with al Qa'ida helped al Shabaab solicit funding from wealthy Arab backers.[28]

As Figure 7.1 highlights, diaspora support to insurgents peaked at the end of the Cold War, occurring in nearly 80 percent of insurgencies. But diaspora support then declined somewhat over the next two decades. Despite these examples, however, diaspora support has rarely been decisive for insurgents, perhaps since most diaspora populations are not able to provide substantial resources.

Refugees: Refugees are often located in neighboring countries, and many retain a close attachment to their homeland. In some cases, insurgents have substantial influence in refugee camps, facilitating recruitment. Refugees can also provide people, intelligence, propaganda, and other types of support.[29]

Unlike broader diaspora populations, refugees often have a closer tie to their homeland, especially those living in neighboring countries. Many may also be more strongly motivated to help insurgents win, leave refugee camps, and return home because their temporary living conditions are untenable. Refugee camps are temporary settlements that are often teeming with people living in squalid conditions and with little food or water, limited shelter, and poor health conditions. While governments back insurgencies for strategic reasons, refugees are often motivated by a desire to support a nearby kinship group or homeland.[30] Refugees are often a good source for recruits, fundraising, intelligence, material, and

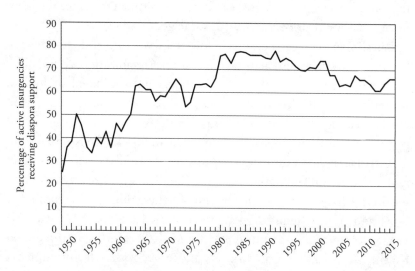

FIGURE 7.1 Diaspora support to insurgents

cross-border sanctuary. Refugee support was critical in a range of cases, from Afghanistan (1978–1992 and 1992–1996) to Cambodia (1970–1975 and 1978–1979) and Mozambique (1964–1974).[31]

There is also a destabilizing aspect of refugee flows for insurgencies. Countries that experience an influx of refugees from neighboring states are significantly more likely to experience insurgencies themselves for several reasons. First, refugee migration leads to the expansion of social networks.[32] Refugee flows can increase the import of combatants, arms, and ideologies from neighboring states, which can facilitate the spread of conflict. In many cases, refugees are able to set up complex political structures in exile and can challenge the host government directly. Tamil refugees were involved in the assassination of India's Prime Minister Rajiv Ghandi in response to his accommodation of the Sri Lankan government. Tutsi refugees in Uganda assisted in the removal of the Obote government. Second, refugee populations can provide resources and support to domestic opposition groups. Somali refugees worked closely with ethnic Somali separatists in the Ogaden region of Ethiopia. Third, refugee flows can change the ethnic balance in a country, sparking discontent among local populations toward the refugees and the government that allows access. Fourth, refugees may pose actual or perceived negative economic externalities. They may compete with locals over scarce resources such as employment, housing, land, and water. Refugees can depress wages if they enter the labor force and impact prices as they consume goods and services.[33]

Palestinian refugees became involved in wars in both Jordan and Lebanon through the Palestine Liberation Organization (PLO). The PLO was organized in the 1960s and was initially based in Jordan, where it frequently engaged in clashes across the border with Israeli forces. Fearing that Palestinian organizations were setting up a rival government and in response to an increase in hijackings, King Hussein of Jordan launched a campaign against the PLO and entered Palestinian refugee camps on September 15, 1980. The PLO subsequently moved to southern Lebanon, where they became further embroiled in conflict.

Rwandan Tutsi refugees in Uganda formed the Rwandan Patriotic Front, reentered the country, and toppled the Hutu government in Kigali, which had instigated the Rwandan genocide. This prompted a mass exodus of Rwandan Hutus—who feared retribution by the new government—into the eastern provinces of the Congo. However, local Tutsis in the Congo were outraged by the sudden entry of more than one million Hutus and mobilized opposition to the Mobutu government, which was seen as siding with the Hutus against the Tutsis.

In the Syrian insurgency that began in 2011, Syrian opposition groups recruited fighters from refugee communities in Jordan, Lebanon, and Turkey. Syrian insurgents also used refugee populations in neighboring countries, such as Turkey, for assistance in military training. To help organize outside assistance, some members of the Syrian opposition created an Assistance Coordination Unit to manage international donations and work with international aid agencies.[34]

Terrorist, insurgent, and criminal groups: External terrorist, insurgent, and criminal organizations can also provide support to rebel groups, though they appear less likely to impact the outcome of insurgencies than great powers. Excluding ongoing cases, insurgent groups won roughly 35 percent of the time when they received support from foreign insurgent or terrorist groups. Much like diaspora populations, the relatively low numbers may be due to the inability of foreign terrorist and insurgent groups to provide significant amounts of aid over a sustained period of time. The low numbers may also be caused by apprehension among insurgent groups, since outside support from militant groups could weaken their domestic and international legitimacy and potentially trigger an international response.

Criminal groups can also provide support. Sierra Leone's civil war, for instance, was sustained by international crime networks that were engaged in arms-for-diamonds trade and the Sierra Leone rebels received direct assistance, fighters, and sanctuary from Liberia's Charles Taylor.[35] In Colombia, the FARC relied on the drug trade to help fund its insurgency, and worked with a wide range of drug cartels.[36] So did the Taliban in Afghanistan, which cooperated with a number of drug-trafficking organizations.

There are numerous examples of insurgent and terrorist groups providing support to insurgents. In Cambodia between 1946 and 1973, for instance, the Khmer Issarak received support from Vietnamese rebels (Viet Minh) and Laotian rebels (Pathet Leo). The Viet Minh also supported the Khmer Rouge in its successful effort to overthrow the Cambodian government between 1970 and 1975. During the insurgency in the Democratic Republic of Congo from 1998 to 2001, Congolese insurgents received support from Angolan rebels such as UNITA. And in Cote d'Ivoire from 2002 to 2004, insurgents received aid from groups like the RUF in Sierra Leone. In Colombia, the FARC received training from the FMLN in El Salvador, who had, in turn, received training from the Viet Cong. It was little surprise, then, that FARC insurgent manuals were similar to those used by FMLN guerrillas.[37]

After its establishment, al Qa'ida became involved in aid to Sunni-led insurgencies. Between 1988 and 2015, al Qa'ida was directly involved in 22 insurgencies in Africa, the Middle East, and Asia. As the war in Syria began to intensify in 2011, al Qa'ida in Iraq leaders utilized established networks that moved fighters from Syria to Iraq and created Jabhat al-Nusrah as their operational arm in Syria. Al Qa'ida in Iraq leader Abu Bakr al-Baghdadi (also known as Abu Du'a), who became the emir of the Islamic State, explained that "we laid for them plans, and drew up for them the policy of work, and gave them what financial support we could every month, and supplied them with men who had known the battlefields of jihad, from the emigrants and the natives."[38] Al Qa'ida in Iraq officials chose Abu Muhammad al-Jawlani as emir. Jawlani pledged allegiance to Baghdadi before taking charge of operations in Syria in late 2011. Al Qa'ida in Iraq then sent small arms and light weapons—including rifles, light machine guns, and rocket-propelled grenades—to its Syrian contingent. It also sent explosive experts to augment Jabhat al-Nusrah's bomb-making capabilities and deployed fighters to boost its ranks. A growing number of donors from the Persian Gulf and Levant began to send financial support. As Jawlani acknowledged, al Qa'ida in Iraq provided a substantial amount of "money, despite the days of difficulties through which they were passing, and he placed his complete trust in me and deputized me to make the policies and the plan, and supported me with some brothers."[39]

As Figure 7.2 shows, outside insurgent and terrorist support to insurgent groups rose beginning in the mid-1950s. There may be several reasons why there was an increase. Throughout the Cold War, for example, some states became sanctuaries for terrorist and insurgent groups, which developed close relations and provided support to each other. In addition, al Qa'ida and the Islamic State evolved into transnational

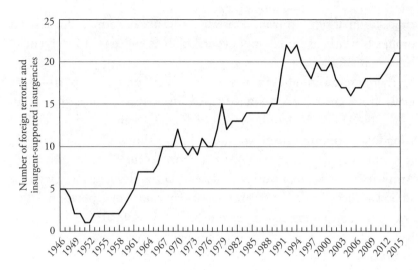

FIGURE 7.2 Outside insurgent and terrorist support to insurgent groups

movements and provided assistance to Islamic insurgences in Africa, the Middle East, and Asia.

TYPES OF OUTSIDE SUPPORT

This section analyzes the types of outside assistance that may be most helpful to insurgents. It examines services (combat support, sanctuary, training, and intelligence) and goods (money, lethal material, and non-lethal material).

Services

Outside state and nonstate actors can provide several types of services, such as combat support, external sanctuary, and training.

Combat support: States sometimes provide direct combat support to groups, using their own militaries to fight alongside insurgents. Such direct assistance is infrequent, occurring in 28 percent of insurgencies since 1946, including ongoing conflicts. But when it occurs, it can have a substantial impact on the fighting by improving insurgent capabilities. Of insurgencies that have terminated, when an insurgent group receives direct combat support from a state, it is victorious almost half the time (48 percent) and battles to a draw another 20 percent of the time. Combat support from nonstate actors like terrorist and insurgent groups is nearly as infrequent, occurring in 30 percent of insurgencies since 1946.

There are multiple examples where direct combat support—especially from great powers—has helped insurgents achieve victory. In Libya, NATO countries like the United States, France, and the United Kingdom supported insurgents to help overthrow Qaddafi's government in 2011. In Kosovo, NATO support to the Kosovo Liberation Army was crucial to insurgent success. US and allied aircrews flew 38,004 sorties during the seventy-eight-day course of Operation Allied Force in 1999, taking out 9 percent of Serbia's soldiers, 42 percent of its aircraft, 25 percent of its armored fighting vehicles, 22 percent of its artillery, and 9 percent of its tanks.[40] During the Cambodian insurgency, Vietnam invaded in December 1978 with 150,000 heavily armed troops in support of insurgents trying to topple the Khmer Rouge government. After a relentless strategic bombing campaign against entrenched Khmer Rouge positions, Cambodian insurgents and Vietnamese forces helped defeat the Khmer Rouge and establish the People's Republic of Kampuchea (PRK). As one assessment bluntly noted, "With Vietnamese military backing, the PRK routed the Khmer Rouge regime."[41]

In Namibia, Angola and Cuba provided support to South West African People's Organization (SWAPO) fighters during the successful insurgency against South Africa, which lasted from 1966 to 1988. A range of other countries, including the Soviet Union, provided assistance to SWAPO rebels. Cuban forces were also directly involved in combat in the neighboring insurgency in Angola.[42] In Afghanistan, a small number of CIA operatives, special operations forces, and air power helped Afghan insurgents overthrow the Taliban regime in less than three months in 2001. They were supported by as many as 100 US combat sorties per day, which destroyed the Taliban's limited communications infrastructure and attacked Taliban ground units, artillery, and other targets.[43]

In some cases, however, combat support to insurgents can be minimized when outside actors support the government or even competing insurgent groups. In Ukraine, Russia provided direct support to pro-Russian insurgents beginning in 2014. Russia deployed elements of twelve battalion tactical groups in eastern Ukraine and sent small numbers of combat support and Spetsnaz, or Russian special forces, to collect intelligence and provide lethal and non-lethal aid to insurgents. The use of masked unmarked soldiers in Ukraine wearing green army uniforms and wielding Russian military weapons led to the term "little green men," or зелёные человечки in Russian, to describe what were later identified as Russian soldiers. Some of this support was blunted by US and other Western covert and overt assistance to the Ukrainian government.

In Lebanon, the Syrian and Israeli armies were heavily involved in the war that lasted from 1975 to 1990, as were smaller contingents of US and French forces. Syria initially supported the traditional Maronite parties, but subsequently shifted its support to groups opposed to the Maronites. Israel invaded Lebanon more than once, with the largest invasion in June 1982. Israel initially supported groups opposed to the Palestinian Liberation Organization and also helped establish the South Lebanon Army composed of Shi'a and Christian fighters, which controlled a southern section of the country until 2000. Throughout the war, there were other types of assistance. Hezbollah received support from Iran. Some insurgent groups received support from the Lebanese and Palestinian populations living outside the country—including financial assistance. As one study concluded, "Repeated and competing external interventions played a major role in provoking, prolonging, and ending the civil war in Lebanon."[44]

While often effective in helping insurgents win, direct combat support can have negative consequences, such as increasing the levels of violence in the conflict and raising the financial, casualty, and political costs for outside patrons.[45] It can also extend the duration of insurgencies by adding another combatant with separate preferences that can complicate peace settlement negotiations.[46] As Figure 7.3 highlights, there was a significant decline in combat support from states as a percentage of active insurgencies, with a notable drop-off beginning around 2001. This may have been caused by several factors, such as a normative stigma attached to state support—including combat support—to insurgent groups, particularly in an era where a range of states focused on counterinsurgency. This bias is perceptible in documents like the

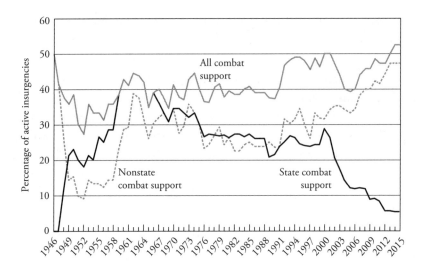

FIGURE 7.3 Combat support to insurgents

US Army and Marine Corps' *Counterinsurgency Field Manual*, which focuses almost exclusively on countering—not supporting—insurgent groups. It characterizes insurgents in a pejorative light and asserts, for example, that they "often carry out barbaric acts and do not observe accepted norms of behavior."[47] With the end of the Cold War, US and Soviet combat support to proxy insurgent groups had also dropped precipitously, with the Soviet Union itself dissolving in 1991.

Figure 7.3 also shows a significant increase in combat support from nonstate actors like insurgent and terrorist groups. This trend may reflect the decision by al Qa'ida, the Islamic State, and other groups to support Islamic insurgencies across Africa, the Middle East, and Asia. According to the data collected for this book, for example, 50 percent of active insurgencies in 2015 were motivated, at least in part, by Islam. Most of them had combat support from outside nonstate actors.

External sanctuary: Numerous studies have stressed the importance of sanctuary for insurgents.[48] Contrary to most of the findings, the data here suggest that external sanctuary is not as helpful to insurgents as other services like great-power combat support. Excluding ongoing cases, when insurgents received outside sanctuary, they won 38 percent of the time and governments won 30 percent of the time. The results are the same whether an outside state willingly provides sanctuary or is too weak to prevent its territory from being used by insurgents.

Despite this cautionary note, external sanctuary can still be helpful if insurgents are unable to control territory in their home country. A group can plot, recruit, proselytize, contact supporters around the world, raise money, regroup, resupply, and—perhaps most important —enjoy a respite from the government's counterinsurgent efforts in a sanctuary.[49] This enables operatives to escape from the constant stress of life underground.[50] Ideally, a sanctuary should be on foreign territory outside the reach of the government forces, yet close enough—such as in a neighboring country—so that it is relatively easy to transit. In addition, some research suggests that sanctuary results in more ferocious conflict and much higher casualties than would otherwise be the case.[51]

There are numerous cases where outside sanctuary has been helpful to insurgents, especially when sanctuary includes insurgent military bases and training camps. In South Africa, for example, the African National Congress had access to a sanctuary in Mozambique, where militants could train, rest, and plan future operations. The Pan-African Congress lacked these safe havens and was forced to fight South African forces without the same opportunity for rest.[52] In Algeria, the National Liberation Front (FLN) benefited from sanctuaries in Egypt, Libya, Tunisia, and Morocco. Approximately 20,000 Algerian guerrillas were concentrated in Tunis alone. As Walter Lacquer argues, it would have been politically infeasible for the French to target FLN guerrillas in these sanctuaries: "Even a minor air attack against an FLN base on the Tunisian side of the border (Sakiet Sidi Yusef) provoked a major international scandal; a massive attack was altogether unthinkable since the French government felt it could not commit such an affront to world public opinion."[53] There are other examples of insurgents effectively using sanctuary to defeat a government, such as the Viet Cong in North Vietnam and Afghan mujahideen in Pakistan.

As noted earlier, however, sanctuary does not necessarily translate into insurgent victory. Not all sanctuaries are equal. Some sanctuaries are far from insurgent-controlled areas or are difficult to reach. During the Malayan Emergency, for example, the Malayan Communist Party had external sanctuaries in Singapore and Thailand. But the British were able to effectively patrol the borders because much of Malaya abuts water.[54] In addition, Tamil insurgents used the southern state of Tamil Nadu in India as a sanctuary for their war against the Sri Lankan government. But Sri Lanka is an island, making it easier for the government to control the border.[55] In their struggle against Turkey, the PKK utilized sanctuaries in neighboring states, including Syria, where PKK leader Abdullah Ocalan was located for years.[56] In Algeria, the French constructed a barrier, the Morice Line, which ran for over 200 miles along the Algerian–Tunisian border. It consisted of an eight-foot electric fenced charged with 5,000 volts, sprinkled with anti-personnel mines, and reinforced by radar and blockhouses.[57] French efforts were fairly successful along the Algerian–Tunisian border, and, according to one estimate, interdiction efforts decreased arms and fighter flow by up to 90 percent.[58]

Training: External actors can also provide training. For US Special Operations Forces, "unconventional warfare" includes activities by outside states to enable a resistance movement to "coerce, disrupt, or overthrow a government or occupying power by operating through or with an underground, auxiliary, and guerrilla force in a denied area."[59] Much like sanctuary, training does not appear to have the same impact as direct combat support. Excluding ongoing cases, insurgent groups that receive training from outside states and nonstate actors win at almost the same rate (39 percent) as those with external sanctuary (38 percent). Militants often need weapons training and instruction in small-unit tactics. Although this is often provided by the militants themselves, the relevant trainings skills are not always available in house.

During the Cold War, for instance, both the United States and Soviet Union provided substantial training to insurgents in Latin America, Africa, the Middle East, and Asia. In 1946, the United States established the School of the Americas, which became increasingly involved in providing anti-communist counterinsurgency training to Latin American governments. In Rhodesia, guerrillas from Joshua Nkomo's Zimbabwe African People's Union (ZAPU) conducted training in Algeria, Egypt, and the Soviet Bloc.[60] China provided training and technical assistance to the Viet Minh during the French–Indochina war from 1946 to 1954.[61] South Africa offered training, financial resources, and logistical support to RENAMO forces in Mozambique. Since the end of the Cold War, terrorist and other groups have provided training to insurgents.

In Nigeria, for example, Boko Haram conducted increasingly sophisticated improvised explosive device attacks because of training from al Qa'ida in the Islamic Maghreb in such countries as Mali. With training, Boko Haram improved its ability to build hollow charges—or directional blast devices—capable of causing substantial damage to structures and lightly armored vehicles.

Goods

States and nonstate actors can also provide a wide range of goods to insurgent groups. This section analyzes three types of goods: money, lethal material, and non-lethal material. It finds that providing any of these goods modestly increases an insurgent group's chances of success, though lethal aid appears to be slightly more helpful.

Lethal material: Lethal aid is more likely to improve an insurgent group's chances of success than other types of goods, though only marginally. With lethal support, insurgent groups won 32 percent of the time and battled to a draw another 24 percent of the time. In particular, there are several types of lethal materials—such as explosively formed penetrators, rocket-propelled grenades, and surface-to-air missiles—that can be extremely useful when insurgents face better-equipped governments that use high-tech vehicles and platforms on the battlefield.[62] Lethal material can include a litany of items such as light weapons, ammunition, improvised explosive device (IED) components, platforms like tanks and aircraft, and heavy weapons (including artillery, surface-to-air missiles, and rocket-propelled grenades).

Some types of lethal aid can be particularly useful to insurgents. In Ukraine, the Russian government provided a range of lethal assistance to rebels in the Donetsk and Luhansk oblasts beginning in 2014, including tanks, armored personnel carriers, surface-to-air missiles, and rocket launchers. There are numerous other historical examples. During the successful insurgency in Afghanistan, the United States exported shoulder-fired Stinger missiles.[63] The Stinger fired an infrared, heat-seeking missile capable of engaging low-altitude, high-speed aircraft. The CIA had initially opposed providing US-manufactured weapons—especially the Stingers—to the mujahideen because they risked starting a major confrontation with the Soviets. The Pentagon had also opposed the deployment of Stingers out of concern that the Soviets would capture one and steal the technology. By 1986, however, US policymakers saw the destruction caused by the Soviet Mi-24 gunships and decided that introducing Stingers would make such a difference on the battlefield that it was worth the risks. In a meeting in January 1986, Pakistani President Zia told CIA Director William Casey that "this is the time to increase the pressure." In mid-February, the US ordered the Defense Department to provide CIA with 400 Stingers for use by the mujahideen.[64]

In September 1986, a force of roughly 35 mujahideen led by a commander named Engineer Ghaffar fired the first Stingers in Afghanistan. They crept through the underbrush and reached a small hill a mile northeast of Jalalabad airfield in eastern Afghanistan. Their target was eight Mi-24 Hind gunships scheduled to land that day. Ghaffar could make out the soldiers in the airfield's perimeter observation posts, and he and his men waited patiently for three hours until the helicopters arrived. They shot five missiles and downed three helicopters, as one mujahideen, shaking nervously with excitement, videotaped the attack. It was the first Stinger attack of the Soviet Afghan conflict and it marked a major turning point in the war. Over the next ten months, 187 Stingers were used in Afghanistan and roughly 75 percent hit aircraft.[65]

Rhodesia and South Africa virtually built from scratch the main insurgent group in Mozambique, RENAMO, and provided significant lethal aid. Both governments were threatened by growing domestic insurgencies, which had set up bases in Angola and Mozambique.[66] In Indochina, the Viet Minh reached a turning point in 1950 when they began receiving lethal aid from China. Although the Viet Minh could have fought a protracted guerrilla war, it would have been difficult to raise a regular army without Chinese aid. By September 1950, 20,000 men in the Viet Minh had been equipped with machine guns, heavy mortars, and anti-aircraft weapons. In 1951, according to French estimates, Chinese aid amounted to 18,000 rifles, 1,200 machine guns, 150 to 200 heavy mortars, and about 50 recoilless guns.[67] Following US intervention in the region, China and the Soviet Union provided lethal aid and other assistance to the Viet Minh. As one study concluded, it is "impossible to argue that the Communist victory in South Vietnam was any thing other than a triumph of foreign help. Indeed, the Communists could not have fought the war or won it the way they did without massive support from China and the Soviet Union."[68]

In Angola, UNITA benefited from lethal material provided by China and Egypt in their successful insurgency from 1961 to 1974. The Chinese, in an effort to expand their foothold in Africa and undermine Western and Soviet interests, provided UNITA with weapons and training.[69] After that, Egypt supported UNITA in the late 1960s and continued to provide military aid through the early 1970s.[70] In Northern Ireland, the first large influx of weapons came from shipments of smuggled Armalite hunting rifles, which were obtained by Republican operatives in the United States through the 1970s. Secret shipments from private individuals in the United States ended by the mid-1980s, but were replaced by a much larger and more significant influx of modern weapons sent by the Libyan government.[71] During the insurgency in North Yemen from 1962 to 1970, Jordan, Saudi Arabia, and Britain supplied military aid to the royalist side, while Egypt and the Soviet Union provided military aid to the republicans.[72]

In Algeria, the FLN imported large amounts of lethal aid. In one three-month span in the winter of 1957–1958, the FLN imported 17,000 rifles, 38 machine guns, 396 automatic rifles, 190 bazookas, 30 mortars, and over 100 million rounds of ammunition.[73] As Figure 7.4 highlights, the FLN benefited early on from logistical facilities outside Algeria that were key to importing weapons and other types of aid. Over time, however, the French successfully cracked down on the Algerian–Tunisian border with construction of the Morice Line.

Money: For insurgents, money is valuable because it can be used for multiple purposes. Insurgents can use money from outside sources for such purposes as buying lethal and non-lethal material, recruiting assets, paying salaries, and building infrastructure like training camps and command-and-control posts. Outside money modestly increases an insurgent group's chances of winning from 28 percent for all insurgencies to 30 percent with financial support from outsiders.

Insurgent groups benefited from financial assistance. In Algeria, for instance, the FLN's successful insurgency against the French government was facilitated by massive financial flows from abroad. The FLN received approximately $1 billion in 1957, $2 billion in 1958, and $3.4 billion in 1959, most of it from Arab countries and China. The FLN also received significant money from Algerian workers in France, who were concentrated in Paris and included students, businessmen, and industrial workers. FLN

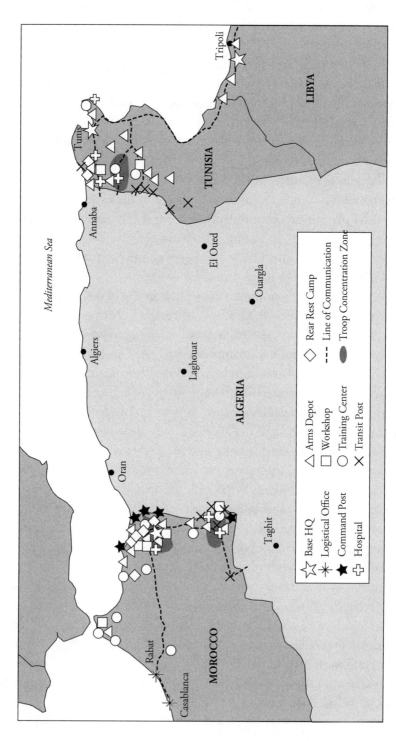

FIGURE 7.4 FLN logistical facilities outside Algeria, 1958[98]

collectors made monthly forced collections from the Algerian diaspora in France, smuggled it out of the country, deposited it in Swiss bank accounts, and used the money to purchase arms and supplies.[74]

In Angola, UNITA rebels received substantial financial aid from at least a dozen foreign governments, including the United States, during its successful insurgency from 1961 to 1974.[75] In Northern Ireland, the Provisional IRA received significant outside money from supporters abroad during its struggle with the British government, which culminated in the Good Friday Agreement in 1998. The diaspora population in the United States established Northern Aid (NORAID) to collect money for the families of dead and imprisoned IRA militants. Between 1970 and 1991, NORAID sent a total of $3.6 million to the IRA.[76]

Even for insurgent groups that eventually lose the war, money may be the difference between a quick defeat and a drawn-out conflict. In Chechnya, rebels began to receive significant sums of money after the first war from 1994 to 1996. According to Russian intelligence estimates, key sources included private donors in the United Arab Emirates, Egypt, Libya, Kuwait, Qatar, Afghanistan, Saudi Arabia, Turkey, and Azerbaijan. In 2000, for instance, the Russians estimated that Chechen rebel groups received an average of $6 million per month.[77] In North Yemen, Saudi Arabia provided money to the royalists, which gave them a temporary boost and helped extend the conflict that eventually lasted from 1962 to 1970.[78]

Non-lethal material: Non-lethal aid can include a wide range of material such as food, intelligence, clothing, medicine, shelter, logistical hubs, gasoline, and water. It can also include material useful for propaganda or intelligence collection such as radios and computers. Though non-lethal aid is not as pivotal to insurgent success as some other types of goods and services, it can still be helpful. In Mozambique, for example, the Rhodesian government sponsored the RENAMO broadcasts *Voz da Africa Livre* (Voice of a Free Africa). RENAMO began sixty-minute transmissions in July 1976 in English, Portuguese, and Swahili. The broadcasts denounced the policies of the Mozambique government under FRELIMO, which had successfully defeated the Portuguese colonial army.[79] In the insurgencies in Libya and Syria, both of which began in 2011, outside supporters provided groups with electronic equipment that facilitated satellite and Internet access.

Non-lethal assistance can also include political and moral support. In Guinea-Bissau, the African Party for the Independence of Guinea and Cape Verde (PAIGC) succeeded in gaining independence from Portugal in 1974. It received a significant boost with political support from abroad. In April 1972, a special United Nations mission visited Guinea-Bissau and issued a report, which led the United Nations Committee on Decolonization to recognize the PAIGC as the only "true and legitimate representative of the peoples of Guinea and the Cape Verde Islands."[80] The United Nations General Assembly then passed a series of resolutions confirming recognition of the PAIGC as the sole legitimate representative of the peoples of Guinea and the Cape Verde Islands, and calling on all state, government, and national and international organizations to strengthen their aid to the PAIGC and to deal exclusively with it. Finally, the United Nations Security Council unanimously adopted a resolution condemning Portuguese colonialism and calling for an end to the war in Guinea-Bissau, withdrawal of the occupation troops, and opening of negotiations.[81] International recognition was also important to insurgents fighting for independence in the Balkans after the end of the Cold War, including in Bosnia, Slovenia, Croatia, and Kosovo.[82]

RISKS OF OUTSIDE SUPPORT

While there may be benefits in gaining outside support, there are also risks for both outside supporters and insurgent groups. Outside supporters face a classical principal–agent problem.[83] Outsourcing military action to an insurgent group entails giving up some control over achieving the outside power's objectives, whether it is a state or nonstate actor. As noted earlier, states are primarily motivated to support insurgents because of geopolitical goals such as weakening rivals or maximizing their security. Instead of deploying large numbers of their own forces and engaging in interstate conflict—which can be expensive, incur large numbers of casualties, and lead to international condemnation—outsiders sometimes choose to work with proxies. Principal–agent theory suggests that delegation is a useful tool that principals use when they wish to avoid the costs—including time and resources—associated with particular tasks.[84]

But if an insurgent group's goals are not closely aligned with that of its foreign patron, or if the group has other sources of international or domestic support, the potential for agency loss is high.[85] Jordan supported and hosted Palestinian insurgents during the 1960s. But the PLO conducted unauthorized cross-border strikes against Israel, provoking Israeli reprisals and eventually leading the Jordanian government to fight the PLO in 1970. In Afghanistan, Abdul Rashid Dostum and other militia commanders that received support from the United States engaged in alleged human rights abuses before—and after—the 2001 US invasion of Afghanistan.[86] Backing insurgent groups can also be politically risky for outside powers. During the Reagan administration, some White House officials provided assistance to the Nicaraguan contras using surplus funds from selling arms to Iran. The "Iran-Contra" scandal was one of America's worst political scandals since Watergate, particularly since it was done in the face of strong congressional opposition.

There are also several costs for insurgent groups. First, accepting aid from foreign patrons often comes with strings attached, since the principal may want some degree of control or influence over the insurgent group's goals or strategy. States and nonstate actors are unlikely to offer resources for free. Relying on external patrons may help augment resources, but it generally means the loss of some autonomy.[87] In Afghanistan, for example, the Taliban received support from the Pakistan government, including from its premier spy agency, the Directorate for Inter-Services Intelligence (ISI). But Pakistan occasionally arrested some Taliban leaders for crossing red lines, such as engaging in peace talks without their involvement.[88]

Second, outside aid can be capricious.[89] Donors often decrease or terminate aid—or even switch sides—if it suits their purpose. In Chad, Libya supported northern insurgent groups in the war that lasted from 1983 to 1990. After intervening, however, Libya annexed the Aouzou Strip, an area in northern Chad that allegedly possessed rich uranium deposits. This annexation led to conflict between Libya and some northern groups who were unwilling to cede control of the Aouzou Strip.[90]

Third, outsiders may become involved in human rights abuses and other activity, undermining local and international legitimacy. Groups that rely on outside support are sometimes populated by opportunists, lack mechanisms for disciplining bad behavior, and commit widespread abuses against civilians.[91] In Sierra Leone, the RUF received some assistance from diaspora populations in neighboring countries like Liberia. But RUF officials had to curtail diaspora involvement in 1992 "when it became a nightmarish experience for our civil population" because they were abusive and difficult to control.[92]

Fourth, the local population may perceive insurgents as puppets of external states or insurgent groups if they rely on outsiders for assistance.[93] Insurgent groups that have a leadership structure outside of the country may also lose legitimacy by being perceived as out of touch with those inside the country. Unlike insurgent groups that rely on the local population for resources and hide among their constituents inside the country, groups with external bases and patrons may be less sensitive to the demands of locals or the costs they bear.[94] The Iranian rebel group Mojahedin-e-Khalq, for example, lost legitimacy in the eyes of some Iranians by allying with Iraq, a longtime Iranian enemy.[95] In the Syrian insurgency that began in 2011, al Qa'ida in Iraq leaders established Jabhat al-Nusrah in late 2011 as their operational arm. But al Qa'ida leaders initially decided not to publicize Jabhat al-Nusrah's links with al Qa'ida in Iraq. They were apparently concerned it would undermine their support among Syrians if they were viewed as foreigners, weaken their relationship with other Syrian opposition groups if they were perceived as too extreme, and dim their prospects for external funding from some sources. Al Qa'ida leaders may also have been concerned that an overt relationship would draw unwelcome attention from Western intelligence agencies. Senior al Qa'ida leaders apparently instructed Jabhat al-Nusrah leaders to refrain from public affiliation with al Qa'ida, sectarian conflict, and disputes with Syrian opposition groups.[96]

Consequently, insurgent groups that are considering outside support should weigh the potential benefits and costs. Some types of outside support may increase their chances of winning, such as aid from great powers. But outside aid sometimes comes at a price, and insurgents should attempt to maximize redundancy and secure funding from multiple channels, ensuring that the loss of one source is not catastrophic.[97]

8

Ending Insurgencies

We know we couldn't have faced down this dictator without America's support—France and the UK, too.[1]

—Yousif Abuleifa, Libyan insurgent

The law governing revolutionary war in our country requires that we become stronger as we fight and take our offensive from a small one to a big one, from a local offensive to a general one so as to conclude the war victoriously. Both the anti-French resistance in the past and the recent fight against US aggression unfolded according to this law.[2]

—General Vo Nguyen Giap

On August 23, 2011, Libyan insurgents in Tripoli overran the fortified perimeter of Muammar al-Qaddafi's headquarters, the Bab al-Aziziya, and brazenly stormed the compound. "It's over! Qaddafi is finished!" announced one fighter over the clamor of celebratory gunfire, as rebels raised their red, green, and black flag over the building.[3] Libyan insurgents, or *thuwwar*, then proceeded to shatter a gilded statue of Qaddafi, tear up a portrait of the Libyan leader, and raze parts of the building. The same day, *thuwwar* also seized control of the Tripoli airport and key neighborhoods of the city, as a growing flock of rebel supporters danced in Tripoli's Green Square.

The insurgent victory was startling in its speed and lethality, overthrowing the Qaddafi government in only six months. Outside combat support was pivotal. Beginning in March 2011, US, French, and British aircraft began targeting Qaddafi's air-defense systems. US and British ships fired 110 Tomahawk missiles that struck Libyan radar, missile, and command-and-control sites. The US flew B-2 stealth bombers from Whiteman Air Force Base in Missouri, which dropped 45 precision-guided bombs on Qaddafi's airfields. Additional cruise missile strikes destroyed Qaddafi's command-and-control facility in Tripoli. Intelligence agencies from NATO countries provided material, money, information, and other assistance to Libyan insurgents. Overall, NATO aircraft conducted a total of 26,500 sorties against the regime's armored vehicles, artillery, and other targets, and provided rebels with an opportunity for victory in Libya. The air campaign also enabled the Benghazi-centered Libyan opposition to survive Qaddafi's offensive in March 2011, which might have overrun the insurgent stronghold and potentially crushed the opposition. In addition, US, French, British, and other special operations forces and intelligence operatives conducted direct-action operations; collected intelligence; trained, advised, and assisted insurgent forces; and provided money and lethal and non-lethal aid.[4]

When the insurgency in Libya started, it was unclear whether it would end because of a military victory by insurgents, a military victory by the Qaddafi government, or a settlement. Both the Libyan opposition and the Qaddafi government wanted a victory. As noted in Chapter 1, the historical data on insurgencies shows that nearly three quarters ended with a battlefield victory by either the government or insurgents. Only 29 percent of insurgencies since World War II ended in a draw.[5] Insurgents are more successful than many policymakers realize.[6] In addition to Libya, prominent historical examples of insurgent victory range from the Khmer Rouge in Cambodia (1970–1975) to insurgent wins in Afghanistan (1978–1992, 1992–1996, and 1996–2001), Cuba (1953–1958), Kosovo (1998–1999), Nicaragua (1978–1979), Sierra Leone (1991–1997), South Africa (1981–1994), and Vietnam (1946–1954 and 1955–1975).

As highlighted by the Libya example, this chapter examines how insurgencies end. It asks, What factors increase an insurgent group's chances of achieving victory by overthrowing the government or seceding from it? To answer this question, this chapter builds on the work in previous chapters, but is different in one important respect. It examines the factors identified in each chapter collectively and more rigorously through a large-N statistical analysis. The analysis involved estimating the correlation between over a dozen factors (or independent variables) and statistically controlling for the influence of other factors in the database. They include such factors as great-power combat support to counterinsurgents and insurgents, insurgent use of sanctuary, insurgent goals like anti-colonialism and secession, and insurgent size. The regression analysis allows us to evaluate the statistical relationship between the factors and insurgent victory. Full results of the analysis are presented in Appendix B.

The findings highlight the importance of great-power support during insurgencies. First, securing combat support from great powers *increases* an insurgent group's chances of achieving victory. Effective combat support often came from a combination of special operations forces, intelligence units, and air power. Examples include the role of US special operations forces, the CIA, and US air power in support of insurgents in Kosovo, Afghanistan, and Libya. In addition, the KGB and Soviet navy provided assistance to insurgents from the Partido Africano da Independencia da Guiné e Cabo Verde (PAIGC) in Guinea-Bissau, which facilitated PAIGC success in gaining independence from Portugal in 1974. Several other factors, such as the number of insurgent groups and the existence of anti-colonial wars, can also increase the odds of insurgent success. Second, several factors *decrease* a group's probability of victory. They include situations when insurgents use a punishment strategy, when insurgents seek secession rather than the overthrow of a regime, and when the government receives great-power combat support. None of these factors is deterministic. They don't guarantee success, but rather they increase (or decrease) the odds of victory. The rest of this chapter is divided into three sections.

The first examines factors that increase the probability of insurgent victory. The second section analyzes factors that decrease the probability of insurgent victory. The third highlights those factors that don't significantly impact the probability of insurgent victory, as well as discusses insurgent draws.

INCREASING INSURGENT ODDS OF VICTORY

Insurgent groups need to think carefully about several issues to achieve victory. First, insurgents can choose from three main strategies: guerrilla warfare, conventional warfare, and punishment. These strategies are not mutually exclusive, and insurgents often use more than one during an insurgency. The choice of strategy has historically depended on such factors as control of territory, performance on the battlefield, and balance of power with the government. Second, groups need to weigh the costs and benefits of a range of tactics, such as ambushes, raids, sabotage, subversion, assassinations, and bombings. Third, insurgents need to think carefully about organizational design, including in insurgencies with multiple groups and factions. Centralized organizational structures are generally more effective because they help insurgent leaders identify and punish those engaged in shirking behavior or defections. Centralization can also help groups better govern territory they control. Fourth, insurgents have a wide range of forums to conduct information campaigns and propaganda, from print and radio to word of mouth. But the Internet, social media, and advanced communications technology can reach a particularly broad audience, help mobilize key populations, and overcome collective action problems by facilitating coordination. Fifth, outside states and nonstate actors can provide a range of services (such as combat support, sanctuary, training, and intelligence) and goods (such as money, lethal material, and non-lethal material) to insurgents.

While all of these factors are important, the statistical analysis indicates that several factors increase the odds of insurgent victory.

Great-power combat support: The first is outside combat support from a great power.[7] This finding is more nuanced than several studies that aggregate external support into one category and don't specify which *types* of support are most important.[8] International relations "realists" have long noted the importance of great powers because these states have the largest impact on what happens in international politics.[9] Most realists agree on several propositions: states are the central actors in international politics; the international political system is anarchic since there is no supranational authority that can enforce rules over states; actors in the international system are rational and sensitive to costs; and states desire power so that they can ensure their own security.[10] The fortunes of states in the international system are determined to a great extent by the actions of those with the most capability. Great powers are largely defined on the basis of their relative military capability.[11] The English historian A. J. P. Taylor noted that the "test of a great power is the test of strength for war."[12] Other kinds of power are also important. The American political scientist Kenneth Waltz used five criteria to determine great powers: military strength, economic capability, size of population and territory, resource endowment, and political stability and competence.[13]

In insurgent warfare, great powers can tip the balance in favor of either side. Great-power support is particularly critical because, by definition, great powers have more military and other resources that they can provide to insurgent groups. Aid from a great power can also serve as an important morale boost for insurgent groups.[14] All great powers, including the United States and the Soviet Union during the Cold War, have historically supported insurgents as a way to expand influence overseas without expending the amount of blood, money, and other costs often involved in interstate war.[15] Proxy war can be relatively cheap for outside powers, even if the costs of war are high for locals.

During the Cold War, states regularly supported insurgent groups. The United States assisted the Nicaraguan contras, Afghan mujahidin, and Tibetan Buddhist fighters among others. The Soviet Union and China backed guerrillas in Angola, Greece, South Africa, Vietnam, and multiple other countries.[16] More broadly, great-power support was critical for insurgent victory in numerous insurgencies, such as Afghanistan, Angola, Cambodia, Chad, Ethiopia, Guinea, Libya, and South Africa. As noted by Mohamad Yousaf, head of the Afghan section of Pakistan's Inter-Services Intelligence Directorate, US support was essential to defeating the Soviet-backed Afghan government:

> [T]he CIA's contributions have played a vital role in the conduct of the Afghan Jehad. Without the backing of the US and Saudi Arabia the Soviet would still be entrenched in that country. Without the intelligence provided by the CIA many battles would have been lost, and without the CIA's training of our Pakistani instructors the Mujahideen would have been fearfully ill-equipped.[17]

In particular, the data indicate that *combat support* from great powers to insurgents increases the likelihood of victory, especially when counterinsurgents don't have support from another great power. As a reminder, combat support refers to the direct involvement of outside militaries, navies, air forces, or intelligence units that fight alongside insurgents. In general, great powers have several options. They can support both insurgents and the government, only insurgents, only governments, or neither side. When insurgents receive combat support from a great power, insurgents are significantly more likely to win.[18] When great powers don't support insurgents but do provide support to the government, insurgents are less likely to win. But when great powers support both sides with combat or noncombat support, insurgents are still more likely to win.

External combat support by great powers can be helpful by allowing states to directly influence the outcome of war through their participation. General assistance is often impersonal and leaves most implementation to insurgents, including how to use outside money, lethal and non-lethal aid, intelligence, and other types of assistance. But direct combat support involves outside powers participating in the struggle. Examples include Indian support to East Pakistan (now Bangladesh) in its war of secession in 1971, NATO support to the Kosovo Liberation Army in 1998 and 1999, US support to Afghan insurgents in 2001, and NATO support to Libyan insurgents in 2011. Several ongoing insurgencies involve direct combat support to insurgent groups, including both Syria (with US and other support to rebels) and Ukraine (with Russian support to rebels).

Great powers often use special operations forces; intelligence units; air power; and airborne intelligence, surveillance, and reconnaissance (ISR) platforms—rather than conventional forces—to support insurgents. This is sometimes referred to as "unconventional warfare," which includes operations conducted by, with, or through insurgent and other irregular forces.[19] In the United States, the definition of unconventional warfare and US support to insurgents evolved over time. The initial doctrinal concept originated with the creation of the Office of Strategic Services during World War II. Unconventional warfare was defined in terms of guerrilla and covert operations in enemy-held territory. One of the first official US Army definitions that highlighted unconventional warfare appeared in 1950 as "partisan warfare."[20] In 1951, the US Army's unconventional warfare capabilities were consolidated under the Office of Psychological Warfare. The US Army published the first two field manuals for the conduct of special operations, with an emphasis on unconventional warfare.[21] By 1955, the first historical manual that specifically linked US Army Special Forces to unconventional warfare declared that unconventional warfare "consists of the three interrelated fields of guerrilla warfare (GW), escape and evasion, and subversion against hostile states."[22]

Over the next several decades, the United States used special operations forces, intelligence operatives, and air power to aid insurgents in Africa, Asia, the Middle East and Latin America. In 1999, after the end of the Cold War, the United States and other NATO countries utilized a combination of these forces in Kosovo during Operation Allied Force.[23] Two years later, approximately 100 CIA officers, 350 special operations forces, and 15,000 Afghans—running as many as 100 combat sorties per day—defeated a Taliban army estimated at 50,000 to 60,000 plus several thousand al Qa'ida fighters.[24]

A decade later in Libya, NATO countries conducted air strikes and deployed covert units to help insurgents overthrow Qaddafi's government. NATO air strikes, which lasted from March to October 2011 under Operation Odyssey Dawn and Operation Unified Protector, were critical for insurgent success. They included air strikes against Libyan government command-and-control sites, maneuver forces, ammunition dumps, SCUD missile garrisons, and surface-to-air missile systems. The air campaign enabled the Benghazi-centered Libyan opposition to survive Qaddafi's offensive in March 2011. American, French, and British air power swiftly destroyed and repelled Qaddafi's tanks, thwarting what could have been a bloody assault on the city. In the face of coalition air power, regime forces could not mass to execute the offensive operations required to overrun Benghazi. In addition, the establishment of a no-fly zone and the beginning—and continuation—of coalition air strikes had a profound effect on the psychology of Libyan rebels, who became increasingly convinced that they could win.[25]

More broadly, NATO combat support helped turn the tide of the Libyan war, enabling the rebels to eventually overthrow Qaddafi's regime. As one study concluded:

> Through its intervention, the coalition stemmed and then reversed the tide of Libya's civil war, preventing Qaddafi from crushing the

nascent rebel movement seeking to overthrow his dictatorship and going on to enable the opposition forces to prevail against an enemy that many had argued the rebels could not defeat without a foreign army invading Libya.[26]

NATO and partner air power worked in concert with rebel forces on the ground to drive Qaddafi's forces back and finally to break their resistance. Overall, NATO maintained an arms embargo, facilitated humanitarian relief, created and sustained a no-fly zone, and helped protect Libya's civilian population from Qaddafi's forces with air strikes. Table 8.1 provides an overview of the air campaigns for Operation Unified Protector in Libya (2011) and Kosovo (1999).[27] Air power, along with external special operations forces and intelligence units, was crucial in both wars in supporting insurgent groups.

Despite these successes, there are several caveats. Combat support from great powers does not always lead to victory, though it does increase the probability of insurgent victory. There are several cases which did not lead to insurgent victory, such as US and other Western support to the Kurdish Democratic Party of Iraq (KDP) and Patriotic Union of Kurdistan (PUK) during the Iraqi Kurdish insurgency that began in 1961. In addition, Chinese combat support to the Communist Party of Burma did not lead to insurgent victory in Myanmar in the war that began in 1948.

TABLE 8.1 Libya and Kosovo air campaigns[63]

Type	Kosovo	Libya (Operation Unified Protector)
Length of operation (days)	78	215
Total sorties	38,004	26,500
Strike sorties	19,484	9,700
Average number of sorties per day	487	123
Civilian deaths	500	60
Cost of operations (billions of 2011 dollars)	$2.7	$1.1

In addition, it is possible that there is some endogeneity with outside support.[28] Some great powers may provide outside support—including direct combat support—in cases where they believe insurgents or counterinsurgents are likely to win. And they may refrain from offering support when insurgents or counterinsurgents are likely to lose. Consequently, some might argue that an insurgent group's prospects for victory influence the degree of outside support, rather than the other way around. Outside powers may not improve the prospects for insurgent victory, but simply join the winning side.[29] While this may be true in some cases, great powers and superpowers are primarily motivated to support insurgents for geopolitical considerations, as the Soviet Union and United States did during the Cold War. This suggests that they may aid insurgents in cases of strategic importance—even where the probability of insurgent success is low. Despite long odds of overthrowing the Castro regime in Cuba, US President John F. Kennedy still supported Operation Zapata—more infamously known as the Bay of Pigs—and anti-Castro insurgents because of Soviet concerns. "In Latin America," Kennedy remarked, "Communist agents seeking to exploit that region's peaceful revolution of hope have established a base on Cuba, only 90 miles from our shore . . . Communist domination in this Hemisphere can never be negotiated."[30]

Still, insurgent lack of outside support from great powers can be catastrophic, especially if groups have limited resources. Without significant support, insurgents in Burundi (1965–1972), the Central African Republic (1996–1997), the Democratic Republic of Congo (1960–1962), the Dominican Republic (1965), Greece (1946–1949), Indonesia (1965–1978), Kenya (1952–1956), Peru (1982–1989), and the Philippines (1946–1954), among others, lacked the resources to overthrow governments.

The Greek case is illustrative. As Joseph Stalin explained to Yugoslav officials in June 1948, the Soviet Union refused to support the Communist insurgents in Greece because "they have no prospect of success at all." The problem, Stalin lectured, was straightforward: "What do you think—that Britain and the US—the US, the most powerful state in the world—will permit you to break their lines of communication in the Mediterranean? Nonsense. And we have no navy."[31] Stalin was perceptive. One now-declassified CIA communiqué concluded that "far more disastrous than the loss of Greece itself would be the psychological and political repercussions [which] could result in international panic."[32] And Under Secretary of State Dean Acheson assessed that the loss of Greece might trigger the loss of states to Communism across "the whole Near and Middle East and North Africa."[33] The failure of Greek groups to secure Soviet support contributed to their ultimate defeat, especially since the United States provided substantial aid to the Greek government.

Number of insurgent groups: In addition to combat support from great powers, the number of insurgent groups matters. As outlined in Chapter 5, there was more than one insurgent group in approximately half of insurgencies since 1946. The percentage of multi-group insurgencies also increased over time. Among those insurgencies that started since 1980, only 36 percent consisted of a single group and 64 percent consisted of multiple groups. While insurgencies with one group or more than five groups do not raise the probability of insurgent victory, those with between two and four insurgent groups over the course of an insurgency are more likely to win. There may be a few reasons. The existence of several groups, for example, may indicate fruitful grounds for an insurgency, such as a weak government, substantial local grievances, or the availability of lootable resources. With too many groups, however, it may be difficult to manage a diffuse coalition.

In insurgencies with two to four groups, insurgent groups may want to establish an umbrella alliance to coordinate political and military activity.[34] An umbrella alliance can also be more effective in dealing with principal–agent problems within the insurgency because it is easier to identify and punish those engaged in shirking or defections. Leaders of umbrella organizations have tighter command and control of their members than without such a structure.[35]

Anti-colonial wars: On a final note, fighting against colonial governments significantly increases the probability of insurgent victory. While this finding is less relevant today, colonial wars were advantageous for insurgents like Mao Tse-Tung in China, Ho Chi Minh in Vietnam, and the Front de Liberation Nationale (FLN) in Algeria. By World War II, the colonial powers like France and Britain were weak, providing an opportunity for budding independence movements. Neither country had the resources or political will to fight prolonged counterinsurgencies in their colonies. As one history of insurgent warfare concluded, "It is vital to understand how weak the two biggest colonial powers were by 1945 in order to understand why decolonization swept the world in the next few years and why anti-Western guerrillas and terrorists appeared to be ascendant."[36] To be sure, a British government publication pointedly declared in 1946, "British 'Imperialism' is dead."[37]

DECREASING INSURGENT ODDS OF VICTORY

There are also several factors that decrease the probability of insurgent victory: the use of punishment strategies, secession, and great-power support to governments.

Punishment: Insurgent groups that use punishment strategies are less likely to achieve victory.[38] Punishment strategies involve deliberately targeting noncombatants in order to raise the societal costs of continued resistance and coerce the government to concede to insurgent demands. The common feature of punishment campaigns is that they inflict suffering on civilians, either directly or indirectly. Their goals may include decreasing civilian morale by exposing large portions of the population to terror or by causing severe shortages of consumer goods and services (such as food, textiles, and industrial goods), as well as deterring the population from cooperating with the government. Insurgent groups used punishment strategies in over one third of insurgencies, often in combination with guerrilla and conventional strategies.

Punishment strategies tend to weaken insurgent support by engendering discontent among civilian populations, undermining hearts and minds, creating high levels of resistance to rebel advances, and damaging the reputation of rebel groups within the country and internationally.[39] Indeed, a punishment strategy risks pushing locals into the arms of the government, rather than cowing them. As one observer remarked about the Viet Cong,

> Returnees reported that indoctrination sessions on the armed struggle cited the Malayan insurgency as a case where ... indiscriminate terror ... failed. "We were told," said one of them, "that in Singapore the rebels on certain days would dynamite every 67th streetcar that passed along a street, the next day it might be every 30th, and so on, but that this hardened the hearts of the people against the rebels."[40]

This is why numerous insurgent groups have struggled to limit—or even refrain from utilizing—strategies and tactics that undermine local support. One member of the Provisional Irish Republican Army noted, for example, that the group should stop using car bombs since "it was too difficult to control and therefore you ended up with civilian casualties which no one wanted, which was (a) a tragedy for the people who were killed and (b) it was a political disaster for the aims of the struggle."[41] In addition, Mao Tse-Tung strongly urged insurgents to obey such rules as "do not steal from the people" and "be neither selfish nor unjust," cautioning them to secure the support—not the ire—of the local population.[42]

Secession: Groups that seek secession—as opposed to overthrowing a regime—are less likely to achieve victory. Secession is harder for insurgents to achieve than regime change, with cases like South Sudan and Kosovo as extreme outliers in their success. Insurgent groups succeeded 43 percent of the time when their goal was to overthrow a regime, and they succeeded 77 percent of the time when their goal was independence from a colonial authority. But secession was only successful 10 percent of the time and led to significantly longer insurgencies—seventeen years for secession wars, compared to ten years for regime change and seven years for independence from a colonial power.

At least two factors may explain the difficulties of secession.[43] International norms generally don't support changing state boundaries and supporting secession. Secessionists tend to find themselves at war against tougher states and fight for ends (redrawing international borders) against which there is a strong taboo in today's international system. In addition, there may be a selection mechanism at work. Groups that seek regime change in weak states, which are favorable to insurgencies, are more likely to win these wars. In these instances, groups don't threaten to change the territorial integrity of international borders. Instead, there may be a selection effect because a notable percentage of groups may only opt for regime change when the government is weak, increasing their odds of victory.[44]

Great-power support to counterinsurgents: Finally, great-power support to governments—particularly combat support—decreases the probability of insurgent victory, particularly in cases where insurgents lack great-power combat support. The logic is similar to great-power combat support to insurgents: great powers are able to provide larger amounts and types of aid to counterinsurgents than other types of outside state and nonstate actors. Waging an insurgency against a better-equipped and richer government is always difficult, but great-power support to governments makes it doubly difficult.

CONCLUSION

Each insurgency is different and ends in a distinct, nuanced way, depending on a range of complex variables, including local conditions. A group's strategy, organizational structure, tactics, outside support, information operations, and other factors are important—including the leadership of insurgent officials and local commanders. So are counterinsurgent decisions and actions, as well as those of outside states and nonstate actors. But there are some generalizable factors that increase—and decrease—an insurgent group's probability of victory. Great-power combat support to groups significantly raises the odds of insurgent victory, as does a modest number of insurgent groups and anti-colonial wars. In addition, several factors decrease a group's probability of victory: when insurgents use a punishment strategy, which weakens their local support; when insurgents seek secession, which undermines Westphalian norms of sovereignty; and when great powers provide combat support to governments.

There are several implications of these findings. To begin with, numerous factors don't affect the probability of insurgent victory. First, there is no evidence that differences in strategies between insurgents and counterinsurgents impact the probability of insurgent outcomes. Some have argued that "strategic interaction"—the relationship between the strategies of both sides—can impact the outcome of insurgencies.[45] Insurgent use of conventional military strategies, even in the face of more conventionally minded adversaries, has little impact on the probability of insurgent victory. Second, some argue that insurgent groups that enjoy sanctuary in neighboring states are more difficult to defeat.[46] Sanctuary allows insurgents to regroup, resupply, and recruit new members. But the ability of insurgents to establish a sanctuary in neighboring states does not increase insurgent probability of victory. Third, Samuel Huntington argued in his book *Clash of Civilizations* that "Islam's borders *are* bloody, and so are its innards" because Islamic societies have cultural and demographic features that make them violence-prone.[47] But insurgencies with Islamic groups are no less or more likely to win. Fourth, the duration of insurgencies does not influence a group's chances of winning.[48]

Fifth, some have argued that the growing "mechanization" of militaries after World War I—including their reliance on armored vehicles and specialized supplies like fuel and spare parts—increases the probability of insurgent victory.[49] Unlike their nineteenth-century predecessors, modern militaries possess force structures that inhibit information collection among local populations. But increasing mechanization does not raise the chances of insurgent victory.[50] Sixth, some have argued that insurgents may perform better against democratic governments.[51] Impatient for success and unwilling to shoulder the required sacrifices of blood and treasure, democracies may be more likely to offer concessions or concede defeat than autocratic states that can safely ignore their publics. But democratic regime type does not appear to impact the outcome of insurgencies.[52]

In addition, though great-power support is more likely to tip the balance in favor of insurgents than support from other actors, great powers have become increasingly reluctant to provide aid. As Figure 8.1 shows, great-power support to insurgents precipitously dropped since the 1970s as a percentage of active insurgencies, but great-power support to governments has remained relatively stable since the mid-1970s. The decrease in great-power support to insurgents may be caused by several factors. In the United States, for example, there was a normative stigma attached to clandestine aid to insurgents from the Church Commission and other investigations in the 1970s.[53] The decline may also be caused, in part, by a decrease in the risk–reward calculations of countries like the United States with the collapse of the Soviet Union and the end of the Cold War.

Finally, it is worth remembering that victory is not always possible for insurgents. As noted at the beginning of this chapter, groups battled to a draw in just over one quarter of the insurgencies that ended since World War II. In a draw, no side wins an outright military victory, but

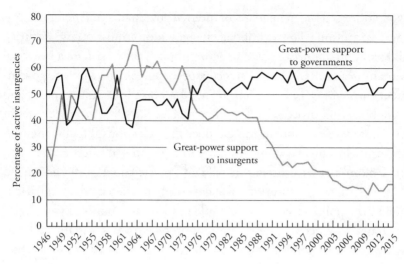

FIGURE 8.1 Great-power support to insurgents and governments, 1946–2015[61]

the war ends because of a negotiated settlement, a sustained cease-fire, or a military stalemate where the violence level dropped to twenty-five deaths per year or less for a sustained period. A government is generally forced to concede to some, but not all, insurgent demands, and neither side obtains its maximal aims. Examples of concessions include disarming, demobilizing, and reintegrating insurgents in exchange for greater participation in the political system (such as forming a legal political party); more autonomy (though not independence); or policy concessions like land reform.[54] In El Salvador, for example, the Chapultepec accords outlined a series of steps such as judicial reform; agrarian reform; a 70 percent reduction of the armed forces; dissolution of the rapid deployment forces, National Guard, National Police, and Treasury Police; and transfer of the state intelligence agencies to the Presidency of the Republic.[55] The FMLN also became a legal political party and eventually won the 2009 presidential elections.

There are numerous other examples where a political settlement occurred between a government and an insurgent group. One is with the Provisional Irish Republican Army, which ended its activity following negotiations with the United Kingdom and Republic of Ireland. The Belfast (Good Friday) Agreement, which was announced on April 10,

1998, addressed the main issues of internal governance and detailed measures concerning constitutional changes, decommissioning, security, and paramilitary prisoners.[56] In Mozambique, the Resistencia Nacional Mozambicana (RENAMO) signed a peace agreement with the government in October 1992, which included a cease-fire, disarmament and demobilization process, and multiparty elections.[57] It won 112 seats in the National Assembly in the October 1994 elections. Finally, the 19th of April Movement (M-19) in Colombia negotiated a settlement with the Colombian government in 1989 and participated in discussions to draw up a new constitution. The government offered M-19 participation in the political system and a role in forming a political party.[58]

Draws have become more common in recent years. Figure 8.2 highlights how insurgencies ended by outcome. One of the most striking developments is that the percentage of insurgencies ending in a draw increased over time, from 25 percent in the early 1980s to 50 percent from 1990 to 1994, 38 percent from 1995 to 1999, 58 percent from 2000 to 2004, 83 percent from 2005 to 2010, and 67 percent from 2010 to 2015. Part of this increase may have been caused by the termination of US and Soviet support to insurgencies at the end of the Cold War. There

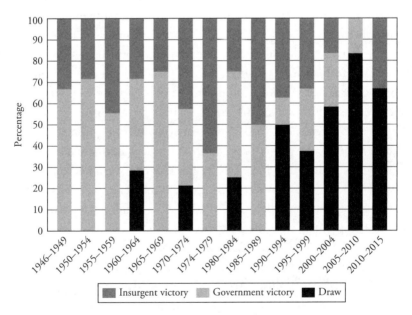

FIGURE 8.2 Insurgency ending by outcome[62]

may be other reasons, such as greater involvement by major powers and the United Nations in brokering peace negotiations.[59]

All insurgencies eventually end with a draw, insurgent victory, or government victory. Whether they end on acceptable terms to insurgent groups is the critical challenge. Still, few insurgent leaders may be as fortunate as General Vo Nguyen Giap, quoted at the beginning of this chapter, who helped win two insurgencies—one against the French and the other against a US-backed government in Saigon.[60]

9

Implications for Counterinsurgency Warfare

*We must have a plan. Secondly we must have a man. When we have a plan
and a man, we shall succeed: not otherwise.[1]*

—Field Marshall Bernard Law Montgomery (during British operations in Malaya)

A DECADE AFTER THE terrorist attacks on September 11, 2001, counterinsurgency had suffered an extraordinary *coup de main* in the West.
Following costly campaigns in Iraq and Afghanistan, there was a pal-
pable revolt against counterinsurgency among Western governments
and populations. As one US Department of Defense document concluded, "the United States will emphasize non-military means and
military-to-military cooperation to address instability" instead of
counterinsurgency operations, though there might be a sporadic need
to conduct "limited counterinsurgency."[2] The US Army and Marine
Corps shifted to a focus on conventional operations, including in
the Asia-Pacific theater against a rising China and in Eastern Europe
against Russia. Key US military training centers like the US Army
War College severely cut back on their number of insurgency and
counterinsurgency classes. In the United Kingdom, a growing contingent of British scholars and practitioners criticized their military's
once-stellar record in counterinsurgency. As one book concluded,
"the British, far from being the counter-insurgent exemplars that history has benevolently cast them, have in fact consistently proven to
be slow learners and slow strategic burners in the realm of counterinsurgency warfare."[3]

There were several possible reasons for this hostility to counterinsurgency.[4] First, there was public aversion to the wars in Iraq and Afghanistan. In 2014, for example, half of Americans said the United States made a mistake sending troops to fight in Afghanistan, up from 6 percent in 2002.[5] The trend was similar in Iraq, where 57 percent of Americans in 2014 believed the United States erred in sending troops to Iraq, up from 23 percent in March 2003.[6] In both Iraq and Afghanistan, the United States fought long, bloody, and expensive counterinsurgency campaigns after overthrowing the Taliban and Saddam Hussein governments. Second, some policymakers and pundits conflated counterinsurgency with the deployment overseas of large numbers of foreign forces.[7] The US Army and Marine Corps' *Counterinsurgency Field Manual* assessed that "a range of 20 to 25 counterinsurgents for every 1,000 residents" was generally necessary for counterinsurgency success.[8] Third, some conflated counterinsurgency to mean the population-centric strategy advocated by US officials in the 2000s.[9]

Yet counterinsurgency simply refers to efforts by a government to degrade or defeat insurgents.[10] It should not be equated with the direct involvement of international forces, which occurred in only one quarter of insurgencies since World War II. In addition, the population-centric strategy adopted by US and other Western militaries was only one of many options Western militaries could have chosen. Indeed, counterinsurgency is a reality of international politics. As long as there are insurgencies, governments will need to conduct counterinsurgency warfare.

This chapter outlines implications for counterinsurgency warfare based on the analysis of insurgent warfare in previous chapters. As noted in Chapter 1, governments defeated insurgents on the battlefield in 36 percent of insurgencies since World War II, roughly similar to insurgent victories (35 percent) and draws (29 percent). This chapter utilizes the quantitative and qualitative findings presented in previous chapters from 181 insurgences since World War II, but applies them to counterinsurgents. It also provides anecdotes to illustrate historical examples. There are several broad themes.

First, political considerations should drive military and other counterinsurgency efforts, including the government's strategy, tactics, resources, and other considerations. Carl von Clausewitz's argument that the "political object . . . will be the standard for determining the aim of the military force and also the amount of effort to be made" is just as relevant for counterinsurgency warfare as it is for conventional warfare.[11] Counterinsurgents should integrate politics into virtually every aspect of their campaign, such as: developing a plan, as noted by Field Marshall Bernard Law Montgomery at the beginning of this chapter; improving governance to deal with the causes of insurgency; mobilizing support from the local population and relevant outside actors; minimizing strategies and tactics that undermine political support; and utilizing information campaigns that maximize political support for counterinsurgents and undermine support for insurgents. Second, several specific steps may reduce the probability of insurgent success and should be a focus of counterinsurgency efforts based on the quantitative analysis in Chapter 8. One is undermining outside support to insurgents, particularly combat support from great powers. Another is securing and maintaining outside support to counterinsurgents, particularly from great powers. An additional step is effectively taking advantage of insurgent use of punishment strategies and tactics, which undermine local support.

The data and findings in previous chapters highlight a range of potential vulnerabilities for insurgents. Governments should identify—and exploit—these weaknesses, particularly those that are likely to decrease insurgent support from the local population. This means better understanding what strategies, tactics, organizational structures, information campaigns, and types of outside support have historically undermined insurgents and their support bases. Table 9.1 provides an overview of steps that counterinsurgents should consider.

This chapter does not offer policy recommendations for specific counterinsurgency campaigns, such as Iraq, Afghanistan, or Syria, in part since wars evolve at such a rapid pace that some recommendations quickly become obsolete. But the conclusions do suggest steps worth considering against groups like the Islamic State.

Based on this analysis, for example, the Islamic State's use of a punishment strategy and punishment tactics is likely a major, long-term vulnerability. The data outlined in Chapter 8 indicate that punishment

TABLE 9.1 Counterinsurgency implications for local governments

Key areas	Example of counterinsurgency steps
Preventing an insurgency	• Strengthen security forces by enhancing civil–military integration, establishing better counterintelligence measures, improving the capacity of security ministries, enacting more aggressive anti-corruption programs, and improving training • Address underlying causes, particularly those related to low per capita income, ethnic polarization, and religious polarization that have a higher probability of triggering an insurgency
Strategies	• Take advantage of poor strategic decisions by insurgents (e.g., weak groups that choose a conventional strategy) • Leverage insurgent use of punishment strategies, which tend to undermine their local support
Tactics	• Take advantage of insurgent use of punishment tactics by fanning local anger against insurgents and encouraging defections • Utilize unconventional warfare designed to undermine the legitimacy and support of insurgent groups in areas they control
Organizational structures	• Conduct aggressive targeting of insurgent leadership, which can force groups to decentralize their organizational structure • Exploit principal–agent fissures and encourage friction *within* groups because of heterogeneous ethnic, religious, and other diversity • Leverage fissures *between* insurgent groups in wars with multiple groups
Information campaigns and propaganda	• Utilize defensive measures such as monitoring insurgent Internet use, chat rooms, radios, cell phones, and social media forums • Conduct offensive campaigns such as targeting the cyber and electronic capabilities of insurgents and spreading information (and disinformation) to discredit them
Outside support	• Interdict outside support to insurgents, particularly from great powers. Examples include identifying and disrupting key routes that insurgents use to transit people, money, and material; improving aerial, ground, and maritime surveillance; strengthening the capacity and resources for border security; constructing physical barriers; and conducting raids against infiltrators • Exploit principal–agent fissures between insurgents and their outside supporters • Increase outside support for counterinsurgents, particularly from great powers

is negatively correlated with insurgent victory. In previous insurgencies, groups that used punishment strategies and tactics almost invariably lost local support, which was so important to such successful insurgents as Mao. Consequently, counterinsurgents should conduct a range of steps—from information campaigns that highlight the Islamic State's brutality against locals to intelligence programs that encourage defections—which exacerbate local unhappiness with the Islamic State and provide opportunities for the reintegration of insurgents. Aggressive and sustained targeting of Islamic State leadership would also likely force the group to decentralize, raising principal–agent costs and undermining the Islamic State's ability to conduct military operations, secure funding, collect and analyze intelligence, and govern areas they control. In addition, outside military involvement from great powers such as the United States should come from special operations and intelligence units, rather than conventional forces. These types of forces are better trained to work with local partners that need to clear and hold territory occupied by the Islamic State. Finally, a key focus of US and other Western efforts should be on helping address the political and other grievances that allowed the Islamic State to secure support in Iraq, Syria, Libya, and other countries. In Iraq, for instance, Sunni hatred of Nouri al-Maliki and his government, which numerous Sunnis perceived as pro-Shia and too closely allied with Iran, contributed to the rise of the Islamic State in 2014.

The rest of this chapter is divided into several sections that correspond to the main chapters of the book. It identifies potential insurgent vulnerabilities and suggests counterinsurgent steps in the following areas: preventing an insurgency, strategies, tactics, organizational structures, information campaigns, and outside support. It does not offer, or intend to offer, a single theory or doctrine of counterinsurgency warfare. After all, there is more than one route to defeat insurgents, and governments have successfully used a wide range of strategies, tactics, and other measures.

PREVENTING AN INSURGENCY

Three sets of factors increase the probability of an insurgency, as discussed in Chapter 2. The first are local grievances, particularly ones associated with low per capita income, ethnic polarization, and religious polarization. Groups need a cause that charismatic leaders can use to help mobilize a local population. Second, a weak government with incompetent police and military forces is generally an important condition for insurgencies. Since insurgents start with few resources, a weak state provides a welcome opportunity for rebellion. A weak state also increases the likelihood of a "security dilemma," in which each side's efforts to increase its own security inadvertently threaten the other side. Third, the availability of lootable resources like oil or drugs increases the probability of an insurgency by creating an opportunity for nonstate actors to challenge the state. In light of these factors, governments have a substantial incentive to prevent an insurgency from beginning and to eliminate armed resistance at the proto-insurgency (or pre-insurgency) phase.[12]

After all, once insurgencies begin they can last more than ten times longer than interstate wars and can severely undermine a state's economy, lead to the death of thousands of innocent civilians, destroy priceless cultural heritage sites, and disrupt life in general.[13] In El Salvador, for example, the planning ministry estimated that the insurgency caused $1.5 billion in infrastructure damages and $1.6 billion in replacement costs, a substantial amount for a population of 5 million by 1990.[14] In addition, the government diverted public resources from investment and social programs to military expenditures. Economic growth, which enjoyed a trend rate of 4.3 percent before the civil war, was negative at -1.4 percent per year between 1978 and 1990. Average real per capita income declined by more than 15 percent between 1981 and 1990. The real minimum wage declined by roughly 50 percent between 1980 and 1988, and the real minimum agricultural wage declined by nearly 70 percent.[15] The percentage of El Salvador's population living in poverty and extreme poverty increased from 51 percent in 1980 to 56 percent in 1990, with the rural population most affected. El Salvador ranked 110 out of 173 countries in the United Nations Development Program's human development rank.[16] To make matters worse, El Salvador emerged from the insurgency heavily dependent on international assistance.[17] Consequently, there are substantial incentives for governments to prevent insurgencies from beginning.

Several factors—such as lootable resources and mountainous terrain—are outside of the control of governments. This makes it

important to focus on controllable factors. At least two are important: addressing underlining causes that may resonate with locals and facilitate insurgent mobilization, and strengthening security institutions.

Underlying causes: One is to deal more effectively with key causes
outlined in Chapter 2, such as low per capita income, ethnic polarization, and religious polarization. Most of these steps are political. The
state's goal should be to prevent nascent insurgents from using these
and other causes to mobilize the local population against the government. Addressing root causes can occur in one of several ways, such as
enacting legislation that addresses income concerns, provides benefits
to large ethnic minority groups that face an ethnic majority, or offers
benefits to a well-organized religious minority that feels excluded from
the political process.

One example was Macedonia in the 1990s. The country had numerous precursor conditions for an insurgency: ethnic polarization, low
per capita income (including a poor economy), ethnic political entrepreneurs, and mountainous terrain. While there was limited violence,
there was no insurgency. One reason was the successful conclusion of
the Ohrid Framework Agreement in August 2001 between representatives of the Albanian and Macedonian communities.[18] The agreement met several of the demands of the Albanian rebels, particularly
the National Liberation Army (NLA). It improved the rights of ethnic
Albanians, removed the constitutional reference to Macedonia as the
"national state of all Macedonian people," increased the proportion of
Albanians in the police force from 5 to 25 percent, and enlarged equita-
ble employment of minorities in state institutions. The agreement also
included provisions to alter the official language of the country, with
any language spoken by over 20 percent of the population (including
Albanian) becoming an official language.[19]

There were other examples. In Singapore in the 1950s and 1960s, the
British helped prevent an insurgency led by the Malayan Communist
Party by supporting a number of political, economic, and ethnic developments that undermined insurgent mobilization. As one assessment
concluded, an insurgency was thwarted, in part, by Lee Kuan Yew and
other members of the People's Action Party who were able to "provide
an honest administration and the huge housing, education and industrial opportunities needed so quickly in order to show the people, even

including many of his wealthy right-wing opponents, where success lay."[20] Beginning in 1959, economic development was overseen by a new Minister of Finance, Goh Keng Swee, who helped raise per capita income and encouraged foreign investment by adopting such measures as tax incentives and establishing a large industrial estate in Jurong. In addition, the People's Action Party initiated a public housing program and constructed more than 25,000 high-rise, low-cost apartments during the first two years of the program.[21] Singapore also became independent in August 1965, further undermining support for the Malayan Communist Party.

Security institutions: Another step is to strengthen security institutions—particularly intelligence units, police, and military forces—and increase the costs of collective action. This is a daunting challenge that academics and practitioners have analyzed and debated for decades. At the proto-insurgency phase, would-be insurgents operate underground, temporarily eschew the use of violence, develop the group's political message, and build a clandestine organizational structure.[22] One goal of government security forces, then, is to crush nascent insurgent cells while they are still weak and vulnerable. This may involve increasing resources, including raising funding levels to security forces and augmenting the number and type of police, soldiers, and intelligence operatives devoted to counterinsurgency efforts. If security forces are weak, it may also mean taking additional steps: enhancing civil–military integration; improving the military, police, and intelligence personnel systems; establishing counterintelligence measures that limit insurgent penetration of counterinsurgent forces; enacting more effective anti-corruption programs; changing legislation to allow police and other security forces greater legal power to target insurgents; and improving training (including with help from outside forces).[23]

As noted in previous chapters, would-be insurgents face a collective action problem in starting an insurgency, though these costs may vary during the war.[24] Individuals have an incentive to let others begin the war—to "free ride" on their activities—because starting an insurgency is dangerous, time-consuming, and sometimes financially onerous. As one study concluded, "While activists might have little trouble persuading a casual acquaintance to sign a petition, they would have great difficulty convincing such a person to risk injury, death, or imprisonment."[25] The collective action problem creates an incentive for government police, military, and intelligence units to put significant pressure on potential rebels by targeting them and raising the costs of collection action. A challenge for insurgents is to rally enough supporters to join the fight, provide resources, and help start a cascade—or tip—that draws in more locals to join the insurgency.[26] The task for security forces, then, is to prevent that tip from ever occurring. Government repression can undermine insurgent recruitment by raising the costs for individuals to join insurgent organizations.[27] Still, governments need to be careful in using excessive violence, since indiscriminate targeting of civilians may increase popular resentment. Indiscriminate action involves the use of violence against individuals based on guilt by association or collective guilt, which can increase grievances and rebellion.[28] This makes it important for governments to use violence selectively, which involves targeting individuals based on a determination of guilt.[29]

There are numerous examples of states responding to potential insurgencies by strengthening security institutions and increasing the costs of collective action, from Macedonia and Singapore to Peru and Egypt. These examples are meant to be illustrative, rather than generalizable. In Peru, the National Liberation Army (ELN) failed to start an insurgency in the 1960s, in part because strengthened Peruvian security forces were effective, capturing or killing most ELN members.[30] In Egypt, Gamaa Islamiya failed to start an insurgency in the 1990s and generate sufficient popular support for an uprising. The Mubarak government, particularly its strengthened security services, crushed the group, and Gamaa Islamiya's campaign of violence alienated most supporters.[31]

Another example is in Saudi Arabia in 2002, where al Qa'ida in the Arabian Peninsula attempted to start an insurgency and which is fleshed out in some detail here. Al Qa'ida's violent campaign began in early 2003 with an operational core of some 50 people and a wider network of between 300 and 700 people who were prepared to take up arms.[32] The Saudi government poured vast resources into preventing an al Qa'ida–backed insurgency. Perhaps the most important organization was the Mubahith al-Amma, Saudi Arabia's domestic intelligence agency, in charge of domestic intelligence-gathering, analysis, counterintelligence operations, criminal investigations, and counter terrorism.

The government's security budget escalated from $8.5 billion in 2004 to $10 billion in 2005 and $12 billion in 2006.[33] Saudi security services offered competitive salaries to security personnel, constructed modern training facilities, and spent considerable sums improving their electronic and signals intelligence capabilities. These developments allowed the Mubahith to conduct a massive intelligence-collection effort that involved listening to phone calls, monitoring email and Internet traffic, recruiting sources (including al Qa'ida operatives), collecting and analyzing intelligence from raids (such as computers, notebooks, and other documents), and interrogating captured al Qa'ida operatives.[34] Several US intelligence and law enforcement agencies, led by the Central Intelligence Agency, provided assistance. British intelligence agencies, led by MI6, also provided aid.

Armed with significant intelligence, the Mubahith led a massive campaign to identify and target al Qa'ida's in-country leadership. They captured or killed a series of leaders: Abd al-Rahim al-Nashiri in November 2002, Yusuf al-Uyayri in May 2003, Hazim al-Sha'ir in April 2004, Abd al-Aziz al-Muqrin (also known as Abu Hajir al-Najdi) in June 2004, and Salih al-Alawi al-Awfi in August 2005. In a controversial step, Saudi security services also detained religious scholars who supported al Qa'ida, including the Burayda and al-Shu'aybi sheikhs. In July 2003, Saudi security forces raided a farm used by al Qa'ida and netted 21 tons of ammonium nitrate fuel oil, 530 blasting caps, 1,000 meters of detonating cord, and 75 kg of RDX-based explosives—enough matèriel to make thirty-five vehicle bombs.[35]

By 2006, the Mubahith and other Saudi security services had foiled more than two dozen attacks and killed or captured more than 260 operatives, including all but one of the twenty-six most wanted al Qa'ida leaders. In November 2007, the Saudi authorities arrested 208 suspects in six cells and thwarted several planned attacks.[36] In fact, the detention of hundreds of suspected al Qa'ida terrorists led to overcrowding prison facilities run by the Mubahith. The Saudi government also targeted charities that were funneling money to al Qa'ida through the newly established National Commission for Relief and Charity Work Abroad, cracked down on the illegal arms market by seizing weapons caches, and increased resources used to conduct airborne and other types of surveillance along the borders with Iraq and Yemen. Over time, these

arrests, killings, and other actions severely undermined al Qa'ida's capabilities by removing its most competent strategists, organizers, and
bomb-makers from the battlefield. By 2008, al Qa'ida was unable to
penetrate any serious attacks in the country.

In addition, the Saudi government ran a sophisticated information campaign that targeted the Saudi population. The Ministry of
Interior, led by Prince Nayef bin Abdulaziz Al Saud, and the Ministry
of Islamic Affairs, run by Saleh bin Abdul-Aziz Al ash-Sheikh, made
extensive use of media and clerical support to denounce al Qa'ida as
dhalla (misguided) and predisposed to kill Muslims and create disorder. They utilized several gruesome bombings to highlight the
"un-Islamic" nature of al Qa'ida. After the November 2003 Muhayya
bombing, for instance, Saudi television and newspapers showed graphic
pictures of wounded children. Saudi media also highlighted the death
of an eleven-year-old Syrian girl in the Washm bombing in April 2004.
With the regime's encouragement, leading sectors of Saudi Arabia's religious establishment—including conservative Sahwist clerics—decried
the bombings as illegitimate.[37]

The Saudi grand mufti, Sheikh Abdulaziz Al Sheikh, disparaged al
Qa'ida and issued a fatwa (religious edict) proclaiming that Saudi youth
had "become a pawn in the hands of foreign apparatuses, which are toying
with them in the name of jihad."[38] In addition, senior Wahhabi clerics
denounced Osama bin Laden and his attacks on the Saudi nation. In
March 2007, the Saudis arrested three al Qa'ida webmasters for their roles
in the online jihadist community in an attempt to weaken al Qa'ida's propaganda operations. These activities weakened al Qa'ida's efforts to garner
popular support and undermine the government's legitimacy, in part by
leveraging the Saudi population's cultural disdain for *fitna* (chaos).[39]

Finally, the regime used its vast wealth to offer exit options for militants. They contacted al Qa'ida operatives, encouraged them to defect,
and established "ports of call" for potential deserters. In mid-2004 and
mid-2006, the Saudi government declared month-long amnesties to
encourage defections. Several influential Islamists—such as Safar al-
Hawali, Muhsin al-Awaji, and Salman bin-Fahd al-Awdah—conducted
low-profile, state-supported mediation efforts with al Qa'ida.[40] When
surrenders occurred, they were highly publicized. In November and
December 2003, the Saudis showed three al Qa'ida operatives—Ali

al-Khudayr, Nasir al-Fahd, and Ahmad al-Khalidi—repenting on television. In addition, Saudi television showed three episodes of a program titled *Inside the Cell* in which captured al Qa'ida operatives spoke of how they had been lured into terrorism—and then repented. The Saudi government set up a reeducation and rehabilitation program to turn captured terrorists into peaceful citizens.[41]

In short, Saudi Arabia significantly strengthened its security institutions. Al Qa'ida in the Arabian Peninsula failed to mobilize the population, and the levels of violence never reached the threshold of an insurgency.[42] The few al Qa'ida operatives that survived resettled in Yemen.

STRATEGIES

As outlined in Chapter 3, insurgent groups can choose from several strategies, such as conventional warfare, punishment, and guerrilla warfare. Groups frequently change their strategies depending on their control of territory, performance on the battlefield, and the balance-of-power ratio with the government. Much like insurgents, counter-insurgents have a range of strategies to choose from, which are not mutually exclusive.

One example is a population-centric strategy, which focuses on winning the hearts and minds—and ultimately the security—of the local population. As the US Army and Marine Corps *Counterinsurgency Field Manual* argued, "The cornerstone of any COIN effort is security for the civilian population."[43] Counterinsurgents that adopt a population-centric strategy concentrate most of their resources on protecting and expanding key population hubs, including building the capacity of the local government.[44] There are numerous variations of population-centric strategies. Some focus more on police and intelligence units, while others concentrate on using military forces. Some governments may also request the help of foreign forces, ranging from small numbers of special operations and intelligence units to larger numbers of conventional forces. Governments may also use various levels of coercion to secure populated areas or forcibly resettle populations. One study of British counterinsurgency during the colonial years bluntly concluded, "The cornerstones of most British counter-insurgency campaigns were coercion and counter-terror, not kindness and economic development."[45]

Another example is an enemy-centric strategy, in which counterinsurgents focus on destroying insurgent groups and their support base. Unlike a population-centric strategy, counterinsurgents channel most of their resources to decimating the capability of insurgent groups, not protecting the population. This may include insurgent military forces, political networks, logistical hubs, financial resources, and other targets that make it difficult for insurgent groups to prosecute the war. The goal is to gain control of the opponent's values in a series of engagements by destroying the insurgent group's physical capacity to resist.[46]

A final example is a punishment strategy, which involves deliberately and often indiscriminately targeting—including killing—noncombatants. The goal is to decrease civilian morale by exposing large portions of the population to terror or by causing severe shortages of consumer goods and services. A decline in civilian morale, it is hoped, then produces internal turmoil, which causes grassroots opposition against insurgents. Unlike a population-centric strategy, the focus of a punishment strategy is not to gain the support of the population, but to use indiscriminate violence to force it into cooperation. Unlike an enemy-centric strategy, the goal is to punish the population.[47]

While this section does not analyze the effectiveness of counterinsurgency strategies, Chapter 3 highlights several lessons that counterinsurgents should consider when weighing options. First is to develop options that take advantage of insurgent weaknesses.[48] Some insurgent strategies make them vulnerable. In cases where weak insurgent groups (relative to the government) choose a conventional strategy, they are often exposed to better-equipped, resourced, and organized government forces. In these instances, one study concludes, counterinsurgents "should win quickly and decisively."[49] In Mali in 2013, French counterinsurgency forces took advantage of the decision by rebels led by Iyad Ag Ghali and jihadist groups to adopt a conventional strategy in the initial stages of the conflict and later in the Ifoghas Mountains. When insurgents massed their forces on the Niger Bend and headed for Bamako, they were a target for French air power and special operations forces. The insurgent's conventional strategy, which may have been sensible against poorly equipped Malian forces, allowed France's air and ground units to inflict maximum damage and ultimately defeat insurgents in Mali.[50]

Second, insurgents that adopt punishment strategies are often susceptible to counterinsurgent propaganda campaigns that undermine insurgent support. Since punishment strategies involve deliberately targeting noncombatants, the suffering these campaigns inflict on civilians can be a source of recruitment for counterinsurgent forces. Since World War II, the probability of insurgent victory was lowest when groups adopted a punishment strategy, almost certainly because it subverted their support base.[51] This may be why the Malayan Communist Party, which was eventually defeated in part because they were starved out of the jungle, put out a directive in October 1951 emphasizing that insurgent actions were undermining their support base:

> Party members are reminded that their primary duty is to expand and consolidate the organization of the masses, which is to take precedence over the purely military objective of destroying the enemy . . . To win the masses, the party must (i) stop seizing identity and ration cards; (ii) stop burning new villages and coolie lines; (iii) stop attacking post offices, reservoirs, power stations, and other public services; (iv) refrain from derailing civilian trains with high explosives; (v) stop throwing grenades and take great care when shooting running dogs found mixing with the masses to avoid stray shots from hurting the masses; and (vi) stop burning religious buildings, sanitary-trucks, Red Cross vehicles, and ambulances.[52]

Third, counterinsurgents need to find ways to interact with the local population and refrain from hunkering down on bases. Insurgent warfare involves dealing with civilians in a direct and consequential manner, creating an "identification problem."[53] Since the government does not have precise information about the allegiances of some locals, counterinsurgent forces may find it difficult to distinguish civilians that support the government or are neutral from those that support insurgents. This makes it essential to understand the local population. Mao's advice is still prescient when he noted that there is an inextricable link in insurgencies "between the people and the troops. The former may be likened to water and the latter to the fish who inhabit it."[54] This reality suggests that counterinsurgents should adapt their strategies, tactics, and even security procedures to collect intelligence, target enemies, disseminate information, and conduct other activity—yet still regularly interact with the local population.

TACTICS

Insurgent groups use an amalgam of ambushes, raids, sabotage operations, assassinations, mutilations, bombings, and other tactics, as highlighted in Chapter 4. In response, counterinsurgents should focus on taking advantage of situations where insurgents use widespread, brutal tactics against civilians that undermine local support. After all, insurgents who use indiscriminate violence often have an underlying preference for violence, which can put them at odds with their leadership.[55] Some tactics, such as suicide attacks, have often been counterproductive, in part because suicide attacks often kill civilians.

In Algeria, the government took advantage of Armed Islamic Group (GIA) indiscriminate tactics by reaching out to disaffected locals. One micro-level example was in the town of Hai Bounab, where a significant component of the population supported the GIA, including the targeting of police and home guards.[56] But the situation shifted in August 1997. "The people in Hai Bounab changed sides the day the five girls were beheaded," recalled one local. "That's when they realized that the same thing could happen to them."[57] That same month, the GIA committed a series of massacres in Rais, Beni Messous, and Bentalha that killed hundreds of civilians. The Algerian government recruited intelligence sources from the disaffected areas and, in some cases, even offered locals weapons to defend themselves. To complicate matters, the Algerian government may have used *agent provocateurs*—including government supporters dressed up as rebels—to conduct attacks and discredit the GIA.[58]

In Northern Ireland, the British government took advantage of several bombings to undermine support for the republican cause. One of the most significant opportunities occurred on August 15, 1998, when the Real IRA detonated a car bomb in Omagh, County Tyrone. It killed 29 people and injured over 200 others, the highest death toll from a single incident during the conflict. The IRA had telephoned police beforehand but gave the wrong location, and police officers inadvertently moved civilians toward the bomb. The Omagh bombing created a domestic and international uproar against the IRA, who made an uncharacteristic statement noting that "we offer our apologies to these civilians."[59] The British government responded with an aggressive campaign that involved publicizing the atrocities using television, print, and radio forums; encouraging a wide range of officials, from Church of Ireland Archbishop of Armagh Robin Earnes and Queen Elizabeth II to US President Bill Clinton and Pope John Paul II, to denounce the bombings; and encouraging Real IRA members to defect from the organization.

In Chechnya, the Russian government developed an effective campaign that painted Chechen insurgents as terrorists, particularly after the attacks at the Dubrovka Theater in October 2002, the August 2004 suicide attacks on two Russian passenger aircraft, and the elementary school in Beslan in September 2004. As Russian President Vladimir Putin remarked after the airplane attacks, "A link with destructive elements, with terrorists who are still active on the territory of Chechnya, has been confirmed again, as one of the international terrorist organizations linked with al-Qaida."[60] The Russian government campaign depicted Chechen insurgents as religiously crazed zealots, undermining domestic and international support.[61]

Counterinsurgents have several options when insurgents use brutal tactics. One is to utilize information campaigns to publicly broadcast atrocities in an effort to undermine insurgent domestic and international support, as explained in the next section. A second is to use local anger against insurgents and to recruit informants, fighters (including moving some into government police, intelligence, and military forces), and political supporters from among the disaffected population. In Iraq, for example, US and Iraqi government officials recruited disgruntled Sunnis after al Qa'ida in Iraq conducted a campaign of attacks against Sunni and Shi'a groups in provinces such as al-Anbar.[62]

Counterinsurgents have frequently developed programs to encourage defections and sow discord. During the insurgency in Oman from 1962 to 1975, for example, the government provided a cash incentive to rebels who surrendered, with a bonus if they brought their weapons. The surrendered rebels formed *firqat* units, irregular units that defended their communities from rebels and were trained by teams from the British Special Air Service.[63] In Malaya, the British were successful in establishing a rewards program for disaffected insurgents. As one analysis concluded, "The heart of the government's psychological warfare was its rewards-for-surrender program."[64] These rewards were sometimes lucrative.[65] Security for defectors was usually critical:

> Above a certain level the amount of money was often less important than the defector or informer's estimate of which side could protect him or hide him better from the other. Until the government could provide a defector or informer the protection he needed, the program got nowhere. But once it could do so—and make this clear to the insurgents—the program not only neutralized a large number of insurgents who might otherwise have continued fighting, but it also provided Special Branch with a large flow of intelligence (full cooperation with the police being the price of the reward).[66]

Third, governments can utilize unconventional-warfare tactics in areas controlled by insurgents. Unconventional warfare involves conducting campaigns by, with, or through irregular forces.[67] Key tactics range from ambushes and raids to subversion and sabotage by surrogate forces, which are designed to undermine the legitimacy of insurgents in areas they control. Since insurgency is, in part, a process of alternative state-building, successful efforts to undermine the legitimacy and governance of insurgents can undercut their popular support.

Governments have often resorted to militias and other nonstate actors as part of unconventional-warfare campaigns because they can help insurgent support and secure the population—especially in rural areas. Militias are rarely used in isolation, but rather as part of a broader civilian-military strategy and often in conjunction with national police and military forces.[68] They can sometimes be helpful. Militias can collect intelligence about insurgent groups. Because of their permanent presence in villages and interaction with the local population, militia members can tap into private information about the structure and organization of insurgent groups, logistics, support networks, collaborators, movement, and tactics and techniques.[69] In Guatemala, one of the main objectives of the Civil Self-Defense Patrols was "to inform on guerrilla sympathizers in the community."[70] They conducted surveillance of the population and reported to the military about insurgent collaboration

and activity in their villages. The Colombian government utilized militias, including the United Self-Defense Forces of Colombia, to collect information on guerrillas from the Revolutionary Armed Forces of
Colombia (FARC) and National Liberation Army (ELN) in rural areas.
These self-defense forces passed it on to state military, police, and intelligence agencies for analysis and operations.[71] They were an integral
component of the state's counterinsurgency campaign, which largely
defeated Colombian insurgents.

In Indonesia, the government relied on some 6,000 militia fighters in
Sumatra to track down guerrillas in the jungle in the 1950s. As one insurgent leader acknowledged, "being local lads they knew every creek and
path just as our people did and could guide the Javanese forces."[72] Even
after the regional rebellions had been extinguished in the 1960s, militias
remained a feature of village life. Civil defense corps, night watchmen,
and local branches of the retired servicemen's association were involved in
collecting information and hunting down thieves and unsanctioned political activists. "The techniques of militia mobilization," one assessment
of Indonesia concluded, "proved valuable for internal pacification."[73]

Militias can be particularly effective in reporting on insurgent activity when they include insurgent defectors. In Turkey, the state mobilized thousands of Kurdish peasants, many of whom had supported
the Kurdistan Worker's Party, into village militias.[74] During the Mau
Mau insurgency in Kenya, Kikuyu populated the Home Guard militia,
which grew to 14,800 full-time and 10,800 part-time guards.[75] In Iraq,
several thousand Sunnis in al-Anbar Province defected from al Qa'ida in
Iraq (AQI) and joined the police and other security forces, significantly
weakening the insurgency. These new forces had joined at the urging of
their tribal leaders in a society where tribal relationships were crucial.
In addition, enough policemen knew the individual members of AQI,
since AQI drew from the same neighborhoods and demographic pool
as the police. The police also brought substantial local intelligence with
them into the force. One US Army lieutenant observed in May 2007
that "about 10 percent of our intelligence is actionable, while 90 percent of their intelligence is actionable."[76]

In addition, militias have sometimes been effective in protecting
and governing the local population by patrolling villages, conducting offensive operations, and performing basic governance functions.

In a range of insurgencies, for instance, states have utilized militias to protect fortified villages.[77] At the heart of the Brigg's Plan during the Malayan Emergency was resettling Chinese squatters, estate workers, and villagers into compact "New Villages" and establishing surrogate Special Constabularies. While resettlement was sometimes harsh, the New Villages and local militias protected the population and were an important component in a counterinsurgency campaign that defeated Communist guerrillas by 1960.[78] As one assessment concluded,

> For the guerrilla it meant that the tide was going out; that he could no longer move among the people as the fish moves through the water; and that when he was now forced to go close inshore he not only gave away his position but ran the risk of being caught in the shallows.[79]

Some states adopted similar programs in Latin America. In Peru, the state helped establish self-defense groups in pro-government Indian villages to provide security from Shining Path guerrillas. Villagers formed *rondas campesinas* that patrolled communities and the puna grasslands, and contributed to the eventual collapse of the insurgency.[80] In Guatemala, the Civil Self-Defense Patrols helped undermine guerrilla support in rural areas and eventually contributed to the 1996 peace accords and collapse of the insurgency. A range of locals viewed the patrols as the "keeper of order and security in the village," despite their brutality against opponents.[81] Another study concluded that "one of the strengths of the counterinsurgency strategy in Guatemala was the involvement of the civil population in the armed conflict by means of the military commissioners and the Civil Self-Defence Patrol—PAC."[82]

In most effective cases, militias worked closely with state police and military forces. In the Philippines, the government used Civilian Home Defense Forces against the Maoist insurgency, which began in 1968. The government became increasingly adept at using regular army forces that conducted clear-and-search operations against New People's Army guerrillas, deployed special forces to set up patrol bases, and established Civilian Home Defense Forces to protect villages once they'd been cleared.[83] The People's Liberation Army (PLA) in China leveraged urban and rural militias during the insurgency from 1946 to 1950. The militias were involved in maintaining law and order, participating in border security in conjunction with PLA forces, and spearheading land reform. The Chinese state also used militias to establish order in later periods.[84] The Sri Lankan government effectively used militias against the Liberation Tigers of Tamil Eelam (LTTE). After his split from the LTTE in 2004, for example, Colonel Karuna created the Tamil Makkal Viduthalai Pulikal to counter the LTTE in the Eastern Province.[85]

Militias, therefore, offer a way for states to recruit local fighters, especially in areas that have been inaccessible to the government. The goal of most governments is to eliminate local support for insurgents through a combination of coercing and co-opting the local population. Militias can be helpful in gaining access to remote areas. Utilizing militias is especially tempting during an insurgency when militia forces already exist in rural areas. Still, the use of militias has sometimes come at a heavy price since some have perpetrated abuses and weakened state power.[86] In Rwanda, *Interahamwe* militia groups created and trained by Hutu extremists tended to see genocide as a "carnival romp," committing grotesque abuses.[87] In Kurdish areas of Turkey, where the government formed village militias to fight Kurdish guerrillas, one assessment noted that the village guards "do as they please under the color of law . . . Reports of rape at the hands of village guards are rising."[88] To deal with these challenges, governments need to establish tight control mechanisms that prevent militias from challenging the state and committing human rights abuses that can undermine local support.

ORGANIZATIONAL STRUCTURES

For insurgent groups, centralized organizational structures are often more effective against counterinsurgents, as outlined in Chapter 5. They can be helpful in identifying and punishing those engaged in shirking or defections. But decentralized groups are more vulnerable and many find it challenging to control territory, since lower-level cells are more likely to usurp power and resources for their own interests. They face organizational challenges accomplishing key tasks, including a principal–agent problem in managing their members. Both challenges impact their ability to achieve key tasks. Counterinsurgents should find ways to weaken centralized control and increase principal–agent problems.

First, aggressive government targeting, particularly by special operations and intelligence forces, can coerce groups to disperse and delegate in order to survive. Government pressure can force insurgent cells and members into hiding, increasing principal–agent problems because of difficulties in communication and coordination between and among insurgent cells. One effective "networked" approach was to quickly process intelligence—from phones, computers, and other sources—from captured or killed insurgents, and use it for rapid targeting. As US General Stanley A. McChrystal argued based on his experience in Afghanistan and Iraq,

> The idea was to combine analysts who found the enemy (through intelligence, surveillance, and reconnaissance); drone operators who fixed the target; combat teams who finished the target by capturing or killing him; specialists who exploited the intelligence the raid yielded, such as cell phones, maps, and detainees; and the intelligence analysts who turned this raw information into usable knowledge.[89]

Second, counterinsurgents may be able to create fissures within groups and exploit principal–agent problems. Insurgent leaders whose members include a heterogeneous mix of ethnic, tribal, religious, cultural and other constituencies may find it difficult to centralize control. They may also be vulnerable to principal–agent fissures between leaders from one constituency and lower-level members from other constituencies, which can be exploited by governments. In some cases, the inclusion of diaspora populations outside the country can increase friction when there are policy differences between diaspora supporters and insurgent leaders. In addition, insurgent groups that receive substantial benefits from natural resources or outside sponsors often encounter difficulties exerting control over their membership. Groups organized largely on the basis of economic endowments have sometimes had difficulty restraining members from committing abuses against civilians and undermining popular support, exacerbating principal–agent problems.[90]

Third, insurgencies with multiple groups may be vulnerable to divide-and-conquer campaigns that turn groups against each other or exacerbate existing fissures. In insurgencies with multiple groups, insurgent leaders can choose from several approaches. They can coordinate with other groups (including by developing an umbrella structure), compete with each other, or stovepipe operations by refraining from competing or coordinating with others. Groups that compete with each other—which occurred in such cases as Sri Lanka, Syria, Palestinian territory, Iraq, Afghanistan in the 1980s and 1990s, and Algeria—were vulnerable to exploitation by governments, as noted in Chapter 5. In fact, groups competed with each other in nearly one third of insurgencies in which there was more than one group. In these cases, counterinsurgents may be able to exacerbate fissures and sow discord among groups by spreading information or disinformation, conducting attacks that appear to come from other insurgent groups, or even providing limited assistance to some groups to encourage in-fighting.

INFORMATION CAMPAIGNS AND PROPAGANDA

Chapter 6 found that while insurgents have long used traditional media such as print, word of mouth, video, and radio, there was a shift beginning in the late 1990s to the Internet and, a decade later, social media. Insurgent groups increasingly used these forums to recruit members, communicate with each other, raise finances, conduct propaganda campaigns, and accomplish other objectives. But these developments also pose risks, since counterinsurgents with signals intelligence capabilities can better monitor their use for intelligence collection and strike operations.

The growth of social media and information technology, including cell phones, provides a range of opportunities to monitor—and counter—insurgent operations and tactics. This includes not only "defensive capabilities" such as monitoring websites, chat rooms, and social media forums like Twitter and Facebook, but also "offensive capabilities" such as targeting the cyber capabilities of insurgents and spreading information to discredit them. Governments need to keep up with insurgent use of encryption, location-masking tools, and other relevant technologies. Technological advances provide counterinsurgents the ability to improve surveillance and data mining, even with insurgent innovations. Mobile technology is a useful example since governments with signals intelligence capabilities can monitor cell and satellite phone use for intelligence collection and targeting. In Iraq, for example, the increase in cell phone use allowed US and Iraqi forces to better track insurgent movement.[91] In the Libyan war in 2011, the Libyan government utilized government and non-governmental hackers to harass bloggers and activists online, monitor them, and collect information to arrest or assassinate them. The Libyan government also periodically turned off the Internet, forcing insurgents to improvise.[92]

In Syria beginning in 2011, the Assad regime closely monitored the online activity of insurgents and used the information collected to target operatives and sympathizers. Government security services also helped establish the Syrian Electronic Army, composed mostly of informal hackers, to launch cyber attacks against insurgents and their supporters, spread false information, block websites, spam targets, and collect intelligence on insurgent activity and locations. Using denial-of-service attacks, defacement, phishing tactics, and other methods, the Syrian Electronic Army targeted political opposition groups and Western websites, including news organizations and human rights groups. It conducted cyber attacks against such news websites as the British Broadcasting Corporation, Forbes, Associated Press, Washington Post, Al Jazeera, the UK's Sunday Times, and Financial Times; companies like Truecaller (home to the world's largest online telephone directory), the video and text messaging service Tango, and free online calling and messaging company Viber; and non-governmental organizations like Human Rights Watch.[93] These attacks provided Syrian intelligence services access to the communications information of millions of individuals, both inside and outside Syria. The Syrian government also periodically shut down the Internet, as one assessment concluded:

> In its campaign to silence media coverage, the [Syrian] government disabled mobile phones, landlines, electricity, and the Internet. Authorities have routinely extracted passwords of social media sites from journalists through beatings and torture. The pro-government online group the Syrian Electronic Army has frequently hacked websites to post pro-regime material, and the government has been implicated in malware attacks targeted at those reporting on the crisis.[94]

In sum, the growing insurgent utilization of the Internet, social media, and mobile technology provides governments with a range of offensive and defensive options to use against insurgents. Governments had mixed success in taking such actions as shutting down the Internet, as illustrated in the Syrian and Libyan cases. But governments still have a range of information and cyber options to consider when waging counterinsurgency warfare.

OUTSIDE SUPPORT

Insurgents frequently seek aid from outside states and nonstate actors, as highlighted in Chapters 7 and 8. Combat support from great powers has been more likely to tip the outcome in favor of insurgents than support from other actors. In addition, lethal material can be particularly useful to insurgents, especially weapons like surface-to-air missiles and rocket-propelled grenades designed to counter a government's sophisticated capabilities. Based on these findings, governments have several options, which are not mutually exclusive.

One is the interdiction of outside aid. Governments can try to stop—or at least diminish—the amount of outside aid coming from great powers and other outside supporters. They can also try to persuade or coerce outside powers into stopping support to rebels. The goal should be to identify key routes that insurgents use to transit people and material; improve aerial, ground, and maritime surveillance; strengthen the capacity and resources of border security personnel; construct barriers where feasible, such as walls and berms; and conduct raids against infiltrators. This approach is generally easier in countries with few or no borders, especially if the borders aren't mountains or jungles. In Sri Lanka, Tamil insurgents used the southern state of Tamil Nadu in India as a sanctuary for their war against the Sri Lankan government, led by the LTTE's maritime force, the Sea Tigers. But Sri Lanka is an island, making it easier for the government to control the border.[95] Indeed, the Sri Lankan Navy conducted an effective maritime interdiction campaign against the LTTE, as highlighted in Figure 9.1. As one study concluded, a "pivotal element of the government victory was the evolution of a successful maritime interdiction strategy by the [Sri Lankan Navy], one

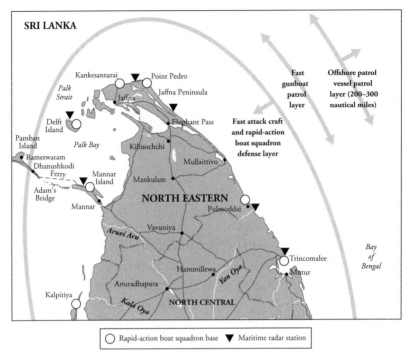

FIGURE 9.1 Sri Lanka's layered defense[110]

that degraded the insurgency's robust maritime logistical network and forced their guerrillas to confront the government's final land offensives with diminished resources."[96] Sri Lankan Navy operations reduced the LTTE's smuggling of arms and other material across Palk Strait, undermined the LTTE's sea lines of communication, and prevented escape of the top LTTE leadership.

In addition to island nations like Sri Lanka, counterinsurgents have conducted numerous border interdiction campaigns in countries with land borders. In some instances—including where there are long mountainous borders, such as along the Afghanistan–Pakistan border—governments have faced extraordinary difficulties trying to stop cross-border movement. But there have been a number of successful border interdiction campaigns. The goal is to make infiltration difficult and raise the costs of external sanctuary by forcing insurgents to navigate perilous minefields and electric fences, elude ground and aerial surveillance, and avoid killing zones. As one assessment concluded,

"Historically, barriers and pursuit forces have been used with great success to counter transnational insurgents."[97]

In Algeria, the French significantly decreased cross-border traffic along the Algerian–Tunisian border after constructing the Morice Line, as noted in Chapter 7. The Morice Line also created a "hunting preserve" where French security forces could identify and target FLN and ALN personnel.[98] The historian Alistair Horne concluded that the Morice Line was "a remarkable and sinister triumph of military technology."[99] In Western Sahara, Morocco constructed a series of berms made of earth and dotted with trenches, bunkers, fences, and land mines to monitor, deter, and interdict cross-border movement. The berm, which was built in six main stages between 1980 and 1987, totaled nearly 1,700 miles and substantially reduced Polisario insurgent activity. In Israel, the fences constructed along the Israel–Gaza, Israel–West Bank, Israel–Lebanon, and Israel–Jordan borders decreased the movement of fighters, arms, and other material. And in Greece, Tito closed Yugoslavia's border with Greece, denying Greek insurgents critical refuge and resupplies.[100]

Second, counterinsurgents can attempt to exploit principal–agent fissures between insurgents and their outside supporters. Accepting aid from foreign patrons often comes with strings attached, since outside patrons may want some degree of control or influence over the insurgent group. While states and nonstate actors are unlikely to offer resources for free, insurgents may have major reservations about the attached strings. In addition, donors can decrease aid—or even switch sides—if it suits their strategic purpose, creating potential friction with insurgents. During the insurgency in the Democratic Republic of Congo in the late 1990s, Rwanda and Uganda intervened to help Joseph Kabila overthrow President Mobutu Sese Seko. There was a year-long break in fighting when Kabila took power in the summer of 1997. But relations eventually soured because Kabila was unwilling to disarm Rwandan and Ugandan insurgents based in Congolese territory. War erupted again in 1998 when Rwanda and Uganda switched sides and backed insurgent groups *opposed* to Kabila, such as the Rally for Congolese Democracy.[101]

The local population may also view insurgents as puppets of external states or insurgent groups by relying on outsiders for assistance, which can be exploited by government forces.[102] Insurgent groups that have a leadership structure outside of the country may lose legitimacy by being perceived as out of touch with those inside the country. Unlike insurgent groups that rely on the local population for resources and hide among their constituents inside the country, groups with external bases and patrons may be less sensitive to the demands of locals or the costs they bear.[103]

A third option is for the government to secure their own outside support, particularly from great powers. Chapter 8 found that outside aid to governments from great powers decreased the probability of insurgent victory. Governments can acquire assistance from great powers, which have access to more resources than other actors in such areas as services (combat support, sanctuary, and training) and goods (money, lethal material, and non-lethal material). Yet outside powers should think carefully before deploying large numbers of conventional forces overseas to conduct counterinsurgency. While outside conventional forces in Iraq and Afghanistan achieved some of their military objectives, the deployment of large numbers of foreign forces also had the unintended consequence of contributing to a new generation of terrorists.

In Iraq, for instance, the large US military presence and such actions as the Abu Ghraib scandal contributed to radicalization. Television images aired daily by Al Jazeera and other channels, which showed suffering Iraqis and Abu Ghraib photos, enraged the Arab street. Public opinion polls reflected deepening anti-Americanism across the Arab world. The percentage of Jordanians who had an unfavorable view of the United States went from 75 percent in the summer of 2002 to 99 percent in May 2003. Unfavorable ratings of the United States jumped from 69 percent to 81 percent in Pakistan, 55 percent to 83 percent in Turkey, and 59 percent to 71 percent in Lebanon over the same time period.[104] Many of the terrorists involved in serious US homeland plots after September 11, 2001—from Major Nidal Hasan, who orchestrated the 2009 mass shooting at Fort Hood, Texas, to Najibullah Zazi, who was arrested in 2009 for plotting suicide attacks in the New York City subway—were motivated, in part, by the deployment of large numbers of US combat troops in Muslim countries and by a conviction, however misplaced, that Muslims were its helpless victims.[105]

Instead of large numbers of outside conventional forces, national and local forces may be more knowledgeable about terrain and more legitimate among the local population. In Iraq, for example, part of the success against insurgents in al-Anbar and other provinces in the mid-2000s was the US military and intelligence community's effective leveraging of tribal leaders and their support networks.[106] In some cases, a better option may be an indirect approach that focuses on small numbers of special operations forces and intelligence units to train, advise, and assist local regular and irregular forces, along with targeted strikes from ground, air, and even sea-based platforms.

POSTMORTEM

Despite Western anxiety about participating in insurgencies and counterinsurgencies, both are a reality of international politics. As John Nagl acknowledged about the post-Vietnam era, American policymakers "decided that the United States should no longer involve itself in counterinsurgency operations."[107] Unfortunately, states and nonstate actors don't have that luxury. Insurgency and counterinsurgency will remain alive and well for the foreseeable future. The challenge, then, is to better understand this type of warfare: what causes insurgencies, how to organize insurgencies and counterinsurgencies, what strategies and tactics to use, how to utilize information operations and propaganda, how to secure outside support, and how insurgencies end. After all, the insurgent allure of trying to create a better world is tempting, as one Sandinista poem in Nicaragua noted:

> One day I put it to all of you:
> Let's fight together for a better world.
> You agreed,
> And from that day on,
> We were brothers.[108]

The world does not lack utopian Che Guevaras that dream about starting insurgencies, as the Sandinista poem above illustrates, even against all odds. What it often lacks, however, is a group of followers willing and able to take the required risks.[109]

Appendix A

Case Study List

Case no.	Case name	Government	Insurgent group(s)	End goal	Outcome
1	Afghan Mujahideen–Soviet War of 1978–1992	Afghanistan	Islamic Unity of Afghan Mujahideen (Pak-based Sunni alliance) Hezbi-Islami (Hekmatyar) Jamiati-Islami (Rabbani) Hezbi-Islami (Khalis) Ittehadi-Islami (Sayyaf) Harkati-Inqilabi-Islami (Nabi) Mahazi-Milli-Islami (Gailani) Jabhai-Nijati-Milli-Afghanistan (Mojaddedi) Harakati-Islami (Mohseni) Hezb-i-Wahdat (Iran-based Shia alliance) Khalqi military faction Dostum military faction	Overthrow incumbent regime	Insurgent victory
2	Afghan–Taliban War of 1992–1996	Afghanistan	Taliban (Omar) Hezbi-Islami (Hekmatyar) Junbish-I Milli-yi Islami (Dostum) Hizbi-Wahdat (Khalili)	Overthrow incumbent regime	Insurgent victory
3	Afghan–Northern Alliance War of 1996–2001	Afghanistan	United Islamic Front for the Salvation of Afghanistan (UIFSA) Jamiati-Islami (Rabbani, Massoud) Junbish-I Milli-yi Islami (Dostum) Hizbi-Wahdat (Kahlili)	Overthrow incumbent regime	Insurgent victory

#	War	Country	Insurgent groups	Aim	Outcome
4	Afghan–Taliban War of 2001–present	Afghanistan	Taliban Hezbi-i-Islami Haqqani Network	Overthrow incumbent regime	Ongoing
5	Algerian Independence War of 1954–1962	Algeria	National Liberation Front (FLN) Algerian National Movement (MNA)	Create new, independent state (from colonial authority)	Insurgent victory
6	Algerian Islamists War of 1991–present	Algeria	Armed Islamic Group (GIA) Armed Islamic Movement (MIA) Islamic Salvation Front (FIS) Islamic Salvation Army (AIS) Takfir wa'l Hijra (Exile & Redemption) Salafist Group for Preaching and Combat (GSPC) Al Qa'ida in the Islamic Maghreb (AQIM)	Overthrow incumbent regime	Ongoing
7	Angolan Independence War of 1961–1974	Angola	Popular Movement for the Liberation of Angola (MPLA) National Union for the Total Independence of Angola (UNITA) National Front for the Liberation of Angola (FNLA)	Create new, independent state (from colonial authority)	Insurgent victory

(continued)

Case no.	Case name	Government	Insurgent group(s)	End goal	Outcome
8	Angolan War of 1975–2002	Angola	National Union for the Total Independence of Angola (UNITA) National Front for the Liberation of Angola (FNLA)	Overthrow incumbent regime	Draw
9	Cabinda Independence War of 1975–2009	Angola	Liberation Front of the Cabinda Enclave (FLEC) Liberation Front of the Cabinda Enclave-Renewed (FLEC-R) Liberation Front of the Cabinda Enclave-Armed Forces of Cabinda (FLEC-FAC) Liberation Front of the Cabinda Enclave-Military Position (FLEC-PM)	Create new, independent state (from sovereign nation)	Draw
10	Argentine Military War of 1955	Argentina	Military faction (Doucet)	Overthrow incumbent regime	Insurgent victory
11	Argentine Leftists War of 1973–1979	Argentina	Revolutionary Worker's Party (ERP) Monteneros Peronist Movement (Monteneros)	Overthrow incumbent regime	Government victory
12	Nagorno–Karabakh Independence War of 1991–1994	Azerbaijan	Republic of Nagorno-Karabakh	Create new, independent state (from sovereign nation)	Draw

13	Chittagong Hill Tracts Independence War of 1975–1997	Bangladesh	Jana Sanghati Samiti/Shanti Bahini (JSS/SB)	Create new, independent state (from sovereign nation)	Draw
14	Bolivian War of 1946	Bolivia	Popular Revolutionary Movement	Overthrow incumbent regime	Insurgent victory
15	Bolivian Leftists War of 1952	Bolivia	Nationalist Revolutionary Movement (MNR)	Overthrow incumbent regime	Insurgent victory
16	Bosnian–Serb Independence War of 1992–1995	Bosnia-Herzegovina	Serbian Republic of Bosnia-Herzegovina (Srpska) Croatian Republic of Bosnia-Herzegovina (HVO) Serbian irregulars Croatian irregulars	Create new, independent state (from sovereign nation)	Government victory
17	Burundi Hutu War of 1965–1972	Burundi	Hutu ethnic majority	Overthrow incumbent regime	Government victory
18	Burundi Hutu War of 1991–2008	Burundi	Party for the Liberation of the Hutu People (Palipehutu) Natonal Council for the Defence of Democracy (CNDD) National Liberation Front (FROLINA) Party for the Liberation of the Hutu People-Forces for National Liberation (Palipehutu-FNL) National Council for the Defense of Democracy–Forces for the Defense of Democracy (CNDD-FDD)	Overthrow incumbent regime	Draw

(*continued*)

Case no.	Case name	Government	Insurgent group(s)	End goal	Outcome
19	Cambodian War of 1970–1975	Cambodia	Khmer Rouge (KR) Sihanouk Royalists National United Front of Kampuchea (FUNK)	Overthrow incumbent regime	Insurgent victory
20	Cambodian War of 1978–1979	Cambodia	Kampuchean National United Front for National Salvation (KNUFNS)	Overthrow incumbent regime	Insurgent victory
21	Cambodian War of 1979–1998	Cambodia	Khmer Rouge (KR) National United Front for an Independent, Neutral, Peaceful, and Cooperative Cambodia (FUNCINPEC) Khmer People's National Liberation Front (KPNLF) Coalition Government of Democratic Kampuchea (CGDK)	Overthrow incumbent regime	Draw
22	Cameroon Independence War of 1957–1961	Cameroon	Union of the Populations of Cameroon (UPC)	Create new, independent state (from colonial authority)	Insurgent victory

23	Central African Republic War of 1996–1997	Central African Republic	Military faction of Cyriac Souke	Overthrow incumbent regime	Government victory
24	Central African Republic War of 2006–present	Central African Republic	Seleka (coalition group) Convention of Patriots for Justice and Peace (CPJP) Convention of Patriots of Salvation and Kodro (CPSK) Union of Democratic Forces for Unity (UFDR) Democratic Front of the Central African People (FDPC) Alliance for Revival and Rebuilding (A2R) Anti-Balaka militias (Christians) Peul militias Revolution Justice	Overthrow incumbent regime	Ongoing
25	Chad War of 1966–1972	Chad	National Liberation Front of Chad (FROLINAT) First Liberation Army Second Liberation Army	Overthrow incumbent regime	Draw
26	Chad War of 1976–1982	Chad	Forces Armees du Nord (FAN)	Overthrow incumbent regime	Insurgent victory
27	Chad War of 1983–1990	Chad	Mouvement Patriotique du Salut (MPS) Mouvement Pour la Salvation Nationale Tchadienne (MOSANAT) Revolutionary Forces of 1 April Islamic Legion Transitional Government of National Unity (GUNT)	Overthrow incumbent regime	Insurgent victory

(continued)

Case no.	Case name	Government	Insurgent group(s)	End goal	Outcome
28	Chad War of 1991–2010	Chad	Mouvement Pour La Democratie et le Development (MDD) Comite National de Redressement (CNR) Conseil de Salut National Pour la Paix et la Democratie (CSNPD) Front National Tchadien (FNT) Forces Armees Pour la Republique Federale (FARF) Mouvement Pour la Democratie et la Justice au Tchad (MJDT) Front Unique Pour la Changement Democratique (FUCD) Forces et le Developpement (UFDD) Rassemblement des Forces Democratiques (RAFD) Alliance National (AN) Union des Forces de Resistance (UFR)	Overthrow incumbent regime	Draw
29	Chilean War of 1973	Chile	Military faction of Augusto Pinochet	Overthrow incumbent regime	Insurgent victory
30	Sino–Communist War of 1946–1949	China	People's Liberation Army (PLA)	Overthrow incumbent regime	Insurgent victory

31	Formosan War of 1947	China	Taiwanese insurgents	Create new, independent state (from sovereign nation)	Government victory
32	Sino–Nationalists War of 1949–1958	China	Kuomintang (KMT)	Overthrow incumbent regime	Government victory
33	Tibetan Independence War of 1950–1951	China	Tibet (Khampas)	Create new, independent state (from sovereign nation)	Government victory
34	Tibetan Independence War of 1956–1959	China	Tibet (Khampas)	Create new, independent state (from sovereign nation)	Government victory
35	Xinjiang Independence War of 1991–present	China	Turkestan Islamic Movement (TIM)	Create new, independent state (from sovereign nation)	Ongoing
36	Colombian "La Violencia" War of 1948–1962	Colombia	"La Violencia" (including numerous nonstate armed groups: local conservative and liberal party organizations, as well as socialists, bandits, peasant organizations, and private armies of large landowners)	Overthrow incumbent regime	Draw

(continued)

Case no.	Case name	Government	Insurgent group(s)	End goal	Outcome
37	Colombian War of 1963–present	Colombia	Revolutionary Armed Forces of Colombia (FARC) National Liberation Army (ELN) April 19 Movement (M-19) Popular Liberation Army (EPL)	Overthrow incumbent regime	Ongoing
38	Congo–Brazzaville War of 1993–1997	Congo	Cobras Ninjas	Overthrow incumbent regime	Insurgent victory
39	Congo–Brazzaville War of 1997–2002	Congo	Cocoyes Ninjas Ntsilouolous	Overthrow incumbent regime	Draw
40	Katanga Independence War of 1960–1962	Congo, Dem. Rep. (Zaire)	State of Katanga	Create new, independent state (from sovereign nation)	Government victory
41	South Kasai Independence War of 1960–1962	Congo, Dem. Rep. (Zaire)	Independent Mining State of South Kasai	Create new, independent state (from sovereign nation)	Government victory
42	Zaire Simba War of 1964–1965	Congo, Dem. Rep. (Zaire)	National Liberation Council (CNL, or Simbas)	Overthrow incumbent regime	Government victory

	War	Country	Combatants	Aim	Outcome
43	Zaire Shaba War of 1977–1978	Congo, Dem. Rep. (Zaire)	Congolese National Liberation Front (FLNC)	Overthrow incumbent regime	Government victory
44	Zaire War of 1996–1997	Congo, Dem. Rep. (Zaire)	Alliance of Democratic Forces for Liberation of Congo (AFDL)	Overthrow incumbent regime	Insurgent victory
45	DRC War of 1998–2001	Congo, Dem. Rep.	Congolese Liberation Movement (MLC) Congelese Rally for Democracy (RCD) RCD-Liberation Movement (RCD-ML)	Overthrow incumbent regime	Draw
46	DRC War of 2006–present	Congo, Dem. Rep.	Mouvement du 23 Mars (M23) Alliance of Patriots for a Free and Sovereign Congo (APCLS) National Congress for the Defence of the People (CNDP)	Overthrow incumbent regime	Ongoing
47	Costa Rican War of 1948	Costa Rica	National Liberation Army (NLA)	Overthrow incumbent regime	Insurgent victory
48	Cote d'Ivoire Military War of 2002–2004	Cote d'Ivoire	Patriotic Movement of Ivory Coast (MPCI) Ivorian Movement for the Greater West (MPIGO) Movement for Justice and Peace (MJP) Forces Republicaines de Cote d'Ivoire (FRCI)	Overthrow incumbent regime	Draw
49	Croatian–Serb Independence War of 1992–1995	Croatia	Serbian Republic of Krajina (Croatian Serb army) Serbian irregulars	Create new, independent state (from sovereign nation)	Government victory

(*continued*)

Case no.	Case name	Government	Insurgent group(s)	End goal	Outcome
50	Cuban Revolution of 1953–1958	Cuba	26 July Movement (M26J)	Overthrow incumbent regime	Insurgent victory
51	Turco–Cypriot War of 1974	Cyprus	Turkish Cypriots	Overthrow incumbent regime	Draw
52	Djibouti War of 1991–1994	Djibouti	Front for the Restoration of Unity and Democracy (FRUD)	Overthrow incumbent regime	Draw
53	Dominican Republic War of 1965	Dominican Rep.	Constitutionalists (leftist faction of military officers) Dominican Revolutionary Party (PRD)	Overthrow incumbent regime	Government victory
54	Egyptian Islamists War of 1992–1998	Egypt	Al-Gama'a al-Islamiyya (the Islamic Group)	Overthrow incumbent regime	Government victory
55	Egyptian Islamists War of 2013–present	Egypt	Sinai Province of the Islamic State (IS) Muslim Brotherhood Mujahideen Shura Council in the Environs of Jerusalem (MSC) Al Qa'ida in the Sinai Peninsula, aka Ansar al Jihad Akfir wal-Hijra, aka At-Takfir Wal-Hijra Jund al Sharia Ansar al-Shariah—Egypt Ansar Bayt al-Maqdis Brigades of Lone Wolves Ajnad Misr Jund al Khilafah Kinana	Overthrow incumbent regime	Ongoing

56	El Salvador War of 1979–1991	El Salvador	Farabundo Marti Front for National Liberation (FMLN) People's Revolutionary Army (ERP) Farabundo Marti Liberation Forces (FPL) Armed Forces of National Resistance (FARN) Salvadoran Communist Party (PCS)	Overthrow incumbent regime	Draw
57	Eritrean Independence War of 1964–1991	Ethiopia	Eritrean Liberation Front (ELF) Eritrean People's Liberation Front (EPLF)	Create new, independent state (from sovereign nation)	Insurgent victory
58	Afar Independence War of 1975–1991	Ethiopia	Afar Liberation Movement (ALF)	Create new, independent state (from sovereign nation)	Draw
59	Ethiopian War of 1976–1991	Ethiopia	Ethiopian People's Revolutionary Democratic Front (EPRDF) Tigray People's Liberation Front (TPLF) Ethiopia People's Revolutionary Party (EPRP) Ethiopia Democratic Union (EDU) Ethiopian People's Democratic Movement (EPDM)	Overthrow incumbent regime	Insurgent victory

(continued)

Case no.	Case name	Government	Insurgent group(s)	End goal	Outcome
60	Ogaden Independence War of 1976–present	Ethiopia	Ogaden National Liberation Front (ONLF) Ogaden National Liberation Army (ONLA) Western Somali Liberation Front (WSLF) Al-Itahad Al-Islami (AIAI)	Create new, independent state (from sovereign nation)	Ongoing
61	Oromo Independence War of 1977–present	Ethiopia	Oromo Liberation Front (OLF)	Create new, independent state (from sovereign nation)	Ongoing
62	South Ossentian Independence War of 1991–1992	Georgia	Republic of South Ossetia	Create new, independent state (from sovereign nation)	Draw
63	Abkhazian Independence War of 1992–1993	Georgia	Republic of Abkahzia	Create new, independent state (from sovereign nation)	Draw

#	War	Country	Insurgent organization	War aim	Outcome
64	Greek Leftists War of 1946–1949	Greece	Democratic Army of Greece (DSE)	Overthrow incumbent regime	Government victory
65	Guatemalan War of 1965–1995	Guatemala	Rebel Armed Forces I (FAR I) Rebel Armed Forces II (FAR II) Guerilla Army of the Poor (EGP) Guatemalan Worker's Party (PGT) Revolutionary Movement November 13 (MR-13) Edgar Ibarra Guerrilla Front (FGEI) Guatemalan National Revolutionary Unity (URNG) Organization of the People in Arms (ORPA)	Overthrow incumbent regime	Draw
66	Guinean War of 2000–2001	Guinea	Rally Democratic Forces of Guinea (RDFG)	Overthrow incumbent regime	Government victory
67	Guinean Independence War of 1962–1974	Guinea Bissau	African Party for the Independence of Guinea and Cape Verde (PAIGC)	Create new, independent state (from colonial authority)	Insurgent victory
68	Guinea-Bissau Military War of 1998–1999	Guinea Bissau	Military Junta for Consolidation of Democracy, Peace, and Justice (MJCDPJ)	Overthrow incumbent regime	Insurgent victory
69	Haitian Democratic War of 1991–1994	Haiti	Supporters of President Jean-Bertrand Aristide's Lavalas Political Organization (OPL)	Overthrow incumbent regime	Insurgent victory

(continued)

Case no.	Case name	Government	Insurgent group(s)	End goal	Outcome
70	Nagaland Independence War of 1956–present	India	Naga Nationalist Council (NCC) National Socialist Council of Nagaland (NSCN) National Socialist Council of Nagaland—Isaac Mulvah (NSCN-IM) National Socialist Council of Nagaland—Khaplang (NSCN-K) National Socialist Council of Nagaland—Khloe-Kitovi faction (NSCN-K-K)	Create new, independent state (from sovereign nation)	Ongoing
71	Indian Naxalite/ Leftist War of 1967–present	India	Communist Party of India-Marxist-Leninist (CPI-ML) Maoist Communist Center (MCC) People's War Group (PWG) Communist Party of India-Maoist (CPI-M)	Overthrow incumbent regime	Ongoing
72	Tripura Independence War of 1978–2006	India	Tripura National Volunteers (TNV) All Tripura Tribal Front (ATTF) National Liberation Front of Tripura (NLFT)	Create new, independent state (from sovereign nation)	Draw
73	Punjabi Sikh Independence War of 1982–1993	India	Sikh insurgents	Create new, independent state (from sovereign nation)	Government victory

74	Manipur Independence War of 1982–present	India	United National Liberation Front (UNLF) People's Revolutionary Party of Kangleipak (PREPAK) Revolutionary People's Front Manipur (RPF) People's Liberation Army (PLA) Kangleipak Communist Party (KCP)	Create new, independent state (from sovereign nation)	Ongoing
75	Bodoland Independence War of 1989–present	India	All Bodo Student Union (ABSU) National Democratic Front for Bodoland (NDFB) NDFB-S NDFB-RD	Create new, independent state (from sovereign nation)	Ongoing
76	Kashmiri Independence War of 1989–present	India	Kashmiri Insurgents (collective) United Jihad Council (UJC) Hizbul-ul-Mujahideen (HM) Lashkar-e-Tayyiba (LeT) Jaish-e-Mohammed (JeM) Harakat-ul-Mujahideen (HuM) Jammu and Kashmir Liberation Front (JKLF) Al-Badhr Tehrik-e-Jihad (TeJ) Tehrik-ul-Muhadiheen (TuM) Jamait-ul-Mujahideen (JuM) Al Jihad Force Al Umar Mujahideen Muslim Janbaz Force	Create new, independent state (from sovereign nation)	Ongoing

(continued)

Case no.	Case name	Government	Insurgent group(s)	End goal	Outcome
77	Assamese Independence War of 1990–present	India	United Liberation Front of Assam (ULFA)	Create new, independent state (from sovereign nation)	Ongoing
78	Indonesian Independence War of 1946–1949	Indonesia	Indonesian People's Army	Create new, independent state (from colonial authority)	Insurgent victory
79	South Moluccas Independence War of 1950	Indonesia	Republic of South Moluccas (RSM)	Create new, independent state (from sovereign nation)	Government victory
80	Sumatra Independence War of 1953–1961	Indonesia	Revolutionary Government of the Republic of Indonesia (PRRI) House of Islam (Darul Islam) Universal Struggle Charter (Permesta)	Create new, independent state (from sovereign nation)	Government victory

	War	Country	Organization	Goal	Outcome
81	West Papuan Independence War of 1965–1984	Indonesia	Organization for a Free Papua (OPM)	Create new, independent state (from sovereign nation)	Draw
82	East Timorese Independence War of 1975–1999	Indonesia	Revolutionary Front for an Independent East Timor (FRETLIN)	Create new, independent state (from sovereign nation)	Draw
83	Acehnese Independence War of 1990–2005	Indonesia	Free Aceh Movement (GAM)	Create new, independent state (from sovereign nation)	Draw
84	Iranian Islamist War of 1978–1979	Iran	Faction of Ayatollah Khomeini	Overthrow incumbent regime	Insurgent victory
85	Iranian Kurdish Independence War of 1979–1996	Iran	Kurdish Democratic Party of Iran (KDPI)	Create new, independent state (from sovereign nation)	Draw
86	Iranian Anti-Khomeini War of 1979–2001	Iran	Mujahideen e Khalq (MEK)	Overthrow incumbent regime	Government victory

(continued)

Case no.	Case name	Government	Insurgent group(s)	End goal	Outcome
87	Iraqi Kurdish Independence War of 1961–1996	Iraq	Kurdish Democatic Party of Iraq (KDP) Patriotic Union of Kurdistan (PUK)	Create new, independent state (from sovereign nation)	Government victory
88	Iraqi Shia War of 1982–1996	Iraq	Supreme Council for the Islamic Revolution in Iraq (SCIRI)	Overthrow incumbent regime	Draw
89	Iraq War of 2003–present	Iraq	Al Qa'ida in Iraq (AQI, ISI, ISIL, ISIS, IS, Da'ish) Soldiers of Islam (Ansar al-Islam/Ansar al-Sunna) Al-Mahdi Army Islamic Army of Iraq (IAI) 1920 Revolution Brigades Jaysh Rijal al-Tariqa al-Naqshbandia (JRTN) Reformation and Jihad Front (RJF) Army of Ansar Al Sunna (JAAS) Organization of Jihad's Base in the Country of Two Rivers (TQJBR) Mujahideen Consultative Council in Iraq (MSC)	Overthrow incumbent regime	Ongoing
90	Occupied Territory Conflict of 1987–present	Israel	Fatah/Palestinian Liberation Organization (PLO) Palestinian National Authority (PNA) Islamic Resistance Movement (HAMAS) Palestinian Islamic Jihad (PIJ) Al Aqsa Martyrs Brigade (AMB)	Create new, independent state (from sovereign nation)	Ongoing

91	Jordanian Palestinian "Black September" War of 1970–1971	Jordan	Palestinian Liberation Organization (PLO)	Overthrow incumbent regime	Government victory
92	Mau Mau Independence War of 1952–1956	Kenya	Kenya Land and Freedom Army (KFLA), or Mau Mau	Create new, independent state (from colonial authority)	Government victory
93	Cheju Independence War of 1948–1950	Korea, South	South Korean Workers' Party Faction of Rhee's military leaders (defected)	Create new, independent state (from sovereign nation)	Government victory
94	Laotian Leftists War of 1959–1973	Laos	Pathet Lao	Overthrow incumbent regime	Insurgent victory
95	Lebanese Nasserite War of 1958	Lebanon	Independent Nasserite Movement (al-Mourabitoun)	Create new, independent state (from sovereign nation)	Government victory
96	Lebanese War of 1975–1990	Lebanon	Lebanese National Movement (LNM) Lebanese Arab Army (LAA) National Union Front (NUF) Palestinian Liberation Organization (PLO) Hezbollah Military Faction of General Aoun Amal Militias	Overthrow incumbent regime	Government victory

(continued)

Case no.	Case name	Government	Insurgent group(s)	End goal	Outcome
97	Liberian War of 1989–1995	Liberia	National Patriotic Front of Liberia (NPFL) Independent National Patriotic Front of Liberia (INPFL)	Overthrow incumbent regime	Insurgent victory
98	Liberian War of 2000–2003	Liberia	Liberians United for Reconciliation and Democracy (LURD) Movement for Democracy in Liberia (MODEL)	Overthrow incumbent regime	Insurgent victory
99	Libyan War of 2011	Libya	National Transitional Council (NTC) Fractious militias	Overthrow incumbent regime	Insurgent victory
100	Libyan Islamists War of 2014–present	Libya	Tripoli Province of the Islamic State (IS) Ansar al-Sharia—Libya Katibat al Muqaoon bil duma Zintan Brigades Libyan Liberation Front (LLF) in Sahel Imprisoned Omar Abdul Rahman Brigades, linked to al Qaʾida Prisoner Omar Abdelrahman Group Rafallah Sahati Islamist Militia Operations Cell of Libyan Revolutionaries Libya Safety and Stability Force Al-Qaqaa Brigade Sumood Front	Overthrow incumbent regime	Ongoing

			Libya Dawn Coalition (Majlis al-Shura, Third Force of the Central Shield, Fajr Libya militia) Tripoli Revolutionary Brigade Islamic Youth Shura Council Shura Mujahidin Council (SMC) The Benghazi Revolutionary Shura February 17 Martyrs Brigade		
101	Madagascar Independence War of 1947	Madagascar	Democratic Movement for Malagasy Renewal (MDRM)	Create new, independent state (from colonial authority)	Government victory
102	Malayan Independence War of 1948–1957	Malaya	Communist Party of Malaya (CPM)	Create new, independent state (from colonial authority)	Government victory

(continued)

Case no.	Case name	Government	Insurgent group(s)	End goal	Outcome
103	Tuareg–Arab War of 1990–1994	Mali	Mouvement Populaire de Liberation de l'Azaouad (MPLA) Azawad People's Movement (MPA) Islamic Arab Front of Azawad (FIAA) Popular Liberation Front of Azawad (FPLA) Azawad Liberation Revolutionary Army (ARLA)	Create new, independent state (from sovereign nation)	Draw
104	Mali Islamists War of 2012–present	Mali	Al Qa'ida in the Islamic Maghreb (AQIM) Movement for Unity and Jihad in West Africa (MUJAO) Al-Mourabitoun Ansar Dine Signed in Blood Battalion	Create new, independent state (from sovereign nation)	Ongoing
105	Dniestr Independence War of 1992	Moldova	Dniestr Republic	Create new, independent state (from sovereign nation)	Draw
106	Moroccan Independence War of 1953–1956	Morocco	Istiqlal	Create new, independent state (from colonial authority)	Insurgent victory

	War	Country	Insurgent organization(s)	Insurgent aim	Outcome
107	Western Sahara Independence War of 1975–1989	Morocco	Popular Front for the Liberation of Saguia el-Hamra and Rio de Oro (POLISARIO)	Create new, independent state (from sovereign nation)	Government victory
108	Mozambique Independence War of 1964–1974	Mozambique	Front for the Liberation of Mozambique (FRELIMO)	Create new, independent state (from colonial authority)	Insurgent victory
109	Mozambique War of 1977–1992	Mozambique	Mozambican National Resistance (RENAMO)	Overthrow incumbent regime	Draw
110	Burmese Leftist War of 1948–1988	Myanmar (Burma)	Communist Party of Burma (CPB); Communist Party of Burma–Red Flag (CPB-RF); Communist Party of Burma–White Flag (CPB-WF); People's Volunteers Organization (PVO)	Overthrow incumbent regime	Government victory
111	Arakan Independence War of 1948–1994	Myanmar (Burma)	Arakan Liberation Party (ALP); Rohingya Patriotic Front (RPF); Arakan Rohingya Islamic Front (ARIF); Rohingya Solidarity Organization (RSO); Arakan National Liberation Party (ANLP); Communist Party of Arakan (CPA); Arakan People's Liberation Party (APLP)	Create new, independent state (from sovereign nation)	Draw

(continued)

Case no.	Case name	Government	Insurgent group(s)	End goal	Outcome
112	Mon Independence War of 1949–1963	Myanmar (Burma)	New Mon State Party (NMSP) Mon Freedom League-Mon United Front (MFL–MUF) Mon People's Front (MPF)	Create new, independent state (from sovereign nation)	Draw
113	Karen Independence War of 1948–present	Myanmar (Burma)	Karen National Union (KNU) Karen National United Party (KNUP) Democratic Karen Buddhist Army (DKBA)	Create new, independent state (from sovereign nation)	Ongoing
114	Shan Independence War of 1959–present	Myanmar (Burma)	Young Warriors (NSH) Shan State Independence Army (SSIA) Shan National United Front (SNUF) Kokang Resistance Force (KRF) Shan State Army (SSA) Shan United Revolutionary Army (SURA) Shan State Nationalities Liberation Organization (SSNLO) Shan United Army (SUA) Mong Tai Army (MTA) Restoration Council of Shan States (RCSS, or SSA-S) Shan State Progress Party (SSPP)	Create new, independent state (from sovereign nation)	Ongoing

115	Kachin Independence War of 1961–1992	Myanmar (Burma)	Kachin Independence Organization/Kachin Independence Army (KIO/KIA)	Create new, independent state (from sovereign nation)	Draw
116	Kachin Independence War of 2011–present	Myanmar (Burma)	Kachin Independence Organization/Kachin Independence Army (KIO/KIA)	Create new, independent state (from sovereign nation)	Ongoing
117	Nepal Maoist War of 1996–2006	Nepal	Communist Party of Nepal—Maoist (CPN-M)	Overthrow incumbent regime	Draw
118	Nicaraguan Sandinista War of 1978–1979	Nicaragua	Sandinista National Liberation Front (FSLN)	Overthrow incumbent regime	Insurgent victory
119	Nicaraguan Contra War of 1982–1990	Nicaragua	Nicaraguan Democratic Forces (Contras/FDN)	Overthrow incumbent regime	Draw
120	Biafra Independence War of 1967–1970	Nigeria	Republic of Biafra	Create new, independent state (from sovereign nation)	Government victory

(continued)

Case no.	Case name	Government	Insurgent group(s)	End goal	Outcome
121	Nigerian Islamists War of 2009–present	Nigeria	Jama'atu Ahlis Sunna Lidda'awati wal-Jihad (Boko Haram) Jama'atu Ansarul Musilimina fi Biladi Sudan (Ansaru)	Overthrow incumbent regime	Ongoing
122	Dhofar Independence War of 1972–1975	Oman	Popular Front for the Liberation of Oman (PFLO)	Overthrow incumbent regime	Government victory
123	Bengali Independence War of 1971	Pakistan	Mukti Bahini (Liberation Force)	Create new, independent state (from sovereign nation)	Insurgent victory
124	Baluchi Independence War of 1973–1977	Pakistan	Baluchi Nationalist Factions, including: Baluch Liberation Front (BLF) Khair Bakhsh Marri (Marri tribal chief) Ataullah Mengal (Mengal tribal chief and deposed Chief Minister) Ghaus Bakhsh Bizenjo (Bizenjo tribal chief and deposed Governor of Baluchistan)	Create new, independent state (from sovereign nation)	Government victory
125	Mohajir Independence War of 1994–1996	Pakistan	Mohajir Quami Movement (MQM)	Create new, independent state (from sovereign nation)	Government victory

126	Baluchi Independence War of 2004–present	Pakistan	Balochistan Liberation Army (BLA) Balochistan Republican Army (BRA) Baloch Ittihad (Baloch Unity) Baluch Liberation Front (BLF) Lashkar-e-Balochistan (LeB)	Create new, independent state (from sovereign nation)	Ongoing
127	Pakistani Islamists War of 2007–present	Pakistan	Tehreek-e-Taliban Pakistan (TTP) Movement for the Enforcement of Islamic Laws (TNSM) Lashkar-e-Islam (LI) Al Qaʾida (core)	Overthrow incumbent regime	Ongoing
128	Bougainville Independence War of 1989–2001	Papua New Guinea	Bougainville Revolutionary Army (BRA)	Create new, independent state (from sovereign nation)	Draw
129	Paraguayan Barefoot Revolution of 1947	Paraguay	Feberista Revolutionary Concentration Liberal Party Paraguayan Communist Party	Overthrow incumbent regime	Government victory
130	Peruvian Shining Path War of 1982–1999	Peru	Shining Path (Sendero Luminoso, SL) Tupac Amaru Revolutionary Movement (MRTA)	Overthrow incumbent regime	Government victory

(*continued*)

Case no.	Case name	Government	Insurgent group(s)	End goal	Outcome
131	Philippine Hukbalahap War of 1946–1954	Philippines	Hukbalahap (HUK)	Overthrow incumbent regime	Government victory
132	Philippine Communist War of 1969–present	Philippines	Communist Party of the Philippines (CPP)	Overthrow incumbent regime	Ongoing
133	Mindanao War of 1970–present	Philippines	Moro National Liberation Front (MNLF) Moro Islamic Liberation Front (MILF) Mindanao Independence Movement (MIM) Abu Sayyaf Group (ASG) Bangsamoro Islamic Freedom Fighters (BIFF) Khalifa Islamiya Mindanao (KIM) Moro National Liberation Front—Nur Misauri Faction (MNLF-NM) Moro National Liberation Front—Habier Malik Faction (MNLF-HM)	Create new, independent state (from sovereign nation)	Ongoing
134	Chechen Insurgency of 1994–present	Russia	Chechen Republic of Ichkeria (ChRI) Imarat Kavkaz (IK, Caucasus Emirate)	Create new, independent state (from sovereign nation)	Ongoing

135	Latvian Independence War of 1946–1947	Russia (Soviet Union)	Latvian National Guerrilla Organization (LNPA) Latvian Fatherland Guards (LTS(p)A)	Create new, independent state (from sovereign nation)	Government victory
136	Lithuanian Independence War of 1946–1948	Russia (Soviet Union)	United Democratic Resistance Movement (BDPS)	Create new, independent state (from sovereign nation)	Government victory
137	Estonian Independence War of 1946–1948	Russia (Soviet Union)	Forest Brothers	Create new, independent state (from sovereign nation)	Government victory
138	Ukrainian Independence War of 1946–1950	Russia (Soviet Union)	Ukrainian Partisan Army (UPA)	Create new, independent state (from sovereign nation)	Government victory
139	Rwandan Tutsi War of 1962–1965	Rwanda	Tutsi ethnic minority	Overthrow incumbent regime	Government victory
140	Rwandan Tutsi War of 1990–1994	Rwanda	Patriotic Rwandan Front (FPR)	Overthrow incumbent regime	Insurgent victory

(continued)

Case no.	Case name	Government	Insurgent group(s)	End goal	Outcome
141	Rwandan Hutu War of 1996–2002	Rwanda	Party for the Liberation of Rwanda (PALIR) Liberation Army of Rwanda (ALIR) Democratic Liberation Forces of Rwanda (FDLR)	Overthrow incumbent regime	Draw
142	Casamance Independence War of 1990–2012	Senegal	Movement of the Democratic Forces of the Casamance (MFDC) Front Nord Front Sud	Create new, independent state (from sovereign nation)	Draw
143	Sierra Leone War of 1991–1997	Sierra Leone	Revolutionary United Front (RUF) Armed Forces Revolutionary Council (AFRC)	Overthrow incumbent regime	Insurgent victory
144	Sierra Leone War of 1997–1998	Sierra Leone	National Provisional Ruling Council (NPRC) Kamajor militias	Overthrow incumbent regime	Insurgent victory
145	Sierra Leone War of 1998–2000	Sierra Leone	Revolutionary United Front (RUF) Armed Forces Revolutionary Council (AFRC)	Overthrow incumbent regime	Government victory
146	Somalia War of 1982–1991	Somalia	Somali Salvation Democratic Front (SSDF) Somali National Movement (SNM) Somali Patriotic Movement (SPM) United Somali Congress (USC)	Overthrow incumbent regime	Insurgent victory
147	Somalia War of 1991–1996	Somalia	United Somali Congress/Somali National Alliance (USC/ SNA)	Overthrow incumbent regime	Draw

148	Somalia War of 2006–present	Somalia	ARS/UIC (Alliance for the Re-Liberation of Somalia/Union of Islamic Courts) SICS (Supreme Islamic Council of Somalia) Al Shabaab Hizbul-Islam Harakat Ras Kamboni	Overthrow incumbent regime	Ongoing
149	Namibian Independence War of 1966–1988	South Africa	South West African People's Organization (SWAPO)	Create new, independent state (from sovereign nation)	Insurgent victory
150	Inkatha–ANC War of 1981–1994	South Africa	African National Congress (ANC) Pan African Congress (PAC) South African Communist Party (SACP) Azanian People's Organization (AZAPO)	Overthrow incumbent regime	Insurgent victory
151	Sri Lankan Leftists War of 1971	Sri Lanka	Janatha Vimukthi Peramuna (JVP)	Overthrow incumbent regime	Government victory
152	Tamil Independence War of 1983–2009	Sri Lanka	Liberation Tigers of Tamil Eelam (LTTE) Tamil Eelam Liberation Organization (TELO) Eelam People's Revolutionary Liberation Front (EPRLF)	Create new, independent state (from sovereign nation)	Government victory

(continued)

Case no.	Case name	Government	Insurgent group(s)	End goal	Outcome
153	Sri Lankan Leftists War of 1987–1989	Sri Lanka	Janatha Vimukthi Peramuna-II (JVP-II)	Overthrow incumbent regime	Government victory
154	Southern Sudan Independence War of 1963–1972	Sudan	Anya Nya	Create new, independent state (from sovereign nation)	Draw
155	South Sudan War of 1983–2004	Sudan	Sudan People's Liberation Movement/Army (SPLM/A) National Democratic Alliance (NDA)	Overthrow incumbent regime	Draw
156	West Sudan–Darfur War of 2003–present	Sudan	Sudanese Revolutinoary Front (SRF) Sudan Liberation Movement/Army (SLM/A) Justice and Equality Movement (JEM) United Resistance Front (URF) Sudan Liberation Movement/Army—Unity (SLM/A-Unity) Sudan Liberation Movement/Army—MM (SLM/A-MM)	Overthrow incumbent regime	Ongoing
157	South Sudanese War of 2011–present	South Sudan	South Sudan Democratic Movement/Army (SSDM/A) South Sudan Liberation Movement/Army (SSLM/A) South Sudan Democratic Movement/Army—Cobra Faction (SSDM/A-Cobra) Sudan People's Liberation Movement/Army—In Opposition (SPLM/A-IO)	Overthrow incumbent regime	Ongoing

158	Syrian Islamist War of 1979–1982	Syria	Muslim Brotherhood (MB)	Overthrow incumbent regime	Government victory
159	Syrian War of 2011–present	Syria	Free Syrian Army (FSA) Al-Nusra Front (AN) Islamic State Syrian Islamic Liberation Front Syrian Islamic Front Ahfad al-Rasul Brigade Democratic Union Party (PYD) Kurdish National Council (KNC) Harakat Ahrah al-Sham al-Islamiyya Liwa al-Islam Liwa al-Tawhid Suqor al-Sham Al-Faruq Brigade	Overthrow incumbent regime	Ongoing
160	Tajik War of 1992–1998	Tajikistan	United Tajik Opposition (UTO)	Overthrow incumbent regime	Draw
161	Thai Leftists War of 1966–1982	Thailand	Communist Party of Thailand (CPT)	Overthrow incumbent regime	Government victory
162	Thailand War of 2003–present	Thailand	Bansan Revolusi Nasional (BRN) Patani United Liberation Organization (PULO-New) National Revolutionary Front-Coordinated (BRN-C) Islamic Mujahideen Movement of Patani (GMIP) Patani Freedom Fighters (village-based militant groups) Small Group Tactic (RKK)	Create new, independent state (from sovereign nation)	Ongoing

(continued)

Case no.	Case name	Government	Insurgent group(s)	End goal	Outcome
163	Tunisian Independence War of 1953–1956	Tunisia	National Liberation Army (NLA)	Create new, independent state (from colonial authority)	Insurgent victory
164	Turkish–Kurdish Independence War of 1984–present	Turkey	Kurdistan Worker's Party (PKK)	Create new, independent state (from sovereign nation)	Ongoing
165	Ugandan War of 1979	Uganda	Front for National Salvation (FRONASA) Kikosi Maalum (KM) Uganda National Liberation Front (UNLF)	Overthrow incumbent regime	Insurgent victory
166	Ugandan "Bush" War of 1980–1986	Uganda	Former Ugandan National Army (FUNA) Uganda National Resistance Front (UNRF) Uganda Freedom Movement (UFM) National Resistance Army (NRA)	Overthrow incumbent regime	Insurgent victory
167	Ugandan War of 1986–present	Uganda	Lord's Resistance Army (LRA) Uganda's People's Army (UPA) Holy Spirit Movement (HSM) Alliance for Democratic Forces (ADF) West Nile Bank Front (WNBF) Uganda National Resistance Front II (UNRF II)	Overthrow incumbent regime	Ongoing

	War	Location	Insurgent group(s)	Goal	Outcome
168	Ukraine War of 2014–present	Ukraine	People's Republic of Donetsk People's Republic of Lugansk Multiple small groups	Create new, independent state (from sovereign nation)	Ongoing
169	Northern Irish Independence War of 1969–1999	United Kingdom	Provisional Irish Republican Army (PIRA/IRA) Real Irish Republican Army (RIRA)	Create new, independent state (from sovereign nation)	Draw
170	French–Indochina Independence War of 1946–1954	Vietnam	Vietnam Independence League (Viet Minh)	Create new, independent state (from colonial authority)	Insurgent victory
171	Vietnamese War of 1955–1975	Vietnam, South	National Liberation Front of South Vietnam (FNL)	Overthrow incumbent regime	Insurgent victory
172	South Yemeni Independence War of 1994	Yemen	Dem. Rep. of Yemen (South Yemen)	Create new, independent state (from sovereign nation)	Government victory
173	Yemeni Houthi War of 2004–present	Yemen	Houthis (Believing Youth, BY, aka al-Shabab al-Mumin)	Overthrow incumbent regime	Ongoing

(continued)

Case no.	Case name	Government	Insurgent group(s)	End goal	Outcome
174	Yemeni Islamist War of 2008–present	Yemen	Al Qa'ida in the Arabian Peninsula (AQAP)	Overthrow incumbent regime	Ongoing
175	North Yemeni Imamate War of 1948	Yemen, North	Opposition Coalition of both secular and Muslim reformists	Overthrow incumbent regime	Government victory
176	North Yemeni Royalists War of 1962–1970	Yemen, North	Imamate Royalists	Overthrow incumbent regime	Government victory
177	Aden Emergency of 1964–1967	Yemen, South	Front for the Liberation of Southern Yemen (FLOSY) National Liberation Front (NLF)	Create new, independent state (from colonial authority)	Insurgent victory
178	South Yemeni Leftists War of 1986	Yemen, South	Yemenite Socialist Party (YSP)	Overthrow incumbent regime	Insurgent victory
179	Croatian/Krajina Independence War of 1991	Yugoslavia	Croatian National Guard Various Croatian nationalist militias, such as the Croatian Defense Forces (HOS)	Create new, independent state (from sovereign nation)	Insurgent victory

180	Kosovar Independence War of 1998–1999	Yugoslavia/ Serbia	Kosovo Liberation Army (KLA)	Create new, independent state (from sovereign nation)	Insurgent victory
181	Rhodesian–Patriotic Front War of 1973–1979	Zimbabwe	Zimbabwe African People's Union (ZAPU) Zimbabwe African National Union (ZANU) Patriotic Front (PF)	Overthrow incumbent regime	Insurgent victory

Sources: The database was built based on author estimates and James D. Fearon and David D. Laitin, "Ethnicity, Insurgency, and Civil War," *American Political Science Review*, Vol. 97, No. 1 (March 2003), pp. 75–90 (replication data available at: http://web.stanford.edu/group/ethnic/publicdata/publicdata.html); Michael W. Doyle and Nicholas Sambanis, "International Peacebuilding: A Theoretical and Quantitative Analysis," *American Political Science Review*, Vol. 94, No. 4 (December 2000), pp. 779–801 (replication data available at: http://econ.worldbank.org/WBSITE/EXTERNAL/EXTDEC/EXTRESEARCH/0,,contentMDK:20701031~pagePK:64214825~piPK:64214943~theSitePK:469382,00.html); Michael W. Doyle and Nicholas Sambanis, *Making War and Building Peace: United Nations Peace Operations* (Princeton, NJ: Princeton University Press, 2006) (replication data available at: http://pantheon.yale.edu/~ns237/DS2006replication.zip); Jason Lyall and Isaiah Wilson III, "Rage against the Machines: Explaining Outcomes in Counterinsurgency Wars," *International Organization*, Vol. 63 (Winter 2009), pp. 67–106 (replication data available at: http://www.jasonlyall.com/publications-data-2/); Kristian Skrede Gleditsch, David Cunningham, and Idean Salehyan, Non-State Actor Data: Version 3.4, November 23, 2013 (available at: http://privatewww.essex.ac.uk/~ksg/eacd.html); Sundberg, Ralph, Kristine Eck, and Joakim Kreutz, "Introducing the UCDP Non-State Conflict Dataset," *Journal of Peace Research*, Vol. 49 (March 2012), pp. 351–362 (available at: http://www.pcr.uu.se/research/ucdp/datasets/ucdp_non-state_conflict_dataset_/); Uppsala Conflict Data Program, "UCDP/PRIO Armed Conflict Dataset v.4-2014, 1946–2013," Uppsala University, 2014 (available at: http://www.pcr.uu.se/research/ucdp/datasets/ucdp_prio_armed_conflict_dataset/); Uppsala Conflict Data Program, "UCDP Conflict Encyclopedia," Uppsala University, 2014 (available at: www.ucdp.uu.se/database); Uppsala Conflict Data Program, "UCDP Battle-Related Deaths Dataset v.5-2014," Uppsala University, 2014 (available at: http://www.pcr.uu.se/research/ucdp/datasets/ucdp_battle-related_deaths_dataset/); Gleditsch, Cunningham, and Idean Salehyan, "It Takes Two: A Dyadic Analysis of Civil War Duration and Outcome," *Journal of Conflict Resolution*, Vol. 53, No. 4 (2009); J. David Singer and Melvin Small, *Resort to Arms: International and Civil War, 1816–1980* (Beverly Hills, CA: Sage, 1982); J. David Singer and Melvin Small, *Correlates of War Project: International and Civil War Data, 1816–1992* (Ann Arbor, MI: Inter-university Consortium for Political and Social Research, 1994); Meredith Reid Sarkees and Frank Whelon Wayman, *Resort to War: 1816–2007, Intra-State War Data (v4.0)* (Washington, D.C.: CQ Press, 2010) (Replication data available at: http://www.correlatesofwar.org); Paul Collier and Anke Hoeffler, "Greed and Grievance in Civil Wars," *Oxford Economic Papers*, Vol. 56, No. 4 (2004), pp. 663–695 (replication data available at: http://users.ox.ac.uk/~ball0144/research.htm); Roy Licklider, "The Consequences of Negotiated Settlements in Civil Wars, 1945–1993," *American Political Science Review*, Vol. 89, No. 3 (1995), pp. 681–690; Stathis Kalyvas, *The Logic of Violence in Civil War* (New York: Cambridge University Press, 2006); Ben Connable and Martin C. Libicki, *How Insurgencies End* (Santa Monica, CA: RAND Corporation, 2010); David Gompert et al., *War by Other Means: Building Complete and Balanced Capabilities for Counterinsurgency* (Santa Monica, CA: RAND Corporation, 2008); Byman, Daniel et al., *Trends in Outside Support for Insurgent Movements* (Santa Monica, CA: RAND Corporation, 2010); Christopher Paul, Colin P. Clarke, and Beth Grill, *Victory Has a Thousand Fathers: Sources of Success in Counterinsurgency* (Santa Monica, CA: RAND Corporation, 2010); Max Boot, *Invisible Armies: An Epic History of Guerrilla Warfare from Ancient Times to the Present* (New York: W.W. Norton 2013); Walter Laqueur, *Guerrilla Warfare: A Historical and Critical Study* (New Brunswick, NJ: Transaction, 1998).

Appendix B

Statistical Results for Ending Insurgencies

Seth G. Jones, Patrick Johnston, and Eric Robinson

THIS APPENDIX DESCRIBES THE methodology and presents the full findings of the analysis in Chapter 8. It describes the variables in the models and the data sources used. It also contains the full results of the regression analysis, as well as a number of robustness checks performed to probe the strength of the findings.

VARIABLE ANALYZED

To identify the set of explanatory variables included in the statistical analysis, we surveyed the literature on insurgency and counterinsurgency to identify key studies and claims about the causes of insurgent victory. This literature included seminal works on insurgent victory and more recent quantitative studies of the correlates of insurgent victory and defeat.[1] Based on the arguments and evidence from the literature, we identified seven categories of explanatory variables for consideration in our analysis.

- **External support**: Outside aid to insurgents is widely thought to increase an insurgent group's chances of victory.[2] The impact of external support to governments in counterinsurgencies might be more muted.[3] We also examined several types of external support to insurgents and incumbent governments fighting against insurgencies, such as combat support, noncombat support, and foreign sanctuary.[4] We also analyzed external support from great-power states, which can allocate more resources to small wars than can other actors.

- **Insurgent strategy and strategic interaction**: We focused on three types of strategies: conventional, guerrilla, and punishment. Each of these strategies has been identified as playing a key role in the success or failure of insurgencies.[5]
- **Regime type**: Democracies are commonly viewed as having less resolve to wage long and costly wars against insurgents, thus increasing the odds of insurgent victory.[6]
- **Insurgent goals**: We examine three primary types of goals: anticolonial, secessionist, and "center-seeking" insurgencies that want to overthrow and replace the incumbent government. We also analyze whether insurgencies had Islamic ideological goals.
- **Counterinsurgent force structure**: The force structure might also affect the performance and effectiveness of counterinsurgents and thus influence the probability of insurgent victory.[7]
- **Insurgent structure**: The insurgent force structure—especially fragmented insurgencies composed of multiple factions—may increase or decrease an insurgent group's odds of victory.
- **Duration**: The duration of insurgencies may influence a group's chances of winning, as insurgents might lack the manpower and resources to survive a protracted war.[8]

DATA AND ANALYSIS

We used the database here to build a multivariate regression model in order to explain the correlation between various traits of governments and insurgent forces with the probability of insurgent victory. The database includes 181 total insurgencies since World War II, of which 38 are still ongoing. In order to avoid biasing our results, we subset our analysis to the 143 insurgencies that reached a definitive conclusion because of insurgent victory, government victory, or draw.

Table B.1 presents the five primary regression models, with marginal effects and standard errors clustered by country per the approach taken by Jason Lyall and Isaiah Wilson.[9] We utilize probit estimation, although the results are robust enough to use a logit estimator. These

TABLE B.1 Main model results

Model	(1)	(2)	(3)	(4)	(5)
Outside support source	Any	Great power	Great-power combat Only	Great-power noncombat vs. combat	Great-power noncombat vs. combat
Outside support type	Any	Any			
GOV–INS interaction	Yes	Yes	No	No	Yes
Outside support to government	−0.295 (0.254)				
Outside support to insurgency	0.153 (0.158)				
Outside support to government and insurgency	0.131 (0.242)				
Great-power support to government		−0.104 (0.111)			
Great-power support to insurgency		0.517*** (0.163)			
Great-power support to government and insurgency		−0.266** (0.127)			
Great-power combat support to government			−0.094 (0.101)		

(continued)

TABLE B.1 Continued

Model	(1)	(2)	(3)	(4)	(5)
Outside support source	Any	Great power	Great-power combat Only	Great-power noncombat vs. combat	Great-power noncombat vs. combat
Outside support type	Any	Any	No	No	Yes
GOV–INS interaction	Yes	Yes			
Great-power combat support to insurgency			0.424** (0.212)		
Great-power combat support to government = none				reference category (omitted)	reference category (omitted)
Great-power combat support to government = noncombat only				−0.169 (0.112)	0.013 (0.143)
Great-power combat support to government = combat				−0.179* (0.0943)	−0.180 (0.114)
Great-power combat support to insurgency = none				reference category (omitted)	reference category (omitted)
Great-power combat support to insurgency = noncombat only				0.303*** (0.102)	0.598*** (0.153)

Great-power combat support to insurgency = combat				0.429**	0.500**
				(0.214)	(0.222)
Great-power noncombat support to government and insurgency					-0.331***
					-0.056
Great-power noncombat support to insurgency and great-power combat support to government					-0.153
					(0.174)
Outside sanctuary support to insurgency	0.0119	0.068	0.076	0.056	0.082
	(0.105)	-0.088	-0.087	-0.09	-0.09
Islamic insurgency	-0.109	-0.108	-0.110	-0.113	-0.115
	(0.130)	(0.128)	(0.121)	(0.123)	(0.123)
Insurgent strategy: conventional	0.102	0.108	0.101	0.102	0.0869
	-0.086	-0.089	-0.088	-0.093	-0.092
Insurgent strategy: punishment	-0.192**	-0.146	-0.154*	-0.152*	-0.166*
	-0.087	-0.09	-0.09	-0.091	-0.087
Insurgent goal: revolution/overthrow	reference category (omitted)	reference category (omitted)	reference category (omitted)	reference category (omitted)	reference category (omitted)
Insurgent goal: colonial independence	0.541***	0.453***	0.480***	0.470***	0.474**
	(0.128)	(0.158)	(0.138)	(0.164)	(0.185)

(continued)

TABLE B.1 Continued

Model	(1)	(2)	(3)	(4)	(5)
Outside support source	Any	Great power	Great-power combat Only	Great-power noncombat vs. combat	Great-power noncombat vs. combat
Outside support type	Any	Any			
GOV–INS interaction	Yes	Yes	No	No	Yes
insurgent goal: sovereignty/secession	-0.343***	-0.363***	-0.314***	-0.333***	-0.390***
	-0.063	-0.062	-0.065	-0.065	-0.06
Insurgent structure: 1 group	reference category (omitted)	reference category (omitted)	reference category (omitted)	reference category (omitted)	reference category (omitted)
Insurgent structure: 2–4 groups	0.235**	0.225**	0.221**	0.242**	0.254**
	(0.104)	(0.108)	(0.103)	(0.104)	(0.116)
Insurgent structure: 5 + groups	0.043	0.098	0.04	0.097	0.152
	(0.140)	(0.140)	(0.143)	(0.146)	(0.131)
Duration of insurgency (years)	-0.008	-0.004	-0.00138	-0.008	-0.006
	-0.017	-0.018	-0.018	-0.018	-0.018
Duration of insurgency (years)—squared	-0.0001	-0.0003	-0.0003	-0.0002	-0.0003
	-0.0004	-0.0005	-0.0004	-0.0005	-0.0005
Democratic government	0.038	-0.013	-0.004	0.0028	0.005
	-0.096	-0.093	-0.095	-0.097	-0.098
Observations	143	143	143	143	143

Note: Marginal effects are presented, with robust standard errors clustered on country in parentheses. ***$p < 0.01$, **$p < 0.05$, *$p < 0.1$.

models are designed to incorporate the existing literature on civil war and insurgency outcomes discussed earlier in the appendix, as well as explore the impact of different types and sources of external support to both governments and insurgents as coded in the database.

In terms of external support, we first assess the extent to which *any outside support* impacts the probability of insurgent victory (in model one). Then we limit this variable (in model two) to assess the specific impact of *great-power support* to both governments and insurgents. In the third model, we focus solely on the impact of great-power *combat support* to both sides on the probability of insurgent victory. Column four breaks out the type of great-power support even further, including dummies for whether a great power provided *noncombat support versus combat support.* The final model assesses the extent to which great-power combat and noncombat *support to governments mediates similar support to insurgents.*

Across each of these models, we also control for a variety of other factors related to both insurgents and counterinsurgents. These include other types of support to insurgents (whether the insurgent has a sanctuary), insurgent strategy (conventional and punishment), insurgent goals (overthrow vs. colonial independence vs. secession), insurgent structure (1 group vs. 2–4 groups vs. 5 or more groups), the duration of the insurgency, and whether the counterinsurgent is democratic.[10] With the exception of this final variable, all covariates are coded within the database. Per similar studies in the literature, the democratic counterinsurgent variable is based on Polity2 scores.[11]

We also conduct five robustness tests of our model results. For ease of interpretation, we utilize the third model from Table B.1 for these tests, which measures the impact of great-power combat support relative to no great-power combat support. More generally, these robustness tests report similar results across each of the main models presented in Table B.1.

First, we assess whether guerrilla strategies affect the probability of insurgent victory.[12] Second, we investigate the Ivan Arreguín-Toft hypothesis that a mismatch between the conventional strategies of insurgents and counterinsurgents affects the probability of insurgent victory.[13] Third, we limit our results to the 72 out of 143 insurgencies that

TABLE B.2 Robustness tests

Robustness test	(1) Guerrilla strategy	(2) Strategic mismatch	(3) Cold War only	(4) Mechanization	(5) Helicopter usage
Great-power combat support to government	-0.086 (0.102)	-0.225 (0.153)	-0.340** (0.146)	-0.007 (0.124)	-0.015 (0.119)
Great-power combat support to insurgency	0.455** (0.189)	0.441** (0.205)	-0.123 (0.344)	0.675*** (0.114)	0.633*** (0.158)
Outside sanctuary support to insurgency	0.074 (0.087)	0.066 (0.089)	0.127 (0.165)	0.087 (0.105)	0.089 (0.104)
Islamic insurgency	-0.01 (0.124)	-0.086 (0.128)	-0.272* (0.139)	-0.115 (0.124)	-0.094 (0.135)
Insurgent strategy: guerrilla	0.081 (0.090)				
Insurgent strategy: conventional		0.045 (0.112)	0.197 (0.138)	0.055 (0.109)	0.052 (0.105)
Insurgent strategy: punishment	-0.147 (0.052)	-0.172* (0.089)	-0.130 (0.156)	-0.168* (0.096)	-0.161* (0.097)
Strategic mismatch		0.229 (0.264)			
Insurgent goal: revolution/overthrow	reference category (omitted)	reference category (omitted)	reference category (omitted)	reference category (omitted)	reference category (omitted)
Insurgent goal: colonial independence	0.424*** (0.152)	0.529*** (0.136)	0.472*** (0.148)	0.421** (0.167)	0.439*** (0.159)

	(1)	(2)	(3)	(4)	(5)
Insurgent goal: sovereignty/secession	-0.330***	-0.325***	-0.422***	-0.240***	-0.249***
	(0.069)	(0.066)	(0.103)	(0.090)	(0.092)
Insurgent structure: 1 group	reference category (omitted)	reference category (omitted)	reference category (omitted)	reference category (omitted)	reference category (omitted)
Insurgent structure: 2–4 groups	0.207**	0.227**	0.141	0.197*	0.211*
	(0.103)	(0.103)	(0.168)	(0.118)	(0.113)
Insurgent structure: 5 + groups	0.032	0.038		-0.190	-0.174
	(0.140)	(0.146)		(0.122)	(0.124)
Duration of insurgency (years)	-0.008	-0.003	0.017	0.025	0.016
	(0.018)	(0.018)	(0.023)	(0.020)	(0.020)
Duration of insurgency (years)—squared	-0.0002	-0.0003	-0.0006	-0.001**	-0.0009
	(0.0005)	(0.0005)	(0.0006)	(0.0006)	(0.0006)
Democratic government	-0.0106	0.000893	0.136	-0.00269	0.00626
	(0.096)	(0.096)	(0.147)	(0.099)	(0.101)
Counterinsurgent mechanization				0.0347	
				(0.046)	
Counterinsurgent helicopter usage					0.165
					(0.130)
	143	143	72	112	112

Note: Marginal effects are presented, with robust standard errors clustered on country in parentheses. ***p < 0.01, **p < 0.05, *p < 0.1.

ended during the Cold War. The fourth and fifth models include Lyall's mechanization and helicopter variables.[14]

Overall, the primary model findings remain robust to these alternative specifications. Guerrilla strategies appear unrelated to the probability of insurgent victory, and do not alter primary model findings. Inclusion of a proxy for Arreguín-Toft's strategic mismatch variable, as well as Lyall's mechanization and helicopter variables, do not impact our main results. On the other hand, limiting our analysis to those insurgencies that ended during the Cold War does alter estimates regarding the impact of great-power combat support to both insurgents and the government. However, given that we restrict our full sample to only those insurgencies ending prior to 1990 (a 50 percent reduction in the sample), we believe that this robustness test does not affect the importance of our main findings and their implications (see Table B.2).

NOTES

⊰——◇◆◇——⊱

Chapter 1

1. Mao Tse-Tung, *On Guerrilla Warfare* (Urbana and Chicago: University of Illinois Press, 2000), p. 73.
2. General Alberto Bayo, *150 Questions for a Guerrilla* (Denver, CO: Cypress, 1963), p. 19.
3. Author interview with US special operations soldier, September 2009.
4. Taliban press release, "Voice of Jihad," April 29, 2009.
5. Richard A. Oppel, Jr. and Rachel Donadio, "Italy Ponders Afghan Pullout After Deadly Blast," *New York Times*, September 17, 2009.
6. Taliban press release, "Voice of Jihad," April 29, 2009.
7. Taliban, "Statement by Leadership Council of Islamic Emirate Regarding Inauguration of Spring Offensive Entitled 'Operation Omari,'" April 2016. The Taliban posted the announcement on their website at: http://shahamat-english.com/statement-by-leadership-council-of-islamic-emirate-regarding-inauguration-of-spring-offensive-entitled-operation-omari/.
8. On ISI support to Afghan insurgents see, for example, Carlotta Gall, *The Wrong Enemy: America in Afghanistan, 2001–2014* (New York: Houghton Mifflin Harcourt, 2014); Seth G. Jones, *In the Graveyard of Empires: America's War in Afghanistan* (New York: W.W. Norton, 2009).
9. On historical accounts of insurgency see Walter Laqueur, *Guerrilla Warfare: A Historical and Critical Study* (New Brunswick, NJ: Transaction, 2010); Max Boot, *Invisible Armies: An Epic History of Guerrilla Warfare from Ancient Times to the Present* (New York: W.W. Norton, 2013).
10. Mean average includes ongoing insurgencies, not just those that have terminated.

11. Alec D. Barker, "Improvised Explosive Devices in Southern Afghanistan and Western Pakistan, 2002–2009," *Studies in Conflict and Terrorism*, Vol. 34, No. 8 (2011), pp. 600–620; Hazard Management Solutions, "Timescale to Develop/Deploy Sophisticated IEDs," unpublished briefing, November 2004.

12. The Field Manual was formally issued on December 15, 2006. The US Army and Marine Corps, *Counterinsurgency Field Manual: US Army Field Manual No. 3–24* and *Marine Corps Warfighting Publication No. 3–33.5* (Chicago: University of Chicago Press, 2007).

13. General Stanley A. McChrystal, "COMISAF's Initial Assessment," Memorandum to the Honorable Robert M. Gates, August 30, 2009, pp. 2–12.

14. See, for example, John A. Nagl, *Learning to Eat Soup with a Knife: Counterinsurgency Lessons from Malaya and Vietnam* (Chicago: University of Chicago Press, 2002); David Kilcullen, *The Accidental Guerrilla: Fighting Small Wars in the Midst of a Big One* (New York: Oxford University Press, 2009); Bard O'Neill, *Insurgency and Terrorism: From Revolution to Apocalypse* (Dulles, VA: Potomac Books, 2005).

15. See, for example, David Galula, *Counterinsurgency Warfare: Theory and Practice* (London: Praeger, 1964); Robert Thompson, *Defeating Communist Insurgency* (St. Petersburg, FL: Hailer, 2005); Charles E. Calwell, *Small Wars: Their Principles and Practice* (Lincoln, NE: University of Nebraska Press, 1996); Frank Kitson, *Low Intensity Operations: Subversion, Insurgency and Peacekeeping* (London: Faber and Faber, 1971); Robert Taber, *War of the Flea: The Classic Study of Guerrilla Warfare* (Washington: Brassey's, 2002); Roger Trinquier, *Modern Warfare: A French View of Counterinsurgency* (London: Praeger, 2006); Walter Lacquer, *Guerrilla Warfare: A Historical and Critical Study* (New Brunswick, NJ: Transaction, 1998).

16. See, for example, David French, *The British Way in Counterinsurgency, 1945–1967* (New York: Oxford University Press, 2011); David Ucko and Robert Egnell, *Counterinsurgency in Crisis: Britain and the Challenges of Modern Warfare* (New York: Columbia University Press, 2013); Fred Kaplan, *The Insurgents: David Petraeus and the Plot to Change the American Way of War* (New York: Simon & Schuster, 2013).

17. The *Counterinsurgency Field Manual*, for example, briefly discusses insurgency but devotes 92 percent of the text to counterinsurgency. Approximately 31 pages (8 percent) out of 372 pages in the *Counterinsurgency Field Manual* are devoted to insurgency.

18. In our dataset, the United States, United Kingdom, and France supported 19 insurgencies (11 percent) since 1946, compared to 68 counterinsurgencies (38 percent). Soviet/Russian support to insurgencies has been on the same order with eighteen cases (an additional nine featured Cuban or Chinese support without Soviet support).

19. Central Intelligence Agency, *Guide to the Analysis of Insurgency* (Washington, D.C.: Central Intelligence Agency, 2012), p. 1.

20. Jeremy Shapiro, *The Terrorist's Dilemma: Managing Violent Covert Organizations* (Princeton, NJ: Princeton University Press, 2013).

21. On the use of violence see, for example, The US Army and Marine Corps, *Counterinsurgency Field Manual*, p. 385.

22. John Shy and Thomas W. Collier, "Revolution War," in Peter Paret, ed., *Makers of Modern Strategy: From Machiavelli to the Nuclear Age* (Princeton, NJ: Princeton University Press, 1986), p. 817. On coups see Edward Luttwak, *Coup d'état: A Practical Handbook* (New York: Alfred A. Knopf, 1969); S. E. Finer, *The Man on Horseback: The Role of the Military in Politics*, 2d ed. (Boulder, CO: Westview, 1988); Eric A. Nordlinger, *Soldiers in Politics: Military Coups and Governments* (Englewood Cliffs, NJ: Prentice-Hall, 1977); Claude E. Welch, Jr. and Arthur K. Smith, *Military Role and Rule: Perspectives on Civil–Military Relations* (North Scituate, MA: Duxbury Press, 1974); and Amos Perlmutter, *The Military and Politics in Modern Times: On Professionals, Praetorians, and Revolutionary Soldiers* (New Haven, CT: Yale University Press, 1977).

23. Kalyvas, *The Logic of Violence in Civil War*, p. 245.

24. Mao Tse-Tung, *On Guerrilla Warfare*, p. 43.

25. In the United States, for instance, some left-wing and right-wing terrorist groups (from radical environmental groups to some white supremacists) used terrorist tactics to advance their political agendas. But their ultimate goal was not to overthrow the US government or to secede from its political boundaries, thus distinguishing them from insurgent organizations. On the definition of insurgent groups see Central Intelligence Agency, *Guide to the Analysis of Insurgency* (Washington, D.C.: Central Intelligence Agency, 2012), p. 1.

26. There are many definitions of terrorism. See, for example, United States Department of State, *Country Reports on Terrorism 2005* (Washington, D.C.: United States Department of States), p. 9; Bruce Hoffman, *Inside Terrorism*, Second Edition (New York: Columbia University Press, 2006), pp. 1–41; Robert A. Pape, *Dying to Win: The Strategic Logic of Suicide Terrorism* (New York: Random House, 2005), p. 9; Audrey Kurth Cronin, "Behind the Curve: Globalization and International Terrorism," *International Security*, Vol. 27, No. 3 (Winter 2002/03), p. 33.

27. Monica Duffy Toft, *Securing the Peace: The Durable Settlement of Civil Wars* (Princeton, NJ: Princeton University Press, 2009); Virginia Page Fortna, *Does Peacekeeping Work? Shaping Belligerents' Choices after Civil War* (Princeton, NJ: Princeton University Press, 2008).

28. Central Intelligence Agency, *Guide to the Analysis of Insurgency*, p. 1; The US Army and Marine Corps, *Counterinsurgency Field Manual: US Army Field Manual*, p. 383.

29. See, for example, US Department of Defense, *Special Operations, Joint Publication 3–05* (Washington, D.C.: Joint Staff, July 16, 2014), p. xi; US Department of the Army, *Army Special Operations Forces Unconventional Warfare* (Washington, D.C.: Headquarters, Department of the Army, September 2008), p. 1–2.

30. See, for example, other data in Monica Toft, *Securing the Peace: The Durable Settlement of Civil Wars* (Princeton, NJ: Princeton University Press, 2010); James D. Fearon, "Iraq's Civil War," *Foreign Affairs*, Vol. 86, No. 2 (March/April 2007), pp. 2–15; Sean M. Zeigler, "Competitive Alliances and Civil War Recurrence," *International Studies Quarterly*, Vol. 1 (2015), pp. 1–14; T. David Mason, Joseph P. Weingarten, Jr., and Patrick J. Fett, "Win, Lose, or Draw: Predicting the Outcome of Civil Wars," *Political Research Quarterly*, Vol. 52, No. 2 (June 1999), pp. 239–268.

31. Exceptions include the data in Jason Lyall and Isaiah Wilson III, "Rage against the Machines: Explaining Outcomes in Counterinsurgency Wars," *International Organization*, No. 63 (Winter 2009), pp. 67–106; Toft, *Securing the Peace*; and Fearon, "Iraq's Civil War."

32. On the transnational movement of terrorists see, for example, Thomas Hegghammer, "Should I Stay or Should I Go? Explaining Variation in Western Jihadists' Choice between Domestic and Foreign Fighting," *American Political Science Review*, Vol. 107, No. 1 (February 2013), pp. 1–15; Hegghammer, "The Rise of Muslim Foreign Fighters: Islam and the Globalization of Jihad," *International Security*, Vol. 35, No. 3 (2011), pp. 53–94.

33. For a list of the sources, see Appendix A.

34. There are a few cases in which data are lacking to definitely determine the number of battle-deaths per year due to poor historical reporting (such as Cabinda/Angola in the early years), or in which casualty numbers dipped into the teens for a few years but then rose again. In these cases, I have coded the war as one continuous insurgency rather than multiple insurgencies because no settlement had been reached, the basic grievances had not yet been resolved, low-level violence continued, and violence soon rose again above twenty-five battle-deaths. If battle-deaths dipped into the teens or lower for five years or longer without again rising above twenty-five battle-deaths (such as in Cabinda/Angola since 2009), I coded the insurgency as terminated even though the basic grievances have yet to be resolved and it remains to be seen if current cease-fires and peace negotiations will be lasting.

35. See, for example, Daniel Byman, *Understanding Proto-Insurgencies* (Santa Monica, CA: RAND, 2007).

Chapter 2

1. Ernesto "Che" Guevara, *Guerrilla Warfare* (Lincoln, NE: University of Nebraska Press, 1998), p. 13.

2. Quoted in Donald L. Barnett and Karari Njama, *Mau Mau from within: Autobiography and Analysis of Kenya's Peasant Revolt* (London: MacGibbon and Kee, 1966), p. 57.

3. David Anderson, *Histories of the Hanged: The Dirty War in Kenya and the End of Empire* (New York: W.W. Norton, 2005), p. 47.

4. Huw Bennett, *Fighting the Mau Mau: The British Army and Counter-Insurgency in the Kenya Emergency* (New York: Cambridge University Press, 2013), p. 1; David Anderson, *Histories of the Hanged: The Dirty War in Kenya and the End of Empire* (New York: W.W. Norton, 2005), pp. 22, 190; Barnett and Njama, *Mau Mau from within*, pp. 33–35.

5. British National Archives, Colonial Office, 822/501. Also see David French, *The British Way in Counter-Insurgency, 1945–1967* (New York: Oxford University Press, 2011), p. 55.

6. Kiboi Muriithi (General Kamwana), *War in the Forest* (Nairobi: Trafford, 1971), pp. 5–6.

7. See Barnett and Karari, *Mau Mau from within*, pp. 55–60; Muriithi, *War in the Forest*, pp. 18–19.

8. The letter is quoted in F. D. Corfield, *Historical Survey of the Origins and Growth of Mau Mau*, Cmnd 1030 (London: Her Majesty's Stationery Office, 1960), pp. 151–152.

9. Bennett, *Fighting the Mau Mau*, p. 12.

10. Proclamation of the State of Emergency, Public Records Office, Colonial Office, 822/444.

11. Daniel Byman, *Understanding Proto-Insurgencies* (Santa Monica, CA: RAND, 2007).

12. Central Intelligence Agency, *Guide to the Analysis of Insurgency* (Washington, D.C.: Central Intelligence Agency, 2012), p. 5.

13. "Fail" in this sense refers to firms that don't return investors' capital. It is based on research from Harvard Business School's Shikhar Ghosh. See Deborah Gage, "The Venture Capital Secret: 3 Out of 4 Start-Ups Fail," *Wall Street Journal*, September 19, 2012.

14. Douglas Holtz-Eakin, David Joulfaian, and Harvey S. Rosen, "Sticking it Out: Entrepreneurial Survival and Liquidity Constraints," *The Journal of Political Economy*, Vol. 102, No. 1 (1994), pp. 53–75; Javier Gimeno, Timothy B. Folta, Arnold C. Cooper, and Carolyn Y. Woo, "Survival of the Fittest? Entrepreneurial Human Capital and the Persistence of Underperforming Firms," *Administrative Science Quarterly*, Vol. 42, No. 4 (1997), pp. 750–783; Arthur L. Stinchcombe, "Social Structure and Organizations," in J. G. March, ed., *Handbook of Organizations* (Chicago, IL: Rand McNally, 1965), pp. 142–193; David M. Townsend, Lowell W. Busenitz, and Jonathan D. Arthurs, "To Start or Not to Start: Outcome and Ability Expectations in the Decision to Start a New Venture," *Journal of Business Venturing*, Vol. 25 (2010), pp. 192–202.

15. Paul Collier, Anke Hoeffler, and Dominic Rohner, "Beyond Greed and Grievance: Feasibility and Civil War," *Oxford Economic Papers*, Vol. 61, No. 2 (2009), p. 1.

16. Mao Tse-Tung, *On Guerrilla Warfare* (Urbana and Chicago: University of Illinois Press, 2000), p. 51.

17. Mao, *On Guerrilla Warfare*, p. 93.

18. See, for example, Stathis N. Kalyvas, *The Logic of Violence in Civil War* (New York: Cambridge University Press, 2006), p. 377.

19. On mobilization see Ted Robert Gurr, *Peoples versus States: Minorities at Risk in the New Century* (Washington, D.C.: United States Institute of Peace, 2000).

20. Guevara, *Guerrilla Warfare*, p. 9.

21. Mao, *On Guerrilla Warfare*, p. 85; Guevara, *Guerrilla Warfare*, pp. 79–80.

22. The list of possible reasons is long. Historical works include Bruce M. Russett, "Inequality and Instability," *World Politics*, Vol. 16, No. 3 (April 1964), pp. 442–454; Edward N. Muller, "Income Inequality, Regime Repressiveness, and Political Violence," *American Sociological Review*, Vol. 50 (1985), pp. 47–61; Samuel Huntington, *The Clash of Civilizations and the Remaking of World Order* (New York: Simon & Schuster, 1996); Huntington, *Political Order in Changing Societies* (New Haven, CT: Yale University Press, 1968); Ted R. Gurr, *Why Men Rebel* (Princeton, NJ: Princeton University Press, 1971); Jeffery M. Paige, *Agrarian Revolution* (New York: Free Press, 1975); Ernest Gellner, *Nations and Nationalism* (Ithaca, NY: Cornell University Press, 1983).

23. David Galula, *Counterinsurgency Warfare: Theory and Practice* (New York: Praeger, 2006), p. 16.

24. Muller, "Income Inequality, Regime Repressiveness, and Political Violence," pp. 47–61; Jeffery M. Paige, *Agrarian Revolution* (New York: Free Press, 1975); Russett, "Inequality and Instability," pp. 442–454; Gurr, *Why Men Rebel*; Huntington, *Political Order in Changing Societies*.

25. Note that Fearon and Laitin use low per capita income as a proxy for governance, including a state's overall financial, administrative, police, and military capabilities. Fearon and Laitin, "Ethnicity, Insurgency, and Civil War," pp. 75–90.

26. Paul Collier and Anke Hoeffler, "Civil War," draft chapter for the *Handbook of Defense Economics*, Department of Economics, University of Oxford, March 2006; Collier, "Economic Causes of Civil Conflict and Their Implications for Policy," pp. 10–11.

27. Fearon and Laitin, "Ethnicity, Insurgency, and Civil War," pp. 75–90; Paul Collier, "Economic Causes of Civil Conflict and Their Implications for Policy," p. 3.

28. See, for example, Havard Hegre and Nicholas Sambanis, "Sensitivity Analysis of Empirical Results on Civil War Onset," *Journal of Conflict Resolution*, Vol. 50, No. 4 (August 2006), pp. 508–535; Fearon and Laitin, "Ethnicity, Insurgency, and Civil War," pp. 75–90.

29. Vladimir Lenin, "Guerrilla Warfare," in Vladimir Lenin, *Collected Works*, 4th English ed. (Moscow: Progress, 1965), pp. 213–223.

30. Guevara, *Guerrilla Warfare*, p. 10.

31. Chin Peng, *My Side of History* (Singapore: Media Masters, 2003). Chin Peng was leader of the Malayan Community Party.

32. CO 717/167/528459/2/1948, f 302, "Declaration of Emergency," in
    A. J. Stockwell, *British Documents on the End of Empire*, Series B,
    Vol. III, Malaya, Part II, *The Communist Insurrection, 1948–1953*
    (London: HMSO, 1995) pp. 19–20. Also see John A. Nagl, *Learning to
    Eat Soup with a Knife: Counterinsurgency Lessons from Malaya and Vietnam*
    (Chicago: University of Chicago Press, 2002), p. 82.

33. Catherine LeGrand, *Frontier Expansion and Peasant Protest in
    Colombia: 1850–1936* (Albuquerque, NM: University of New Mexico Press,
    1986); Fabio Sánchez, Andrés Solimano, and Michel Formisano, "Conflict,
    Violence, and Crime in Colombia," in Paul Collier and Nicholas
    Sambanis, eds., *Understanding Civil War*, Vol. 2, *Europe, Central Asia, and
    Other Regions* (Washington, D.C.: World Bank, 2005), pp. 120–121.

34. José Carlos Mariátegui, *Siete ensayos de interpretación de la realidad peruana*
    (Lima: Empresa Editora Amauta, 1965); José Carlos Mariátegui, *José Carlos
    Mariátegui: An Anthology*, ed. and trans. by Harry E. Vanden and Marc
    Becker (New York: Monthly Review Press, 2011).

35. Bennett, *Fighting the Mau Mau*, p. 1; Anderson, *Histories of the Hanged*,
    pp. 22, 190; Barnett and Njama, *Mau Mau from within*, pp. 33–35.

36. British National Archives, Colonial Office, 822/501. Also see French,
    The British Way in Counter-Insurgency, p. 55.

37. See, for example, Fearon and Laitin, "Ethnicity, Insurgency, and Civil
    War," pp. 75–90; Paul Collier and Anke Hoeffler, "Greed and Grievance in
    Civil Wars," *Oxford Economic Papers*, Vol. 56 (2004), pp. 563–595; Robert
    H. Bates, *When Things Fell Apart: State Failure in Late Century Africa*
    (New York: Cambridge University Press, 2008); Nicholas Sambanis and
    Moses Shayo, "Social Identification and Ethnic Conflict," draft paper,
    September 12, 2012.

38. Jose G. Montalvo and Marta Reynal-Querol, "Ethnic Polarization,
    Potential Conflict, and Civil Wars," *The American Economic Review*, Vol.
    95, No. 3 (June 2005), pp. 796–816; Ravi Bhavnani and Dan Miodownik,
    "Ethnic Polarization, Ethnic Salience, and Civil War," *Journal of Conflict
    Resolution*, Vol. 53, No. 1 (February 2009), pp. 30–49. Also see Halvard
    Buhaug, Lars-Erik Cederman, and Jan Ketil Røda, "Disaggregating Ethno-
    Nationalist Civil Wars: A Dyadic Test of Exclusion Theory," *International
    Organization*, Vol. 62, No. 3 (July 2008), pp. 531–551; Andreas Wimmer
    and Brian Min, "Why Do Ethnic Groups Rebel? New Data and Analysis,"
    World Politics, Vol. 62, No. 1 (January 2010), pp. 87–119.

39. Paul Collier and Anke Hoeffler, "On Economic Causes of Civil War,"
    Oxford Economic Papers, Vol. 50, No. 4 (1998), pp. 563–573.

40. Donald L. Horowitz, *Ethnic Groups in Conflict* (Berkeley: University of
    California Press, 1985); Rui J. P. de Figueiredo Jr. and Barry R. Weingast,
    "The Rationality of Fear: Political Opportunism and Ethnic Conflict,"
    in Barbara F. Walter and Jack Snyder, eds., *Civil Wars, Insecurity and
    Intervention* (New York: Columbia University Press, 1999), pp. 261–302;

Chaim Kaufmann, "Possible and Impossible Solutions to Ethnic Civil Wars," *International Security*, Vol. 20, No. 4 (Spring 1996), pp. 136–175; David A. Lake and Donald Rothchild, "Containing Fear: The Origins and Management of Ethnic Conflict," *International Security*, Vol. 21, No. 2 (Fall 1996), pp. 41–75; Stephen M. Saideman, *The Ties That Divide: Ethnic Politics, Foreign Policy, and International Conflict* (New York: Columbia University Press, 2001); Tatu Vanhanen, "Domestic Ethnic Conflict and Ethnic Nepotism: A Comparative Analysis," *Journal of Peace Research*, Vol. 36, No. 1 (January 1999), pp. 55–73.

41. Sambanis and Shayo, "Social Identification and Ethnic Conflict."
42. Montalvo and Reynal-Querol, "Ethnic Polarization, Potential Conflict, and Civil Wars," pp. 796–816.
43. Sambanis and Shayo, "Social Identification and Ethnic Conflict."
44. Central Intelligence Agency, *World Factbook 1984* (Washington, D.C.: Central Intelligence Agency, 1985), p. 213.
45. Central Intelligence Agency, *World Factbook 1994* (Washington, D.C.: Central Intelligence Agency, 1995).
46. David Kilcullen, *The Accidental Guerrilla: Fighting Small Wars in the Midst of a Big One* (New York: Oxford University Press, 2009), p. 213.
47. Christopher Zurcher, Pavel Baev, and Jan Koehler, "Civil Wars in the Caucasus," in Collier and Sambanis, eds., *Understanding Civil War*, Vol. 2, pp. 259–298.
48. Collier and Hoeffler, "Greed and Grievance in Civil Wars," pp. 563–595.
49. See the discussion in Kalyvas, *The Logic of Violence in Civil War*, pp. 74–76.
50. On religious polarization see Montalvo and Reynal-Querol, "Ethnic Polarization, Potential Conflict, and Civil Wars," pp. 796–816. Also see the discussion in Collier, "Economic Causes of Civil Conflict and Their Implications for Policy."
51. Samir Makdisi and Richard Sadaka, "The Lebanese Civil War, 1975–90," in Collier and Sambanis, eds., *Understanding Civil War*, Vol. 2, pp. 62–63.
52. Sayyid Qutb, *Ma'alam fi al-tariq* [*Milestones*] (New Delhi: Islamic Book Service, 2007).
53. Ayman al-Zawahiri, *Knights Under the Prophet's Banner*, trans. by Laura Mansfield (Old Tappan, NJ: TLG, 2002), p. 201.
54. 'Abd Al-'Aziz Al-Muqrin, *A Practical Course for Guerrilla Warfare*, trans. by Norman Cigar (Washington, D.C.: Potomac Books, 2009), p. 89.
55. Fearon and Laitin, "Ethnicity, Insurgency, and Civil War," pp. 75–90.
56. James D. Fearon, *Governance and Civil War Onset*, World Development Report 2011 Background Paper (Washington, D.C.: World Bank, August 31, 2010); Fearon and Laitin, "Ethnicity, Insurgency, and Civil War," pp. 75–90; Ann Hironaka, *Neverending Wars: The International Community, Weak States, and the Perpetuation of Civil War* (Cambridge, MA: Harvard University Press, 2005). On the importance of building institutions, see Roland Paris, *At War's End: Building Peace After Civil Conflict* (New York: Cambridge University Press, 2004).

57. World Bank, *Governance Matters 2006: Worldwide Governance Indicators* (Washington, D.C.: World Bank, 2006), p. 2.
58. Max Weber, "Politics as a Vocation," in H. H. Gerth and C. Wright Mills, eds., *From Max Weber: Essays in Sociology* (New York: Oxford University Press, 1958), p. 78.
59. On governance see Daniel Kaufman, Aart Kraay, and Massimo Mastruzzi, *Governance Matters III: Governance Indicators for 1996–2002* (Washington, D.C.: World Bank, 2002); Daniel Kaufmann, "Myths and Realities of Governance and Corruption," in *The World Economic Forum, Global Competitiveness Report 2005–2006* (Geneva: World Economic Forum, 2005), pp. 81–98; Paris, *At War's End*.
60. Daniel Kaufmann, Aart Kraay, and Massimo Mastruzzi, *Governance Matters V: Aggregate and Individual Governance Indicators for 1996–2005* (Washington, D.C.: The World Bank, 2006), p. 4.
61. World Bank, *Reforming Public Institutions and Strengthening Governance* (Washington, D.C.: World Bank, 2000); Jessica Einhorn, "The World Bank's Mission Creep," *Foreign Affairs*, Vol. 80, No. 5 (2001), pp. 22–35.
62. Hironaka, *Neverending Wars*, pp. 42–46.
63. Stathis N. Kalyvas, *The Logic of Violence in Civil War* (New York: Cambridge University Press, 2006), p. 216; Timothy P. Wickham-Crowley, *Guerrillas and Revolution in Latin America: A Comparative Study of Insurgents and Regimes Since 1956* (Princeton, NJ: Princeton University Press, 1992), p. 35.
64. Fearon and Laitin, "Ethnicity, Insurgency, and Civil War," pp. 75–90; Collier, Hoeffler, and Rohner, "Beyond Greed and Grievance: Feasibility and Civil War," p. 16. Some research has found little or no correlation between mountainous terrain and insurgency. See, for example, Collier and Hoeffler, "Greed and Grievance in Civil War"; Nicholas Sambanis, "What Is a Civil War? Conceptual and Empirical Complexities of an Operational Definition," *Journal of Conflict Resolution*, Vol. 48 (2004), pp. 814–848.
65. Fearon and Laitin, "Ethnicity, Insurgency, and Civil War," p. 85.
66. James C. Scott, *The Art of Not Being Governed: An Anarchist History of Upland Southeast Asia* (New Haven, CT: Yale University Press, 2009).
67. Fear and Laitin, "Ethnicity, Insurgency, and Civil War," p. 81.
68. Jon Lee Anderson, *Guerrilla: Journeys in the Insurgent World* (New York: Penguin, 2004), pp. 212–213.
69. Jane Stromseth, David Wippman, and Rosa Brooks, *Can Might Make Rights? Building the Rule of Law after Military Interventions* (New York: Cambridge University Press, 2006), pp. 137–140.
70. Daniel L. Byman, "Friends Like These: Counterinsurgency and the War on Terrorism," *International Security*, Vol. 31, No. 2 (Fall 2006), pp. 79–115; Byman, *Going to War with the Allies You Have: Allies, Counterinsurgency, and the War on Terrorism* (Carlisle, PA: US Army War College, November 2005).

71. Roger Trinquier, *Modern Warfare: A French View of Counterinsurgency*, trans. Daniel Lee (New York: Praeger, 2006), p. 43; David Galula, *Counterinsurgency Warfare: Theory and Practice* (New York: Praeger, 2006), p. 31.

72. The security dilemma literature is quite large. Some of the basic works include John Herz, "Idealist Internationalism and the Security Dilemma," *World Politics*, Vol. 2, No. 2 (January 1950), pp. 157–180; Robert Jervis, "Cooperation Under the Security Dilemma"; Charles L. Glaser, "Realists as Optimists: Cooperation as Self-Help," *International Security*, Vol. 19, No. 3 (Winter 1994/95), pp. 50–90; Randall L. Schweller, "Neorealism's Status-Quo Bias: What Security Dilemma?" *Security Studies*, Vol. 5, No. 3 (Spring 1996), pp. 90–121; Andrew Kydd, "Sheep in Sheep's Clothing: Why Security Seekers Do Not Fight Each Other," *Security Studies*, Vol. 7, No. 1 (Autumn 1997), pp. 114–154; Charles L. Glaser, "The Security Dilemma Revisited," *World Politics*, Vol. 50, No. 1 (October 1997), pp. 171–201.

73. Barry Posen, "The Security Dilemma and Ethnic Conflict," in Michael E. Brown, ed., *Ethnic Conflict and International Security* (Princeton, NJ: Princeton University Press, 1993), pp. 103–124; James D. Fearon, "Rationalist Explanations for War," *International Organization*, Vol. 49, No. 3 (Summer 1995), pp. 379–414.

74. Posen, "The Security Dilemma and Ethnic Conflict," pp. 103–124.

75. Fearon and Laitin, "Ethnicity, Insurgency, and Civil War," pp. 75–76.

76. Michael W. Doyle and Nicholas Sambanis, *Making War and Building Peace* (Princeton, NJ: Princeton University Press, 2006), p. 5.

77. Hironaka, *Neverending Wars*, p. 45.

78. Hironaka, *Neverending Wars*, p. 51.

79. Jeremy M. Weinstein and Laudemiro Francisco, "The Civil War in Mozambique: The Balance between Internal and External Influences," in Paul Collier and Nicholas Sambanis, eds., *Understanding Civil War*, Vol. 1, *Africa* (Washington, D.C.: World Bank, 2005), pp. 157–192.

80. Zurcher, Baev, and Koehler, "Civil Wars in the Caucasus," p. 273.

81. Doyle and Sambanis, *Making War and Building Peace*, pp. 162–163.

82. Stathis N. Kalyvas and Nicholas Sambanis, "Bosnia's Civil War: Origins and Violence Dynamics," in Collier and Sambanis, eds., *Understanding Civil War*, Vol. 2, p. 210.

83. Makdisi and Sadaka, "The Lebanese Civil War, 1975–1990."

84. Zurcher, Baev, and Koehler, "Civil Wars in the Caucasus."

85. Mark Kramer, "The Perils of Counterinsurgency: Russia's War in Chechnya," *International Security*, Vol. 29, No. 3 (Winter 2004/05), pp. 5–63.

86. See, for example, Galula, *Counterinsurgency Warfare*, pp. 36–37.

87. Guevara, *Guerrilla Warfare*, p. 20.

88. Waruhiu Itote (General China), *"Mau Mau" General* (Nairobi: East African Publishing House, 1967).

89. Baya Gacemi, *I, Nadia, Wife of a Terrorist* (Lincoln, NE: University of Nebraska Press, 2006), p. xi.

90. Quoted in Aliza Marcus, *Blood and Belief: The PKK and the Kurdish Fight for Independence* (New York: New York University Press, 2007), p. 76.

91. Omar Cabezas, *Fire from the Mountain: The Making of a Sandinista* (New York: Crown, 1985), p. 200.

92. Thomas Hegghammer, *Jihad in Saudi Arabia: Violence and Pan-Islamism since 1979* (New York: Cambridge University Press, 2010); Bruce Riedel and Bilal Y. Saab, "Al Qaeda's Third Front: Saudi Arabia," *Washington Quarterly*, Vol. 31, No. 2 (Spring 2008), pp. 33–46; John R. Bradley, "Al Qaeda and the House of Saud: Eternal Enemies or Secret Bedfellows?" *The Washington Quarterly*, Vol. 28, No. 4 (Autumn 2005), pp. 139–152.

93. Collier, Hoeffler, and Rohner, "Beyond Greed and Grievance," pp. 3–4; Collier, "Economic Causes of Civil Conflict and Their Implications for Policy," pp. 1, 3; Paul Staniland, "Organizing Insurgency," *International Security*, Vol. 37, No. 1 (Summer 2012), pp. 142–177; Michael L. Ross, "A Closer Look at Oil, Diamonds, and Civil War," *Annual Review of Political Science*, Vol. 9 (June 2006), pp. 265–300.

94. Collier and Hoeffler, "Civil War."

95. Collier, Hoeffler, and Rohner, "Beyond Greed and Grievance," pp. 1–27.

96. Collier, Hoeffler, and Rohner, "Beyond Greed and Grievance," p. 4; Strategic Foresight Group, *Cost of Conflict in Sri Lanka* (Mumbai: Strategic Foresight Group, 2006).

97. Collier, Hoeffler, and Rohner, "Beyond Greed and Grievance," p. 4.

98. See, for example, Collier, "Economic Causes of Civil Conflict and Their Implications for Policy," p. 3.

99. Michael L. Ross, "Resources and Rebellion in Aceh, Indonesia," in Collier and Sambanis, eds., *Understanding Civil War*, Vol. 2, pp. 40–41, 48–49.

100. "Violence at Multinationals," *Tempo*, March 20, 2001.

101. See, for example, Michael Freeman, ed., *Financing Terrorism: Case Studies* (Burlington, VT: Ashgate, 2012), pp. 199–215.

102. Gordon H. McCormick, *The Shining Path and Peruvian Terrorism* (Santa Monica, CA: RAND, 1987), p. 12.

103. Gacemi, *I, Nadia, Wife of a Terrorist*, p. 47.

104. Mancur Olson, *The Logic of Collective Action* (Cambridge, MA: Harvard University Press, 1971).

105. See, for example, Collier, "Economic Causes of Civil Conflict and Their Implications for Policy," p. 3.

106. Stathis N. Kaylvas and Matthew Adam Kocher, "How 'Free' is Free Riding in Civil Wars? Violence, Insurgency, and the Collective Action Problem," *World Politics*, Vol. 49, No. 2 (January 2007), pp. 177–216.

107. Peng, *My Side of History*, p. 201.

108. Héctor Béjar, *Peru 1965: Notes on a Guerrilla Experience*, translated by William Rose (New York: Monthly Review Press, 1970), p. 118.

109. Béjar, *Peru 1965*, p. 74.
110. Richard Clutterbuck, *Conflict and Violence in Singapore and Malaysia 1945–1983* (Boulder, CO: Westview Press, 1985), p. 269.
111. Clutterbuck, *Conflict and Violence in Singapore and Malaysia*, p. 268.
112. Michael S. Lund, "Greed and Grievance Diverted: How Macedonia Avoided Civil War, 1990–2001," in Collier and Sambanis, eds., *Understanding Civil War*, Vol. 2, pp. 231–257.
113. James D. Fearon and David D. Laitin, "Explaining Interethnic Cooperation," *The American Political Science Review*, Vol. 90, No. 4 (December 1996), pp. 715–735.
114. Guevara, *Guerrilla Warfare*, p. 13.

Chapter 3

1. Chin Peng, *My Side of History* (Singapore: Media Masters, 2003), p. 207.
2. Peng, *My Side of History*, p. 195; "Pontian Tragedy," *The Straits Times*, November 6, 1947, p. 1.
3. Peng, *My Side of History*, p. 207.
4. On strategy see, for example, Lawrence Freedman, *Strategy: A History* (New York: Oxford University Press, 2013), pp. ix–xvi.
5. John J. Mearsheimer, *Conventional Deterrence* (Ithaca, NY: Cornell University Press, 1983), pp. 2, 28–29. For insurgent and asymmetric strategies see Ivan Arreguín-Toft, *How the Weak Win Wars: A Theory of Asymmetric Conflict* (New York: Cambridge University Press, 2005); Jerry M. Tinker, ed., *Strategies of Revolutionary Warfare* (New Delhi: S. Chand & Co., 1969); Gérard Chaliand, *Guerrilla Strategies: An Historical Anthology from the Long March to Afghanistan* (Berkeley, CA: University of California Press, 1982).
6. B. H. Liddell Hart, *Strategy: The Indirect Approach* (London: Faber, 1967), p. 335.
7. On grand strategy see Barry R. Posen, *The Sources of Military Doctrine: France, Britain, and Germany between the World Wars* (Ithaca, NY: Cornell University Press, 1984), p. 13; Hart, *Strategy*, pp. 335–336.
8. On insurgent strategies see Chaliand, *Guerrilla Strategies*; Arreguín-Toft, *How the Weak Win Wars*, pp. 23–47; Brian Crozier, *The Rebels: A Study of Post-War Insurrections* (London: Chatto and Windus, 1960); Thomas Perry Thornton, "Terror as a Weapon of Political Agitation," in Harry Eckstein, ed., *Internal War: Problems and Approaches* (New York: Free Press, 1964), p. 91; Tinker, ed., *Strategies of Revolutionary Warfare*.
9. Arreguín-Toft, *How the Weak Win Wars*, pp. 32–33.
10. Robert Taber, *War of the Flea: The Classic Study of Guerrilla Warfare* (Washington, D.C.: Potomac Books, 2002).
11. Walter Laqueur, *Guerrilla Warfare: A Historical and Critical Study* (New Brunswick, NJ: Transaction, 2010); John Shy and Thomas W. Collier, "Revolution War," in Peter Paret, ed., *Makers of Modern Strategy: From*

Machiavelli to the Nuclear Age (Princeton, NJ: Princeton University Press, 1986), pp. 815–862; Hart, *Strategy*; Chaliand, *Guerrilla Strategies*.

12. Sun Tzu, *The Art of War*, trans. Ralph D. Sawyer (Boulder, CO: Westview Press, 1994).

13. Chaliand, *Guerrilla Strategies*, p. 3.

14. Camille Rougeron, *La prochaine guerre* (Paris: Berger-Levrault, 1948).

15. Weinstein, *Inside Rebellion*, p. 29.

16. Mao, *On Guerrilla Warfare*, p. 51. Emphasis added.

17. Commander Prachanda, "Some Ideological and Military Questions Raised by People's War," in Prachanda et al., *Problems and Prospects of Revolution in Nepal* (Nepal: Janadisha, 2004), chapter 15.

18. See, for example, Robert Taber, *War of the Flea: The Classic Study of Guerrilla Warfare* (Washington, D.C.: Potomac Books, 2002), p. 6.

19. African National Congress, "Operation Mayibuye," Part I, 1963.

20. Joe Slovo, *The Unfinished Biography* (London: Hodder and Stoughton, 1996), pp. 145–146.

21. See, for example, Prachanda's comments on urban guerrilla warfare. Prachanda, "Some Ideological and Military Questions Raised by People's War."

22. See the discussion on political networks in Roger Trinquier, *Modern Warfare: A French View of Counterinsurgency*, trans. Daniel Lee (New York: Praeger, 2006), pp. 9–13.

23. O'Neill, *Insurgency and Terrorism*, pp. 49–55.

24. Mao Tse-Tung, "On Protracted War," in *Selected Works of Mao Tse-Tung*, Vol. II (Peking: Foreign Languages Press, 1967).

25. Anna Simons, "War: Back to the Future," *Annual Reviews of Anthropology*, Vol. 28, 1999, pp. 73–108.

26. Stathis N. Kalyvas and Laia Balcells, "International System and Technologies of Rebellion: How the End of the Cold War Shaped Internal Conflict," *American Political Science Review*, Vol. 104, No. 3 (August 2010), pp. 415–429.

27. General Alberto Bayo, *150 Questions for a Guerrilla* (Denver, CO: Cypress, 1963), p. 31.

28. T. E. Lawrence, *The Evolution of a Revolt*, CSI Reprint (Fort Leavenworth, KS: Combat Studies Institute, 1990), p. 22. The document was printed with permission from the *Army Quarterly and Defence Journal*, October 1920.

29. Commander Prachanda, "War Policy of Nepalese New Democratic Revolution in the Context of Historical Development," in Prachanda, *Problems and Prospects of Revolution in Nepal*, Chapter 14.

30. Mao, *On Guerrilla Warfare*, p. 46.

31. Don Barnett and Roy Harvey, *The Revolution in Angola: MPLA, Life Histories and Documents* (New York: The Bobbs-Merrill Company, 1972), p. 8.

32. H. D. S. Greenway, "A 'Sign of Weakness' in the Propaganda of War," *Boston Globe*, August 2, 2011; Eric Schmitt and David Rohde, "Taliban Fighters Increase Attacks, with Troubling Toll among G.I.s and Afghans," *New York Times*, August 1, 2004.

33. Mao, *On Guerrilla Warfare*, p. 46.

34. Weinstein, *Organizing Rebellion*, p. 69.

35. Mao, "On Protracted War."

36. Chaliand, *Revolution in the Third World*, pp. 74–87.

37. Tim Pat Coogan, *The IRA: A History* (Niwot, CO: Roberts Rinehart, 1994), p. 366.

38. Irish Republican Army, *Green Book* (Belfast: Irish Republican Army, 1977), p. 7.

39. The term comes from the Spanish word *foco*, which means "center" or "focal point." Building off of Che Guevara's Guerrilla Warfare, the term was first coined in Régis Debray, *Revolution in the Revolution? Armed Struggle and Political Struggle in Latin America* (New York: Grove Press, 1967), p. 22.

40. Guevara, *Guerrilla Warfare*, p. 7.

41. Gérard Chaliand, *Revolution in the Third World: Currents and Conflicts in Asia, Africa, and Latin America* (New York: Penguin, 1989), pp. 43–44; Lacquer, *Guerrilla Warfare*, pp. 330–338.

42. John Shy and Thomas W. Collier, "Revolution War," in Peter Paret, ed., *Makers of Modern Strategy: From Machiavelli to the Nuclear Age* (Princeton, NJ: Princeton University Press, 1986), p. 850.

43. Chaliand, *Revolution in the Third World*, p. 44.

44. Chaliand, *Revolution in the Third World*, pp. 44–45; Chaliand, *Guerrilla Strategies*, p. 27.

45. Quoted in Arne Westad, *The Global Cold War* (New York: Cambridge University Press, 2007), p. 179.

46. On attrition strategies see, for example, Mearsheimer, *Conventional Deterrence*, pp. 29–30, 33–35.

47. See, for example, Gil Merom, *How Democracies Lose Small Wars: State, Society, and the Failures of France in Algeria, Israel in Lebanon, and the United States in Vietnam* (New York: Cambridge University Press, 2003), p. 33; Chaliand, *Guerrilla Strategies*. Chaliand excludes cases like Biafra "since the war there was essentially fought on conventional lines" (p. 21).

48. Arreguín-Toft, *How the Weak Win Wars*, pp. 30–31.

49. O'Neill, *Insurgency and Terrorism*, p. 50.

50. Kalyvas and Balcells, "International System and Technologies of Rebellion."

51. Daniel Byman, *Deadly Connections: States That Sponsor Terrorism* (New York: Cambridge University Press, 2005); James D. Fearon and David D. Laitin, "Ethnicity, Insurgency, and Civil War," *American Political Science Review*, Vol. 97, No. 1 (February 2003), p. 86; Stathis N. Kalyvas,

The Logic of Violence in Civil War (New York: Cambridge University Press, 2006).

52. David Galula, *Counterinsurgency Warfare: Theory and Practice* (St. Petersburg, FL: Hailer, 2005), pp. 53–58.

53. Abdul Haris Nasution, *Fundamentals of Guerrilla Warfare* (New York: Praeger, 1965), p. 17.

54. Laqueur, *Guerrilla Warfare*, pp. 284–285.

55. Captain Labignette, "Casconcrete de guerre révolutionnaire," *Revue demilitaire l'information*, No. 281 (February–March 1957); Chaliand, *Guerrilla Strategies*, p. 266.

56. "An Interview of King Paul of Greece," *US News & World Report*, April 21, 1950, p. 29.

57. General Vo Nguyen Giap and Van Tien Dung, *How We Won the War* (Philadelphia: RECON, 1976), p. 40. Emphasis added.

58. Ibid., p. 35.

59. John de St. Jorre, *The Nigerian Civil War* (Toronto: Ernest Benn, 1960); O'Neill, *Insurgency and Terrorism*, pp. 56–57.

60. Robert Asprey, *War in the Shadows: The Guerrilla in History* (New York: William Morrow and Company, 1994), pp. 1188–1189.

61. Chester Crocker, *High Noon in Southern Africa: Making Peace in a Rough Neighborhood* (New York: W.W. Norton, 1992).

62. Revolutionary United Front, *Footpaths to Democracy: Toward a New Sierra Leone*, 1995.

63. Barnett and Harvey, *The Revolution in Angola*, p. 276.

64. Central Intelligence Agency, *Balkan Battlegrounds: A Military History of the Yugoslav Conflict, 1990–1995* (Washington, D.C.: Central Intelligence Agency, Office of Russian and European Analysis, 2002), p. xiii.

65. Laura Silver and Allan Little, *Yugoslavia: Death of a Nation* (New York: Penguin, 1997); Steven L. Burg and Paul S. Shoup, *The War in Bosnia-Herzegovina: Ethnic Conflict and International Intervention* (Armonk, NY: M.E. Sharpe, 1999); Central Intelligence Agency, *Balkan Battlegrounds*.

66. Gary C. Schroen, *First In: An Insider's Account of How the CIA Spearheaded the War on Terror in Afghanistan* (New York: Ballantine Books, 2005), pp. 161–162.

67. 'Abd Al-'Aziz Al-Muqrin, *A Practical Course for Guerrilla Warfare*, trans. by Norman Cigar (Washington, D.C.: Potomac Books, 2009), p. 90.

68. See "Islamic State," Jane's World Insurgency and Terrorism Data Base. Accessed on November 8, 2015.

69. Arreguín-Toft, *How the Weak Win Wars*, pp. 31–32; Robert B. Asprey, *War in the Shadows: The Classic History of Guerrilla Warfare from Ancient Persia to the Present* (New York: Little, Brown and Company, 1994), p. 108; Nathan Leites and Charles Wolf, Jr., *Rebellion and Authority: An Analytic Essay on Insurgent Conflicts* (Santa Monica, CA: RAND, February 1970), pp. 90–131.

70. Robert A. Pape, *Bombing to Win: Air Power and Coercion in War* (Ithaca, NY: Cornell University Press, 1996), pp. 13–18.

71. Thomas C. Schelling, *Arms and Influence* (New Haven: Yale University Press, 1966).

72. On punishment campaigns and air power see Pape, *Bombing to Win: Air Power and Coercion in War*, pp. 66–69.

73. Weinstein, *Inside Rebellion*, p. 206; Kalyvas, *The Logic of Violence in Civil War*, pp. 153–154.

74. Kalyvas, *The Logic of Violence in Civil War*.

75. Leites and Wolf, *Rebellion and* Authority, p. 96.

76. David Zucchino, "Sorting Friends from Foes," *Los Angeles Times*, November 1, 2004, pp. A8–A9.

77. Kalyvas, *The Logic of Violence in Civil War*, p. 209.

78. Quoted in Leites and Wolf, *Rebellion and Authority*, p. 100.

79. Gonzalo Sánchez, "Introduction: Problems of Violence, Prospects for Peace," in Charles Bergquist, Ricardo Penaranda, and Gonzalo Sánchez, eds., *Violence in Colombia, 1990–2000: Waging War and Negotiation Peace* (Wilmington, DE: Scholarly Resources, 2001), p. 30.

80. Chaliand, *Revolution in the Third World*, p. 57.

81. Richard Stubbs, *Hearts and Minds in Guerrilla Warfare: The Malayan Emergency, 1948–1960* (New York: Oxford University Press, 1989), p. 105; Robert Thompson, *Defeating Communist Insurgency* (St. Petersburg, FL: Hailer, 2005), p. 25.

82. John P. Cann, *Counterinsurgency in Africa: The Portuguese Way of War, 1961–1974* (Westport, CT: Greenwood Press, 1997), p. 157.

83. Lynn Horton, *Peasants in Arms: War and Peace in the Mountains of Nicaragua, 1979–1984* (Athens, OH: Ohio University Center for International Studies, 1998), p. 167; Clifford Krauss, *Zimbabwe's Guerrilla War: Peasant Voices* (New York: Cambridge University Press, 1999); Ponciano H. Del Pino, "Family, Culture, and 'Revolution': Everyday Life with Sendero Luminoso," in Steven J. Stern, ed., *Shining and Other Paths: War and Society in Peru, 1980–1995* (Durham, NC: Duke University Press, 1998), pp. 172, 189; Nelson Manrique, "The War for the Central Sierra," in Stern, *Shining and Other Paths*, p. 218; Paul Richards, *Fighting for the Rain Forest: War, Youth, and Resources in Sierra Leone* (Oxford: James Currey, 1966), pp. 181–182; Mauricio Rubio, *Crimen e impunidad: precisiones sobre la violencia* (Santafé de Bogotá: Tercer Mundo, 1999), p. 120.

84. Faith J. H. McDonnell and Grace Akallo, *Girl Soldier: A Story of Hope for Northern Uganda's Children* (Grand Rapids, MI: Chosen, 2007), p. 100.

85. Kalyvas, *The Logic of Violence in Civil War*, p. 224.

86. David Anderson, *Histories of the Hanged: The Dirty War in Kenya and the End of Empire* (New York: W.W. Norton, 2005), p. 118.

87. Stathis N. Kaylvas and Matthew Adam Kocher, "How 'Free' is Free Riding in Civil Wars? Violence, Insurgency, and the Collective Action Problem," *World Politics*, Vol. 49, No. 2 (January 2007), pp. 189–190.

88. Russell Crandall, *America's Dirty Wars: Irregular Warfare from 1776 to the War on Terror* (New York: Cambridge University Press, 2014), p. 179.

89. Weinstein, *Inside Rebellion*, pp. 204–206.

90. Quoted in Anders Nilsson, *Peace in Our Time* (Gothenburg, Sweden: Padrigu, 1999), p. 115. Also see Weinstein, *Inside Rebellion*, p. 230.

91. Weinstein, *Inside Rebellion*, pp. 79, 229–239.

92. Thomas Perry Thornton, "Terror as a Weapon of Political Agitation," in Harry Eckstein, ed., *Internal War: Problems and Approaches* (New York: Free Press, 1964), p. 83.

93. One of the classical works on the psychology of terrorism is Hannah Arendt, "Ideologie und Terror," in Klaus Piper, ed., *Offener Horizont: Festschrift für Karl Jaspers* (Munich, Germany: Piper, 1953), pp. 229–254.

94. Ayman al-Zawahiri, *A Treatise on the Exoneration of the Nation of the Pen and Sword of the Denigrating Charge of Being Irresolute and Weak*, March 2008, p. 40.

95. Ibid., p. 41.

96. Ibid., p. 41.

97. National Counterterrorism Center, *2009 Report on Terrorism* (Washington, D.C.: National Counterterrorism Center, April 2010), p. 28; National Counterterrorism Center, *2007 Report on Terrorism* (Washington, D.C.: National Counterterrorism Center, April 2008), pp. 11, 36.

98. On the end of insurgencies see, for example, Jason Lyall and Isaiah Wilson III, "Rage against the Machines: Explaining Outcomes in Counterinsurgency Wars," *International Organization*, No. 63 (Winter 2009), pp. 67–106.

99. Barry Posen, "The Security Dilemma and Ethnic Conflict," in Michael E. Brown, ed., *Ethnic Conflict and International Security* (Princeton, NJ: Princeton University Press, 1993), pp. 103–124; James D. Fearon, "Rationalist Explanations for War," *International Organization*, Vol. 49, No. 3 (Summer 1995), pp. 379–414.

100. On hybrid warfare see, for example, David Kilcullen, *The Accidental Guerrilla: Fighting Small Wars in the Midst of a Big One* (New York: Oxford University Press, 2009), pp. 4–6, 25, 148–154, 188, 294–300; Peter Pindják, "Deterring Hybrid Warfare: A Chance for NATO and the EU to Work Together?" *NATO Review*, 2014; David E. Johnson, *Military Capabilities for Hybrid Warfare: Insights from the Israel Defense Forces in Lebanon and Gaza* (Santa Monica, CA: RAND, 2010); Frank G. Hoffman, "Hybrid Warfare and Challenges," *Joint Forces Quarterly*, No. 52 (2009), pp. 34–39.

101. Revolutionary United Front, *Footpaths to Democracy: Toward a New Sierra Leone*.

102. Mao, "On Protracted War," p. 138.

103. Mao, "On Protracted War," p. 139.

104. On the three phases see Mao, "On Protracted War," pp. 136–145.

105. Kalyvas, *The Logic of Violence in Civil War*, p. 221.

106. Mean averages include ongoing insurgencies.

Chapter 4

1. Mao Tse-Tung, *On Guerrilla Warfare*, translated by Samuel B. Griffith II (Urbana, IL: University of Illinois Press, 2000), p. 46.

2. Irish Republican Army, *Green Book* (Belfast: Irish Republican Army, 1977), p. 6. The *Green Book* was a training and induction manual issued by the Irish Republican Army to new volunteers.

3. Isabel Nassief, *The Campaign for Homs and Aleppo: The Assad Regime's Strategy in 2013* (Washington, D.C.: Institute for the Study of War, January 2014), pp. 27–28; Damien McElroy, "Syrian Rebels Use Captured Army Tanks to Attack Aleppo Airforce Base," *Telegraph* (UK), August 2, 2012.

4. "Government Airstrike in Northern Syria Reportedly Kills 14 as Rebels Attack Airbase," *Associated Press*, December 28, 2012.

5. Joby Warrick, "Second Wind for Syrian rebels?" *Washington Post*, August 21, 2013; Loveday Morris, "Syrian Rebels Claim Key Air Base, Other Gains," *Washington Post*, August 7, 2013.

6. Video uploaded to YouTube on August 6, 2013. Accessed on February 20, 2014. The link (www.youtube.com/watch?v=SG87ZafxSHs) was eventually taken down.

7. See, for example, Department of Defense, *Joint Publication 1–02: Department of Defense Dictionary of Military and Associated Terms* (Washington, D.C.: Department of Defense, 2012), p. 259; Lawrence Freedman, *Strategy: A History* (New York: Oxford University Press, 2013), pp. 72–75.

8. Karl von Clausewitz, *On War*, edited and translated by Michael Howard and Peter Paret (Princeton, NJ: Princeton University Press, 1989), p. 128.

9. Quoted in Herman Hattaway, *Reflections of a Civil War Historian: Essays on Leadership, Society, and the Art of War* (Columbia, MO: University of Missouri, 2004), p. 200.

10. *Direct fire* refers to launching a projectile by relying on a direct line of sight between an individual and the target. It can come from a range of weapons, such as rifles, rocket-propelled grenades, and handguns. *Indirect fire* refers to launching a projectile without relying on a direct line of sight, in which the individual aims by calculating azimuth and elevation angles. Examples include missiles and mortars.

11. US Department of the Army, *FM 3–90–1: Offense and Defense, Volume 1* (Washington, D.C.: Headquarters, Department of the Army, March 2013), pp. 3–23. Also see, for example, 'Abd Al-'Aziz Al-Muqrin, *A Practical Course for Guerrilla War*, translated by Norman Cigar (Washington, D.C.: Potomac Books, 2009), pp. 118–119.

12. See, for example, Department of Defense, *Joint Publication 1–02: Department of Defense Dictionary of Military and Associated Terms* (Washington, D.C.: Department of Defense, 2012), p. 219; Al-Muqrin, *A Practical Course for Guerrilla War*, p. 119.

13. Al-Muqrin, *A Practical Course for Guerrilla War*, p. 119.
14. M. Anderson, M. Arnsten, and H. Averch, *Insurgent Organization and Operations: A Case Study of the Viet Cong in the Delta, 1964–1966* (Santa Monica, CA: RAND, August 1967), pp. 107–108, 113.
15. Don Barnett and Roy Harvey, *The Revolution in Angola: MPLA, Life Histories and Documents* (New York: Bobbs-Merrill, 1972), p. 17.
16. This paragraph and the following two paragraphs draw heavily from Mark Kramer, "The Perils of Counterinsurgency: Russia's War in Chechnya," *International Security*, Vol. 29, No. 3 (2005/2006), p. 19.
17. Col. Gennadii Zhilin, "Opyt boevogo primeneniya voisk na Severnom Kavkaze" [Experience with the combat employment of troops in the North Caucasus], part 3, *Soldat Otechstva*, No. 47 (June 16 2004), p. 5; Mark Kramer, "The Perils of Counterinsurgency: Russia's War in Chechnya," *International Security*, Vol. 29, No. 3 (2005/2006), p. 19.
18. Quoted from a set of "instructions on the waging of combat operations" issued by the Chechen guerrilla commander Hattab in 2002. The document was captured by Russian forces after Hattab was killed. Kramer, "The Perils of Counterinsurgency," p. 20.
19. Quoted in Vladimir Mukhin, "Chechnya kak obshchevoiskovoi poligon" [Chechnya as a combined-forces training ground], *Nezavisimoe voennoe obozrenie*, No. 42 (November 28 2003), p. 2; Kramer, "The Perils of Counterinsurgency," pp. 19–20.
20. Interview transcribed in Andrei Pilipchuk, "General-polkovnik Vladimir Boldyrev: My—lyudi derzhavnye, i Otechestvo sumeem zashchitit" [Colonel General Vladimir Boldyrev: We are people who serve a great power, and the Fatherland will be able to defend us], *Krasnaya zvezda* (October 16 2003), p. 1. Kramer, "The Perils of Counterinsurgency," p. 24.
21. Vadim Solovev, "Severnyi Kavkaz: Retsidiv 22 iyunya 1941 goda" [The North Caucasus: A Reprise of June 22, 1941], *Nezavisimoe voennoe obozrenie*, No. 24 (June 25 2004), p. 3; Kramer, "The Perils of Counterinsurgency," p. 24.
22. Jerry Meyerle and Carter Malkasian, *Insurgent Tactics in Southern Afghanistan, 2005–2008* (Alexandria, VA: Center for Naval Analysis, August 2009), pp. 3–8.
23. Thomas Marks, *Colombian Army Adaptation to FARC Insurgency* (Carlisle, PA: Strategic Studies Institute, US Army War College, 2002), p. 8.
24. Kiboi Muriithi (General Kamwana), *War in the Forest* (Nairobi: Trafford, 1971); David Anderson, *Histories of the Hanged: The Dirty War in Kenya and the End of Empire* (New York: W.W. Norton, 2005), pp. 252–257.
25. United States Army Special Operations Command, *Undergrounds in Insurgent, Revolutionary, and Resistance Warfare* (Fort Bragg, NC: United States Army Special Operations Command, January 2013), p. 80.
26. Ron Buikema and Matt Burger, "Farabundo Martí Frente Para La Liberación Nacional (FMLN)," in *Casebook on Insurgency and*

Revolutionary Warfare, Volume II: 1962–2009 (Laurel, MD: Johns Hopkins University Applied Physics Laboratory, 2010).

27. Ron Buikema and Matt Burger, "Sendero Luminoso," in *Casebook on Insurgency and Revolutionary Warfare, Volume II: 1962–2009*, p. 64.

28. Barak Salmoni, Bryce Loidolt, and Madeleine Wells, *Regime and Periphery in Northern Yemen: The Huthi Phenomenon* (Santa Monica, CA: RAND, 2010), pp. 197–204.

29. Waruhiu Itote (General China), *"Mau Mau" General* (Nairobi: East African Publishing House, 1967), p. 97.

30. Joint Publication 3–24, *Counterinsurgency Operations* (Washington, D.C.: Department of Defense, 2009), GL-9.

31. United States Army Special Operations Command, *Undergrounds in Insurgent, Revolutionary, and Resistance Warfare* (Fort Bragg, NC: United States Army Special Operations Command, January 2013), p. 171.

32. Al-Muqrin, *A Practical Course for Guerrilla War*, p. 128.

33. Barnett and Harvey, *The Revolution in Angola*, p. 2.

34. James I. Wirtz, *The Tet Offensive: Intelligence Failure in War* (New York: Cornell University Press, 1991), p. 22.

35. United States Army Special Operations Command, *Undergrounds in Insurgent, Revolutionary, and Resistance Warfare* (Fort Bragg, NC: United States Army Special Operations Command, January 2013), p. 38. On Vietnam, see James I. Wirtz, *The Tet Offensive: Intelligence Failure in War* (New York: Cornell University Press, 1991), p. 22.

36. Omar Cabezas, *Fire from the Mountain: The Making of a Sandinista* (New York: Crown, 1985), p. 44.

37. US Special Operations Command, *Unconventional Warfare*, Draft Document, Joint Publication, 2013.

38. United States Army Special Operations Command, *Undergrounds in Insurgent, Revolutionary, and Resistance Warfare* (Fort Bragg, NC: United States Army Special Operations Command, January 2013), p. 38.

39. Department of Defense, Joint Publication 1–02, *Department of Defense Dictionary of Military and Associated Terms* (Washington, D.C.: Department of Defense, 2012), p. 291.

40. United States Army Special Operations Command, *Undergrounds in Insurgent, Revolutionary, and Resistance Warfare*, p. 178.

41. US Special Operations Command, *Unconventional Warfare*, Draft Document, Joint Publication, 2013.

42. African National Congress, "Operation Mayibuye," Part V, 1963.

43. Ronnie Kasrils, *Armed and Dangerous: From Undercover Struggle to Freedom* (Auckland Park, South Africa: Jacana Media, 2013), p. 35.

44. Joe Slovo, *The Unfinished Biography* (London: Hodder and Stoughton, 1996), p. 152.

45. Thomas C. Schelling, *Arms and Influence* (New Haven, CT: Yale University Press, 1966), p. 3.

46. General Alberto Bayo, *150 Questions for a Guerrilla* (Denver, CO: Cypress Printing, 1963), p. xiv.

47. Ernesto "Che" Guevara, *Guerrilla Warfare* (Thousand Oaks, CA: BN Publishing, 2007), pp. 17–18.

48. Joaquin Villalobos, "Popular Insurrection: Desire or Reality?" *Latin American Perspectives*, Vol. 62, No. 3 (Summer 1989), pp. 5–37.

49. United States Army Special Operations Command, *Undergrounds in Insurgent, Revolutionary, and Resistance Warfare*, p. 178.

50. "Infijar 'Anif Yahazz Madinat Baqim bi-Muhafazat Sa'da," al-Ayyam, December 10, 2006. On broader Huthi insurgent tactics see Salmoni, Loidolt, and Wells, *Regime and Periphery in Northern Yemen*.

51. Coalition Provisional Authority, Pipeline Sabotage, October 28, 2003. From the Coalition Provisional Authority Archives.

52. Memo from James Ellery to Ambassador Bremer, Subject: Read Ahead for Ambassador Bremer: Infrastructure Security Strategy, January 11, 2004. From the Coalition Provisional Authority Archives.

53. Infrastructure Security Planning Group, Infrastructure Security Strategy, January 12, 2004. From the Coalition Provisional Authority Archives.

54. Info Memo from Darrell Trent to the Administrator, Subject: Ministry of Transportation Issues Update, December 15, 2003. From the Coalition Provisional Authority Archives.

55. Memorandum from United States Central Command to Secretary of Defense, Subject: Energy Systems Stability and Security in Iraq, August 28, 2003. From the Coalition Provisional Authority Archives.

56. Gordon H. McCormick, *The Shining Path and Peruvian Terrorism* (Santa Monica, CA: RAND, 1987), pp. 4, 11.

57. See Al-Muqrin, *A Practical Course for Guerrilla War*, p. 141.

58. Itote, *"Mau Mau" General*, p. 43. Also see Anderson, *Histories of the Hanged*, p. 87.

59. Baya Gacemi, *I, Nadia, Wife of a Terrorist* (Lincoln, NE: University of Nebraska Press, 2006), p. 65.

60. Salmoni, Loidolt, and Wells, *Regime and Periphery in Northern Yemen*, p. 206.

61. Faith J. H. McDonnell and Grace Akallo, *Girl Soldier: A Story of Hope for Northern Uganda's Children* (Grand Rapids, MI: Chosen, 2007), p. 118.

62. Tim Pat Coogan, *The IRA: A History* (Niwot, CO: Roberts Rinehart, 1994), p. 290.

63. Article 3 of the Geneva Conventions prohibits the "violence to life and person, in particular murder of all kinds, mutilation, cruel treatment and torture." See Article 3 in the Convention (IV) Relative to the Protection of Civilian Persons in Time of War, Geneva, 12 August 1949.

64. Anthony Vinci, "The Strategic Use of Fear by the Lord's Resistance Army," *Small Wars and Insurgencies*, Vol. 16, No. 3, December 2005, p. 370.

65. Faith J. H. McDonnell and Grace Akallo, *Girl Soldier: A Story of Hope for Northern Uganda's Children* (Grand Rapids, MI: Chosen, 2007), pp. 100–102.

66. Kiboi Muriithi (General Kamwana), *War in the Forest* (Nairobi: Trafford, 1971), p. 56.

67. Coogan, *The IRA: A History*, p. 355.

68. Gacemi, *I, Nadia, Wife of a Terrorist*, p. 74.

69. See Al-Muqrin, *A Practical Course for Guerrilla War*, p. 156.

70. United States Army Special Operations Command, *Undergrounds in Insurgent, Revolutionary, and Resistance Warfare* (Fort Bragg, NC: United States Army Special Operations Command, January 2013), p. 38. On Vietnam, see James I. Wirtz, *The Tet Offensive: Intelligence Failure in War* (New York: Cornell University Press, 1991), p. 32.

71. United States Army Special Operations Command, *Undergrounds in Insurgent, Revolutionary, and Resistance Warfare*, p. 38. On Vietnam, see Wirtz, *The Tet Offensive*, p. 67.

72. Rukmini Callimachi, "Paying Ransoms, Europe Bankrolls Qaeda Terror," *New York Times*, July 29, 2014.

73. Ibid.

74. Stephen Phillips, "Fuerzas Armadas Revolutionarias—FARC," in Chuck Crossett, ed., *Assessing Revolutionary and Insurgent Strategies* (Laurel, MD: Johns Hopkins Applied Physics Laboratory, 2009), p. 23.

75. Abubakar Shekau, statement on video released on multiple jihadist websites circa May 12, 2014.

76. McDonnell and Akallo, *Girl Soldier*, p. 99.

77. Russell Crandall, *America's Dirty Wars: Irregular Warfare from 1776 to the War on Terror* (New York: Cambridge University Press, 2014), p. 284.

78. Robert W. Schaefer, *The Insurgency in Chechnya and the North Caucasus: From Gazavat to Jihad* (Santa Barbara, CA: ABC-CLIO, 2011), pp. 195–232.

79. Adam Dolnik, *Understanding Terrorist Innovation: Technology, Tactics and Global Trends* (New York: Routledge, 2007); Paul Gill, John Horgan, and Jeffrey Lovelace, "Improvised Explosive Device: The Problem of Definition," *Studies in Conflict and Terrorism*, Vol. 34, No. 9 (September 2011), pp. 732–748.

80. See, for example, Alec D. Barker, "Improvised Explosive Devices in Southern Afghanistan and Western Pakistan, 2002–2009," *Studies in Conflict and Terrorism*, Vol. 34, No. 8 (2011), pp. 600–620.

81. On the vulnerability of high-tech vehicles in insurgencies, see, for example, Lyall and Wilson, "Rage against the Machines," pp. 67–106. On foraging, see Martin L. Van Creveld, *Supplying War: Logistics from Wallenstein to Patton* (London: Cambridge University Press, 1977).

82. Kramer, "The Perils of Counterinsurgency," p. 25. The proportion of casualties was cited by Col. Vladimir Trushkov, head of engineering forces

of the Russian airborne commando staff in Chechnya, in "Za vremya kontrterroristicheskoi operatsii na Severnom Kavkaze pogibli 22 sapera desantnika" [During the counterterrorist operation in the North Caucasus, 22 of the paratroop mine-clearers have perished], Agenstvo voennykh novostei [Military News Agency], April 19, 2001, item 9.

83. See Serdtsev's remarks in the series of untitled commentaries by senior military and MVD officers under the rubric "Kontrterroristicheskaya operatsiya na Severnom Kavkaze: Osnovnye uroki i vyvody—Kruglyi stol" [The counterterrorist operation in the North Caucasus: The main lessons and conclusions—A roundtable], *Voennaya mysl*, No. 4 (July–August 2000), pp. 5–24. Serdtsev's commentary is on pp. 21–24. Kramer, "The Perils of Counterinsurgency," pp. 25–26.

84. Alec D. Barker, "Improvised Explosive Devices in Southern Afghanistan and Western Pakistan, 2002–2009," *Studies in Conflict and Terrorism*, Vol. 34, No. 8 (2011), pp. 600–620; Hazard Management Solutions, "Timescale to Develop/Deploy Sophisticated IEDs," unpublished briefing, November 2004.

85. Barker, "Improvised Explosive Devices in Southern Afghanistan and Western Pakistan, 2002–2009," pp. 600–620.

86. See, for example, Bruce Hoffman, *Inside Terrorism* (New York: Columbia University Press, 2006), pp. 1–40.

87. Trinquier, *Modern Warfare*, p. 17.

88. On suicide terrorism see Bruce Hoffman, *Inside Terrorism*, revised ed. (New York: Columbia University Press, 2006), pp. 131–171; Mia Bloom, *Dying to Kill: The Allure of Suicide Terror* (New York: Columbia University Press, 2005); Robert A. Pape, *Dying to Win: The Strategic Logic of Suicide Terrorism* (New York: Random House, 2005); Pape and James K. Feldman, *Cutting the Fuse: The Explosion of Global Suicide Terrorism and How to Stop It* (Chicago: University of Chicago Press, 2010).

89. Pape, *Dying to Win*, p. 22.

90. These data have been calculated from the CPOST Suicide Attack Database. From 1982 to 2014, the CPOST dataset recorded 4,620 total suicide attacks worldwide, of which 4,532 suicide attacks (98 percent) occurred in campaigns included in this book's universe of insurgencies. Excluded are attacks by core al Qa'ida against the US homeland (e.g., the 9/11 attacks) and US military and diplomatic installations abroad that took place outside of war zones (e.g., USS *Cole* and the Tanzanian and Kenyan US embassy bombings). Including all attacks in the CPOST dataset through 2014, these averages rise to 9.9 killed and 25.5 wounded per suicide attack. These averages are largely consistent with data recorded in START's Global Terrorism Database (GTD) hosted by the University of Maryland.

91. On the Anbar Awakening see, for example, Mitchell B. Reiss, *Negotiating with Evil: When to Talk to Terrorists* (New York: Open Road, 2010), pp.

177–220; Austin Long, "The Anbar Awakening," *Survival*, Vol. 50, No. 2 (April–May 2008), pp. 67–94.

92. In this context, outside support included both combat support (boots on the ground and/or drone strikes) as well as lethal and non-lethal aid. For instance, Russia, China, and India all faced suicide attackers in their domestic insurgencies (Chechnya, Xinjiang, Kashmir, Assam, Sri Lanka). The United States, France, NATO, and Russia faced suicide attackers in conflicts in which they had deployed boots on the ground in support of governments (Iraq, Afghanistan, Mali, Syria, Lebanon) and in which they provided lethal air support (Yemen, Somalia, Pakistan, Algeria, Nigeria), as well as other forms of training, equipping, and intelligence-sharing (Israel, the Philippines, Turkey).

93. The one exception was Pakistan versus Baluchi separatists. However, given the fungibility of US defense aid to Pakistan, this might reasonably also be coded as a case involving outside US support.

94. Major Raymond M. Longabaugh, "Incorporating MRAPs into the Army Force Structure," *Army Sustainment*, September–October 2011, p. 28.

95. Mao, *On Guerrilla Warfare*, pp. 92–93.

96. Mao, *On Guerrilla Warfare*, p. 92.

97. Max Abrahms similarly finds that terrorist targeting of civilians undermines their support—and, ultimately, their ability to achieve objectives. See Max Abrahms, "Why Terrorism Does Not Work," *International Security*, Vol. 31, No. 2 (Fall 2006), pp. 42–78.

98. Gacemi, *I, Nadia, Wife of a Terrorist*, p. 141.

99. See, for example, Gilles Kepel, *Jihad: The Trail of Political Islam* (Cambridge, MA: Harvard University Press, 2002), p. 271.

100. The quote comes from Article 78 in Islamic Emirate of Afghanistan [Taliban], *Layha* [Code of Conduct], 2010.

101. United Nations Assistance Mission in Afghanistan, *Afghanistan: Midyear Report 2015, Protection of Civilians in Armed Conflict* (Kabul: United Nations Assistance Mission in Afghanistan, 2015), p. 2.

102. David Kilcullen, *Out of the Mountains: The Coming Age of the Urban Guerrilla* (New York: Oxford University Press, 2013).

103. Gordon H. McCormick, *From the Sierra to the Cities: The Urban Campaign of the Shining Path* (Santa Monica, CA: RAND, 1992), p. 5.

104. McCormick, *From the Sierra to the Cities*, p. 8.

105. Anderson, *Histories of the Hanged*, pp. 181–229, 190–192.

106. Kilcullen, *Out of the Mountains*.

107. Al-Muqrin, *A Practical Course for Guerrilla Warfare*, p. 131.

108. Paul Staniland, "Cities on Fire: Social Mobilization, State Police, and Urban Insurgency," *Comparative Political Studies*, Vol. 43, No. 12 (June 2010), p. 1630.

109. See, for example, Michael Orr, "Better or Just Not So Bad? An Evaluation of Russian Combat Effectiveness in the Second Chechen War," in Anne Aldis, ed., *The Second Chechen War* (Camberley, UK: Conflict Studies Research Centre, 2000); Mark Kramer, "The Perils of Counterinsurgency," pp. 5–63.

110. Austin Long, "Swimming through Concrete: Enduring Barriers to Urban Insurgency," Draft Document, April 2013.
111. Al-Muqrin, *A Practical Course for Guerrilla Warfare*, p. 171.
112. Long, "Swimming through Concrete."
113. Al-Muqrin, *A Practical Course for Guerrilla Warfare*, p. 120.
114. Guevara, *Guerrilla Warfare*, p. 28.
115. Irish Republican Army, *Green Book*, p. 7.
116. Meyerle and Malkasian, *Insurgent Tactics in Southern Afghanistan*, p. 25.
117. The data are from the University of Maryland's START database, but using only the groups in our insurgent database.
118. The Chicago Project on Security and Terrorism (CPOST) Suicide Attack Database, University of Chicago; START Global Terrorism Database (GTD), University of Maryland. These datasets are largely in agreement about the case list of insurgencies involving use of suicide tactics, with a few minor exceptions. The START dataset records a small number of suicide attacks in the conflicts in Assam, Mindanao, and Baluchistan, which are not included in the CPOST dataset.
119. The wars in India/Assam and Turkey/Kurdistan involved low levels of violence (i.e., less than 100 battle-deaths per year), but were judged to be unresolved and to possess a reasonable probability of near-future escalation given a number of qualitative and quantitative factors.
120. The data are from the Chicago Project on Security and Terrorism (CPOST) Suicide Attack Database, University of Chicago (September 30, 2015 release).
121. Includes delivery by cart, animal, scuba, backpack, airplane (not including 9/11), and unidentified methods.
122. The data are from the University of Maryland's START Global Terrorism Database (GTD), but using only the groups in our insurgent database.
123. The START database labels ambushes and raids as "armed/unarmed assaults."
124. The START database labels sabotage operations as "facility/infrastructure sabotage." In addition, it does not have data on other subversive acts.
125. The START database did not have data on mutilations.
126. I used the number of hostages taken, rather than the number killed, since most insurgent groups released hostages in exchange for money or prisoners.
127. In the START database, suicide attacks are coded as a subtype and they can come from multiple categories. Approximately 93 percent of suicide attacks are coded as bombings/explosions. Of the remaining 7 percent, most are assassinations.

Chapter 5

1. Mohammad Yousaf and Mark Adkin, *Afghanistan the Bear Trap: The Defeat of a Superpower* (Havertown, PA: Casemate, 2001), p. 39.
2. Mao Tse-Tung, *On Guerrilla Warfare* (Urbana and Chicago: University of Illinois Press, 2000), p. 77.

3. Yousaf and Adkin, *Afghanistan the Bear Trap*, pp. 38–39.

4. Jeremy M. Weinstein, *Inside Rebellion: The Politics of Insurgent Violence* (New York: Cambridge University Press, 2007), p. 19.

5. On organizational challenges see Charles Tilly, *From Mobilization to Revolution* (Reading, MA: Addison-Wesley, 1978).

6. Jeremy Shapiro, *The Terrorist's Dilemma: Managing Violent Covert Organizations* (Princeton, NJ: Princeton University Press, 2013).

7. Mancur Olson, *The Logic of Collective Action: Public Goods and the Theory of Groups* (Cambridge: Harvard University Press, 1965).

8. Omar Cabezas, *Fire from the Mountain: The Making of a Sandinista* (New York: Crown, 1985), p. 9.

9. Stathis N. Kaylvas and Matthew Adam Kocher, "How 'Free' is Free Riding in Civil Wars? Violence, Insurgency, and the Collective Action Problem," *World Politics*, Vol. 49, No. 2 (January 2007), pp. 177–216.

10. Irish Republican Army, *Green Book* (Belfast: Irish Republican Army, 1977), p. 2.

11. Waruhiu Itote (General China), *"Mau Mau" General* (Nairobi: East African Publishing House, 1967), p.45.

12. Paul Collier, "Economic Causes of Civil Conflict and Their Implications for Policy," in Chester A. Crocker, Fen Osler Hampson, and Pamela Aall, eds., *Turbulent Peace: The Challenges of Managing International Conflict* (Washington, D.C.: United States Institute of Peace Press, 2001), p. 150.

13. Mark Irving Lichbach, *The Rebel's Dilemma* (Ann Arbor: University of Michigan Press, 1995), pp. 215–238.

14. William H. McNeil, *The Greek Dilemma: War and Aftermath* (Philadelphia, PA: J.B. Lippincott, 1947), pp. 80–81.

15. Edward N. Muller and Karl-Dieter Opp, "Rational Choice and Rebellious Collective Action," *American Political Science Review*, Vol. 80 (June 1986); Charles D. Brocket, *Political Movements and Violence in Central America* (New York: Cambridge University Press, 2005); Elisabeth Jean Wood, *Insurgent Collective Action and Civil War in El Salvador* (New York: Cambridge University Press, 2003); Roger D. Petersen, *Resistance and Rebellion: Lessons from Eastern Europe* (New York: Cambridge University Press, 2001); Samuel Popkin, *The Rational Peasant: The Political Economy of Rural Society in Vietnam* (Berkeley: University of California Press, 1979); Norman Frolich, Joseph Oppenheimer, and Oran Young, *Political Leadership and Collective Goods* (Princeton, NJ: Princeton University Press, 1971); Michael Taylor, "Rationality and Revolutionary Collective Action," in Michael Taylor, ed., *Rationality and Revolution* (New York: Cambridge University Press, 1988), pp. 63–97; and Michael Hechter, *Principles of Group Solidarity* (Berkeley: University of California Press, 1987).

16. Kaylvas and Kocher, "How 'Free' is Free Riding in Civil Wars?" pp. 177–216.

17. On principal–agent problems and insurgency see Shapiro, *The Terrorist's Dilemma*; Weinstein, *Inside Rebellion*, p. 130.

18. Weinstein, *Inside Rebellion*, pp. 129–130.

19. Weinstein, *Inside Rebellion*, pp. 43–44; Abdulkader H. Sinno, *Organizations at War in Afghanistan and Beyond* (Ithaca, NY: Cornell University Press, 2008), p. 70.

20. Mark Moyar, *Phoenix and the Birds of Prey: The CIA's Secret Campaign to Destroy the Viet Cong* (Annapolis, MD: Naval Institute Press, 1997), pp. 250–251.

21. Robert Thompson, *Defeating Communist Insurgency* (St. Petersburg, FL: Hailer, 1966), p. 25.

22. Bard E. O'Neill, *Insurgency and Terrorism: From Revolution to Apocalypse* (Washington, D.C.: Potomac Books, 2005), pp. 115–116.

23. Roderick Kiewiet and Mathew McCubbins, *The Logic of Delegation: Congressional Parties and the Appropriations Process* (Chicago: University of Chicago Press, 1991); Idean Salehyan, "The Delegation of War to Rebel Organizations," *Journal of Conflict Resolution*, Vol. 54, No. 3 (2010), pp. 493–515.

24. Weinstein, *Inside Rebellion*, pp. 42–43.

25. Interview with Abimael Guzman, July 15, 1988, printed in *El Diario*, July 24, 1988, p. 15.

26. Don Barnett and Roy Harvey, *The Revolution in Angola: MPLA, Life Histories and Documents* (New York: Bobbs-Merrill, 1972), p. 13.

27. General Vo Nguyen Giap and Van Tien Dung, *How We Won the War* (Philadelphia: RECON, 1976), p. 41.

28. Weinstein, *Inside Rebellion*, p. 44.

29. Mao, *On Guerrilla Warfare*, pp. 71–87; Ernesto Che Guevara, *Guerrilla Warfare* (Thousand Oaks, CA: BN Publishing, 2007), pp. 61–86.

30. Paul Collier, Anke Hoeffler, and Dominic Rohner, "Beyond Greed and Grievance: Feasibility and Civil War," *Oxford Economic Papers*, Vol. 61, No. 1 (January 2009), pp. 1–27; Collier, "Economic Causes of Civil Conflict and Their Implications for Policy," pp. 1, 3; Paul Staniland, "Organizing Insurgency," *International Security*, Vol. 37, No. 1 (Summer 2012), pp. 142–177; Michael L. Ross, "A Closer Look at Oil, Diamonds, and Civil War," *Annual Review of Political Science*, Vol. 9 (June 2006), pp. 265–300.

31. Aliza Marcus, *Blood and Belief: The PKK and the Kurdish Fight for Independence* (New York: New York University Press, 2007), pp. 181–184.

32. On insurgent intelligence see, for example, Lincoln B. Krause, "Insurgent Intelligence: The Guerrilla Grapevine," *International Journal of Intelligence and Counterintelligence*, Vol. 9, No. 3 (1996), pp. 291–311; J. Bowyer Bell, "The Armed Struggle and Underground Intelligence: An Overview," *Studies in Conflict and Terrorism*, Vol. 17, No. 2 (1994), pp. 115–150; William Rosenau, "Understanding Insurgent Intelligence Operations," *Marine Corps University Journal*, Vol. 2, No. 1 (Spring 2011), pp. 1–32.

33. General Alberto Bayo, *150 Questions for a Guerrilla* (Denver, CO: Cypress Printing, 1963), p. 21.

34. Omar Cabezas, *Fire from the Mountain: The Making of a Sandinista* (New York: Crown, 1985), p. 225.

35. Kiboi Muriithi (General Kamwana), *War in the Forest* (Nairobi: Trafford, 1971), p. 93.

36. Weinstein, *Inside Rebellion*, p. 44.

37. Stathis N. Kalyvas, *The Logic of Violence in Civil War* (New York: Cambridge University Press, 2006), p. 218.

38. Nelson Manrique, "The War for the Central Sierra," in Steve J. Stern, ed., *Shining and Other Paths: War and Society in Peru, 1980–1995* (Durham: Duke University Press, 1998), p. 204.

39. Giap and Dung, *How We Won the War*, p. 56.

40. Baya Gacemi, *I, Nadia, Wife of a Terrorist* (Lincoln, NE: University of Nebraska Press, 2006), p. 46.

41. Patrick B. Johnston et al., *Foundations of the Islamic State: Management, Money, and Terror in Iraq, 2005–2010* (Santa Monica, CA: RAND, 2016).

42. Harmony documents NMEC-2009-636065, NMEC-2009-636153, and NMEC-2009-634370. The Harmony documents are located at the Combating Terrorism Center at West Point (https://www.ctc.usma.edu/programs-resources/harmony-program).

43. Harmony document NMEC-2009-636153.

44. On hierarchy and centralization see Shapiro, *The Terrorist's Dilemma*, pp. 1–25.

45. Sinno, *Organizing to Win*, p. 11.

46. Shapiro, *The Terrorist's Dilemma*.

47. On interconnectedness and specialization see, for example, John Horgan and Max Taylor, "The Provisional Irish Republican Army: Command and Functional Structure," *Terrorism and Political Violence*, Vol. 9, No. 3 (1997), pp. 1–32; Phil Williams, "Transnational Criminal Networks," in John Arquilla and David Ronfeldt, eds., *Networks and Netwars* (Santa Monica, CA: RAND 2002); Andrew Silke, "In Defense of the Realm: Financing Loyalist Terrorism in Northern Ireland—Part One: Extortion and Blackmail," *Studies in Conflict and Terrorism*, Vol. 21 (1998), pp. 331–361; Silke, "Drink, Drugs, and Rock'n'Roll: Financing Loyalist Terrorism in Northern Ireland—Part Two," *Studies in Conflict and Terrorism*, Vol. 23 (2000), pp. 107–127; Brian A. Jackson et al., *Aptitude for Destruction: Organizational Learning in Terrorist Groups and Its Implications for Combating Terrorism* (Santa Monica, CA: RAND, 2005).

48. Shapiro, *The Terrorist's Dilemma*, pp. 1–13, 15–17; Weinstein, *Inside Rebellion*, pp. 133–134.

49. Shapiro, *The Terrorist's Dilemma*, p. 17; Gery J. Miller, *Managerial Dilemmas* (New York: Cambridge University Press, 1992).

50. Data adapted from Kristian Skrede Gleditsch, David Cunningham, and Idean Salehyan, *Non-State Actor Data: Version 3.4*, November 23, 2013,

available at http://privatewww.essex.ac.uk/~ksg/eacd.html. In insurgencies with multiple groups, coding is based upon the structure of the dominant group. Nine cases in my dataset are coded as "not available (n/a)" either because the insurgency does not appear in the UCDP database (e.g., Ukraine, 2014–present) or because UCDP codes the degree of centralization as "n/a."

51. The high, moderate, and low codings come from the Non-State Actor Data Set. See David E. Cunningham, Kristian Skrede Gleditsch, and Idean Salehyan, *Codebook for the Non-State Actor Data*, University of North Texas, Version 3.3, January 2012.

52. 'Abd Al-'Aziz Al-Muqrin, *A Practical Course for Guerrilla War*, translated by Norman Cigar (Washington, D.C.: Potomac Books, 2009), p. 103.

53. General Alberto Bayo, *150 Questions for a Guerrilla* (Denver, CO: Cypress Printing, 1963), p. 21.

54. Weinstein, *Inside Rebellion*, p. 134.

55. Front de Liberation Nationale, Plateforme de la Soummam, August 1956; Commandant en Chef des Forces en Algérie, État-Major Interarmées, 2e Bureau, Section "Opérations," *Evolution des structures et des methods de la rébellion de 1957 à 1960*, No. 4515/EMI/2/OPE (Alger, 18 août 1960), 1, in folder, "10e Région Militaire, État-Major Interarmées, 3e Bureau— Enseignements de la lute contre les rebelles d'AFN-ESG, 10 mars 1958," Dossier 1H1942 d. 3, Fonds Algérien, SHAT.

56. Charles R. Schrader, *The First Helicopter War: Logistics and Mobility in Algeria, 1954–1962* (Westport, CT: Praeger, 1999), pp. 137–40.

57. Schrader, *The First Helicopter War*, pp. 149–151.

58. On the intelligence network see Norman C. Walpole et al., *US Army Handbook for Algeria*, Department of the Army Pamphlet No. 550-44 (Washington, D.C.: Headquarters, Department of the Army, January 1965); Commandant en Chef des Forces en Algérie, État-Major Interarmées, 2e Bureau, Section "Opérations," *Evolution des structures et des methods de la rébellion de 1957 à 1960*, No. 4515/EMI/2/OPE (Alger, 18 août 1960), 1, in folder, "10e Région Militaire, État-Major Interarmées, 3e Bureau— Enseignements de la lute contre les rebelles d'AFN-ESG, 10 mars 1958," Dossier 1H1942 d. 3, Fonds Algérien, SHAT.

59. Gordon H. McCormick, *The Shining Path and Peruvian Terrorism* (Santa Monica, CA: RAND, 1987), p. 5.

60. María Eugenia Vázquez Perdomo, *My Life as a Colombian Revolutionary: Reflections of a Former Guerrillera*, translated by Lorena Terando (Philadelphia: Temple University Press, 2005), p. 87.

61. Gacemi, *I, Nadia, Wife of a Terrorist* (Lincoln, NE: University of Nebraska Press, 2006), p. 44.

62. M. Anderson, M. Arnsten, and H. Averch, *Insurgent Organization and Operations: A Case Study of the Viet Cong in the Delta, 1964–1966* (Santa Monica, CA: RAND, August 1967), p. ix.

63. Anderson, Arnsten, and Averch, *Insurgent Organization and Operations*, p. xi.

64. Joanna Nathan, "Reading the Taliban," in Antonio Giustozzi, ed., *Decoding the New Taliban: Insights from the Afghan Field* (New York: Columbia University Press, 2009), pp. 23–42. Also see, for example, Austin Long, "Whack-a-Mole or Coup de Grace? Institutionalization and Leadership Targeting in Iraq and Afghanistan," *Security Studies*, Vol. 23, No. 3 (2014), pp. 471–512.

65. On the challenge of hierarchical structures, including for counterinsurgency and counterterrorist operations, see John Arquilla and David Ronfeldt, eds., *Networks and Netwars: The Future of Terror, Crime, and Militancy* (Santa Monica, CA: RAND, 2001), pp. 15–16; Weinstein, *Inside Rebellion*, pp. 127–159.

66. Mia Bloom, *Dying to Kill: The Allure of Suicide Terror* (New York: Columbia University Press, 2005), p. 60.

67. K. M. de Silva, *Sri Lanka and the Defeat of the LTTE* (New York: Penguin, 2012).

68. Data adapted from Gleditsch, Cunningham, and Salehyan, *Non-State Actor Data: Version 3.4*, http://privatewww.essex.ac.uk/~ksg/eacd.html.

69. Sinno, *Organizing to Win*, p. 11.

70. Audrey Kurth Cronin, *How Terrorism Ends: Understanding the Decline and Demise of Terrorist Campaigns* (Princeton, NJ: Princeton University Press, 2009), pp. 13–34.

71. Shapiro, *The Terrorist's Dilemma*, pp. 26–62.

72. Richard Clutterbuck, *Conflict and Violence in Singapore and Malaysia, 1945–1983* (Boulder, CO: Westview Press, 1985), pp. 170–171.

73. Clutterbuck, *Conflict and Violence in Singapore and Malaysia*, pp. 198–199.

74. Weinstein, *Inside Rebellion*, pp. 7–16.

75. John Howell, "Horn of Africa: Lessons from the Sudan Conflict," *International Affairs*, Vol. 54, No. 3 (1978), p. 425.

76. Phyllis M. Martin, "The Cabinda Connection: An Historical Perspective," *African Affairs*, Vol. 76, No. 302 (January 1977), pp. 47–59.

77. Michael C. Lambert, "Violence and the War of Words: Ethnicity v. Nationalism in the Casamance," *Africa: Journal of the International African Institute*, Vol. 68, No. 4 (1998), p. 598.

78. Tekle Mariam Woldemikael, "Political Mobilization and Nationalist Movements: The Case of the Eritrean People's Liberation," *Africa Today*, Vol. 38, No. 2 (1991), pp. 31–42; Haggai Erlich, *The Struggle Over Eritrea 1962–1978* (Stanford: Hoover Institution Press, 1982); David Pool, "Revolutionary Crisis and Revolutionary Vanguard: The Emergence of the Eritrean People's Liberation Front," *Review of African Political Economy*, No. 19 (Sep.–Dec. 1980), pp. 33–47.

79. David Anderson, *Histories of the Hanged: The Dirty War in Kenya and the End of Empire* (New York: W.W. Norton, 2005), p. 244.

80. See, for example, the primary source accounts in Donald L. Barnett and Karari Njama, *Mau Mau from within: Autobiography and Analysis of Kenya's*

Peasant Revolt (New York: Monthly Review Press, 1966), pp. 103–104, 114, 126–127, 134; H. Kahinga Wachanga, *The Swords of Kirinyaga: The Fight for Land and Freedom* (Nairobi,: Kenya Literature Bureau, 1975).

81. David Anderson, *Histories of the Hanged: The Dirty War in Kenya and the End of Empire* (New York: W.W. Norton, 2005), p. 249.

82. Barak Salmoni, Bryce Loidolt, and Madeleine Wells, *Regime and Periphery in Northern Yemen: The Huthi Phenomenon* (Santa Monica, CA: RAND, 2010), pp. 189–241.

83. Don Barnett and Roy Harvey, *The Revolution in Angola: MPLA, Life Histories and Documents* (New York: Bobbs-Merrill, 1972), p. 13.

84. Anderson, Arnsten, and Averch, *Insurgent Organization and Operations: A Case Study of the Viet Cong in the Delta, 1964–1966* (Santa Monica, CA: RAND, August 1967), p. 16.

85. Special Operations Research Office, *Ethnographic Study Series: Selected Groups in the Republic of Vietnam: Binh Xuyen* (Washington, D.C.: American University, 1966).

86. Special Operations Research Office, *Binh Xuyen*, pp. 5–6.

87. On the use of local militias in insurgencies, see Ariel I. Ahram, *Proxy Warriors: The Rise and Fall of State-Sponsored Militias* (Stanford, CA: Stanford University Press, 2011); Austin Long, Stephanie Pezard, Bryce Loidolt, and Todd C. Helmus, *Locals Rule: Historical Lessons for Creating Local Defense Forces for Afghanistan and Beyond* (Santa Monica, CA: RAND 2012).

88. Shapiro, *The Terrorist's Dilemma*, pp. 26–62. Shapiro also includes the level of government pressure, which is discussed earlier in this subsection.

89. Mean averages include ongoing insurgencies.

90. Michael C. Horowitz and Philip B. K. Potter, "Allying to Kill: Terrorist Intergroup Cooperation and the Consequences for Lethality," *Journal of Conflict Resolution*, forthcoming; Bruce Hoffman and Gordon H. McCormick, "Terrorism, Signaling, and Suicide Attack," *Studies in Conflict and Terrorism*, Vol. 27, No. 4 (2004), pp. 243–81; Marc Sageman, *Understanding Terror Networks* (Philadelphia: University of Pennsylvania Press, 2004).

91. Horowitz and Potter, "Allying to Kill."

92. Yousaf and Adkin, *Afghanistan the Bear Trap*, pp. 38–43; Sinno, *Organizations at War*, pp. 119–172.

93. Christopher S. Chivvis, *Toppling Qaddafi: Libya and the Limits of Liberal Intervention* (New York: Cambridge University Press, forthcoming).

94. See Hassan Abbas, "Increasing Talibanization in Pakistan's Seven Tribal Agencies," *Terrorism Monitor*, Vol. 5, No. 18 (September 27 2007), pp. 1–5; Hassan Abbas, "A Profile of Tehrik-i-Taliban Pakistan," *CTC Sentinel*, Vol. 1, No. 2 (January 2008), pp. 1–4; Syed Shoaib Hasan, "Profile: Baitullah Mehsud," *BBC News*, December 28, 2007; Saeed Shah, "Taliban Rivals Unite to Fight US Troop Surge," *The Guardian*, March 3, 2009.

95. Author fieldwork in Pakistan in February and April 2009.
96. See such articles as Asad Hashim, "Pakistan Taliban Splits into Factions," *Al Jazeera*, May 28, 2014.
97. Quoted in Jon B. Perdue, *The War of All the People: The Nexus of Latin American Radicalism and Middle Eastern Terrorism* (Dulles, VA: Potomac Books, 2012), p. 144.
98. Elizabeth O'Bagy, *The Free Syrian Army* (Washington, D.C.: Institute for the Study of War, March 2013).
99. Bill Roggio, "Al Nusrah Front Poised to Take Over Last Major City on Euphrates River," *Long War Journal*, March 13, 2013.
100. Bloom, *Dying to Kill*, p. 51.
101. Bloom, *Dying to Kill*, p. 59.
102. Kingsley de Silva, "Terrorism and Political Agitation in Post-Colonial South Asia: Jammu-Kashmir and Sri Lanka," in Ramesh Thakur and Oddny Wiggen, eds., *South Asia in the World: Problem Solving Perspectives on Security, Sustainable Development, and Good Governance* (New York: United Nations University Press, 2004), p. 95.
103. Walpole et al., *US Army Handbook for Algeria*, pp. 38–39; Edgar O'Ballance, *The Algerian Insurrection, 1954–62* (Hamden, CT: Archon Books, 1967), pp. 89–90; Schrader, *The First Helicopter War*, p. 143.
104. Raul Gonzalez, "Sendero vs. MRTA," *QueHacer*, No. 46 (April–May 1987), pp. 47–53.
105. Statement from the Army of Islam on Bombings of Muslim Targets, Harmony Database, NMEC-2007-639043, May 4, 2007.
106. Disavowals of Who Oppose ISI and Pledges of Allegiance to ISI, Harmony Database, NMEC-2007-636883, date unknown.
107. Régis Debray, *Revolution in the Revolution? Armed Struggle and Political Struggle in Latin America* (New York: Grove Press, 1967), pp. 72–73.
108. On decentralized, network groups see, for example, John Arquilla and David Ronfeldt, eds., *Networks and Netwars: The Future of Terror, Crime, and Militancy* (Santa Monica, CA: RAND, 2001); Arquilla and Ronfeldt, eds., *In Athena's Camp: Preparing for Conflict in the Information Age* (Santa Monica, CA: RAND, 1997).
109. Louis Beam, "Leaderless Resistance," *Seditionist*, Issue 12, February 1992, p. 5.
110. Arquilla and Ronfeldt, "The Advent of Netwar," in Arquilla and Ronfeldt, eds., *In Athena's Camp*, p. 280.
111. On al Qa'ida's organizational structure see, for example, Bruce Hoffman, *Inside Terrorism*, revised ed. (New York: Columbia University Press, 2006), p. 285; Daniel Byman, *Breaking the Bonds between Al-Qa'ida and Its Affiliate Organizations* (Washington, D.C.: Brookings Institution, 2013).
112. See, for example, letter from Ayman al-Zawahiri to Abu Bakr al-Baghdadi and Abu Muhammad al-Jawlani, May 2013.
113. As used here, an "allied" group indicates that there are ties with al Qa'ida or one of its affiliates because of training, operations, or other joint endeavors.

114. Shapiro, *The Terrorist's Dilemma*, p. 7.
115. Thanks to Howard Shatz and Erin-Elizabeth Johnson for helping design the organizational structure of the Islamic State of Iraq in al-Anbar, based on captured documents.
116. Schrader, *The First Helicopter War*, p. 140.
117. Schrader, *The First Helicopter War*, p. 149.

Chapter 6

1. T. E. Lawrence, "The Evolution of a Revolt," *Army Quarterly and Defence Journal* (October 1920), p. 11.
2. United States Army Special Operations Command, *Undergrounds in Insurgent, Revolutionary, and Resistance Warfare* (Fort Bragg, NC: United States Army Special Operations Command, January 2013), p. 112.
3. See, for example, United States Army, *Case Study: Terrorist Attack on Westgate Mall, Nairobi, Kenya: 21–24 September 2013*, Washington, D.C., 2014; Kevin Yorke, *Analysis of Al-Shabaab's Attack at the Westgate Mall in Nairobi, Kenya*, New York: New York City Police Department, 2013.
4. The tweets were downloaded from al Shabaab's Twitter site, @HSM_Press, in September 2013.
5. "From the Editor," *Gaidi Mtaani*, Dhul Hijra 1434, toleo 4, p. 1.
6. See, for example, the definition for strategic communications at US Department of Defense, *Department of Defense Dictionary of Military and Associated Terms*, Joint Publication 1-02 (Washington, D.C.: US Department of Defense, November 8, 2010 (as amended through March 15, 2014)), p. 250.
7. Lawrence, "The Evolution of a Revolt," p. 11.
8. Jeremy Weinstein, *Inside Rebellion: The Politics of Insurgent Violence* (New York: Cambridge University Press, 2007), pp. 7–8.
9. Mao Tse-Tung, *On Guerrilla Warfare* (Urbana and Chicago: University of Illinois Press, 2000), p. 85.
10. Ernesto "Che" Guevara, *Guerrilla Warfare* (Lincoln, NE: University of Nebraska Press, 1998), p. 79.
11. General Alberto Bayo, *150 Questions for a Guerrilla* (Denver, CO: Cypress Printing, 1963), p. 78.
12. Omar Cabezas, *Fire from the Mountain: The Making of a Sandinista* (New York: Crown, 1985), p. 209.
13. Cabezas, *Fire from the Mountain*, p. 210.
14. Barak Salmoni, Bryce Loidolt, and Madeleine Wells, *Regime and Periphery in Northern Yemen: The Huthi Phenomenon* (Santa Monica, CA: RAND, 2010), pp. 216–222.
15. Russell Crandall, *America's Dirty Wars: Irregular Warfare from 1776 to the War on Terror* (New York: Cambridge University Press, 2014), p. 316.
16. John D. Waghelstein, *El Salvador: Observations and Experiences in Counterinsurgency* (Carlisle Barracks, PA: US Army War College, January 1, 1985).

17. United States Marine Corps, *After Action Report on Operations in Afghanistan* (Camp Lejeune, NC: United States Marine Corps, August 2004); *Operation Enduring Freedom: Tactics, Techniques, and Procedures* (Fort Leavenworth, KS: US Army Training and Doctrine Command, December 2003); United Nations Department of Safety and Security, *Half Year Review of the Security Situation in Afghanistan* (Kabul, Afghanistan: United Nations, August 13, 2007).

18. See, for example, Thomas H. Johnson, "The Taliban Insurgency and an Analysis of Shabnamah (Night Letters)," *Small Wars and Insurgencies*, Vol. 18, No. 3 (September 2007), pp. 317–344.

19. "Taliban Military Chief Threatens to Kill US Captives, Views Recent Attacks, Al-Qa'ida," Interview with Al Jazeera TV, July 18, 2005.

20. National Directorate for Security, *Strategy of Insurgents and Terrorists in Afghanistan* (Kabul: National Directorate for Security, 2006), p. 8.

21. José Ignacio López Vigil, *Rebel Radio: The Story of El Salvador's Radio Venceremos*, trans. Mark Fried (Willimantic, CT: Curbstone Press, 1994).

22. SITE Intelligence Group, *Islamic State Launches Radio Station in ar-Raqqah* (Bethesda, MD: SITE, June 30, 2014).

23. Weinstein, *Inside Rebellion*, p. 72.

24. US Special Operations Command, *Unconventional Warfare: Initial Draft*, Joint Publication, March 2014, p. I-15.

25. Author interview with L. Paul Bremer III, November 15, 2007; author interview with Dan Senor, October 31, 2008.

26. Memo from the Scott Carpenter to the Administrator, Re: Daily Governing Council Sitrep, September 22, 2003, Coalition Provisional Authority (CPA) archives.

27. Email from Gary Thatcher to Daniel Senor and Nabeel A. Khoury, Subject: Taking on Al Jazeera, September 13, 2003, Coalition Provisional Authority (CPA) archives; Cable from CPA to SECDEF WASHDC, SECSTATE WASHDC, NSC WASHDC, AMEMB DOHA, IRAQ COLLECTIVE, TREASURY WASHDC, Subject: The CPA and Al Jazeera, September 30, 2003, Coalition Provisional Authority (CPA) archives.

28. African National Congress, "Operation Mayibuye," 1963.

29. African National Congress, "Operation Mayibuye," 1963.

30. The data for both Internet and mobile cellular subscriptions were from ITU World Telecommunication/ICT Indicators database, accessed June 2014.

31. Gabriel Weimann, *Terror on the Internet: The New Arena, the New Challenges* (Washington, D.C.: US Institute of Peace, 2006).

32. The dates for the creation of the websites are based on an analysis of digital archives, such as Wayback Machine at www.archive.org and WHOIS at www.whois.net. WHOIS, for example, was standardized in the early 1980s to look up domains, people, and other resources related to domain registrations.

33. See, for example, Weimann, *Terror on the Internet*, pp. 49–110.
34. Gabriel Weimann, "Terror on Facebook, Twitter, and YouTube," *Brown Journal of World Affairs*, Vol. 16, No. 2 (Spring/Summer 2010), p. 45.
35. Ibid., p. 45.
36. Yuki Noguchi and Evan Kohlman, "Tracking Terrorists Online," *Washington Post*, April 19, 2006; Weimann, "Terror on Facebook, Twitter, and YouTube," pp. 45–54.
37. Chad Hurley, Steve Chen, and Jawed Karim launched YouTube in 2005.
38. Quoted in Weimann, "Terror on Facebook, Twitter, and Youtube," p. 49.
39. Elizabeth Dickinson, *Playing with Fire: How Gulf Financing for Extremist Rebels Risks Igniting Sectarian Conflict at Home* (Washington, D.C.: Brookings Institution, 2013).
40. Marc Lynch, Deen Freelon, and Sean Aday, "Social Media and Transnational Involvement in Civil War," Working Paper, January 5, 2004.
41. Marc Lynch, Deen Freelon, and Sean Aday, *Blogs and Bullets III: Syria's Socially Mediated Civil War* (Washington, D.C.: United States Institute of Peace, 2014).
42. Christopher Zambelis, "Information Wars: Assessing the Social Media Battlefield in Syria," *Combating Terrorism Sentinel*, Vol. 5, No. 7 (July 2012), pp. 19–21.
43. On the effects of cell phone coverage on political violence in Africa see Jan H. Pierskalla and Florian M. Hollenbach, "Technology and Collective Action: The Effect of Cell Phone Coverage on Political Violence in Africa," *American Political Science Review*, Vol. 107, No. 2 (2013), pp. 1–18.
44. Lynch, Freelon, and Aday, "Social Media and Transnational Involvement in Civil War."
45. See, for example, United States Army, *Case Study: Terrorist Attack on Westgate Mall, Nairobi, Kenya: 21–24 September 2013*, Washington, D.C., 2014; Kevin Yorke, *Analysis of Al-Shabaab's Attack at the Westgate Mall in Nairobi, Kenya*, New York: New York City Police Department, 2013.
46. Pierskalla and Hollenbach, "Technology and Collective Action," pp. 207–224.
47. Pierskalla and Hollenbach, "Technology and Collective Action," p. 220.
48. Stathis N. Kaylvas and Matthew Adam Kocher, "How 'Free' is Free Riding in Civil Wars? Violence, Insurgency, and the Collective Action Problem," *World Politics*, Vol. 49, No. 2 (January 2007), pp. 177–216; Elisabeth Jean Wood, *Insurgent Collective Action and Civil War in El Salvador* (New York: Cambridge University Press, 2003); Mancur Olson, *The Logic of Collective Action: Public Goods and the Theory of Groups* (Cambridge: Harvard University Press, 1965).
49. Mehdi Shadmehr and Dan Bernhardt, "Collective Action with Uncertain Payoffs: Coordination, Public Signals, and Punishment Dilemmas," *American Political Science Review*, Vol. 105, No. 4 (November 2011), pp. 829–851.
50. Pierskalla and Hollenbach, "Technology and Collective Action," pp. 207–224.

51. Cell phones also have numerous societal benefits. Cell phone usage, the availability of hotlines to voters, and text messaging can have positive effects on the political information available to voters as well as their political participation. Cell phones can also decrease corruption among government officials, including during elections. In addition, cell phone technology can facilitate peaceful protests, particularly in authoritarian regimes. Increased cell phone coverage in developing countries has been associated with higher levels of market efficiency, especially across labor markets and private goods markets. Cell phones decrease information asymmetries between market participants and facilitate economic exchange. See, for example, Jenny C. Aker, Paul Collier, and Pedro C. Vincente, "Is Information Power? Using Cell Phones during an Election in Mozambique," Working Paper, May 2011; Catie Now Bailard, "Mobile Phone Diffusion and Corruption in Africa," *Political Communication*, Vol. 26, No. 3 (July 2009), pp. 333–353; Larry Diamond and Marc F. Plattner, eds., *Liberation Technology: Social Media and the Struggle for Democracy* (Baltimore, MD: Johns Hopkins University Press, 2012); Richard Lapper, "Youthful Protesters Help Shape New Kind of Politics," *Financial Times*, January 28, 2010; Pierskalla and Hollenbach, "Technology and Collective Action," pp. 207–224.

52. Pierskalla and Hollenbach, "Technology and Collective Action," pp. 207–224.

53. Pierskalla and Hollenbach, "Technology and Collective Action," pp. 207–224.

54. Timur Kuran, "Now Out of Never: The Element of Surprise in the East European Revolution of 1989," *World Politics*, Vol. 44, No. 1 (October 1991), pp. 7–48; Susanne Lohmann, "Dynamics of Informational Cascades: The Monday Demonstrations in Leipzig, East Germany, 1989–1991," *World Politics*, Vol. 47, No. 1, October 1994, pp. 42–101.

55. Pierskalla and Hollenbach, "Technology and Collective Action," pp. 207–224.

56. Scott Peterson, "Syria's iPhone Insurgency Makes for Smarter Rebellion," *Christian Science Monitor*, August 1, 2012.

57. William Reno, *Warfare in Independent Africa* (New York: Cambridge University Press, 2011).

58. Eric von Hippel, *Democratizing Innovation* (Cambridge, MA: MIT Press, 2005).

59. Author interview with US Special Operations Forces deployed to southern and eastern Afghanistan, March 2012.

60. Jennifer Yang Hui, "The Internet in Indonesia: Development and Impact of Radical Websites," *Studies in Conflict and Terrorism*, Vol. 33 (2010), pp. 171–191.

61. See, for example, www.hide-my-ip-address.com.

62. Jacob N. Shapiro and Nils B. Weidmann, "Is the Phone Mightier than the Sword? Cell Phones and Insurgent Violence in Iraq," Working Paper, September 2012.

63. Irish Republican Army, *Green Book* (Belfast: Irish Republican Army, 1977), p. 2.

64. Irish Republican Army, *Green Book*, p. 2.

65. Irish Republican Army, *Green Book*, p. 13.

66. Gordon H. McCormick, *The Shining Path and Peruvian Terrorism* (Santa Monica, CA: RAND, 1987), p. 5.

67. Cabezas, *Fire from the Mountain*, p. 14.

68. Ayman al-Zawahiri, "Truth Has Come and Falsehood Has Perished," Ansar al-Mujahidin Network, September 2012.

69. Letter from Nasir al-Wahishi to Emir of Al Qa'ida in the Islamic Maghreb, May 21, 2012, Associated Press collection. The document is part of a cache of documents that the Associated Press found on the floor in a building occupied by al Qa'ida fighters in Mali.

70. ITU World Telecommunication/ICT Indicators database, accessed June 2014.

Chapter 7

1. Danna Harman, "Ortega Hoping for a Second Act in Nicaragua," *USA Today*, October 6, 2005.

2. Christopher Andrew and Vasili Mitrokhin, *The World Was Going Our Way: The KGB and the Battle for the Third World* (New York: Basic Books, 2005), pp. 40–50.

3. Andrew and Mitrokhin, *The World Was Going Our Way*, pp. 42–43.

4. Christopher Andrew and Vasili Mitrokhin, *The Sword and the Shield: The Mitrokhin Archive and the Secret History of the KGB* (New York: Basic Books, 1999), p. 386.

5. As used here, a superpower refers to the Soviet Union and United States. Great powers include the United States, China, United Kingdom, Russia/Soviet Union, Japan, Saudi Arabia, France, Germany, India, and Brazil based on military and economic might. This list represents a fair approximation of powers that had significant international and regional influence. On great powers see, for example, John J. Mearsheimer, *The Tragedy of Great Power Politics* (New York: W.W. Norton, 2001), p. 5.

6. I have coded refugees as a subset of diasporas.

7. Ben Connable and Martin C. Libicki, *How Insurgencies End* (Santa Monica, CA: RAND Corporation, 2010), p. 62; Jason Lyall and Isaiah Wilson, "Rage against the Machines: Explaining Outcomes in Counterinsurgency Wars," *International Organization*, Vol. 63, No. 1 (Winter 2009), pp. 67–106.

8. Lyall, "Rage against the Machines," pp. 67–106. External support is defined as the insurgent group having an international patron that provided material support, a rear base across international borders that could serve as a sanctuary in which to organize and train fighters and evade government countermeasures, or both.

9. These data should be taken as preliminary. A later version will conduct a more robust statistical analysis of types of outside support, which includes other factors that could contribute to insurgent victory and defeat (including outside support to governments).

10. Daniel L. Byman, *Deadly Connections: States That Sponsor Terrorism* (Cambridge University Press, 2005), p. 67; and Bruce Hoffman, "Rethinking Terrorism and Counterterrorism Since 9/11," *Studies in Conflict & Terrorism*, Vol. 25, No. 5 (2002), p. 311.

11. Daniel Byman et al., *Trends in Outside Support for Insurgent Movements* (Santa Monica, CA: RAND, 2001), p. 10.

12. David E. Cunningham, "Blocking Resolution: How External States Can Prolong Civil Wars," *Journal of Peace Research*, Vol. 47, No. 2 (2010), pp. 115–127; Byman, *Trends in Outside Support for Insurgent Movements*, p. 23.

13. Ahmed Rashid, *Taliban: Militant Islam, Oil and Fundamentalism in Central Asia* (New Haven, CT: Yale University Press, 2000), p. 18; Barnett R. Rubin, *The Fragmentation of Afghanistan: State Formation and Collapse in the International System* (New Haven, CT: Yale University Press, 1995), p. 20.

14. Robert M. Gates, *From the Shadows: The Ultimate Insider's Story of Five Presidents and How They Won the Cold War* (New York: Simon & Schuster, 1996), pp. 251, 319–321, 348–249. Also see Steve Coll, *Ghost Wars: The Secret History of the CIA, Afghanistan, and Bin Laden, from the Soviet Invasion to September 10, 2001* (New York: Penguin, 2004).

15. Mohammad Yousaf and Mark Adkin, *Afghanistan—The Bear Trap: The Defeat of a Superpower* (Havertown, PA: Casemate, 1992), pp. 78–112; Gates, *From the Shadows*, p. 349.

16. William G. Thom, "Trends in Soviet Support for African Liberation," *Air University Review* (July–August 1974). Emphasis added.

17. Central Intelligence Agency, *Soviet Support for International Terrorism and Revolutionary Violence: Special National Intelligence Estimate* (Washington, D.C.: Central Intelligence Agency, May 27, 1981).

18. Robert Thompson, *Defeating Communist Insurgency* (St. Petersburg, FL: Hailer, 2005), p. 28.

19. Russell Crandall, *America's Dirty Wars: Irregular Warfare from 1776 to the War on Terror* (New York: Cambridge University Press, 2014), p. 201.

20. Lars-Erik Cederman et al., "Transborder Ethnic Kin and Civil War," *International Organization*, Vol. 67, No. 2 (April 2013), pp. 389–410; Paul Collier, Anke Hoeffler, and Nicholas Sambanis, "The Collier–Hoeffler Model of Civil War Onset and the Case Study Project Research Design," in Paul Collier and Nicholas Sambanis, eds., *Understanding Civil War, Volume 2: Europe, Central Asia, and Other Regions* (Washington, D.C.: The World Bank, 2005), p. 9.

21. Douglas Woodwell, "Unwelcome Neighbors: Shared Ethnicity and International Conflict during the Cold War," *International Studies Quarterly*, Vol. 48 (2004), pp. 197–223.

22. Revolutionary United Front, *Footpaths to Democracy: Toward a New Sierra Leone*, 1995.

23. Stathis N. Kalyvas and Nicholas Sambanis, "Bosnia's Civil War: Origins and Violence Dynamics," in Collier and Sambanis, eds., *Understanding Civil War, Volume 2: Europe, Central Asia, and Other Regions* (Washington, D.C.: The World Bank, 2005), pp. 209–210.

24. Christoph Zurcher, Pavel Baev, and Jan Koehler, "Civil Wars in the Caucasus," in Paul Collier and Nicholas Sambanis, eds., *Understanding Civil War, Volume 2*, pp. 292–293.

25. Byman, *Trends in Outside Support for Insurgent Movements*, pp. 42–49.

26. Aliza Marcus, *Blood and Belief: The PKK and the Kurdish Fight for Independence* (New York: New York University Press, 2007), p. 230.

27. Ken Menkhaus, "Al-Shabab's Capabilities Post-Westgate," *CTC Sentinel*, March 24, 2014.

28. Rob Wise, "Al-Shabaab," AQAM Future Project Case Studies Report, Center for Strategic and International Studies (CSIS), July 2011.

29. Michael Hechter, *Containing Nationalism* (Oxford: Oxford University Press, 2001); Woodwell, "Unwelcome Neighbors."

30. Roger Petersen, *Resistance and Rebellions: Lessons from Eastern Europe* (New York: Cambridge University Press, 2001); Idean Salehyan and Kristian Skrede Gleditsch, "Refugees and the Spread of Civil War," *International Organization*, Vol. 60, No. 2 (April 2006), pp. 335–366.

31. Examples include Afghanistan (1978–1992 and 1992–1996), Cambodia (1970–1975 and 1978–1979), Chad (1983–1990), Congo-Brazzaville (1993–1997), Zaire (1996–1997), Eritrea (1964–1991), Ethiopia (1976–1991), Kosovo (1998–1999), Laos (1959–1973), Liberia (1989–1995 and 2000–2003), Mozambique (1964–1974), Pakistan (1971), Rwanda (1990–1994), Sierra Leone (1991–1997 and 1997–1998), Somalia (1982–1991), South Africa/Namibia (1966–1988), Uganda (1980–1986), and Vietnam (1955–1975).

32. Petersen, *Resistance and Rebellions*.

33. Salehyan and Gleditsch, "Refugees and the Spread of Civil War."

34. US Department of State, *US Government Assistance to Syria* (Washington, D.C.: Office of the Spokesperson, US Department of State, February 22, 2013).

35. Victor Davies and Abie Fofana, "Diamonds, Crime and Civil War in Sierra Leone," Paper prepared for the Yale University and World Bank Case Study Project on the Political Economy of Civil Wars, 2002.

36. See, for example, Michael Freeman, ed., *Financing Terrorism: Case Studies* (Burlington, VT: Ashgate, 2012), pp. 199–215.

37. Thomas Marks, *Colombian Army Adaptation to FARC Insurgency* (Carlisle, PA: Strategic Studies Institute, US Army War College, 2002), p. 22.

38. Audio Statement by Abu Bakr al-Baghdadi, April 10, 2013.

39. Thomas Joscelyn, "Al Nusrah Front Leader Renews Allegiance to al Qaeda, Rejects New Name," *Long War Journal*, April 10, 2013.

40. Benjamin S. Lambeth, *NATO's Air War for Kosovo: A Strategic and Operational Assessment* (Santa Monica, CA: RAND, 2001), p. 61.

41. MacAlister Brown and Joseph J. Zasloff, *Cambodia Confounds the Peacemakers, 1979–1998* (Ithaca, NY: Cornell University Press, 1998), p. 9. Also see, for example, Grant Curtis, *Cambodia Reborn? The Transition to Democracy and Development* (Washington, D.C.: Brookings Institution Press, 1998); Evan Gottesman, *Cambodia After the Khmer Rouge: Inside the Politics of Nation-Building* (New Haven, CT: Yale University Press, 2003).

42. Robert B. Asprey, *War in the Shadows: The Guerrilla in History* (New York: William Morrow, 1994), pp. 1188–1192.

43. On the overthrow of the Taliban regime, see Gary C. Schroen, *First In: An Insider's Account of How the CIA Spearheaded the War on Terror in Afghanistan* (New York: Ballantine, 2005); Stephen Biddle, *Afghanistan and the Future of Warfare: Implications for Army and Defense Policy* (Carlisle, PA: Strategic Studies Institute, US Army War College, November 2002); Gary Berntsen and Ralph Pezzullo, *Jawbreaker: The Attack on Bin Laden and Al-Qaida* (New York: Crown, 2005); Bob Woodward, *Bush at War* (New York: Simon & Schuster, 2002); Stephen D. Biddle, "Allies, Airpower, and Modern Warfare: The Afghan Model in Afghanistan and Iraq," *International Security*, Vol. 30, No. 3 (Winter 2005/2006), pp. 161–176; and Richard B. Andres, Craig Wills, and Thomas E. Griffith, Jr., "Winning with Allies: The Strategic Value of the Afghan Model," *International Security*, Vol. 30, No. 3 (Winter 2005/2006), pp. 124–160.

44. Samir Makdisi and Richard Sadaka, "The Lebanese Civil War, 1975–90," in Collier and Sambanis, eds., *Understanding Civil War, Volume 2*, p. 81.

45. Lindsay Heger and Idean Salehyan, "Ruthless Rulers: Coalition Size and the Severity of Civil Conflict," *International Studies Quarterly*, Vol. 51 (2007), pp. 385–403.

46. Patrick M. Regan, "Third-Party Interventions and the Duration of Intrastate Conflicts," *Journal of Conflict Resolution*, Vol. 46, No. 1 (February 2002), pp. 55–73; Cunningham, "Blocking Resolution."

47. The US Army and Marine Corps, *Counterinsurgency Field Manual: US Army Field Manual No. 3-24 and Marine Corps Warfighting Publication No. 3-33.5* (Chicago: University of Chicago Press, 2007), p. liv.

48. See, for example, Connable and Libicki, *How Insurgencies End*, pp. 34–49; O'Neill, *Insurgency and Terrorism*, pp. 145–148; Byman, *Trends in Outside Support for Insurgent Movements*, pp. 84–86.

49. Byman, *Deadly Connections*, pp. 53–78.

50. For an argument on the importance of such stress, see Hoffman, "The Modern Terrorist Mindset," p. 88.

51. Ariel E. Levite, Bruce W. Jentleson, and Larry Berman, eds., *Foreign Military Intervention: The Dynamics of Protracted Conflict* (New York: Columbia University Press, 1992); Patrick M. Regan, *Civil*

Wars and Foreign Powers: Outside Intervention in Intrastate Conflict (Ann Arbor, MI: University of Michigan Press, 2000).

52. Byman, *Trends in Outside Support for Insurgent Movements*, p. 10.
53. Lacquer, *Guerrilla Warfare*, p. 295.
54. Richard Clutterbuck, *Conflict and Violence in Singapore and Malaysia, 1945–1983* (Boulder, CO: Westview Press, 1985), pp. 195–210; Chin Peng, *My Side of History* (Singapore: Media Masters, 2003).
55. O'Neill, *Insurgency and Terrorism*, p. 147.
56. Marcus, *Blood and Belief*, p. 81.
57. Alistair Horne, *A Savage War of Peace: Algeria 1954–1962* (New York: The Viking Press, 1977), pp. 263–264.
58. John Talbott, *The War without a Name: France in Algeria 1954–1962* (New York: Knopf, 1980), p. 184. On the Morice Line, also see Constantin Melnik, *Insurgency and Counterinsurgency in Algeria* (Santa Monica, CA: RAND, April 23, 1964).
59. US Special Operations Command, *Unconventional Warfare: Initial Draft*, Joint Publication, March 2014, pp. 11–12.
60. J. R. T. Wood, "Countering the Chimurenga: The Rhodesian Counterinsurgency Campaign 1962–80," in Daniel Marston and Carter Malkasian, eds., *Counterinsurgency in Modern Warfare* (New York: Osprey, 2008), p. 186.
61. Galula, *Counterinsurgency Warfare*, pp. 40–41.
62. On the evolution of mechanized warfare by counterinsurgents see Lyall and Wilson, "Rage against the Machines," pp. 67–106.
63. There is some debate about how effective the Stinger missiles were against the Soviets. See, for example, Alan J. Kuperman, "The Stinger Missile and US Intervention in Afghanistan," *Political Science Quarterly*, Vol. 114, No. 2 (1999), pp. 219–263.
64. Gates, *From the Shadows*, pp. 349–350.
65. Yousaf and Adkin, *Afghanistan—The Bear Trap*, p. 184.
66. Arnold, *Wars in the Third World*; Alex Vines, *Renamo: Terrorist in Mozambique* (Bloomington, IN: Indiana University Press, 1991).
67. Galula, *Counterinsurgency Warfare*, pp. 40–41; Bernard Fall, *Le Viet-Minh* (Paris: Libraire Armand Colin, 1960), p. 195;
68. Jeffrey Record, *Beating Goliath: Why Insurgencies Win* (Washington, D.C.: Potomac Books, 2007), p. 48.
69. Qiang Zhai, *China and the Vietnam War, 1950–1975* (Chapel Hill, NC: University of North Carolina Press, 2000), pp. 140–143; Connable and Libicki, *How Insurgencies End*, p. 68.
70. John A. Marcum, "Lessons of Angola," *Foreign Affairs*, Vol. 54, No. 3 (April 1976), p. 406; Jakkie Potgieter, "Taking Aid from the Devil Himself: UNITA's Support Structures," in Jakkie Cilliers and Christian Dietrich, eds., *Angola's War Economy: The Role of Oil and Diamonds* (Pretoria: Institute for Security Studies, 2000), pp. 256–258.

71. Bowyer J. Bell, "The Irish War," *Studies in Conflict and Terrorism*, Vol. 24 (1999), pp. 475–484; Douglas Woodwell, "The 'Troubles' of Northern Ireland: Civil Conflict in an Economically Well-Developed State," in Collier and Sambanis, *Understanding Civil War, Volume 2*, p. 171.

72. Paul Dresch, *A History of Modern Yemen* (New York: Cambridge University Press, 2002), p. 91.

73. Alistair Horne, *A Savage War of Peace: Algeria 1954–1962* (New York: The Viking Press, 1977), pp. 263–264.

74. Charles R. Shrader, *The First Helicopter War: Logistics and Mobility in Algeria, 1954–1962* (Westport, CT: Praeger, 1999), pp. 166–167; Galula, *Counterinsurgency Warfare*, p. 39.

75. Connable and Libicki, *How Insurgencies End*, pp. 67–75.

76. John Horgan and Max Taylor, "Playing the 'Green Card'—Financing the Provisional IRA: Part 1," *Terrorism and Political Violence*, Vol. 11, No. 2 (1999), pp. 1–38; Woodwell, "The 'Troubles' of Northern Ireland," p. 171.

77. Christoph Zurcher, Pavel Baev, and Jan Koehler, "Civil Wars in the Caucasus," in Collier and Sambanis, *Understanding Civil War, Volume 2*, p. 283.

78. Saeed Badeeb, *The Saudi–Egyptian Conflict over North Yemen, 1962–1970* (Boulder, CO: Westview Press, 1986), pp. 37, 55.

79. Weinstein, *Inside Rebellion*, p. 72.

80. Chaliand, *Revolution in the Third World*, p. 181.

81. Ibid., p. 181.

82. See, for example, Susan Woodward, *Balkan Tragedy: Chaos and Dissolution After the Cold War* (Washington, D.C.: Brookings Institutions, 1995).

83. Idean Salehyan, Kristian Skrede Gleditsch, and David E. Cunningham, "Explaining External Support for Insurgent Groups," *International Organization*, Vol. 65, No. 4 (Fall 2011), pp. 709–744.

84. Darren G. Hawkins et al., eds., *Delegation and Agency in International Organizations* (Cambridge: Cambridge University Press, 2006); Roderick D. Kiewiet and Mathew D. McCubbins, *The Logic of Delegation: Congressional Parties and the Appropriations Process* (Chicago: University of Chicago Press, 1991).

85. Salehyan, Gleditsch, and Cunningham, "Explaining External Support for Insurgent Groups," pp. 709–744.

86. Human Rights Watch, *Seductions of "Sequencing": The Risks of Putting Justice Aside for Peace* (New York: Human Rights Watch, December 2010), pp. 5–6; Human Rights Watch, *Afghanistan: Poor Rights Record of Opposition Commanders* (New York: Human Rights Watch, October 2001).

87. Idean Salehyan, "The Delegation of War to Rebel Organizations," *Journal of Conflict Resolution*, Vol. 54, No. 3 (2010), pp. 493–515; Salehyan, Gleditsch, Cunningham, "Explaining External Support for Insurgent Groups," pp. 709–744.

88. See, for example, Thomas Ruttig, "The Taliban Arrest Wave in Pakistan," *CTC Sentinel*, Vol. 3, No. 3 (March 2010), pp. 5–7; Ashley J. Tellis,

Beradar, Pakistan, and the Afghan Taliban: What Gives? (Washington, D.C.: Carnegie Endowment for International Peace, March 2010); Seth G. Jones, *In the Graveyard of Empires: America's War in Afghanistan* (New York: W.W. Norton, 2009), pp. 256–278.

89. Byman, *Trends in Outside Support for Insurgent Movements*; O'Neill, *Insurgency and Terrorism*, p. 140.

90. O'Neill, *Insurgency and Terrorism*, p. 150; Cunningham, "Blocking Resolution," p. 117.

91. Weinstein, *Inside Rebellion*, p. 14.

92. Revolutionary United Front, *Footpaths to Democracy: Toward a New Sierra Leone*, 1995.

93. Karl W. Deutsch, "External Involvement in Internal War," in Harry Eckstein, ed., *Internal War: Problems and Approaches* (New York: The Free Press of Glencoe, 1964), pp. 100–110; David M. Edelstein, *Occupational Hazards: Success and Failure in Military Occupation* (Ithaca, NY: Cornell University Press, 2010).

94. Chaliand, *Revolution in the Third World*, p. 181; Salehyan, Gleditsch, and Cunningham, "Explaining External Support for Insurgent Groups," pp. 709–744.

95. Salehyan, Gleditsch, and Cunningham, "Explaining External Support for Insurgent Groups," pp. 709–744.

96. Author interview with government officials from Europe and the Middle East, April and May 2013.

97. Salehyan, Gleditsch, and Cunningham, "Explaining External Support for Insurgent Groups," pp. 709–744.

98. Charles R. Shrader, *The First Helicopter War: Logistics and Mobility in Algeria, 1954–1962* (Westport, CT: Praeger, 1999), p. 173.

Chapter 8

1. David Zucchino, "Libyan Rebels Embrace US and Its Flag," *Los Angeles Times*, August 5, 2011.

2. General Vo Nguyen Giap and Van Tien Dung, *How We Won the War* (Philadelphia: RECON, 1976), p. 38.

3. Peter Graff, "Libyan Rebels Overrun Gaddafi HQ, Say He's 'Finished,'" *Reuters*, August 23, 2011.

4. See, for example, Christopher S. Chivvis, *Toppling Qaddafi: Libya and the Limits of Liberal Intervention* (New York: Cambridge University Press, 2013); Karl Mueller, ed., *Precision and Purpose: Airpower in the Libyan Civil War* (Santa Monica, CA: RAND 2015).

5. I have coded cases as a draw if they ended because of a negotiated settlement, a sustained cease-fire, or the violence level dropped to twenty-five deaths per year for a sustained period (but there was no settlement).

6. The data indicate that fifty insurgencies ended with an insurgent victory and fifty-two ended with a government victory, out of a total of 143

insurgencies that terminated between 1946 and 2015. In addition, forty-one insurgencies ended with a draw.

7. Great powers include the United States, China, United Kingdom, Russia/Soviet Union, Japan, Saudi Arabia, France, Germany, India, and Brazil based on military and economic might. This list represents a fair approximation of powers that had significant international and regional influence. On great powers see, for example, John J. Mearsheimer, *The Tragedy of Great Power Politics* (New York: W.W. Norton, 2001), p. 5.

8. See, for example, Ben Connable and Martin C. Libicki, *How Insurgencies End* (Santa Monica, CA: RAND Corporation, 2010), p. xiii; Jason Lyall and Isaiah Wilson III, "Rage against the Machines: Explaining Outcomes in Counterinsurgency Wars," *International Organization,* Vol. 63 (Winter 2009), pp. 67–106.

9. Hans J. Morgenthau, *Politics among Nations: The Struggle for Power and Peace* (New York: Alfred A. Knopf, 1963).

10. See, for example, Kenneth Waltz, *Theory of International Politics* (New York: McGraw-Hill, 1979); Mearsheimer, *The Tragedy of Great Power Politics.*

11. Mearsheimer, *The Tragedy of Great Power Politics*, p. 5.

12. A. J. P. Taylor, *The Struggle for Mastery in Europe 1848–1918* (New York: Oxford University Press, 1980), p. xxiv.

13. Kenneth N. Waltz, *Theory of International Politics* (New York: McGraw-Hill, 1979), p. 131.

14. See, for example, Daniel Byman et al., *Trends in Outside Support for Insurgent Movements* (Santa Monica, CA: RAND, 2001), p. xiv. They note: "The encouragement or example of the state is enough to convince individuals to take up arms and join, or otherwise support, an insurgent movement."

15. On great powers and insurgencies see Steven R. David, "Why the Third World Matters," *International Security*, Vol. 14, No. 1 (Summer), 1989, pp. 50–85; Mark P. Lagon, "The International System and the Reagan Doctrine: Can Realism Explain Aid to 'Freedom Fighters'?" *British Journal of Political Science*, Vol. 22, No. 1 (January 1992), pp. 39–70; William Rosenau, "The Kennedy Administration, US Foreign Internal Security Assistance and the Challenge of 'Subterranean War,' 1961–63," *Small Wars and Insurgencies*, Vol. 14, No. 3 (Autumn 2003), pp. 65–99.

16. Byman, *Trends in Outside Support for Insurgent Movements*, p. 1.

17. Mohammad Yousaf and Mark Adkin, *Afghanistan the Bear Trap: The Defeat of a Superpower* (Havertown, PA: Casemate, 2001), p. 97.

18. Note that the significance of great-power support to insurgents alone disappears during Cold War insurgencies only (those that ended prior to 1989). This could be for a range of reasons, such as the importance of anti-colonial wars. Insurgents fighting against colonial powers, for example, had a high probability of winning regardless of whether they received

support from great powers. Still, the importance of great-power support to insurgents in the post–Cold War era has relevant implications for contemporary insurgencies.

19. See, for example, US Department of Defense, *Special Operations, Joint Publication 3-05* (Washington, D.C.: Joint Staff, July 16, 2014), p. xi; US Department of the Army, *Army Special Operations Forces Unconventional Warfare* (Washington, D.C.: Headquarters, Department of the Army, September 2008), pp. 1–2.

20. US Army, *Dictionary of United States Army Terms* (Washington, D.C.: Headquarters, Department of the Army, August 1950).

21. Department of the Army, *Organization and Conduct of Guerilla Warfare*, FM 31-21 (Washington, D.C.: Headquarters, Department of the Army, October 1951); Department of the Army, *Operations against Guerilla Forces*, FM 31-20 (Washington, D.C.: Headquarters, Department of the Army, February 1951).

22. Department of the Army, *US Army Special Forces Group (Airborne)*, FM 31–20 (Washington, D.C.: Headquarters, Department of the Army, August 1955).

23. Benjamin S. Lambeth, *NATO's Air War for Kosovo: A Strategic and Operational Assessment* (Santa Monica, CA: RAND, 2001); Ivo H. Daalder and Michael E. O'Hanlon, *Winning Ugly: NATO's War to Save Kosovo* (Washington, D.C.: Brookings Institution Press, 2000).

24. On the overthrow of the Taliban regime see Gary Schroen, *First In: An Insider's Account of How the CIA Spearheaded the War on Terror in Afghanistan* (New York: Ballantine Books, 2005); Stephen Biddle, *Afghanistan and the Future of Warfare: Implications for Army and Defense Policy* (Carlisle, PA: Strategic Studies Institute, US Army War College, November 2002); Gary Berntsen and Ralph Pezzullo, *Jawbreaker: The Attack on Bin Laden and Al Qa'ida* (New York: Crown, 2005); Bob Woodward, *Bush at War* (New York: Simon & Schuster, 2002); Henry A. Crumpton, "Intelligence and War: Afghanistan 2001–2002," in Jennifer E. Sims and Burton Gerber, eds., *Transforming US Intelligence* (Washington, D.C.: Georgetown University Press, 2005).

25. Mueller, *Precision and Purpose*; Chivvis, *Toppling Qaddafi*.

26. Mueller, *Precision and Purpose*, p. 1.

27. Odyssey Dawn was the US code name for the initial stages of the Libyan operation; some of the other coalition members used it as well, but others adopted their own names for their national efforts in Libya, including Operation Ellamy (United Kingdom), Operation Harmattan (France), and Operation Mobile (Canada). After command of the operation was transferred to NATO on March 31, 2011, it became Operation Unified Protector.

28. On endogeneity see, for example, Gary King, Robert O. Keohane, and Sidney Verba, *Designing Social Inquiry: Scientific Inference in Qualitative Research* (Princeton, NJ: Princeton University Press, 1994).

29. I thank Daniel Byman for this point.

30. John F. Kennedy, State of the Union Address, January 30, 1961.

31. Lars Baewrentzen, John O. Iatrides, and Ole L. Smith, eds., *Studies in the History of the Greek Civil War, 1945–1949* (Copenhagen: Museum Tusculanum Press, 1987), p. 273.

32. Quoted in Michael D. Shafer, *Deadly Paradigms: The Failure of US Counterinsurgency Policy* (Princeton, NJ: Princeton University Press, 1988), p. 178; Russell Crandall, *America's Dirty Wars: Irregular Warfare from 1776 to the War on Terror* (New York: Cambridge University Press, 2014), p. 168.

33. Quoted in Shafer, *Deadly Paradigms*, p. 177; Crandall, *America's Dirty Wars*, p. 168.

34. David E. Cunningham, *Barriers to Peace in Civil War* (New York: Cambridge University Press, 2011).

35. Virginia Page Fortna, *Peace Time: Cease-Fire Agreements and the Durability of Peace* (Princeton, NJ: Princeton University Press, 2004).

36. Max Boot, *Invisible Armies: An Epic History of Guerrilla Warfare from Ancient Times to the Present* (New York: W.W. Norton, 2013), p. 322.

37. Ronald Hyam, *Britain's Declining Empire: The Road to Decolonization, 1918–1968* (New York: Cambridge University Press, 2006), p. 94.

38. According to the statistical analysis, punishment is negative and marginally significant.

39. Weinstein, *Inside Rebellion*, p. 206; Kalyvas, *The Logic of Violence in Civil War*, pp. 153–154.

40. Douglas Pike, *Viet Cong: The Organization and Techniques of the National Liberation Front of South Vietnam* (Cambridge, MA: MIT Press, 1966), p. 251.

41. Quoted in Rogelio Alonso, *The IRA and Armed Struggle* (New York: Routledge, 2007), p. 157.

42. Mao Tse-Tung, *On Guerrilla Warfare*, p. 92.

43. Thanks to Patrick Johnston and Nathan Chandler for these points.

44. On insurgency and weak states see James D. Fearon and David D. Laitin, "Ethnicity, Insurgency, and Civil War," *American Political Science Review*, Vol. 97, No. 1 (March 2003), pp. 75–90. The selection logic is roughly consistent with core elements of Dan Reiter and Allan Stam's theory of why democracies tend to win interstate wars. They argue that democracies are less likely to initiate wars they are unlikely to win because they have more at stake if they lose. The same might be true of insurgencies seeking regime change in a well-defined territory. Dan Reiter and Allan C. Stam III, "Democracy, War Initiation, and Victory," *American Political Science Review*, Vol. 92, No. 2 (June 1998), pp. 377–389.

45. Andrew J. R. Mack, "Why Big Nations Lose Small Wars: The Politics of Asymmetric Conflict," *World Politics*, Vol. 27, No. 2 (January 1975), pp. 175–200; Arreguín-Toft, *How the Weak Win Wars*, pp. 23–47; Lincoln B.

Krause, "Playing for the Breaks: Insurgent Mistakes," *Parameters*, Vol. 39, No. 3 (Autumn 2009), pp. 49–64.

46. See, for example, Connable and Libicki, *How Insurgencies End*, pp. 34–49; Bard O'Neill, *Insurgency and Terrorism: From Revolution to Apocalypse* (Dulles, VA: Potomac Books, 2005), pp. 145–148; Byman, *Trends in Outside Support for Insurgent Movements*, pp. 84–86.

47. Samuel P. Huntington, *The Clash of Civilizations and the Remaking of World Order* (New York: Simon & Schuster, 1996), p. 258.

48. Connable and Libicki, *How Insurgencies End*.

49. Lyall and Wilson, "Rage against the Machines," pp. 67–106.

50. On critiques of Lyall's argument see Paul K. MacDonald, "'Retribution Must Succeed Rebellion': The Colonial Origins of Counterinsurgency Failure," *International Organization*, Vol. 67, No. 2 (April 2013), pp. 253–286.

51. Gil Merom, *How Democracies Lose Small Wars: State, Society, and the Failures of France in Algeria, Israel in Lebanon, and the United States in Vietnam* (New York: Cambridge University Press, 2003).

52. See, for example, Jason Lyall, "Do Democracies Make Inferior Counterinsurgents? Reassessing Democracy's Impact on War Outcomes and Duration," *International Organization*, Vol. 64, No. 1 (Winter 2010), pp. 167–192.

53. See, for example, *The Final Report of the Select Committee to Study Governmental Operations with Respect to Intelligence Activities* (Washington, D.C.: US Government Printing Office, 1976).

54. Lyall and Wilson, "Rage against the Machines," p. 71.

55. "Letter dated 27 January 1992 from the Permanent Representative of El Salvador to the United Nations Addressed to the Secretary-General," A/46/864, S/23501, January 30, 1992, Annex: Peace Agreement.

56. See, for example, Douglas Woodwell, "The 'Troubles' of Northern Ireland: Civil Conflict in an Economically Well-Developed State," in Paul Collier and Nicholas Sambanis, eds., *Understanding Civil War: Evidence and Analysis, Vol. II* (Washington, D.C.: World Bank, 2005), pp. 161–190.

57. Chris Alden, *Mozambique and the Construction of the New African State: From Negotiations to Nation Building* (New York: Palgrave, 2001); United Nations Department of Public Information, *The United Nations and Mozambique* (New York: United Nations, 1995).

58. María Eugenia Vásquez Perdomo, *My Life as a Colombian Revolutionary: Reflections of a Former Guerrillera*, trans. Lorena Terando (Philadelphia: Temple University Press, 2005); Americas Watch, *The Killings in Colombia* (New York: Americas Watch, 1989).

59. See, for example, Michael W. Doyle and Nicholas Sambanis, *Making War and Building Peace: United Nations Peace Operations* (Princeton, NJ: Princeton University Press, 2006).

60. This chapter was drafted with the extraordinary help of Patrick Johnston and Eric Robinson, along with a close review by Sean Zeigler.

61. It is worth noting that my codings don't distinguish between changes in support levels throughout the insurgency. Even if a great power supports an insurgent group for only a fraction of the insurgency, the time series reflects support for the entire duration. I considered breaking great-power support into time-series increments, but the data are too poor.

62. The figure excludes ongoing cases.

63. Chivvis, *Toppling Qaddafi*, p. 177.

Chapter 9

1. Oliver Lyttelton *The Memoirs of Lord Chandos: An Unexpected View from the Summit* (New York: New American Library, 1963), p. 364.

2. US Department of Defense, *Sustaining Global Leadership: Priorities for 21st Century Defense* (Washington, D.C.: US Department of Defense, January 2012), p. 6.

3. Andrew Mumford, *The Counter-Insurgency Myth: The British Experience of Irregular Warfare* (New York: Routledge, 2012), p. 1. Also see, for example, such books as David French, *The British Way in Counter-Insurgency, 1945–1967* (New York: Oxford University Press, 2011).

4. On the visceral reaction to counterinsurgency, see Fred Kaplan, *The Insurgents: David Petraeus and the Plot to Change the American Way of War* (New York: Simon & Schuster, 2013).

5. Frank Newport, "More Americans Now View Afghanistan War as a Mistake," *Gallup*, February 19, 2014.

6. "Iraq," Gallup, 2014. The article was accessed on September 10, 2014 at: www.gallup.com/poll/1633/iraq.aspx.

7. On a critique of the *Counterinsurgency Field Manual* and its force ratios see Jeffrey A. Friedman, "Manpower and Counterinsurgency: Empirical Foundations for Theory and Doctrine," *Security Studies*, Vol. 20, No. 4 (2011), pp. 556–591.

8. The US Army and Marine Corps, *Counterinsurgency Field Manual: US Army Field Manual No. 3-24 and Marine Corps Warfighting Publication No. 3-33.5* (Chicago: University of Chicago Press, 2007), p. 23.

9. See, for example, Karl W. Eikenberry, "The Limits of Counterinsurgency Doctrine in Afghanistan: The Other Side of the COIN," *Foreign Affairs*, Vol. 92, No. 5 (September/October 2013), pp. 59–74.

10. On definitions of counterinsurgency see, for example, Central Intelligence Agency, *Guide to the Analysis of Insurgency* (Washington, D.C.: Central Intelligence Agency, 2012), p. 1; British Army Field Manual, *Countering Insurgency*, Volume 1, Part 10 (London: UK Ministry of Defence, October 2009), pp. 1–6; US Army and Marine Corps, *Counterinsurgency Field Manual*, p. 2.

11. Carl von Clausewitz, *On War* (New York: Penguin, 1968), p. 109.

12. On the proto-insurgency or pre-insurgency stages, see Daniel Byman, *Understanding Proto-Insurgencies* (Santa Monica, CA: RAND, 2007); Central Intelligence Agency, *Guide to the Analysis of Insurgency* (Washington, D.C.: Central Intelligence Agency, 2012).

13. Paul Collier, Anke Hoeffler, and Dominic Rohner, "Beyond Greed and Grievance: Feasibility and Civil War," *Oxford Economic Papers*, Vol. 61, No. 2 (2009), p. 1.

14. Alexander Segovia, "The War Economy of the 1980s," in James K. Boyce, ed., *Economic Policy for Building Peace: The Lessons of El Salvador* (Boulder, CO: Lynne Rienner, 1996), p. 31; John Eriksson, Alcira Kreimer, and Margaret Arnold, *El Salvador: Post-Conflict Reconstruction* (Washington, D.C.: World Bank 2000), p. 18.

15. Eriksson, Kreimer, and Arnold, *El Salvador: Post-Conflict Reconstruction*, pp. 19, 21.

16. M. Pastor and M. E. Conroy, "Distributional Implication," in Boyce, ed., *Economic Policy for Building Peace*, p. 157; Jenny Pearce, "From Civil War to 'Civil Society': Has the End of the Cold War Brought Peace to Central America?" *International Affairs*, Vol. 74, No. 3 (1998), pp. 591–592; Graciana del Castillo, "Post-Conflict Reconstruction and the Challenge to International Organizations: The Case of El Salvador," *World Development*, Vol. 29, No. 12, p. 1972.

17. The figure for US aid includes remittances sent by its citizens in the United States. C. Vilas, *Between Earthquakes and Volcanoes: Market, State, and the Revolutions in Central America* (New York: Monthly Review Press, 1995), p. 161.

18. Ohrid Framework Agreement, August 13, 2001.

19. Michael S. Lund, "Greed and Grievance Diverted: How Macedonia Avoided Civil War, 1990–2001," in Paul Collier and Nicholas Sambanis, eds., *Understanding Civil War, Vol. 2: Europe, Central Asia, and Other Regions* (Washington, D.C.: World Bank, 2005), pp. 231–257.

20. Quoted in Richard Clutterbuck, *Conflict and Violence in Singapore and Malaysia 1945–1983* (Boulder, CO: Westview Press, 1985), p. 63.

21. Barbara Leitch Lepoer, ed., *Singapore: A Country Study* (Washington: Government Printing Office, 1989).

22. Central Intelligence Agency, *Guide to the Analysis of Insurgency*, p. 5; Daniel Byman, *Understanding Proto-Insurgencies* (Santa Monica, CA: RAND, 2007).

23. Byman, *Going to War with the Allies You Have*, p. 26.

24. Stathis N. Kaylvas and Matthew Adam Kocher, "How 'Free' is Free Riding in Civil Wars? Violence, Insurgency, and the Collective Action Problem," *World Politics*, Vol. 49, No. 2 (January 2007), pp. 177–216.

25. Roger V. Gould, *Insurgent Identities: Class, Community, and Protest in Paris from 1848 to the Commune* (Chicago: University of Chicago Press, 1995), p. 204.

26. See, for example, Paul Collier, "Economic Causes of Civil Conflict and Their Implications for Policy," Draft Paper, Department of Economics, Oxford University, April 2006, p. 3.

27. Gordon Tullock, "The Paradox of Revolution," *Public Choice*, Vol. 11 (September 1971), p. 90.

28. Mark Irving Lichbach and Ted Gurr, "The Conflict Process: A Formal Model," *Journal of Conflict Resolution*, Vol. 25 (March 1981), pp. 3–29; David T. Mason and Dale A. Krane, "The Political Economy of Death Squads: Toward a Theory of the Impact of State-Sanctioned Terror," *International Studies Quarterly*, Vol. 33, No. 2 (June 1989), pp. 175–198.

29. Kaylvas and Kocher, "How 'Free' is Free Riding in Civil Wars?" pp. 177–216.

30. Héctor Béjar, *Peru 1965: Notes on a Guerrilla Experience*, translated by William Rose (New York: Monthly Review Press, 1970).

31. See, for example, Gilles Kepel, *Jihad: The Trail of Political Islam* (Cambridge, MA: Harvard University Press, 2002), pp. 276–298.

32. Hegghammer, *Jihad in Saudi Arabia*, p. 181. On al Qa'ida estimates, also see Nawaf Obaid and Anthony Cordesman, *Al-Qaeda in Saudi Arabia: Asymmetric Threats and Islamic Extremists* (Washington, D.C.: Center for Strategic and International Studies, 2005), p. 20. On other aspects of the al Qa'ida threat to Saudi Arabia see George Tenet with Bill Harlow, *At the Center of the Storm: My Years at the CIA* (New York: HarperCollins, 2007), p. 248; Ron Suskind, *The One Percent Doctrine* (New York: Simon & Schuster, 2006), p. 148.

33. Hegghammer, "The Failure of Jihad in Saudi Arabia," p. 19; Nawaf Obaid, "Remnants of al Qaeda in Saudi Arabia: Current Assessment," Presentation at Center for Strategic and International Studies, Washington, November 2006.

34. Author interview with US government official deployed to Saudi Arabia during this period, August 2014.

35. Author interview with US government official deployed to Saudi Arabia during this period, July 2014.

36. Riedel and Saab, "Al Qaeda's Third Front," pp. 38–39.

37. Hegghammer, *Jihad in Saudi Arabia*, p. 220.

38. Sheikh Abd Al-'Aziz bin Abdallah Aal Al-Sheikh, *Al-Sharq Al-Awsat* (London), October 2, 2007. The editor of *Al-Sharq Al-Awsat*, Tareq Al-Humaid, commented that the fatwa "called a spade a spade" since some Saudi youth "have become enslaved by Al-Qaeda and its ideology," making it important that the fatwa was directed at Saudi youth and, just as significant, their fathers and mothers. See the comments by Tareq Al-Humaid in *Al-Sharq Al-Awsat* (London), October 2, 2007.

39. Author interview with US government official deployed to Saudi Arabia during this period, August 2014.

40. Hegghammer, *Jihad in Saudi Arabia*, p. 218.

41. Riedel and Saab, "Al Qaeda's Third Front," pp. 33–46.
42. There were not, for example, anywhere near 1,000 combat battle-deaths sustained over the course of the conflict, including 100 combatant battle-deaths sustained by each side over the course of the conflict.
43. The US Army and Marine Corps, *Counterinsurgency Field Manual*, p. 42.
44. Some of the key historical texts for population-centric counterinsurgency include David Galula, *Counterinsurgency Warfare: Theory and Practice* (London: Praeger, 1964); Robert Thompson, *Defeating Communist Insurgency* (St. Petersburg, FL: Hailer, 2005); Charles E. Calwell, *Small Wars: Their Principles and Practice* (Lincoln, NE: University of Nebraska Press, 1996); Frank Kitson, *Low Intensity Operations: Subversion, Insurgency and Peacekeeping* (London: Faber and Faber, 1971); and Roger Trinquier, *Modern Warfare: A French View of Counterinsurgency* (London: Praeger, 2006).
45. French, *The British Way in Counter-Insurgency*, p. 65.
46. Arreguín-Toft, *How the Weak Win Wars*, pp. 30–31.
47. T. X. Hammes, "Counterinsurgency: Not a Strategy, But a Necessary Capability," *Joint Forces Quarterly*, No. 65 (April 2012), pp. 48–52.
48. Andrew J. R. Mack, "Why Big Nations Lose Small Wars: The Politics of Asymmetric Conflict," *World Politics*, Vol. 27, No. 2 (January 1975), pp. 175–200; Arreguín-Toft, *How the Weak Win Wars*, pp. 23–47; Lincoln B. Krause, "Playing for the Breaks: Insurgent Mistakes," *Parameters*, Vol. 39, No. 3 (Autumn 2009), pp. 49–64.
49. Arreguín-Toft, *How the Weak Win Wars*, p. 38.
50. Christopher Chivvis, *Wildcat: The French War on Al Qaida in Africa* (New York: Cambridge University Press, forthcoming).
51. Insurgents achieved victory 20 percent of the time when they utilized a punishment strategy, compared to 38 percent for conventional strategies and 25 percent for guerrilla strategies.
52. Quoted in Victor Purcell, *Malaya: Communist or Free* (Stanford, CA: Stanford University Press, 1955), p. 69. The complete text was published in *The Times*, December 1, 1952.
53. Stathis N. Kalyvas, *The Logic of Violence in Civil War* (New York: Cambridge University Press, 2006).
54. Mao, *On Guerrilla Warfare*, p. 93.
55. Jeremy Shapiro, *The Terrorist's Dilemma: Managing Violent Covert Organizations* (Princeton, NJ: Princeton University Press, 2013), pp. 44–49.
56. Edmund Burke III and David N. Yaghoubian, eds., *Struggle and Survival in the Modern Middle East* (Berkeley and Los Angeles, CA: University of California Press, 2006), p. 384.
57. Baya Gacemi, *I, Nadia, Wife of a Terrorist* (Lincoln, NE: University of Nebraska Press, 2006), p. 141.
58. See the allegations in, for example, Omar Nasiri, *Inside the Jihad: My Live with Al Qaeda* (New York: Basic Books, 2006), p. 278.

59. "Real IRA Apologises for Omagh Bomb," BBC, August 18, 1998.

60. Nick Paton Walsh, "Women Moved by Family Not Ideology," *The Guardian* (London), September 1, 2004, p. 13.

61. Robert W. Schaefer, *The Insurgency in Chechnya and the North Caucasus: From Gazavat to Jihad* (Santa Barbara, CA: ABC-CLIO, 2011), pp. 221–222.

62. On the Anbar Awakening see, for example, Mitchell B. Reiss, *Negotiating with Evil: When to Talk to Terrorists* (New York: Open Road, 2010), pp. 177–220.

63. Frank Kitson, *Gangs and Counter-Gangs* (London: Barrie and Rockliff, 1960); Calvin H. Allen and W. Lynn Rigsbee, *Oman under Qaboos: From Coup to Constitution, 1970–1996* (New York: Routledge, 2000); Major-General Tony Jeapes, *SAS Secret War* (London: Greenhill Books, 2005).

64. Robert W. Komer, *The Malayan Emergency in Retrospect: Organization of a Successful Counterinsurgency Efforts* (Santa Monica, CA: RAND, 1972), p. 72.

65. On an overview of Komer's argument and contemporary implications see Austin Long, *On "Other War": Lessons from Five Decades of RAND Counterinsurgency Research* (Santa Monica, CA: RAND, 2006), pp. 48–49.

66. Komer, *The Malayan Emergency in Retrospect*, p. 74.

67. See, for example, US Department of Defense, *Special Operations, Joint Publication 3-05* (Washington, D.C.: Joint Staff, July 16, 2014), p. xi; US Department of the Army, *Army Special Operations Forces Unconventional Warfare* (Washington, D.C.: Headquarters, Department of the Army, September 2008), pp. 1–2.

68. Adrian H. Jones and Andrew R. Molnar, *Internal Defense against Insurgency: Six Cases* (Washington, D.C.: Center for Research in Social Systems, 1966), p. 25.

69. Kalyvas, *The Logic of Violence in Civil Wars*, p. 107.

70. Robert M. Carmack, "Editor's Preface to the First Edition," in Carmack, ed., *Harvest of Violence: The Maya Indians the Guatemalan Crisis* (Norman, OK: University of Oklahoma Press, 1988), p. 63.

71. Nazih Richani, "Caudillos and the Crisis of the Colombian State: Fragmented Sovereignty, the War System and the Privatization of Counterinsurgency in Colombia," *Third World Quarterly*, Vol. 28, No. 2 (2007), pp. 403–417.

72. Cited in Audrey Kahin, *Rebellion to Integration: West Sumatra and the Indonesian Polity, 1926–1998* (Amsterdam: Amsterdam University Press, 1999), p. 221.

73. Ahram, *Proxy Warriors*, p. 47.

74. Stathis N. Kalyvas, "Ethnic Defection in Civil War," *Comparative Political Studies*, Vol. 41, No. 8 (August 2008), pp. 1043–1068.

75. Daniel Branch, "The Enemy Within: Loyalists and the War against Mau Mau in Kenya," *Journal of African History*, Vol. 48, No. 2 (2007), pp. 291–315; Kalyvas, "Ethnic Defection in Civil War," p. 1053.
76. Chris Kraul, "In Ramadi, A Ragtag Solution with Real Results," *Los Angeles Times*, May 7, 2007.
77. John A. Armstrong, "Introduction," in Armstrong, ed., *Soviet Partisans in World War II* (Madison: University of Wisconsin Press, 1964), p. 30; Eva-Lotta Hedman, "State of Siege: Political Violence and Vigilante Mobilization in the Philippines," in Bruce B. Campbell and Arthur D. Brenner, eds., *Death Squads in Global Perspective: Murder with Deniability* (New York: St. Martin's Press, 2000), p. 133; Fred H. Barton, *Salient Operational Aspects of Paramilitary Warfare in Three Asian Areas*, ORO-T-228 (Chevy Chase, MD: Operations Research Office, 1953).
78. John A. Nagl, *Learning to Eat Soup with a Knife: Counterinsurgency Lessons from Malaya to Vietnam* (Chicago: University of Chicago Press, 2002), pp. 75, 98–99; Hamzah-Sendurt, "A Resettlement Village in Malaya," *Asian Survey*, Vol. 1, No. 9 (November 1961), pp. 21–26; Robert O. Tilman, "The Non-Lessons of the Malayan Emergency," *Asian Survey*, Vol. 6, No. 8 (August 1966), pp. 407–419.
79. Quoted in Nagl, *Learning to Eat Soup with a Knife*, p. 75.
80. Kimberly Theidon, "Justice in Transition: The Micropolitics of Reconciliation in Postwar Peru," *The Journal of Conflict Resolution*, Vol. 50, No. 3 (June 2006), pp. 433–457; Thomas A. Marks, *Maoist Insurgency since Vietnam* (Portland, OR: Frank Cass, 1996), pp. 279–280.
81. Simone Remijnse, "Remembering Civil Patrols in Joyabaj, Guatemala," *Bulletin of Latin American Research*, Vol. 20, No. 4 (2001), p. 463.
82. Matilde González, "The Man Who Brought the Danger to the Village: Representations of the Armed Conflict in Guatemala from a Local Perspective," *Journal of Southern African Studies*, Vol. 26, No. 2 (June 2000), pp. 317–335. Also see, for example, Michael Richards, "Cosmopolitan World View and Counterinsurgency in Guatemala," *Anthropological Quarterly*, Vol. 58, No. 3 (July 1985), pp. 90–107.
83. David Kowalewski, "Counterinsurgent Paramilitarism: A Philippine Case Study," *Journal of Peace Research*, Vol. 29, No. 1 (February 1992), pp. 71–84; Jose P. Magno, Jr. and A. James Gregor, "Insurgency and Counterinsurgency in the Philippines," *Asian Survey*, Vol. 26, No. 5 (May 1986), pp. 501–517.
84. James C. F. Wang, "The Urban Militia as a Political Instrument in the Power Contest in China in 1976," *Asian Survey*, Vol. 18, No. 6 (June 1978), pp. 541–559.
85. Neil DeVotta, "The Liberation Tigers of Tamil Eelam and the Lost Quest for Separatism in Sri Lanka," *Asian Survey*, Vol. 49, No. 6 (November/December 2009), pp. 1021–1051.
86. Russell Crandall, *Driving by Drugs: US Policy toward Colombia*, 2nd ed. (Boulder, CO: Lynne Rienner, 2008); Frank Stafford and Marco

Palacios, *Colombia: Fragmented Land, Divided Society* (New York: Oxford University Press, 2002); and Max. G. Manwaring, *Non-State Actors in Colombia: Threat and Response* (Carlisle, PA: US Mary War College Strategic Studies Monograph, 2002); Kimberly Marten, "Warlordism in Comparative Perspective," *International Security*, Vol. 31, No. 3 (Winter 2006/07), pp. 41–73.

87. Philip Gourevitch, *We Wish to Inform You That Tomorrow We Will Be Killed with Our Families: Stories from Rwanda* (New York: Farrar, Straus and Giroux, 1998), p. 93.

88. Karl Vick, "In Kurdish Turkey, a New Enemy," *Washington Post*, October 31, 2002, p. A18.

89. Stanley A. McChrystal, "It Takes a Network: The New Front Line of Modern Warfare," *Foreign Policy*, February 21, 2011.

90. Weinstein, *Inside Rebellion*, pp. 7–16.

91. Jacob N. Shapiro and Nils B. Weidmann, "Is the Phone Mightier Than the Sword? Cell Phones and Insurgent Violence in Iraq," Working Paper, September 2012.

92. John Scott-Railton, *Revolutionary Risks: Cyber Technology and Threats in the 2011 Libyan Revolution* (Newport, RI: United States Naval War College, 2013).

93. See, for example, Andy Greenberg, "How the Syrian Electronic Army Hacked Us: A Detailed Timeline," *Forbes*, February 2, 2014; Kenneth Geers and Ayed Alqarteh, *Syrian Electronic Army Hacks Major Communications Websites* (Milpitas, CA: FireEye, July 30, 2013); Roy Greenslade, "Syrian Hackers Attack Websites of the Sun and Sunday Times," *Guardian*, June 18, 2014; Craig Timberg, "Hackers Break Into Post's Servers, Gain Access to Employee Passwords," *Washington Post*, December 19, 2013.

94. Committee to Protect Journalists, *10 Most Censored Countries* (New York: Committee to Protect Journalists, 2012).

95. O'Neill, *Insurgency and Terrorism*, p. 147.

96. Justin O. Smith, "Maritime Interdiction in Sri Lanka's Counterinsurgency," *Small Wars & Insurgencies*, Vol. 22, No. 3 (July 2011), p. 449.

97. Paul Staniland, "Defeating Transnational Insurgencies: The Best Offense Is a Good Fence," *Washington Quarterly*, Vol. 29, No. 1 (2005–2006), p. 32.

98. Russell Crandall, *America's Dirty Wars: Irregular Warfare from 1776 to the War on Terror* (New York: Cambridge University Press, 2014), pp. 181–182.

99. Alistair Horne, *A Savage War of Peace: Algeria 1954–1962* (New York: Viking Press, 1978), p. 263.

100. Staniland, "Defeating Transnational Insurgencies," pp. 21–40.

101. David E. Cunningham, "Blocking Resolution: How External States Can Prolong Civil Wars," *Journal of Peace Research*, Vol. 47, No. 2 (2010), p. 117.

102. Karl W. Deutsch, "External Involvement in Internal War," in Harry Eckstein, ed., *Internal War: Problems and Approaches* (New York: The Free

Press of Glencoe, 1964), pp. 100–110; David M. Edelstein, *Occupational Hazards: Success and Failure in Military Occupation* (Ithaca, NY: Cornell University Press, 2010).

103. Chaliand, *Revolution in the Third World*, p. 181; Salehyan, Gleditsch, and Cunningham, "Explaining External Support for Insurgent Groups," pp. 70 9–744.

104. Pew Global Attitudes Project, *US Image up Slightly, but Still Negative* (Washington, D.C.: Pew Global Attitudes Project, June 2005), p. 41.

105. Seth G. Jones, *Hunting in the Shadows: The Pursuit of Al Qa'ida Since 9/11* (New York: W.W. Norton, 2012).

106. Mitchell B. Reiss, *Negotiating with Evil: When to Talk to Terrorists* (New York: Open Road, 2010), pp. 177–220; Major Neil Smith and Colonel Sean MacFarland, "Anbar Awakens: The Tipping Point," *Military Review* (March–April 2008), pp. 41–52. For a slightly different view which adds the role of US "surge" forces see Stephen Biddle, Jeffrey A. Friedman, and Jacob N. Shapiro, "Testing the Surge: Why Did Violence Decline in Iraq in 2007?" *International Security*, Vol. 37, No. 1 (Summer 2012), pp. 7–40.

107. Nagl, *Learning to Eat Soup with a Knife*, p. 207.

108. Omar Cabezas, *Fire from the Mountain: The Making of a Sandinista* (New York: Crown, 1985), p. 98.

109. Kaylvas and Kocher, "How 'Free' is Free Riding in Civil Wars?" p. 182.

110. Smith, "Maritime Interdiction in Sri Lanka's Counterinsurgency," p. 459.

Appendix B

1. See, for example, Andrew J. R. Mack, "Why Big Nations Lose Small Wars: The Politics of Asymmetric Conflict," *World Politics*, Vol. 27, No. 2 (January 1975), pp. 175–200; Gil Merom, *How Democracies Lose Small Wars: State, Society, and the Failures of France in Algeria, Israel in Lebanon, and the United States in Vietnam* (New York: Cambridge University Press, 2003); Ivan Arreguín-Toft, *How the Weak Win Wars: A Theory of Asymmetric Conflict* (New York: Cambridge University Press, 2005); Karl R. DeRouen, Jr. and David Sobek, "The Dynamics of Civil War Duration and Outcome," *Journal of Peace Research*, Vol. 41, No. 3 (2004), pp. 303–320; Jason Lyall and Isaiah Wilson III, "Rage against the Machines: Explaining Outcomes in Counterinsurgency Wars," *International Organization*, No. 63 (Winter 2009), pp. 67–106; Ben Connable and Martin C. Libicki, *How Insurgencies End* (Santa Monica, CA: RAND, 2010); Paul K. MacDonald, "'Retribution Must Succeed Rebellion': The Colonial Origins of Counterinsurgency Failure," *International Organization*, Volume 67, No. 2 (April 2013), pp. 253–286; Anna Getmansky, "You Can't Win if You Don't Fight: The Role of Regime Type in Counterinsurgency Outbreaks and Outcome," *Journal of Conflict Resolution*, Vol. 57, No. 4 (August 2013), pp. 709–734.

2. Jeffrey Record, "External Assistance: Enabler of Insurgent Success," *Parameters*, Vol. 36, No. 3 (Autumn 2006), pp. 36–49; Record, *Beating Goliath: Why Insurgencies Win* (Washington, D.C.: Potomac Books, 2007); Lyall and Wilson, "Rage against the Machines."

3. Connable and Libicki, *How Insurgencies End*.

4. Connable and Libicki, *How Insurgencies End*; Jason Lyall, "Do Democracies Make Inferior Counterinsurgents? Reassessing Democracy's Impact on War Outcomes and Duration," *International Organization*, Vol. 64, No. 1 (Winter 2010), pp. 167–192; Lyall and Wilson, "Rage against the Machines," pp. 89–91.

5. On strategy, see Arreguín-Toft, *How the Weak Win Wars*; Stathis N. Kalyvas and Laia Balcells, "International System and Technologies of Rebellion: How the End of the Cold War Shaped Internal Conflict," *American Political Science Review*, Vol. 104, No. 3 (August 2010), pp. 415–429. On the use of terrorism—a component of an insurgent punishment strategy—see Virginia Page Fortna, "Do Terrorists Win? Rebels' Use of Terrorism and Civil War Outcomes," *International Organization*, Vol. 69, No. 3 (June 2015), pp. 519–556; Connable and Libicki, *How Insurgencies End*.

6. Mack, "Why Big Nations Lose Small Wars"; Merom, *How Democracies Lose Small Wars*. For an alternative view on democratic effectiveness in countering insurgencies, Lyall, "Do Democracies Make Inferior Counterinsurgents?"

7. Lyall and Wilson, "Rage against the Machines," pp. 89–91.

8. Connable and Libicki, *How Insurgencies End*.

9. Lyall and Wilson, "Rage against the Machines," pp. 89–91.

10. Consistent with extant studies, we include the squared version of duration to adequately capture nonlinear time effects. See, for example, Govinda Clayton, "Relative Rebel Strength and the Onset and Outcome of Civil War Mediation," *Journal of Peace Research*, Vol. 50, No. 5 (2013), p. 616; and Thomas Edward Flores and Irfan Nooruddin, "Democracy Under the Gun: Understanding Postconflict Economic Recovery," *Journal of Conflict Resolution*, Vol. 53, No. 1 (2009), pp. 3–29.

11. See, for example, Lyall and Wilson III, "Rage against the Machines," p. 85; Simon Collard-Wexler, Costantino Pischedda, and Michael G. Smith, "Do Foreign Occupations Cause Suicide Attacks?" *Journal of Conflict Resolution*, Vol. 58, No. 4 (2014), pp. 625–657. Polity2 scores range from 10 (Highly Autocratic) to + 10 (Highly Democratic), and are intended to capture the democratic nature of a government. We code democracies as having a Polity2 score greater than or equal to zero. However, our results are robust to a more stringent threshold using scores of seven or higher to define democracies.

12. We do not include insurgent use of a guerrilla strategy in our main model, given that this variable is highly negatively correlated ($p = 0.689$)

with insurgent use of a conventional strategy. Inclusion of both variables introduces significant heteroscedasticity.

13. The database identifies whether the insurgent pursued a conventional strategy, but does not code the strategy pursued by the primary counterinsurgent. As a result, the strategic mismatch variable included in the model is an interaction between great-power combat support to the government and insurgent use of a conventional strategy. This assumes, imperfectly, that counterinsurgent size and resource strength will adequately capture any strategic overlap with a more conventionally minded insurgent. Coefficient estimates in column two suggest that insurgencies using a conventional strategy to fight a counterinsurgent supported by a great power are no less likely to lose or win, countering Arreguín-Toft's hypothesis.

14. We merge these variables directly from the replication data provided by Lyall and Wilson in "Rage against the Machines." Due to differing definitions of insurgency and differing time periods used within each dataset, we subset this regression to only the 112 cases that exist in both datasets.

ACKNOWLEDGMENTS

───◈───

I first considered writing about insurgent warfare following a series of pointed classroom discussions with students in my insurgency and counterinsurgency course in the Strategic Studies Program at Johns Hopkins University's School of Advanced International Studies (SAIS). As we collectively recognized, there was a cacophony of books on counterinsurgency, particularly after the US and allied campaigns in Afghanistan and Iraq. But there was a dearth of recent work that looked comprehensively at how insurgents—not counterinsurgents—conducted warfare, other than a handful of specific case studies. From its inception, *Waging Insurgent Warfare* was designed to help fill this vacuum.

When it came time to research and write the book, no one was as valuable as Nathan Chandler. He helped compile the database on insurgencies, tirelessly reviewed hundreds of cases, tracked down countless sources, and served as a friend and colleague. I could not have written the book without his able assistance. Several individuals reviewed all or part of the manuscript and provided outstanding comments: Daniel Byman, Christopher Chivvis, Rafi Cohen, Austin Long, and Andrew Radin. Not to be outdone, Patrick Johnston, Eric Robinson, and Sean Zeigler were extraordinarily helpful with the quantitative analysis, and they provided helpful comments on the manuscript as well. Discussions with several others—such as Scott Mann, Carlos Perez, David Phillips, Travis Schweizer, and Mike Waltz—helped shape my thoughts along the way. Mary Wrazen from RAND did excellent work on the figures.

Several others had a significant impact on my understanding of insurgency over the years, particularly Steve Biddle, Lieutenant General Charles Cleveland, Eliot Cohen, T.X. Hammes, Bruce Hoffman, Major General Scott Howell, David Kilcullen, Steve Metz, Lieutenant General Scott Miller, Admiral Eric Olson, General David Petraeus, Major General Ed Reeder, Jacob Shapiro, General Tony Thomas, Mike Vickers, and General Joseph Votel. At RAND, I am indebted to a range of individuals who influenced my thinking on insurgency and counterinsurgency, particularly Jason Campbell, Colin Clarke, Ben Connable, Kim Cragin, Lynn Davis, James Dobbins, Daniel Egel, Gian Gentile, David Gompert, Todd Helmus, Rich Girven, John Gordon, Steve Hosmer, Terry Kelly, Andy Liepman, Mike McNerney, Arturo Muñoz, David Ochmanek, John Parachini, Linda Robinson, Christopher Paul, Howard Shatz, Greg Treverton, Steve Watts, Henry Willis, and Rebecca Zimmerman. In addition, the Insurgency Board Panel of Experts at RAND was a priceless venue to debate the complexities and nuances of insurgent warfare. I thank Michael Rich, Andy Hoehn, and Jack Riley at RAND for their extraordinary support over the years and their commitment to rigorous and objective analysis. Joy Merck was exceptional during the entire manuscript process as my assistant and gatekeeper.

In addition, numerous US soldiers—particularly US Special Operations Forces—had a profound impact on my understanding of insurgent warfare. They included colleagues from US Special Operations Command, Joint Special Operations Command, Special Operations and Low Intensity Conflict in the Office of the Secretary of Defense, US Army Green Berets, US Navy SEALs, US Army Rangers, US Marine Special Operations Command, and US Air Force Special Operations Command. I also thank friends and colleagues from the US Intelligence Community, US State Department, US Agency for International Development, and allied governments for their tireless work, sacrifice, and insights over the years about insurgency and counterinsurgency. There are far too many of them to thank by name, and most of these patriots would prefer to remain nameless.

The team at Oxford University Press was outstanding, including David McBride, Kathleen Weaver, and Emma Clements. I am also extremely grateful for the generous support from the Smith Richardson Foundation, particularly from Marin Strmecki and Allan Song, which helped make this book possible.

Finally, my parents, brothers, and broader family in the United States and Canada have been a constant source of inspiration and friendship over the years. My wife and daughters have been my rock and foundation. They have been far too patient on myriad trips overseas and countless hours toiling away on the manuscript. I dedicate this book to them.

INDEX